ANTIME
ASPBERRY
RIDGEWA
WHOLE LEAF HOPS
CW00322324
HATHERN BREWERY
GWOOD
FFKIN
AUTUMN
ALE
4.4% ABV
WERY
VALE BREWERY Co.
BUCKS
BLACK BEAUTY
www.valebrewery.co.uk
PORTER
Hand Crafted
500 ml ℮
Alc. 4.3% Vol.
Wholesome and full bodied, detect the hop character through the dominant complex malt flavours.
A Dark Horse!
Bottle Conditioned for Flavour
ORIGINAL
BOB
BRAND OAK BITTER
WICKWAR BREWING Co
NOTED BEERS
GLOUCESTE
Taiphoon
LEMONGRASS BEER
A FINE PALE GOLD BEER
WITH HINTS OF
LEMONGRASS AND CORIANDER
500mL ℮
ALC VOL 4.2%
EXCELLENT WITH SPICY AND ORIENTAL FOOD
BOTTLE CONDITIONED FOR QUALI
ALL GRAIN BEER
50 cl
Pen-lon
3.8%
ABV
Cottage Brewery
TIPSY TUP
Bottle Conditioned
PALE ALE
GLEYS
ST. 2003
GBURY
TER
% ABV
crafted in
ry, Northants
CWRW CYMREIG DA
BRAGDY MŴS PIWS
CWRW ERYRI
ABV 3.6%
SNOWDONIA
ALE
BREWERY
HOPDAEMON
LEVIATHAN
ale 6% alc./vol.

GOOD BOTTLED BEER GUIDE

JEFF EVANS

SPONSORED BY

Sainsbury's

Contents

Published by CAMRA Books, 230 Hatfield Road, St Albans, Hertfordshire AL1 4LW.
Tel. (01727) 867201
Fax (01727) 867670
e-mail: camra@camra.org.uk

ISBN 1-85249-226-0
Author: Jeff Evans
Design: Rob Howells
Cover design: Paul Welti
Printed and bound in Great Britain by William Clowes Ltd, Beccles, Suffolk

Great effort has gone into researching the contents of this book, but no responsibility can be taken for errors.

Foreword

I HAVE OFTEN HEARD IT REMARKED that beer is the new bread. While you might be able to buy a bottle of beer for next to nothing, it'll probably be flavourless and of poor quality, whereas for a few extra pence you can pick up something truly amazing. What's more, the one next to it will be entirely different in flavour, but just as good to drink!

I have only joined the world of beer in the last year and nothing could have prepared me for the journey – or for such an exciting postbox full of new beers each morning. I am sent beers from all across the country – from Rock to Arran, from Chiswick to Wainfleet – all distinctly different and superb in their own way.

I've visited many of the breweries of Britain and spoken with all their head brewers. I am constantly astounded by the passion and attention to detail displayed by all. Each beer, each bottle, each label has every last detail considered prior to being put on display to the public. The most exciting development is the inclusion of more and more beer and food matching ideas on the back of labels, in stores and especially throughout the media. This, for me, is going to be the key if we are to take beer to a wider audience, to keep an industry that has been enjoyed by millions, for centuries, brewing. So it is encouraging to see beer appearing on more and more dinner tables throughout the country, at home and in restaurants.

Another heartening development is the constant influx of foreign beers, which add yet another dimension to the wealth of flavours available. Some people are Trappist enthusiasts and will drink nothing else; others simply love the variety to be found by switching from one bottle to the next, in a quest to find their own Utopia.

There hasn't been a more exciting time in bottled beer than right now, so, as we like to say at Sainsbury's, 'Try Something New Today'. I shall, and this book is a great place to start.

Neil Whelpton
Beer Buyer: Sainsbury's

Introduction

IT'S BEEN TWO YEARS since the last edition of the *Good Bottled Beer Guide* but it seems like ten. So much has changed in such a short period of time, not least the format of the book. We hope you like it.

Of more importance, however, are developments in the world of bottled beer. First the good news. There are more breweries producing bottle-conditioned beer than ever before and there are more bottle-conditioned beers for you to enjoy. When the first *Good Bottled Beer Guide* was published in 1998, we could count on only around 180 beers that were naturally conditioned in the bottle. Two years ago, we were astounded to find that the number had risen to well over 600. Now we can reveal that we've tracked down nearly 800 for this book, and there's no sign that the trend is petering out. Exciting times, then, for lovers of good bottled beer.

Real ale in a bottle

But what do we mean by bottle-conditioned beer? In simple terms, we're talking about real ale in a bottle, beer that, just like real ale on draught in a pub, contains yeast and therefore continues fermenting after leaving the brewery. It is not pasteurized, so it's a living beer, with all the benefits for taste that this brings – notably freshness and full, complex flavours. It's not artificially carbonated either, which means the only fizz is the natural effervescence created by fermentation.

We don't include filtered or pasteurized beers in this book. Bottle-conditioned beer, being a living product, is by definition more difficult to create and handle. It demands absolute hygiene in the brewhouse, and it needs to be treated like all good foodstuffs once it has left the brewery. But the benefits are substantial. If you want boring consistency, stick to dead, pasteurized beer, but if you want complex, intriguing, multi-dimensional flavours, then bottle-conditioned beer is the first choice. Some people balk at the sediment in the bottle, but this is harmless and is what makes the beer so special. That's the yeast that provides the rich, fresh flavours. If the beer takes a little more care to pour, so what if it tastes so much better in the glass?

It's clear that thousands of drinkers share our views. The ever-increasing number of bottle-conditioned beers on sale and the expanding number of bottled beer retailers are evidence of this. There is, unfortunately, some less happy news to impart. In March 2006, Gale's Brewery in Horndean, Hampshire, was closed by its new owner, Fuller's. Gale's had long been one of the stalwarts of traditional bottled beer, with an interesting range of strong beers intriguingly packaged in little corked bottles. Pick of the pack was the famous Prize Old Ale, a beer that had been in production since the 1920s and was one of only five bottle-conditioned beers regularly available when CAMRA was founded in 1971. With the transfer of Gale's production to Fuller's Chiswick brewery, all Gale's bottled beers have been lost, except for Prize Old Ale, which has already been bottled for this year. Next year's

Buying and Storing Real Ale in a Bottle... Because it is a living, working product, real ale in a bottle needs a little extra attention before you drink it. Just like cask ale in a pub, it benefits from care and respect, but a few ground rules make it simple.

Firstly, always buy fresh stock. Although bottle-conditioned beers sometimes mature beautifully in the bottle (particularly strong, malty ales), buy the freshest beer you can (check the best before dates) and, with only a few exceptions, drink it sooner, rather than later. When you get the beer home, keep it in the dark. Most beer bottles are dark brown. This is for a purpose. The opacity of the glass protects the beer from being 'sunstruck' — a chemical reaction caused by bright light that leads to unpleasant flavours and 'skunky' aromas. To help the bottles do their job, store them in a dark place. Be particularly careful with clear- or green-glass bottles, which may look nice but are woefully inadequate in protecting beer.

It's also vital to store your beer cool, as low temperatures preserve beer. When it comes to serving temperatures, follow the advice on the label. Finally, unless the bottle has a cork, in which case it is best stored lying down to keep the cork moist, bottled beers should be stored upright. If you do lay down a beer, remember to put it back vertical a few days before drinking to give the sediment time to settle.

brew is in its maturation stage and will be bottled by Fuller's in due course. The future of the beer after that remains uncertain, but we hope Fuller's will keep faith with this classic beer.

Turning back to the plus points, however, it is encouraging to see more major brewers joining microbreweries in putting their trust in real ale in a bottle. Shepherd Neame, which was one of the first to lend its weight to the bottle-conditioned beer revival in the early 1990s, only to pull out when production problems struck, is now back in the fold, and a more surprising newcomer to the territory is Indian lager company Cobra, which has recognized that some curry lovers are looking for more than a standard lager when they go for a meal.

Allied to the growth in bottle-conditioned beers is the expansion in the number of shops that sell them. The Beer Shops section of this book is bigger than ever, and mail order beer services add another dimension. CAMRA is actively supporting retailers who sell bottle-conditioned beer. Since early 2005, it has provided – free of charge – a range of branded materials to promote bottle-conditioned beers. Training and advice sheets, explanatory leaflets and 'Buy Real Ale in a Bottle Here' window stickers are all available to interested retailers, who can also buy real ale in a bottle carry packs for their customers' use.

This initiative follows up CAMRA's real ale in a bottle accreditation scheme, launched in 2004, which allows brewers of bottle-conditioned beers to use a special 'CAMRA says this is real ale' logo on their labels. More than a hundred breweries have so far signed up to the scheme, which is intended to help shoppers identify bottled real ale from filtered bottled beers and to educate them about the properties of a bottled real ale.

Looking for the best

A further initiative launched by CAMRA has centred on the quality of bottle-conditioned beers. Through the *Good Bottled Beer Guide* and other work, CAMRA has helped to dramatically increase the number of bottled real ales in production. Now the aim is to ensure that the quality remains as high as the quantity.

The *Good Bottled Beer Guide* is an inclusive guide, covering all bottle-conditioned beers brewed in the UK, but, with the numbers growing every year, and in response to reader requests, we feel it is time to recognize the very best producers. There are numerous brewers who make consistently excellent bottle-conditioned beer, and when the process is allied to a remarkable recipe, the final product is outstanding, way surpassing anything else in the bottled beer world. CAMRA now wants to encourage all brewers to hit these highest standards and it begins with this edition of the book.

Rosettes and stars

As you turn the pages you will discover two new symbols. The first is a rosette next to the names of some breweries. The rosette indicates that, in our opinion – after years of tasting bottle-conditioned beers – a brewery delivers not just a good beer but an outstandingly high quality product. We have not awarded this rosette lightly. The aim is to recognize excellence. The award will remain under constant review and may be taken away in the next edition if standards slip, but similarly the incentive is there for breweries that have not claimed a rosette on this occasion to join the elite. Some new bottling brewers in particular have been impressive, but we'd like a little more time to confirm the consistency.

The second new symbol highlights outstanding individual beers, beers that are not only to be found constantly in top order but which are truly great examples of a bottle-conditioned beer. Again, we have set the benchmark high. We have been sparing in our selection and look forward to adding more stars in future editions.

Supporting the drive for the highest standards is a quality feedback card produced by CAMRA. The card has been designed to collect information that can be relayed to the brewers about their products. It prompts responses about both the quality of the beer and the way in which it was sold. The cards are free to all beer lovers, whether or not CAMRA members, and can be obtained from: RAIB Quality Scheme, CAMRA, 230 Hatfield Road, St Albans AL1 4LW, or via e-mail at: camra@camra.org.uk. The more people who fill in these cards, the better picture of the quality of bottled beer we can obtain, and the more information brewers will have to make their products even better.

We encourage you to have your say, but the very least you can do is to keep on buying and enjoying bottle-conditioned beers. With nearly 800 to look for, it'll keep you busy until the next edition of this book.

The Champions

Below is a list of the most recent winners of CAMRA's *Champion Bottle-Conditioned Beer of Britain* contest, which began in 1991 and is now sponsored by *The Guardian* newspaper. Judging takes place during the Great British Beer Festival, held in London in August each year.

1994
1 Courage Imperial Russian Stout
2 King & Barnes Festive
3 Shepherd Neame Spitfire

1995
1 King & Barnes Festive
2 Gale's Prize Old Ale
3 Bass Worthington's White Shield

1996
1 Marston's Oyster Stout
2 Bass Worthington'sWhite Shield
3 Courage Imperial Russian Stout

1997
1 Hop Back Summer Lightning
2 King & Barnes Festive
3 Fuller's 1845

1998
1 Fuller's 1845
2 Burton Bridge EmpirePale Ale
3 Hampshire Pride of Romsey

1999
1 Young's Special London Ale
2 Salopian Entire Butt
3 Hampshire Pride of Romsey

2000
1 King & Barnes Worthington's White Shield
2 Hampshire Pride of Romsey
3 King & Barnes Festive

2001
1 RCH Ale Mary
2 Hop Back Summer Lightning
3 Fuller's 1845

2002
1 Fuller's 1845
2 Brakspear Live Organic
3 Hop Back Summer Lightning

2003
1 O'Hanlon's Original Port Stout
2 Fuller's 1845
3 RCH Old Slug Porter

2004
1 Titanic Stout
2 Young's Special London Ale
3 Yates' YSD

2005
1 Durham Evensong
2 Young's Special London Ale
3 Titanic Stout

Brewing Bottled Beer

THE PROCESS OF BREWING begins with malt. Malt is barley grain that has been partially germinated to help release sugars and enzymes needed for the brewing process and then kilned to prevent further germination. The degree of kilning also dictates the character of the malt; the more 'baked' the malt, the darker the colour and the more roasted the taste. Some malts are toasted dark for bitter, coffeeish flavours; others are just lightly crisped for a sweeter, nuttier taste. At the brewery, the malt is crushed and then combined in a vessel called a mash tun with hot water (known as 'liquor' in the trade), which has usually been treated to adjust its chemical balance.

The beauty of hops

After roughly an hour and a half's mashing and stirring, a thick, sweet liquid called wort is formed. This is run off from the mash tun and diverted into a boiler known as a copper. Here the wort is boiled up with hops which add bitterness and sometimes herbal, spicy, citrus or floral characters. Like malts, hops come in many varieties. Some are very bitter; others milder. Some make themselves known in the aroma; others are expressed in the taste. Hops also act as a preservative. They can be added as whole hop flowers or as compressed pellets. Some brewers use hop oils (concentrated extract), but these can be astringent. The hops are added at various stages of the boil and sometimes 'adjuncts' are introduced in the copper, or earlier in mash tun, too. These include sugars, which add to the fermentability of the wort, and maize, which helps produce a good head on the beer.

After an hour or two in the copper, the hops are strained out and the wort is run off and cooled, before being pumped into a fermenting vessel, where yeast is added ('pitched'). Yeast is a single-celled fungus that turns the sugars in the wort into alcohol and carbon dioxide (the gas that gives beer its natural effervescence). Each yeast, however, also

HOW REAL ALE IN A BOTTLE IS BREWED

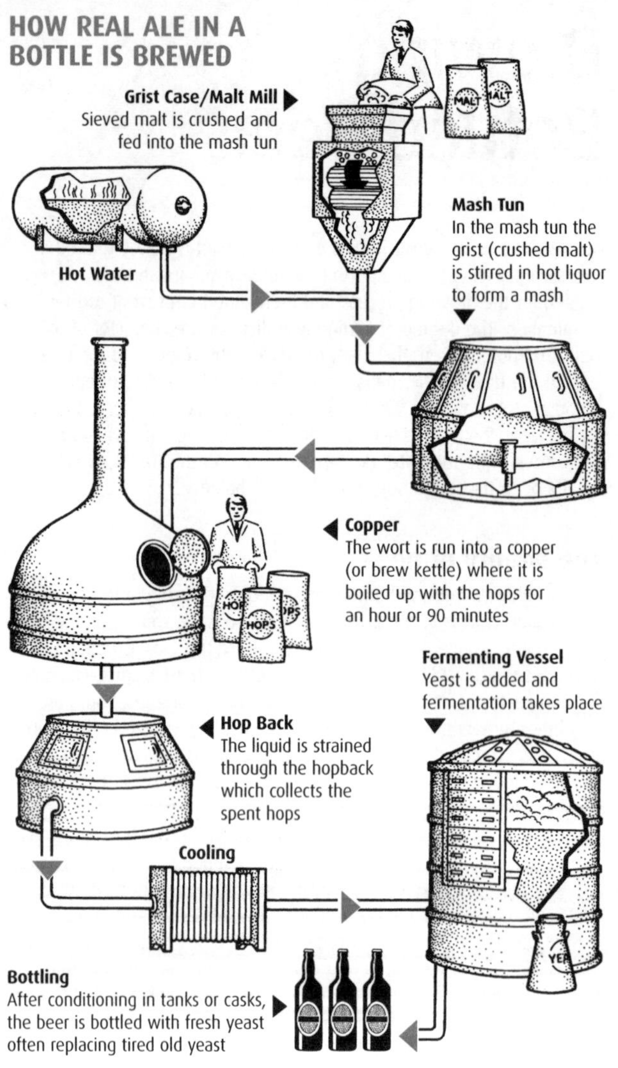

has its own character which is harnessed and preserved by brewery chemists. Many breweries use the same yeast for decades.

During the first few days of fermentation, the yeast works furiously with the wort, growing quickly and covering the top with a thick, bubbly layer of foam. Most is skimmed off, but some sinks into the brew and continues to work, eating up the sugars and generating more carbon dioxide and alcohol. Lager beers are known as 'bottom fermenting', because the yeast they use sinks to the bottom of the wort, rather than lying on the top. A few days later, this 'primary fermentation' is deemed over and bottle-conditioned beers and processed bottled beers go their separate ways.

The living and the dead

Processed, or 'bright', beers are chilled, filtered and pasteurized, killing off and removing any yeast still in the brew. They are then put into bottles and carbonated. Some of these beers are given time at the brewery beforehand to mature. Other breweries follow a halfway-house system whereby the beer is sterile filtered to remove the yeast, but is not pasteurized. Such beers, strictly speaking, do not condition in the bottle and have a fairly short shelf-life, but they do have a fresher taste than heavily pasteurized beers.

For bottle-conditioned beers, however, the next stage varies from brewery to brewery. Some adopt the simplest form of bottle conditioning, running the beer from a cask or tank into the bottle, yeast and all. This can be a rather hit and miss affair, as not enough yeast may get into the bottle to ensure a good secondary fermentation and the beer may be rather flat when opened. Other breweries take greater pains to ensure their beers have the right level of fizz. They fine or filter out the tired old yeast and replace it with fresh yeast, which may be a special strain that works well in bottles. The technically precise check the yeast and fermentable sugar levels to guarantee that the right amounts are present.

Some brewers 'kräusen' the beer ready for bottling. This involves adding some partially fermented wort to the beer to give the yeast new sugars to react with. Others prime the beer, using sugar solutions for the same purpose. Once capped and labelled, bottles are often warm-conditioned at the brewery for a few weeks, to ensure that the secondary fermentation gets off to a good start.

The Trappists' Tale

OUR UNDERSTANDING OF BOTTLE-CONDITIONED BEER may only just be re-awakening in the UK, but in Belgium they've never lost their love for natural bottled beer. Most of the country's finest beers mature in the bottle and, intriguingly, at the heart of the country's bottled beer industry is a small core of brewing monks. There are six monasteries in Belgium (plus one in the Netherlands) that produce beer on a commercial basis. They belong to an offshoot of the Cistercian brotherhood known as the Trappists, and they make heavenly beer.

Some people think it odd that monks have anything to do with beer, that the Church and brewing do not mix. It's an attitude that combines ignorance with prejudice. The same people think nothing of the fact that the clergy uses wine in its rituals. Beer, it seems, is below the salt, but don't tell the holy brothers in Belgium this.

Historic roots

The brothers revere the beer they create. Its production dates back to the Middle Ages when monasteries operated partly as resting places for pilgrims and beer was produced to serve to the guests. Beer also played a role in the monks' own lives. Although they are allowed one glass a day under the rule of St Benedict, the original founder of the order, most now save their indulgence for high days and holidays. Traditionally, however, beer was a boon in times of fasting, when solid food was off the menu, and nutrients needed to be found somewhere.

Nominally, the six Trappist monastery-breweries are Chimay, Orval, Westmalle, Westvleteren, Achel and Rochefort. They belong to a Trappist federation but are independently operated. Lay workers are brought in to do most of the brewhouse tasks but, in order to maintain the Trappist accreditation, brewing has to be overseen by the monks themselves. The brothers are more than happy to do this. Their lifestyle is based around St Benedict's ordnance that the day be divided into three equal periods: eight hours of work, eight hours of prayer and eight hours of rest. The work element may involve other duties around the abbey – in the gardens or in the kitchens, perhaps – but brewing is as good as any option. Another requirement for retaining the Trappist title is that the profits from beer production be used only for the upkeep of the abbey and for good causes. That's why the six abbeys are closely linked to charitable work in their neighbourhoods.

So brewing at a Trappist monastery is quite unlike any other type of brewing. It may be a commercial enterprise to a degree, but it's not a capitalist venture in the recognized sense. Most only brew enough to satisfy their needs. Their beers may be magnificent, but they won't increase production just to meet demand. Also, they sell very little of their production in draught form. For the Trappists, the bottle is the key.

Holy Wednesday

At Rochefort abbey in the south of Belgium, the brewing week revolves around Wednesday. That's the day when bottling takes place. Every other aspect of the brewing process – the mashing, the boiling, the cooling and the fermenting – has to fit around this vital day. There are three beers here, all dark, rich ales. They are labelled simply 6, 8 and 10 – a relic of an old system of assessing a beer's gravity. Most of the production is given over to 8, a joyous 9.2% elixir that warms the spirit as well as the throat. At a daunting 11.3% stands the mighty 10, described in some circles as the 'Burgundy of beers', and then there is 6, a junior member of the team at a mere 7.5%, which is less easy to find outside its home town. All the beers have a distinctive malty, peppery character, with varying degrees of fruitiness, sweetness and warmth. There is definitely something saintly about them.

The beers are only sold in bottle and gain much of their character while in the bottle, as there is no maturation at the brewery. After primary fermentation, the beer is centrifuged, sugar and fresh yeast are added and the bottles are filled. Consequently, there is a marked change of flavour between young and older examples, with the yeast working its miracles in the bottle, swooping on those luscious sugars and drying out the beer. There's no talk of pasteurization here. There are no gas bottles to swamp dead, filtered beer with carbon dioxide. There is no rush to turn over pallet after pallet of mass-marketed 'brands'. This is bottled beer brewing at its purest. The dirty fingers of the commercial world are kept well away from the production process.

Thus Trappist beer is holy beer in more than one sense. Other brewers interested in producing truly great bottled beer, take note.

How the Guide Is Organised

THE *GOOD BOTTLED BEER GUIDE* contains details of all known bottle-conditioned beers being brewed in the UK. The beers are listed by brewery (which is briefly described), and within each brewery beers are listed in increasing order of strength. For each beer the following information is given: alcohol by volume percentage (ABV – the beer's strength), bottle size and ingredients. Suggested serving temperatures have been simplified to 'cold', 'cool' and 'room temperature'. Cool is estimated to be around 12°C, or the correct temperature for cask ale in a pub. A rosette symbol is awarded to breweries that, we consider, produce consistently good bottle-conditioned beer. A star is shown next to a beer's name if we believe it to be a particularly outstanding beer. The tasting notes are purely the views of the author. Because bottle-conditioned beers are likely to change character during their shelf life, these notes are therefore offered only as a basic guide.

Beers featured in this book are mostly sold locally, through farmers' markets, small grocers, craft shops and delicatessens. Some breweries also sell direct to the public, but this may be by the case only, and some offer a mail order service, which is mentioned if relevant. Otherwise beers can be obtained through specialist off-licences or mail order companies (see the Beer Shops section at the back of the book). If a beer has a listing with a major retailer (supermarket or off-licence chain), this is indicated. However, where beers are actually sold is subject to change, so it is suggested that readers contact the breweries for up-to-date details of retailers.

Much appreciation is offered to numerous people for their assistance in the compilation of this book. These include CAMRA's brewery liaison officers, and brewers who kindly forwarded details of their beers and sample bottles. Brewers who would like to make sure their beers are featured in the next edition are invited to contact the author, Jeff Evans, via CAMRA at: 230 Hatfield Road, St Albans, Hertfordshire AL1 4LW. Alternatively, they can e-mail Jeff via camra@camra.org.uk.

Alcazar

Alcazar Brewery, Church Street, Old Basford, Nottingham NG6 0GA.
Tel. (0115) 978 2282 Fax (0115) 978 9666
E-mail: alcazarbrewery@tiscali.co.uk
Website: www.alcazarbrewery.co.uk
Mail order service

Alcazar Brewery was set up behind the Fox & Crown pub in 1999 and is run by Canadian David Allen. The brewery has a series of filtered bottled beers but added these bottle-conditioned brews in 2006.

Mocha Stout

● **ABV 5%** ● **BOTTLE SIZE 500 ml** ● **SERVE cool**
● **INGREDIENTS Maris Otter pale malt/crystal malt/chocolate malt/roasted barley/Target and Golding hops/chocolate and coffee essences**

To enhance the richness of this stout, chocolate and coffee essences are added to the copper boil. Like the other Alcazar bottle-conditioned beers, Mocha Stout is bottled in house, after being filtered and re-seeded with fresh yeast (the same as used for primary fermentation).

TASTING NOTES

Dark ruby, with bitter dark malts and light chocolate in the nose and dark, nutty chocolate and light coffee in the bitter taste and dry finish.

Maple Magic

● **ABV 5.5%** ● **BOTTLE SIZE 500 ml** ● **SERVE cool**
● **INGREDIENTS Maris Otter pale malt/crystal malt/amber malt/chocolate malt/roasted barley/Fuggle, Golding, Challenger and Northdown hops/maple syrup/nutmeg/cinnamon/cloves**

This is Alcazar's dark winter ale, exposing David Allen's Canadian roots. A selection of spices are added to the copper for a seasonal effect.

TASTING NOTES

A deep ruby beer with vinous dark malts and sweet spices throughout, before a dry, coffeeish, spicy, bitter aftertaste.

Bombay Castle IPA

● **ABV 6.5%** ● **BOTTLE SIZE 500 ml** ● **SERVE cool**
● **INGREDIENTS Maris Otter pale malt/Progress and Golding hops**

This new IPA was inspired by a recipe in *Homebrew Classics: India Pale*

Ale, one of two histories of beer styles written by Roger Protz and Clive La Pensée for CAMRA Books. Bombay Castle was an East India Company merchant ship from the 18th and 19th centuries.

TASTING NOTES

A golden ale with a hoppy, citrus nose and a big, tangy hop taste, with bitter orange and other citrus. Dry, very hoppy finish. Lightly warming.

Ales of Scilly

Ales of Scilly Brewery, Higher Trenoweth, St Mary's, Isles of Scilly TR21 0NS. Tel. (01720) 422419
E-mail: mark@alesofscilly.co.uk

Opened in 2001 and expanded to a five-barrel plant in 2004, Ales of Scilly is the most southwesterly brewery in the UK.

Scuppered

● ABV 4.6% ● BOTTLE SIZE 500 ml ● SERVE cool
● INGREDIENTS Maris Otter pale malt/crystal malt/black malt/ Challenger hops

A premium ale bottled just in the winter months and mostly sold on the Isles of Scilly. The beer is filled from a settling tank after fermentation and allowed three months in bottle prior to going on sale.

Atlantic

Atlantic Brewery, Treisaac Farm, Treisaac, Newquay, Cornwall TR8 4DX. Tel. (01637) 880326 Fax (07092) 869242
E-mail: stuart@atlanticbrewery.com
Website: www.atlanticbrewery.com

This small, farm-based brewery began production in 2005 and so far has concentrated on bottled beers. The beers are all Soil Association-accredited organic and are left unfined (thus acceptable to vegans). They are filled directly on site from the tank and are allowed three months to mature in bottle. Best before dates are set at one year.

Gold

● ABV 4.6% ● BOTTLE SIZE 330 ml ● SERVE cool
● INGREDIENTS Pale malt/wheat malt/Fuggle and First Gold hops/ root ginger

Gold Organic Summer Ale, to give it its full title. The crisp, clean palate and ginger accent ensure it goes well with spicy foods, according to brewer Stuart Thomson. Best served cooler than the other two beers.

TASTING NOTES

An orange-amber beer with a spicy, perfumed aroma of fresh ginger. The gently bitter taste is also ginger-accented, perfumed and lightly warming. More ginger warmth develops in the dry, bitter finish.

Blue

● **ABV 4.8%** ● **BOTTLE SIZE 330 ml** ● **SERVE cool**

● **INGREDIENTS Pale malt/crystal malt/chocolate malt/black malt/wheat malt/Fuggle and First Gold hops**

Described as organic dark ale, this beer should really have been named Black, says Stuart – except that Atlantic Blue sounds much better.

TASTING NOTES

A ruby beer with a chocolaty, oaty malt and light orangey hop nose. The taste is bitter yet creamily malty, with gentle tropical fruits. The darker malts bring a little dryness, which continues in the bitter finish, although sweet malt remains, along with a hint of plain chocolate.

Red

● **ABV 5%** ● **BOTTLE SIZE 330 ml** ● **SERVE cool**

● **INGREDIENTS Pale malt/crystal malt/wheat malt/Fuggle and First Gold hops**

This one is fully known as Red Organic Celtic Ale and was Atlantic's first ever beer, introduced in January 2005. Because of its strength and full body, Stuart thinks it marries well with red meats and game.

TASTING NOTES

True to its name, with nutty malt and a creamy, oaty note in the nose, with hop resins and light fruit emerging. There's plenty of malt in the mouth but also a firm, hoppy bitterness. Dry, bitter finish of nutty malt.

B&T

B&T Brewery Ltd., The Brewery, Shefford, Bedfordshire SG17 5DZ.
Tel. (01462) 815080 Fax (01462) 850841
E-mail: brewery@banksandtaylor.com
Website: www.banksandtaylor.com
Mail order service

This Bedfordshire brewery was founded as Banks & Taylor in 1981 and rescued from receivership by new ownership in 1994, when the company name was shortened to B&T. The name Banks & Taylor is still used on the bottle labels. Bottling takes place on site after one month's maturation in the cask. The beer is allowed to drop bright and then re-seeded with new yeast and primed with sugar. Much of the bottled production is now sold at farmers' markets.

Shefford Bitter

● ABV 3.8% ● BOTTLE SIZE 500 ml ● SERVE cool
● INGREDIENTS Pearl pale malt/crystal malt/Golding, Fuggle and Challenger hops

Brewed first on 14 August 1982, the day the brewery opened, and taking its name from the brewery's home village. Shefford Bitter has been added to the regular bottled beer range in the past two years.

TASTING NOTES

A dark golden ale with a soft, fruity aroma of pears and citrus. Light, tinned fruit flavours lead the way in the mouth over a gentle malty base. There's a fine hop edge and then some bittersweet notes on the swallow. Drying, hoppy and bitter finish.

Golden Fox

● ABV 4.1% ● BOTTLE SIZE 500 ml ● SERVE cool
● INGREDIENTS Pearl pale malt/wheat malt/Styrian Golding hops

Originally brewed as Millennium Gold in time for the year 2000 celebrations, when a fox featured on the pump clip. Bottled since 2004.

TASTING NOTES

A golden ale with a mellow fruity (tinned peaches) aroma. The taste is crisp, with sharp citrus hop bitterness and underlying sweet 'fruit cocktail' flavours. Drying, bitter, hoppy aftertaste.

Black Dragon Mild

● ABV 4.3% ● BOTTLE SIZE 500 ml ● SERVE cool
● INGREDIENTS Mild ale malt/crystal malt/black malt/roasted barley/wheat malt/Golding hops

Brewed initially as a cask beer for CAMRA's May Mild Month in 2001.

TASTING NOTES

A deep ruby beer with biscuity dark grains leading in the aroma, providing gentle chocolate, coffee and caramel notes. There's more smooth, dark malt in the taste supported by light fruit. Gentle bitterness builds in the dry, roasted grain finish.

Dragonslayer

● ABV 4.5% ● BOTTLE SIZE 500 ml ● SERVE cool
● INGREDIENTS Pearl pale malt/wheat malt/Challenger and Golding hops

Based on the legend of St George, Dragonslayer was first brewed in cask form in 1992 and is a particularly suitable accompaniment for white meats and pasta dishes, say the brewers.

TASTING NOTES

A golden ale with delicate malt and light lemon in the aroma. The bittersweet taste is delicately malty, with hops bringing more gentle lemon notes. Dry, hoppy finish.

Edwin Taylor's Extra Stout

● ABV 4.5% ● BOTTLE SIZE 500 ml ● SERVE cool
● INGREDIENTS Pearl pale malt/brown malt/roasted barley/ Challenger hops

Named after the great-grandfather of brewery founder Martin Ayres, Edwin Taylor's Extra Stout has been on sale in cask since 1991 and in bottle since 1998. Mr Taylor was, as the label declares, involved in brewing in London in the 1890s. He was in fact a drayman for Fremlins.

TASTING NOTES

Dark ruby, with dark malts and faint liquorice in the aroma, and a bitter taste of biscuity dark malts and hops. Lingering, dry, bitter finish of roasted grain, with coffee notes.

SOD

● ABV 5% ● BOTTLE SIZE 500 ml ● SERVE cool
● INGREDIENTS Pearl pale malt/crystal malt/black malt/Challenger and Golding hops

Short for Shefford Old Dark, SOD was one of the first draught beers the brewery ever produced. It has been in bottle since 2004.

SOS

● ABV 5% ● BOTTLE SIZE 500 ml ● SERVE cool
● INGREDIENTS Pearl pale malt/crystal malt/Golding and Fuggle hops

Shefford Old Strong: winner of the *Tesco Beer Challenge* in 2002.

Ballard's

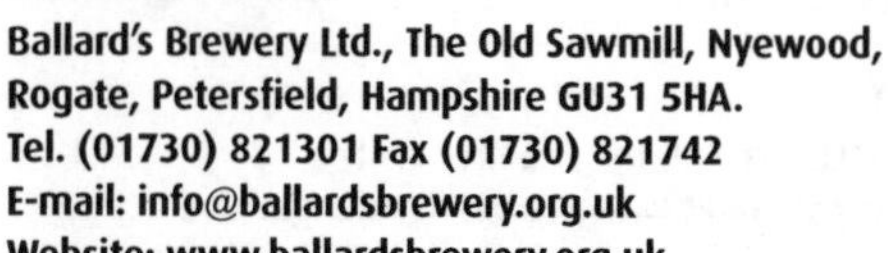

Ballard's Brewery Ltd., The Old Sawmill, Nyewood, Rogate, Petersfield, Hampshire GU31 5HA.
Tel. (01730) 821301 Fax (01730) 821742
E-mail: info@ballardsbrewery.org.uk
Website: www.ballardsbrewery.org.uk
Mail order service

Founded in 1980 at Cumbers Farm, Trotton, Ballard's has been trading at Nyewood in West Sussex since 1988 and bottle conditioning for a number of years. All the beers are matured for ten days, fined in a conditioning tank, sterile filtered and re-seeded with dried yeast before bottling. They carry a nine-month best before date, although the strongest beer should mature beautifully well beyond this time.

Best Bitter

● **ABV 4.2%** ● **BOTTLE SIZE 500 ml** ● **SERVE cool**
● **INGREDIENTS Pearl pale malt/crystal malt/Fuggle and Golding hops**

Ballard's first ever beer, and its consistent best seller, was only introduced in bottled form in 2001.

TASTING NOTES

An amber beer with a malty, lightly fruity nose. The taste is quite dry and bitter with malt sweetness and some soft fruit character. Dry, bitter finish with lingering malt and hops.

Major stockists Local Asda and Budgens

Nyewood Gold

● **ABV 5%** ● **BOTTLE SIZE 500 ml** ● **SERVE cool**
● **INGREDIENTS Pearl pale malt/Phoenix hops**

'Nye', as in the brewery address and the name of this beer, is a collective noun for a group of pheasants, which appear on the label. This beer was first brewed for the 1997 *Beauty of Hops* competition, where it took top honours in the category for Phoenix hops. The same draught beer then claimed the *Best Strong Bitter* prize at the *Champion Beer of Britain* contest in 1999. It was bottled for the first time the same year. Ballard's recommends serving Nyewood Gold at a slightly lower temperature than its other beers.

TASTING NOTES

A dark golden ale with a soft malt and fruit nose (oranges and tinned

fruit salad), before a bitter taste of grassy hop resins and light, smooth malt. Dry, hoppy and bitter aftertaste.
Major stockists Local Asda and Budgens

Wassail

ABV 6% • BOTTLE SIZE 500 ml • SERVE cool
• INGREDIENTS Pearl pale malt/crystal malt/Fuggle and Golding hops
Wassail is a drinking salutation, translating as 'Be whole' from Old English. This winter warmer first appeared in cask in 1980, and in bottle in 1995. The label shows Hengist, the 5th-century leader of the Jutes, toasting Vortigern, King of the Britons. Rowena, Hengist's daughter, who seduced Vortigern, is also depicted.
TASTING NOTES
A russet-coloured strong ale with a creamy, malt and fruit nose. Soft in the mouth, it tastes fruity, malty and strong. The bitter, fruity, hoppy finish leaves a little tingle on the gums.
Major stockist Local Asda

Poms' Delight

ABV 9.6% • BOTTLE SIZE 275 ml • SERVE cool
• INGREDIENTS Pearl pale malt/crystal malt/Fuggle and Golding hops
Poms' Delight (think of the Ashes) is the latest in the Ballard's series of 'Old Bounder' beers – strong beers in the same style but with different names and strengths. The brewery has been producing these for 18 years. The first batch of each of new beer rolls out on the first Sunday in December (to tie in with a charity 'beer walk') and the brew is then repeated about six months later. There is a draught version, too (available over Christmas), which is aged for at least two months before dispatch to the pub. The bottled version is conditioned for two weeks before bottling. Although each bottle carries a 12-month best before date, the beer is likely to remain drinkable for much longer. Add a little to a Christmas pudding, or treat it like port, says brewery owner Carola Brown. She also suggests you mull it with sugar and spices.
TASTING NOTES
A ruby ale with vinous fruits (sultanas), a little treacle and a touch of liquorice in the aroma. The taste is surprisingly bitter, even though there's plenty of sweetness lingering on the lips. Creamy in places, with more vinous fruit. The finish is warming and drying, with bitterness lasting longest, but there's just a little vinous catch in the throat, too.

Bartrams

Bartrams Brewery, Rougham Estate, Rougham, Bury St Edmunds, Suffolk IP30 9LZ. Tel. (01449) 737655

Marc Bartram set up his own brewery in an industrial unit in 1999 and moved into new premises, on an old airfield, in 2004. An earlier Bartrams Brewery operated in Tonbridge, Kent, between 1894 and 1920. It was run by Captain Bill Bartram, whose image Marc wanted to use on his beer labels and pump clips. No photograph was found, however, so Marc grew a beard, became Captain Bill and now features on all his beers. Each beer is filtered and re-seeded with fresh yeast prior to bottling. The bottles are mostly sold in local farmers' markets.

Marld

● **ABV 3.4%** ● **BOTTLE SIZE 500 ml** ● **SERVE cool**
● **INGREDIENTS Mild ale malt/amber malt/roasted barley/flaked barley/Galena and Golding hops**

Marc's dark ruby mild.

TASTING NOTES

Spicy malt and a hint of chocolate in the aroma are followed by a malty taste, with faint fruit. Lightly roasted, dry finish with growing bitterness.

Rougham Ready

● **ABV 3.6%** ● **BOTTLE SIZE 500 ml** ● **SERVE cool**
● **INGREDIENTS Pale malt/crystal malt/hops vary**

A light beer, made from organic ingredients.

Premier Bitter

● **ABV 3.7%** ● **BOTTLE SIZE 500 ml** ● **SERVE cool**
● **INGREDIENTS Maris Otter pale malt/crystal malt/chocolate malt/Challenger, Fuggle and Golding hops**

PMs Thatcher and Churchill have featured on the pumpclips for the cask version of this ale, as did the contenders at the last General Election.

Little Green Man

● **ABV 3.8%** ● **BOTTLE SIZE 500 ml** ● **SERVE cool**
● **INGREDIENTS Pale malt/First Gold hops/coriander**

A more quaffable version of the 4% Green Man (see opposite), also produced with organic ingredients.

TASTING NOTES
A golden, bitter ale with the peppery, orangey notes of subtle coriander and hops throughout. Dry, bitter, spicy, hoppy finish.

Red Queen

● **ABV 3.9%** ● **BOTTLE SIZE 500 ml** ● **SERVE cool**
● **INGREDIENTS Maris Otter pale malt/crystal malt/chocolate malt/ Challenger, Fuggle and Golding hops**
A rich amber-coloured session ale.
TASTING NOTES
Chocolate maltiness, a little hop spice and citrus notes feature in the aroma. Balanced malt and bitterness combine in the taste, with a clean, sweet, hoppy-citrus edge. Bitterness grows in the fruity, hoppy finish.

Green Man

● **ABV 4%** ● **BOTTLE SIZE 500 ml** ● **SERVE cool**
● **INGREDIENTS Pale malt/First Gold hops/coriander**
A golden best bitter made with organic ingredients. These may vary, depending on what becomes available.
TASTING NOTES
A fuller version of Little Green Man, with more malty sweetness. Sappy hops give way to a peachy/orangey fruitiness in the nose but re-emerge in the mouth. Dry, bitter, lightly fruity and spicy, hop finish.

Headway

● **ABV 4%** ● **BOTTLE SIZE 500 ml** ● **SERVE cool**
● **INGREDIENTS Pale malt/crystal malt/hops vary**
Headway is an organic charity beer, with 10p per bottle sold being donated to Headway, the brain injury association.

Pierrot

● **ABV 4%** ● **BOTTLE SIZE 500 ml** ● **SERVE cool**
● **INGREDIENTS Maris Otter pale malt/caramalt/Fuggle, Golding, Saaz and Tettnang hops**
An ale inspired by a visit Marc made to a Croatian brewery.
TASTING NOTES
A golden ale with a complex, hoppy nose. Hops and bitterness are balanced by malt in the taste. Long, hoppy finish. A hint of bubblegum throughout adds a something of a Belgian ale character.

The Bee's Knees

● ABV 4.2% ● BOTTLE SIZE 500 ml ● SERVE cool
● INGREDIENTS Maris Otter pale malt/carapils malt/Challenger, Ahtanum and Fuggle hops/wildflower honey/coriander
As for Pierrot overleaf, a very pale-coloured malt forms the basis of the mash for this honey-flavoured beer.
TASTING NOTES
An amber beer with a floral, honeyed, hoppy aroma. There's a honey softness throughout the taste, which is otherwise crisp and bitter, with good malt balance. Dry, bitter finish with the smoothness of honey.

Catherine Bartram's IPA

● ABV 4.3% ● BOTTLE SIZE 500 ml ● SERVE cool
● INGREDIENTS Pale malt/First Gold and Fuggle hops
Catherine Bartram was apparently a survivor of the Siege of Lucknow (1857–8) and her diary helped paint a picture of what went on during the conflict. Her Indian connections inspired this IPA.
TASTING NOTES
A golden ale with an initial malty aroma which soon gives way to light, fruity hop. Tangy hop leads over malt in the taste and dominates the dry and increasingly bitter aftertaste.

Jester Quick One

● ABV 4.4% ● BOTTLE SIZE 500 ml ● SERVE cool
● INGREDIENTS Maris Otter pale malt/crystal malt/chocolate malt/ Ahtanum hops
A sweet, reddish bitter using American hops. Its name comes from the 'signature' (a drawn jester) of an artist who produces Marc's pumpclips.

Coal Porter

● ABV 4.5% ● BOTTLE SIZE 500 ml ● SERVE cool
● INGREDIENTS Pale malt/crystal malt/barley extract/hops vary
Another organic beer, originally a one-off for a beer festival.

Stingo!

● ABV 4.5% ● BOTTLE SIZE 500 ml ● SERVE cool
● INGREDIENTS Pale malt/Hallertau and Perle hops/honey/coriander
Another honey beer, made using organic ingredients. A Norwich Beer Festival winner in its cask version.

TASTING NOTES
A sweetish and fruity bitter with a hoppy nose and a floral honey note on the swallow. Light honey softens the mostly bitter aftertaste.

Captain Bill Bartram's Best Bitter

● **ABV 4.8%** ● **BOTTLE SIZE 500 ml** ● **SERVE cool**
● **INGREDIENTS Maris Otter pale malt/crystal malt/Fuggle and Golding hops**
A tawny beer named after the man who inspired the brewery.
TASTING NOTES
Red berries lead in the nose, edging out lightly toasted, slightly treacly malt. Fruit, malt and bitterness are all to the fore in the taste and nicely balanced. The finish has toasted malt, hops, fruit and a hint of almond.

The Captain's Cherry Stout

● **ABV 4.8%** ● **BOTTLE SIZE 500 ml** ● **SERVE cool**
● **INGREDIENTS Mild ale malt/crystal malt/black malt/chocolate malt/smoked malt/Galena, Fuggle and Golding hops/cherries**
An award-winning ruby beer, based on the stout below. Marc is pleased with the way in which he processes the fruit for this beer and the Damson Stout overleaf, but he declines to reveal his secret.
TASTING NOTES
Cherry fruit leads over dark, lightly smoky malt in the aroma. The flavours of Captain's Stout are all here, too, but with light cherry adding a touch more sweetness. Subtle cherry lingers in the aftertaste, which is bittersweet, smoky and marked by roasted malt.

Captain's Stout

● **ABV 4.8%** ● **BOTTLE SIZE 500 ml** ● **SERVE cool**
● **INGREDIENTS Mild ale malt/crystal malt/black malt/chocolate malt/smoked malt/Galena, Fuggle and Golding hops**
A ruby-coloured stout made using Bavarian smoked malt and (in part) American hops.
TASTING NOTES
Biscuity dark malt leads in the lightly smoky aroma with just a hint of vanilla. There is plenty of roasted malt character in the taste, with coffee notes and a whiff of smoke, but a light, sweet fruitiness ensures it is neither too bitter nor heavy. Bittersweet, roasted malt and a lingering smokiness run into the aftertaste.

Damson Stout

● ABV 4.8% ● BOTTLE SIZE 500 ml ● SERVE cool
● INGREDIENTS Mild ale malt/crystal malt/black malt/chocolate malt/smoked malt/Galena, Fuggle and Golding hops/damsons

A variation on the Cherry Stout, already mentioned, incorporating different fruit.

Beer Elsie Bub

● ABV 4.8% ● BOTTLE SIZE 500 ml ● SERVE cool
● INGREDIENTS Maris Otter and Halcyon pale malt/amber malt/torrefied wheat/Challenger, Golding and Fuggle hops/wildflower honey/coriander

A strong honey beer originally brewed for a pagan wedding ceremony and now produced for other pagan festivals, including Hallowe'en. The back label features an amusing, not entirely (if at all) truthful, account of how the beer got its name.

TASTING NOTES

A dark golden ale with a mellow honey note to the citrus, floral nose. Slightly earthy bitterness leads over spicy orange in the mouth, with more honey emerging softly on the swallow to linger lightly in the bitter, hoppy aftertaste.

Suffolk 'n' Strong

● ABV 5% ● BOTTLE SIZE 500 ml ● SERVE cool
● INGREDIENTS Pale malt/crystal malt/hops vary

Another organic strong ale, introduced a couple of years ago.

Xmas Holly Daze

● ABV 5% ● BOTTLE SIZE 500 ml ● SERVE cool
● INGREDIENTS Maris Otter pale malt/crystal malt/Golding and Fuggle hops

A light-coloured bitter only on sale at Christmas.

New Year Daze

● ABV 5.2% ● BOTTLE SIZE 500 ml ● SERVE cool
● INGREDIENTS Maris Otter pale malt/crystal malt/roasted malt/Golding and Fuggle hops

A deep reddish, strong bitter generally made available only over the Christmas and New Year holiday period.

Mother in Law's Tongue Tied

● ABV 9% ● BOTTLE SIZE 500 ml ● SERVE cool
● INGREDIENTS Maris Otter pale malt/Galena, Tettnang and Hallertau hops
Brewed to celebrate Marc's mother-in-law's 90th birthday.

Bazens'

Bazens' Brewery, The Rees Bazen Brewing Co. Ltd., Unit 6, Knoll Street Industrial Park, Knoll Street, Salford, Greater Manchester M7 2BL. Tel. (0161) 708 0247
Website: www.bazensbrewery.co.uk
Bazens' was set up in 2002 by Richard Bazen, formerly of Phoenix and other breweries, and his wife, Jude. Bottling commenced in 2006 and the bottles are filled direct from the fermenter, without the use of finings (so making them acceptable to vegans).

Flatbac

● ABV 4.2% ● BOTTLE SIZE 500 ml ● SERVE cool
● INGREDIENTS Maris Otter pale malt/Hallertau, Cascade and Styrian Golding hops
Richard is a former professional mandolin player and this beer takes its name from one of his instruments, a flatback mandolin. The unusual spelling is the result of a typo in a local newspaper when it carried a picture of Richard with the mandolin. The Bazens liked the look of it and kept it for the beer. The hops include Hallertau from New Zealand.
TASTING NOTES
A pale golden beer with a spicy, honeyed citrus hop aroma. The taste is crisp with spicy hops, delicate malt and more honey, before a dry, bitter, hoppy, honey-malty finish.

Knoll St Porter

● ABV 5.2% ● BOTTLE SIZE 500 ml ● SERVE cool
● INGREDIENTS Maris Otter pale malt/chocolate malt/smoked malt/ chocolate wheat malt/crystal wheat malt/rye malt/oat malt/Green Bullet hops
Knoll Street is the road on which the brewery stands, but this award-winning porter (CAMRA's *Champion Stout and Porter* in 2006 in its cask form) was originally created as Knoll's Porter at its previous site. The

family that owned the old mining land on which the brewery stood was named Knoll. More New Zealand hops feature in the recipe.

Bells

Bells Brewery & Merchants, The Workshop, Lutterworth Road, Ullesthorpe, Leicestershire LE17 5DR. Tel. (01455) 209940
E-mail: sales@bellsbrewery.co.uk
Website: www.bellsbrewery.co.uk
Mail order service

Brewery set up by former Man in the Moon and Everards brewer Jon Hutchinson in 2004. The company has moved since, just along the road to a new site next to a garden centre. The new premises include a bottled beer shop, featuring bottle-conditioned beers from numerous microbreweries.

Rainmaker

● ABV 4.1% ● BOTTLE SIZE 500 ml ● SERVE cool
● INGREDIENTS Maris Otter pale malt/crystal malt/wheat malt/ Bramling Cross and Fuggle hops

Rainmaker, like the other Bells beers, is also available in cask form.

Victor

● ABV 4.1% ● BOTTLE SIZE 500 ml ● SERVE cool
● INGREDIENTS Maris Otter pale malt/crystal malt/wheat malt/ Cascade and Columbus hops

Bells is located near Buntingthorpe RAF base, hence the naming of two of the beers, Victor and Vulcan, after Cold War bomber aircraft.

Vulcan

● ABV 4.1% ● BOTTLE SIZE 500 ml ● SERVE cool
● INGREDIENTS Maris Otter pale malt/crystal malt/Cascade and Bramling Cross hops

The second bomber beer, bottled, like all the beers, straight from the cask with no primings or fresh yeast additions.

Smalley's Stout

● ABV 4.2% ● BOTTLE SIZE 500 ml ● SERVE cool
● INGREDIENTS Maris Otter pale malt/roasted barley/Golding hop

This beer was originally named after the third V bomber, the Valiant, but as Batemans already owns a brand of that name, its title was changed to Smalley's Stout.

TP Buck

● ABV 4.3% ● BOTTLE SIZE 500 ml ● SERVE cool
● INGREDIENTS Maris Otter pale malt/crystal malt/torrefied wheat/ Cascade hops

A new beer, named after a well-known brewery in Lutterworth, now sadly long closed.

Dreamcatcher

● ABV 4.6% ● BOTTLE SIZE 500 ml ● SERVE cool
● INGREDIENTS Maris Otter pale malt/chocolate malt/Saaz and Fuggle hops

By Jon's own admission, there's nothing particularly relevant about the name of Dreamcatcher, or Rainmaker, What the Duck or Mucky Dog for that matter: he just likes the sound of them.

India Pale Ale

● ABV 4.8% ● BOTTLE SIZE 500 ml ● SERVE cool
● INGREDIENTS Maris Otter pale malt/crystal malt/Columbus and Challenger hop

An IPA seasoned with citrus American hops as well as more familiar British Challengers.

What the Duck

● ABV 5.5% ● BOTTLE SIZE 500 ml ● SERVE cool
● INGREDIENTS Maris Otter pale malt/crystal malt/wheat malt/ Bramling Cross hops

A strong bitter, light and slightly spicy according to Jon. Look out for two new fruit beers based on What the Duck with cherries and raspberries added to the cask.

Mucky Dog

● ABV 6% ● BOTTLE SIZE 500 ml ● SERVE cool
● INGREDIENTS Maris Otter pale malt/crystal malt/Fuggle and Cascade hops

Be careful with this strong ale. Jon reckons it's all too moreish.

Belvoir

Belvoir Brewery Ltd., Woodhill, Nottingham Lane,
Old Dalby, Leicestershire LE14 3LX.
Tel./Fax (01664) 823455
E-mail: sales@belvoir-brewery.go-plus.net
Website: www.belvoirbrewery.co.uk

Established in 1995 by Colin Brown, who used to brew with both Shipstone's and Theakston, this brewery sits in the Vale of Belvoir (pronounced 'beaver'). As well as three regular cask ales, five bottled beers are now in production, each being filtered and re-seeded with fresh yeast prior to bottling. Small runs are filled on site, with larger runs handled by Branded Drinks in Gloucestershire.

Star Bitter

● **ABV 3.9%** ● **BOTTLE SIZE 500 ml** ● **SERVE cool**
● **INGREDIENTS Maris Otter pale malt/crystal malt/chocolate malt/ torrefied wheat/Target, Golding and Progress hops**

Introduced in spring 2004, the star in this beer's name alludes to the emblem of Colin's former employer, the much-missed Shipstone's Brewery in Nottingham. Not so regularly produced now that a stronger version, Super Star, has been added to the range.

TASTING NOTES

A dark golden beer with a hoppy nose and taste, and a dry, hoppy, bitter finish.

Beaver Bitter

● **ABV 4.3%** ● **BOTTLE SIZE 500 ml** ● **SERVE cool**
● **INGREDIENTS Maris Otter pale malt/crystal malt/chocolate malt/ Challenger, Progress, Bramling Cross and Golding hops**

One of the brewery's first ever cask beers, making a play on the often-mispronounced name of the brewery.

Peacock's Glory

● **ABV 4.7%** ● **BOTTLE SIZE 500 ml** ● **SERVE cool**
● **INGREDIENTS Maris Otter pale malt/crystal malt/Target, Progress and Golding hops**

The agricultural pastures of the Vale of Belvoir are overlooked by battlemented Belvoir Castle (seat of the Duke of Rutland), where the grounds are home to a fine collection of peacocks. Their splendour is echoed in the name of this brew.

TASTING NOTES

Golden, with a hoppy aroma. Robust and full-bodied, it features lots of bitter hops but also good malty balance. Dry, bitter, hoppy aftertaste.

Old Dalby

● ABV 5.1% ● BOTTLE SIZE 500 ml ● SERVE cool
● INGREDIENTS Maris Otter pale malt/crystal malt/chocolate malt/ Challenger, Progress, Bramling Cross and Golding hops

Old Dalby is the name of the village where Belvoir Brewery has set up home. This strong ale is generally only made available in winter.

Super Star

● ABV 5.6% ● BOTTLE SIZE 500 ml ● SERVE cool
● INGREDIENTS Maris Otter pale malt/crystal malt/chocolate malt/ torrefied wheat/Target, Golding and Progress hops

A new addition to the range, a beefed-up version of Star Bitter.

Beowulf

Beowulf Brewing Co., Chasewater Country Park, Pool Road, Brownhills, Staffordshire WS8 7NL. Tel./Fax (01543) 454067
E-mail: beowulfbrewing@yahoo.co.uk

Beowulf was founded in a converted shop in Birmingham in 1997. In 2003 owner Philip Bennett moved the business to new premises at a country park. He's been producing one bottle-conditioned beer since 2005, but only in small quantities.

Dragon Smoke Stout

● ABV 5.3% ● BOTTLE SIZE 500 ml ● SERVE cool
● INGREDIENTS Pearl pale malt/black malt/roasted barley/flaked barley/Northern Brewer and Golding hops

Brewed as for the cask equivalent (4.7%), but primed with sugar to ensure a good bottle fermentation. Therefore a touch stronger and drier.

TASTING NOTES

Dark ruby with creamy dark malts and a hint of vanilla in the nose. Bitter dark malts lead in the taste with a little sweetness and touches of vanilla and chocolate. Dry, smoky, roasted, bitter, lightly chocolaty finish.

Betwixt

The Betwixt Beer Co., New Ferry, Wirral, Cheshire. Tel. (07792) 967414
E-mail: brewer@betwixtbeer.co.uk
Website: www.betwixtbeer.co.uk

Taking its name from its location, 'betwixt the Mersey and the Dee', this Wirral-based business is run by brewer Mike McGuigan, formerly of Wolf, Brakspear and Zero Degrees. He currently has no brewery of his own, but uses equipment at Northern Brewing in Cheshire to produce beer for sale in local pubs and at farmers' markets.

Sunlight

● **ABV 4.3%** ● **BOTTLE SIZE 500 ml/1 litre** ● **SERVE cool**
● **INGREDIENTS Maris Otter pale malt/Golding hops**

A pale best bitter that was test brewed at the house of a friend in Port Sunlight, hence the name. The beer is bottled straight from a cask, without primings or re-seeding with yeast. It is sold in one-litre plastic bottles but 500 ml glass bottles are planned. A version brewed with wild hops has been produced occasionally under the name of BeWilder.

Black Isle

Black Isle Brewery, Old Allangrange, Munlochy, Highland IV8 8NZ.
Tel. (01463) 811871 Fax (01463) 811875
E-mail: info@blackislebrewery.com
Website: www.blackislebrewery.com
Mail order service

Converted farm buildings in the Highlands of Scotland provide a home for Black Isle Brewery, which was set up 1998. The Black Isle itself is a peninsula across the Moray Firth from Inverness, with an ancient history of barley production and a spectacular coastline. The brewery runs a mail order service, selling the following Soil Association-accredited organic beers by the case and also other bottled beers (filtered but not pasteurized). Organic Blonde (4.5%), listed in previous editions of this book, is now only occasionally bottled. Another occasional bottling is Hibernator (7%), a deep red ale described by brewer David Gladwin as 'liquid fruit cake'. The beers are also sanctioned by the Vegetarian Society. The ones listed below are kräusened in a conditioning tank prior to bottling. Best before dates are marked at 12 months after filling.

Organic Porter

● ABV 4.5% ● BOTTLE SIZE 500 ml ● SERVE cool

● INGREDIENTS Pale malt/crystal malt/chocolate malt/wheat malt/ oat malt/Challenger, Golding and Styrian Golding hops

A Salisbury Beer Festival champion in 2002 under its original cask name of Wagtail, this dark brew is suggested by David as a perfect match for seafood like oysters, crab and smoked salmon.

TASTING NOTES

A dark ruby porter with a mellow, biscuity, coffee nose. The taste is creamy and coffeeish but bittersweet, with a restrained hoppy fruitiness behind. Bitter, roasted finish.

Organic Scotch Ale

● ABV 4.5% ● BOTTLE SIZE 500 ml ● SERVE cool

● INGREDIENTS Pale malt/crystal malt/peat-smoked malt/wheat malt/Challenger and Golding hops/bog myrtle

A beer – recommends the brewer – to savour with haggis, black pudding or even apple strüdel! Apart from peat-smoked malt (more familiar to whisky drinkers), the unusual ingredient in Scotch Ale is bog myrtle. It may sound like the moaning ghost who hides in a lavatory in the Harry Potter books, but this is an aromatic marshland shrub (also known as sweet gale) that was often used to season beer before the arrival of hops some 500 years ago. First produced in 2002.

TASTING NOTES

A red ale with a big malty nose, with a hint of mint toffee, spice and smoke. The taste is spicy, smoky and malty with a cool 'peppermint' note. The finish has toasted malt, cool spice, smoke and bitterness.

Organic Wheat Beer

● ABV 4.5% ● BOTTLE SIZE 500 ml ● SERVE cool

● INGREDIENTS Pale malt/wheat malt/Challenger and Hallertau hops/coriander/orange peel/lemon peel

Brewed initially in 2001, this Belgian-style wheat beer was runner-up in 2002's SIBA *Wheat Beer Challenge*. David Gladwin suggests that it should served with fresh Scottish mussels or Black Isle raspberries.

TASTING NOTES

A hazy, yellow beer with lemon, orange and gingery spice in the aroma. The taste is peppery and bittersweet with a tart lemon accent. Dry, increasingly bitter finish of lemon and spice.

Blackawton

**Blackawton Brewery, Unit 7, Peninsula Park,
Moorlands Trading Estate, Saltash, Cornwall PL12 6LX.
Tel./Fax (01752) 848777
E-mail: steve@blackawtonbrewery.eclipse.co.uk**

Blackawton Brewery was set up in 1977, one of the first of the new wave of microbreweries founded after the early successes of CAMRA. Until 2001 it was the longest established brewery in Devon, but then it was sold and the new owners moved it across the River Tamar to Cornwall. The brewery moved yet again in 2003, but this time just around the corner to larger premises. The beers are bottled for Blackawton by Country Life Brewery.

Winter Fuel

● **ABV 5%** ● **BOTTLE SIZE 500 ml** ● **SERVE cool**
● **INGREDIENTS Pale malt/crystal malt/chocolate malt/torrefied wheat/Progress and Golding hops/mace/ginger/lemons**

The label of this seasonal warmer declares that it conceals a 'secret wintery twist'. Now the secret is out: brewer Steve Brooks adds whole lemons to the copper for a citrus edge and seasons the beer not only with hops but with Christmas spices, too.

TASTING NOTES

A tawny ale with an aroma of citrus and Christmas cake spices. The taste is malty but spicy, dry and bitter, with a ginger warmth poking through. Bitter, Christmas spice finish with lingering lemon.

Head Strong

● **ABV 5.2%** ● **BOTTLE SIZE 500 ml** ● **SERVE cool**
● **INGREDIENTS Pale malt/crystal malt/torrefied wheat/Progress, Challenger and Styrian Golding hops**

Head Strong is one of the beers Steve inherited when the company was purchased and it dates right back to the brewery's formative days (it was first mentioned in the *Good Beer Guide*'s 1979 edition). Steve, however, has personalised the beer a little by adding Challenger hops to the recipe.

TASTING NOTES

Golden, with a piney, citrus aroma. Spicy, citrus, piney hops dominate the taste until toasted malt emerges. Bitter, toasted malt finish.

Blue Anchor

Blue Anchor Inn, 50 Coinagehall Street, Helston, Cornwall TR13 8EL.
Tel. (01326) 562821 Fax (01326) 565765
Mail order service

Famous as one of the handful of home-brew houses still in operation when CAMRA took up the challenge of preserving British brewing heritage in 1971, The Blue Anchor is one of the UK's classic pubs. The thatched building began life as a monks' resting place in the 15th century. Its brewery – famous for its 'Spingo' ales – has been refurbished in recent years. Bottling now takes place in house.

Jubilee Ale

● ABV 4.5% ● BOTTLE SIZE 275 ml ● SERVE cool
● INGREDIENTS Pipkin pale malt/Golding hops

An IPA first brewed for The Queen's Golden Jubilee in 2002. May also be sold simply as 'IPA'.

Spingo Middle

● ABV 5% ● BOTTLE SIZE 275 ml ● SERVE cool
● INGREDIENTS Pipkin pale malt/Golding hops

Spingo has been on tap at The Blue Anchor for centuries, the pub claims. The origin of the name is the Old English 'stingo', a term for strong beer.

TASTING NOTES

A dark amber, robust ale with an earthy, spicy malt aroma. The distinctive taste merges earthy maltiness and spice, before a dry, thick, bittersweet, spicy finish.

Spingo Bragget

● ABV 6% ● BOTTLE SIZE 275 ml ● SERVE cool
● INGREDIENTS Pipkin pale malt/honey/apple juice

A hop-less, honey-flavoured brew that was originally sold under the name of Spingo 800 when it was introduced in 2001 to commemorate the 800th anniversary of the granting of the royal charter to the town of Helston by King John.

TASTING NOTES

A golden drink with a herbal aroma of honey and green apples. The same flavours come through in the sweet taste and aftertaste.

Spingo Special

● ABV 6.6% ● BOTTLE SIZE 275 ml ● SERVE cool
● INGREDIENTS Pipkin pale malt/Golding hops

This is a stronger version of Spingo Middle and, like its stablemate, may be found in dishes like beef in Spingo and Spingo burgers at the pub.

TASTING NOTES

A powerful ruby ale with an earthy, appley, spicy nose. Sweet malt is well to the fore in the mouth, allowing the earthy, bitter spiciness to provide a nice contrast. Bittersweet, fruity, spicy aftertaste.

Christmas Special/Easter Special

● ABV 7.6% ● BOTTLE SIZE 275 ml ● SERVE cool
● INGREDIENTS Pipkin pale malt/crystal malt/Golding hops

A seasonal draught ale available in bottle for a month either side of the two holidays and labelled up under the appropriate name.

TASTING NOTES

A strong ruby ale with a peppery, malt and fruit nose and the distinctive Blue Anchor spiciness in the sweet and malty taste. Red fruit and oranges lurk in the background before a sweetish, fruity finish.

Blythe

Blythe Brewery, Blythe House Farm, Lichfield Road,
Hamstall Ridware, Staffordshire WS15 3QQ.
Tel. (07773) 747724
E-mail: info@blythebrewery.plus.com
Website: www.blythebrewery.co.uk

After working for 27 years in the fluorochemical industry, it came as a welcome change when Robert Greenway began brewing in 2003, using two-and-a-half-barrel equipment in a converted barn on a Staffordshire farm. His vegan-friendly bottled beers – conditioned first in cask, racked bright then kräusened using the same yeast as used in the primary fermentation – are sold at local farmers' markets, with best before dates of six months. All are also available as draught products.

Blythe Bitter

● ABV 4% ● BOTTLE SIZE 500 ml ● SERVE cool
● INGREDIENTS Pale malt/Golding, Fuggle and Cascade hops

Like the brewery, this beer takes its name from the River Blythe that runs at the back of the brewhouse. The cask version was runner-up for West Midlands CAMRA's Beer of the Year award in 2005.

TASTING NOTES

Golden, with an aroma of sweet oranges, grapefruit and other citrus fruits. The taste is crisp and hoppy with grapefruit notes. It's sweeter on the swallow but bitterness builds quickly in the finish as hop dominate.

Chase Bitter

● ABV 4.4% ● BOTTLE SIZE 500 ml ● SERVE cool

● INGREDIENTS Pale malt/crystal malt/Challenger and Golding hops

Chase Bitter is named after Cannock Chase, Staffordshire's famous area of forest and heathland.

TASTING NOTES

A copper-coloured best bitter with a floral, citrus-fruity aroma with mellow malt. On the palate, it is bitter and lightly fruity, featuring perfumed citrus notes and gentle malty sweetness. Light body. Dry, bitter, hoppy finish.

Staffie

● ABV 4.4% ● BOTTLE SIZE 500 ml ● SERVE cool

● INGREDIENTS Pale malt/torrefied wheat/Chinook and Cluster hops

Celebrating the Staffordshire bull terrier, this best bitter has an American accent, thanks to the inclusion of Chinook and Cluster hops.

TASTING NOTES

A golden bitter with a light, hoppy, citrus aroma. The taste is crisp, clean and hoppy with delicate malty sweetness for balance and more bitter citrus fruit. Dry, bitter and hoppy aftertaste.

Palmer's Poison

● ABV 4.5% ● BOTTLE SIZE 500 ml ● SERVE cool

● INGREDIENTS Pale malt/crystal malt/black malt/flaked maize/ Challenger and Golding hops

This dark best bitter has an equally dark connection with Staffordshire's history: it recalls in its name Dr William Palmer, a notorious serial killer from Rugeley who was hanged in Stafford in 1856.

TASTING NOTES

Amber in colour, with gentle malt and light spice in the nose. It is malty, yet mostly bitter, in the mouth, with light toffee and a gentle fruity sharpness. Dry, malty, but increasingly hoppy and bitter finish.

Old Horny

● ABV 4.6% ● BOTTLE SIZE 500 ml ● SERVE cool
● INGREDIENTS Pale malt/crystal malt/black malt/torrefied wheat/ Challenger, Golding and Styrian Golding hops

Blythe's strongest bottled beer celebrates the Horn Dance, a morris dancing-type ritual that dates back to medieval times and is performed every autumn in and around the village of Abbots Bromley.

TASTING NOTES

An amber ale with light malt and citrus in the aroma. The taste is fairly crisp and bitter, supported by sweetish malt. Dry, malty finish with hops soon taking over. Rather bitter in the end.

Bradfield

Bradfield Brewery, Watt House Farm, High Bradfield, Sheffield, South Yorkshire S6 6LG. Tel./Fax (0114) 285 1118
E-mail: info@bradfieldbrewery.com
Website: www.bradfieldbrewery.com

Bradfield Brewery was set up in 2005 on a working dairy farm in Derbyshire's Peak District, and uses the farm's own bore-hole water supply. The beers are bottled direct from conditioning tanks, but filtered versions also exist. Best before dates are set at six–eight months.

Farmers Stout

● ABV 4.5% ● BOTTLE SIZE 500 ml ● SERVE cool
● INGREDIENTS Fanfare pale malt/crystal malt/chocolate malt/ roasted barley/Fuggle and Golding hops

First brewed in May 2005, this beer is said to be perfect with meat and potato pie with mushy peas!

TASTING NOTES

Deep ruby with a white collar, this stout has a grainy, biscuity aroma of dark malt and plain chocolate. More bitter, dark chocolate leads in the mouth with some herbal hop. Dry, biscuity, bitter finish of roasted grain.

Farmers Pale Ale

● ABV 5% ● BOTTLE SIZE 500 ml ● SERVE cool
● INGREDIENTS Fanfare pale malt/Fuggle and Golding hops

Also brewed first in May 2005, Pale Ale is one to try with spicy foods and curries, according to brewer Paul Ward.

TASTING NOTES
Golden, with grassy, herbal hops and light, sharp citrus in the aroma. The taste is bitter and hoppy, with strong herbal flavours and a bitter grapefruit note. Dry, bitter, herbal finish with more bitter citrus notes.

Brakspear

Brakspear Brewing Co., Eagle Maltings, The Crofts, Witney, Oxfordshire OX28 4DP. Tel. (01993) 890800 Fax (01993) 772553 E-mail: sales@brakspear-beers.co.uk Website: www.brakspear-beers.co.uk

After the closure of Brakspear's Henley brewery in 2002, brewing of the beers was moved to Burtonwood in Cheshire. In 2004, however, Refresh UK, a marketing company that had acquired the rights to brew and sell the brands, re-constructed elements of the Brakspear brewhouse at its Wychwood Brewery in Witney, so returning the beers to Oxfordshire.

Organic Beer

● ABV 4.6% ● BOTTLE SIZE 500 ml ● SERVE cool ● INGREDIENTS Pale malt/crystal malt/Hallertau, Golding and Target hops

As Live Organic, this ale won the first ever *Organic Beer Challenge*, in 2000. The beer is now brewed in Witney, although bottled at Hepworth & Co. in Horsham, where the beer is filtered and re-seeded with fresh Brakspear yeast. The best before date is set at ten months, although the beer is best drunk young. Acceptable to vegans.

TASTING NOTES
A copper ale with a rich, orange and apricot aroma. The taste is fairly bitter with lots of fruity, tangy hops (more orange and apricot) and a spicy overlay. Dry, bitter, tangy-hop finish.

Major stockists Asda, Booths, Budgens, Morrisons, Sainsbury's, Waitrose

Triple ★

● ABV 7.2% ● BOTTLE SIZE 500 ml ● SERVE cool ● INGREDIENTS Maris Otter pale malt/crystal malt/black malt/ Northdown and Cascade hops

First brewed in March 2005 as a celebratory brew to mark the successful return of Brakspear brewing to Oxfordshire, Triple takes its name from two sources. Firstly, it is hopped three times – twice in the copper (Northdowns early for bitterness and Cascades late for aroma) and finally in the fermenter with more Cascades after the beer has 'dropped' (Brakspear beers are known for their 'double dropping' system of fermentation, where the beer begins fermenting in an upper tank and then drops through to a second tank, leaving behind tired yeast and unwanted proteins). Secondly, it is thrice fermented – once during primary fermentation, a second time during a long maturation period and finally in the bottle (with the addition of fresh yeast). Triple is brewed at Witney and bottled for Brakspear by Thwaites in Lancaster. The best before date is set at ten months, but this beer should mature nicely beyond this period. Each bottle is individually numbered and, if you want to know when it was bottled, you can look it up on the Brakspear website. Like its Belgian namesakes, this English Triple is best served in a chalice-style glass and makes an excellent accompaniment to cheeses and nuts.

TASTING NOTES

Amber, with pineapple, citrus and a hint of liquorice in the full, malty aroma. Rich, malty sweetness is matched by tangy hops and tropical fruit in the taste, backed by butterscotch. Gently warming, hoppy, bittersweet finish, drying all the time, with the malty, slightly salty character of Brakspear's beers in evidence.

Major stockists Sainsbury's, Waitrose

Where to buy real ale in a bottle...

Beers in this book are generally sold locally, through farmers' markets, small grocers, craft shops, delicatessens and some restaurants. Some breweries also sell direct to the public, but this may be by the case only, and some offer a mail order service, which is mentioned in each entry, if relevant. Otherwise beers can be obtained through specialist off-licences or mail order companies, many of which are listed in the Beer Shops section at the back of the book. If a beer has a listing with a major supermarket or off-licence chain, this is indicated at the end of the entry.

Brancaster

The Brancaster Brewery, The Jolly Sailors, Main Road, Brancaster Staithe, King's Lynn, Norfolk PE31 8BJ.
Tel. (01485) 210314 Fax (01485) 210414
E-mail: enquiries@jollysailors.co.uk
Website: www.jollysailors.co.uk

Brewery set up in 2003 at The Jolly Sailors pub in the Norfolk seaside town of Brancaster Staithe. Both bottled beers are also sold on draught.

IPA

● **ABV 3.7%** ● **BOTTLE SIZE 500 ml** ● **SERVE cool**
● **INGREDIENTS Maris Otter pale malt/caramalt/Fuggle and Brewer's Gold hops**

A session bitter, rather than a genuine IPA. As with Old Les, below, the beer is allowed to drop bright and then bottled by hand by Iceni Brewery. The best before date for IPA is six months.

TASTING NOTES

A crisp and easy-drinking, golden bitter with a clean, lightly hoppy-fruity aroma. Well-balanced malt and fruity hops follow in the taste, rounded off by a dry, bitter, hoppy finish. Good body for the strength.

Old Les

● **ABV 5%** ● **BOTTLE SIZE 500 ml** ● **SERVE cool**
● **INGREDIENTS Maris Otter pale malt/caramalt/roasted barley/ Challenger and Fuggle hops**

This strong ale was named in memory of a Brancaster Staithe character who died a few years ago. The best before date for Old Les is one year.

TASTING NOTES

Orange-amber with a malty, toffeeish aroma with a little hop resin. The taste is also malty, but not too sweet, with sappy hops for balance and a touch of astringency. Dry, malty, increasingly bitter and hoppy finish.

Branscombe Vale

Branscombe Vale Brewery, Great Seaside Farm, Branscombe, Devon EX12 3DP. Tel. (01297) 680511
E-mail: branscombebrewery@yahoo.co.uk

It was in 1992 that Branscombe Vale set up home in an old farm that is now owned by the National Trust. It has dabbled in bottled beers in the past but only in 2002 did it make the move into regular bottle-conditioned beer production, with beer brewed at Branscombe and bottled by Devon neighbour O'Hanlon's, without filtration or re-seeding of yeast. The best before dates are set at 12 months.

Drayman's Best Bitter

● ABV 4.2% ● BOTTLE SIZE 500 ml ● SERVE cool
● INGREDIENTS Pipkin pale malt/chocolate malt/Phoenix and Bramling Cross hops

Brewed with spring water and also sold in cask form.

TASTING NOTES

An amber ale with a malty, lightly citrus nose, a bittersweet, citrus, hoppy taste and a dry, bitter finish.

Breconshire

The Breconshire Brewery, Ffrwdgrech Industrial Estate, Brecon, Powys LD3 8LA.
Tel. (01874) 623731 Fax (01874) 611434
E-mail: sales@breconshirebrewery.com
Website: www.breconshirebrewery.com
Mail order service

Breconshire was opened in 2002 to expand the business of CH Marlow, a beer wholesaler which has supplied pubs in South, Mid and West Wales for more than 30 years. The bottled beers are bottled at an undisclosed Shropshire brewery (our guess is Hobson's). They are cold conditioned for a week before filling, sterile filtered and re-seeded with fresh yeast, without primings. Best before dates stand at 12 months.

Golden Valley

● ABV 4.2% ● BOTTLE SIZE 500 ml ● SERVE cool
● INGREDIENTS Optic pale malt/crystal malt/Progress hops

First bottled in 2003, award-winning Golden Valley was *Champion Beer of Wales* in 2004–5 in its cask form.

TASTING NOTES

A golden ale with spicy hops and hints of orange, melon and grapefruit in the nose. Bitterness leads sweet malt in the taste, with hop resins and citrus fruit throughout. Bitter, dry and hoppy finish.

Brecknock Best

● ABV 4.5% ● BOTTLE SIZE 500 ml ● SERVE cool
● INGREDIENTS Optic pale malt/dark crystal malt/black malt/Pilot and Bramling Cross hops

Originally brewed as a seasonal ale to mark the 250th anniversary of the Brecknockshire Agricultural Society (Britain's oldest such body) in 2005, this best bitter was added to the bottled beer range later the same year. One for pork, hams and cheeses, says brewer Buster Grant.

TASTING NOTES

An amber beer with a malty, fruity and floral nose. Fruity hops (hints of lemon and blackcurrant) provide a sharp, refreshing lead in the mouth, with malt behind. Dry, hoppy finish with lingering malt.

Red Dragon

● ABV 4.7% ● BOTTLE SIZE 500 ml ● SERVE cool
● INGREDIENTS Optic pale malt/crystal malt/dark crystal malt/wheat malt/Pioneer, Golding and First Gold hops

A red ale suited to washing down game pies or strong Welsh cheeses, claims Buster, or even as a base for cawl (Welsh soup). The beer up to now has also included the trial hop known as 93/50, or Susan, but this is no longer grown, so the recipe will be modified in due course. First bottled in winter 2004.

TASTING NOTES

A red ale with chocolate following hop and fruit in the aroma. Fruity, bitter hops lead over sweet malt and a little roasted grain in the taste, before a hoppy, nutty finish.

Ramblers Ruin

● ABV 5% ● BOTTLE SIZE 500 ml ● SERVE cool
● INGREDIENTS Optic pale malt/crystal malt/black malt/Golding, Progress and First Gold hops

Like Red Dragon, Ramblers Ruin – a strong bitter – was first bottled in spring 2005. A beer for bangers and mash or roast beef, says Buster.

Winter Beacon

● ABV 5.3% ● BOTTLE SIZE 500 ml ● SERVE cool
● INGREDIENTS Optic pale malt/low colour malt/crystal malt/black malt/wheat malt/First Gold, Fuggle and Golding hops

Best enjoyed after a long walk in the Brecon Beacons, Buster says. This pale winter ale was first added to the range in 2003 and, while the cask version remains seasonal, this bottled equivalent is sold all year.

TASTING NOTES

Amber in colour, this strong ale has a fruity aroma (oranges and other citrus fruit). The taste is malty and sweetish with light countering hop. Fruit comes from both hops and fermentation, and there's a gentle alcoholic warmth that continues into the drying, bittersweet finish.

Brewster's

Brewster's Brewing Company Ltd., Lodge Farm, Penn Lane, Stathern, Leicestershire LE14 4JA. Tel. (01949) 861868 Fax (01949) 861901
E-mail: sara@brewsters.co.uk
Website: www.brewsters.co.uk

In centuries past, brewsters were female brewers and their work was prolific, many brewing beer for consumption at home when drinking water supplies were unreliable. There is a small core of professional women brewers employed today in breweries across Britain, but the brewster in the name of this Leicestershire business is Sara Barton. Sara used to work for Courage, brewing some of the biggest names in world beer. Leaving it all behind, she returned to her native Vale of Belvoir, setting up this microbrewery in 1998.

Jezebel

● **ABV 4.8%** ● **BOTTLE SIZE 500 ml** ● **SERVE cool**
● **INGREDIENTS Maris Otter pale malt/caramalt/Bramling Cross hops**

One of the features of Brewster's cask beer output has been a range of 'Wicked Women' beers, each featuring a notorious female figure from the past. These beers are now being introduced in bottle form, largely for export to the USA (through Shelton Brothers), but with some supplies made available in the UK. These are brewed at Brewster's but bottled and marketed by Peter Scholey of Ridgeway Brewing, who was once a colleague of Sara's at Courage in Reading. Each beer has a 12-month best before date. Four beers are planned but only two are available so far.

TASTING NOTES

A dark golden ale with biscuity malt and citrus hops in the spicy aroma. The taste is hoppy and mostly bitter, with the pithy bitterness of citrus fruit. Dry, hoppy, bitter citrus aftertaste.

Mata Hari

● ABV 4.8% ● BOTTLE SIZE 500 ml ● SERVE cool
● INGREDIENTS Maris Otter pale malt/crystal malt/Fuggle, Progress and Northdown hops
The second of the Wicked Women to be bottled, Mata Hari is a stronger version of Brewster's award-winning session ale, Marquis.

Vale Pale Ale

● ABV 4.5% ● BOTTLE SIZE 500 ml ● SERVE cool
● INGREDIENTS Maris Otter pale malt/caramalt/Northdown, Golding and Cascade hops
Belvoir Castle features on the label of this beer inspired by the vale in which the brewery sits. It was one of Sara's first beers, launched in cask in 1998 and released in bottle in summer 2003. Drink with white meat and fish dishes is her recommendation.

TASTING NOTES
Light copper, showcasing Cascade hops right from the juicy grapefruit aroma, through the zesty, bitter taste to the tangy grapefruit finish.
Major stockist Local Asda

Bridge of Allan

Bridge of Allan Brewery and Visitor Centre, The Brewhouse, Queens Lane, Bridge of Allan, Stirlingshire FK9 4NY.
Tel. (01786) 834555 Fax (01786) 833426
E-mail: brewery@bridgeofallan.co.uk
Website: www.bridgeofallan.co.uk
Mail order service
Founded in 1997, Bridge of Allan has now relocated its commercial brewing into Stirling. However, the original site, in the Victorian spa town called Bridge of Allan, is still open and welcomes visitors. A range of bottled beers is sold, but only the following are bottle conditioned.

Brig O'Allan

● ABV 4.1% ● BOTTLE SIZE 500 ml ● SERVE cool
● INGREDIENTS Maris Otter pale malt/crystal malt/chocolate malt/ wheat malt/Hallertau and Golding hops
This traditional 80/- style beer was introduced in 2001. As for the other bottle-conditioned beers, it is allowed two weeks in conditioning tanks

after fermentation, then two further weeks of cold conditioning, so that it drops bright. No finings are used, making it safe for vegetarians. The beer is then primed with sugar and re-seeded with fresh yeast. Winner of CAMRA's *Scottish Bottle-Conditioned Beer Championship* in 2004.

TASTING NOTES

A dark amber ale with a malty nose. The taste is surprisingly crisp and bitter with a toasted malt flavour. Bitter, toasted malt finish.

Sporran Warmer

● ABV 4.8% ● BOTTLE SIZE 500 ml ● SERVE cool
● INGREDIENTS Maris Otter pale malt/crystal malt/caramalt/chocolate malt/torrefied wheat/Golding and Sterling hops

Sporran Warmer is a traditional 80/- ale enhanced by the inclusion of some unusual American Sterling hops.

Organic Blonde

● ABV 5% ● BOTTLE SIZE 500 ml ● SERVE cool
● INGREDIENTS Pale malt/crystal malt/wheat malt/Hallertau hops

Made with organic ingredients and certified by the Soil Association, this golden beer was introduced in 2004 and the same year was runner-up to Brig O'Allan in the *Scottish Bottle-Conditioned Beer Championship.*

Beerjolais Nouveau

● ABV 5% ● BOTTLE SIZE 500 ml ● SERVE cool
● INGREDIENTS Maris Otter pale malt/crystal malt/caramalt/chocolate malt/torrefied wheat/Saaz hops

A novel twist on the Auld Alliance. Scotland meets France in this ruby ale that is matured in Beaujolais casks for three months before going on sale on Beaujolais Nouveau day (third Thursday in November).

Scottish Bramble Ale

● ABV 5% ● BOTTLE SIZE 500 ml ● SERVE cool
● INGREDIENTS Maris Otter pale malt/crystal malt/amber malt/chocolate malt/wheat malt/First Gold hops/blackberries

The unusual ingredient here is fresh blackberries, tossed into the fermenting vessel and also crushed for juice to add to the bottle. Gentle hopping allows the fruit to shine through. Available from blackberry season (August) until supplies are exhausted. Runner-up in the CAMRA *Scottish Bottle-Conditioned Beer Championship* in 2005.

Burrington

Burrington Brewery, Homelands Business Centre, Burrington, Devon EX37 9JJ. Tel. (01805) 622813
Email: info@burringtonbrewery.co.uk
Website: www.burringtonbrewery.co.uk

This small brewery was set up in 2003 in the village of Burrington. Brewer Craig Carter has trialled a number of bottle-conditioned beers to add to his cask beer range, but only one is now regularly produced.

DNA (Dark Newt Ale)

● **ABV 4.4%** ● **BOTTLE SIZE 500 ml** ● **SERVE cool**
● **INGREDIENTS Maris Otter pale malt/crystal malt/dark crystal malt/wheat malt/wheat crystal malt/torrefied wheat/First Gold and Willamette hops**

Several of Burrington's beers feature the humble newt in their title, but the name of this one tends to be shortened to DNA. The bottles are filled directly from a cask, with primary fermentation yeast carried over.

Burton Bridge

Burton Bridge Brewery, 24 Bridge Street, Burton upon Trent, Staffordshire DE14 1SY. Tel. (01283) 510573 Fax (01283) 515594

Burton Bridge Brewery, a microbrewery in the pale ale capital, was established in 1982 by former Allied Breweries employees Bruce Wilkinson and Geoff Mumford. They began bottling in the same year.

Burton Porter ★

● **ABV 4.5%** ● **BOTTLE SIZE 500 ml** ● **SERVE cool**
● **INGREDIENTS Pale malt/crystal malt/chocolate malt/Challenger and Target hops**

The simple yellow paint and rubber stamp label that used to adorn bottles of this popular porter has long given way to a more sophisticated paper badge. However, inside the bottle the beer is just the same as before, following the same recipe as draught Burton Porter. Bottles are filled from one-week-old casks, and the beer is said to be on form at any stage from one- to six-months-old (the period indicated by the best before date). Bottling is handled within the brewery.

TASTING NOTES
A dark red, almost black, porter with an aroma of malt and chocolate. Dry roasted malt in the taste is backed by gentle, sweet malt, with dryness, roasted malt and bitterness coming through to dominate the finish, which also has a little liquorice.

Bramble Stout

● ABV 5% ● BOTTLE SIZE 500 ml ● SERVE cool
● INGREDIENTS Pale malt/chocolate malt/Challenger hops/ blackberry juice
Introduced in 1999, Bramble Stout is the brewery's Top Dog Stout with blackberry juice added to the cask before bottling.
TASTING NOTES
A deep red beer, with a smoky, biscuity, fruity aroma. In the mouth it is bitter, blackberry-fruity and roasty. Bitter, fruity, strong roasted finish.

Empire Pale Ale ★

● ABV 7.5% ● BOTTLE SIZE 500 ml ● SERVE cool
● INGREDIENTS Pipkin pale malt/invert sugar/Challenger and Styrian Golding hops
The Guardian's Best Bottle-Conditioned Beer 1997, and runner-up in the joint *Guardian*/CAMRA competition a year later, Empire, first brewed in 1996, is a re-creation of the classic IPAs which once sailed out to the far corners of the Empire from Burton. Being strong, bitter and hoppy, it fits the bill admirably. The days of the Raj are recalled on the label, too. After primary fermentation, it is conditioned in cask for six months and then dry hopped with Styrian Goldings two weeks before being primed and bottled. The yeast carried over from the cask takes care of the bottle fermentation. B United is the US distributor.
TASTING NOTES
Bitter oranges are prominent in this heady, copper-coloured IPA. They feature, with hops, in the nose; they figure highly in the malty taste, again with powerful hops on the side; and carry right through to the warming, mouth-tingling finish.

Tickle Brain

● ABV 8% ● BOTTLE SIZE 500 ml ● SERVE cool
● INGREDIENTS Pale malt/crystal malt/invert sugar/Northdown hops
At 8%, this beer – first brewed in 1996, as the intended first of a series

of beer style re-creations – more than tickles the brain. However, the brewery gives credit for this euphemism to Shakespeare, from whose writings the name is derived. The ale is an interpretation of an early (16th-century) hopped beer, as might have been produced by brewer monks. To emphasise the era it comes from (at least in spirit), Henry VIII, the king who ordered the dissolution of the monasteries, is shown on the label. Best drunk about two months into its 12-month shelf life.

TASTING NOTES

Dark red with a malty, fruity (raspberries) aroma. The taste is sweetish, malty and very fruity (more hints of raspberries), with good bitterness to ensure it is not cloying. Mouth-numbing, fruity and bitter finish.

Butts

Butts Brewery Ltd., Northfield Farm,
Great Shefford, Hungerford, Berkshire RG17 7BY.
Tel. (01488) 648133 Fax (01488) 648134
E-mail: enquiries@buttsbrewery.com
Website: www.buttsbrewery.com

Butts Brewery was established in 1994 in converted farm buildings north of Hungerford and the M4 motorway by Chris Butt. His organic (Soil Association-accredited) beers now find their way into around 80 outlets. Two bottled beers, Barbus Barbus and Blackguard, were introduced in 1999, and three more have followed since. Each beer is primed, filtered and then re-seeded with Butts's own yeast prior to bottling on site. The beers are then conditioned in the bottle for at least a month before they are released for sale.

Blackguard

● **ABV 4.5%** ● **BOTTLE SIZE 500 ml** ● **SERVE cool**
● **INGREDIENTS Not declared**

Blackguard (pronounced 'blaggard') is Butts's porter, introduced as a winter brew but now found all year round. The label features a variation on the brewery's playing card joker logo, showing a 'jester with attitude', as Chris describes it. Ingredients-wise, the only information Mr Butt will supply is that he uses British malt and British hops.

TASTING NOTES

A deep ruby-coloured beer with a contrasting white head. The appetising aroma features orange hop fruit and a peppery roastiness,

while the soft, bittersweet, roasted malt taste has a touch of liquorice and more fruit. Long, dry, bitter, charcoal-like roast finish.
Major stockists Local Somerfield and Waitrose

Barbus Barbus ★

● **ABV 4.6%** ● **BOTTLE SIZE 500 ml** ● **SERVE cool**
● **INGREDIENTS Not declared**

Barbus Barbus is the Latin name for the barbel fish and this beer celebrates the sport of coarse fishing, Chris's chief pastime. In cask form, it has quickly become the brewery's most popular ale. Three hop strains contribute to the flavour.

TASTING NOTES

An attractive bronze beer with a full hoppy nose backed with juicy orange fruit notes. The orange-citrus theme continues on the palate, but with hop bitterness quickly taking over. Very hoppy, dry fruity finish.
Major stockists Local Somerfield and Waitrose

Golden Brown

● **ABV 5%** ● **BOTTLE SIZE 500 ml** ● **SERVE cool**
● **INGREDIENTS Not declared**

Chris Butt confesses to being a Stranglers fan, hence the use of one of their song titles for this beer's name. In the lyrics there is reference to 'tied to a mast', which explains the girl tied to a mast of a ship on the label. The beer contains three different malts and just one hop strain.

TASTING NOTES

A light ruby ale with a chocolaty aroma and a chocolaty, malty taste with a hint of pear. Silky smooth, it also has a pleasant tang of hop before a long, nutty, bitter finish.
Major stockist Local Somerfield

Le Butts

● **ABV 5%** ● **BOTTLE SIZE 500 ml** ● **SERVE cold**
● **INGREDIENTS Pale malt/wheat malt/hops not declared**

Le Butts is produced with lager yeast and a lager hop to parody the efforts of the booze cruisers who cross the Channel to pick up car-loads of cheap French lager. Through its name, it also pokes fun at the Canadian lager giant Labatt in the process.

TASTING NOTES

A golden beer with a pronounced hoppy, lime-like aroma. Lots of tangy,

herbal, lime-like hops dominate a delicate sweet maltiness in the taste, before a dry, bitter, hoppy and tangy aftertaste.
Major stockist Local Somerfield

Coper

● ABV 6% ● BOTTLE SIZE 500 ml ● SERVE cool
● INGREDIENTS Malts not declared/Fuggle and Golding hops
'A coper is a ship employed in surreptitiously supplying strong drink to deep sea fishermen,' declares the bottle. 'Not a lot of people know that.' The name was suggested by Chris Butt's father while he was doing a crossword, so Chris asked him to draw the boat on the bottle, too. The beer doubled as the brewery's tenth anniversary ale in 2004.
TASTING NOTES
An unusual ruby ale with rich malt, a touch of roasted grain, hints of liquorice and a little vinous fruit in the aroma. Vinous fruit comes through strongly in the mouth (sultanas and oranges), but, with dark malt flavours and an almost liquorice-like bitterness fighting back, it's not particularly sweet. Softly bitter finish with grainy dark malts.
Major stockist Local Somerfield

Castle Rock

Castle Rock Brewery, Queensbridge Road, Nottingham NG2 1NB.
Tel. (0115) 985 1615 Fax (0115) 985 1611
E-mail: castle.rock@btconnect.com
Website: www.castlerockbrewery.co.uk
Founded as Bramcote Brewery in 1996, Castle Rock moved to new premises next to Nottingham's Vat & Fiddle pub in 1998 (when the new name was adopted), and was then taken over by the Tynemill pub company in 2001. Considerable expansion has since taken place. For the bottle, the beers are fined, re-seeded with special bottling yeast and primed with sugars. Bottling takes place at an unnamed outside contractor, with 12-month best before dates applied.

Hemlock Bitter

● ABV 4.1% ● BOTTLE SIZE 500 ml ● SERVE cool
● INGREDIENTS Maris Otter pale malt/crystal malt/torrefied wheat/ Fuggle and Golding hops
Forget Socrates. This beer was named after the Hemlock Stone, a

bizarre natural rock formation in nearby Bramcote. It was first brewed in 1997. Like Elsie Mo, Hemlock is also sold in cask-conditioned format.

TASTING NOTES

A mid-brown beer with malt, fruit and developing toffee and butterscotch in the aroma. The taste is bitter up front, with dark malt behind and fruity notes at all times. Bitter, dry finish of dark malt.

Major stockist Local Asda

Elsie Mo

● ABV 4.7% ● BOTTLE SIZE 500 ml ● SERVE cool

● INGREDIENTS Low colour Maris Otter malt/torrefied wheat/ Challenger, Styrian Golding and Golding hops

Who, precisely, was Elsie Mo? A pointless question. The name simply comes from the type of malt used: low colour Maris Otter, or LCMO.

TASTING NOTES

A golden ale with pungent lemon and grapefruit in the nose and taste. Lots of zesty citrus hops dominate a clean, smooth malt base. Dry, bitter finish with lingering citrus fruit.

Major stockist Local Asda

Ceredigion

Bragdy Ceredigion, Brynhawk, New Road, Newquay, Ceredigion SA45 9SB. Tel. (01239) 654888

Mail order service

This brewery was constructed in a converted barn on a working West Wales farm in 1997. The address above is the office address: the brewery itself is in the village of Pentregat. The beers are targeted at the local tourist trade and have bilingual Welsh/English labels, hand-drawn by Julia Tilby, wife of brewer Brian Tilby. Each beer is siphoned into bottles direct from the fermenter, or from a cask, and is primed with raw demerara sugar. Best before dates are 12–18 months after bottling. All the beers are declared suitable for vegetarians.

Gwrach Ddu

● ABV 4% ● BOTTLE SIZE 500 ml ● SERVE cool

● INGREDIENTS Maris Otter pale malt/crystal malt/amber malt/First Gold hops

Translated as 'Black Witch', Gwrach Ddu was first brewed in 1998, for

Hallowe'en. The cask version is dry hopped and sold as a 'dark porter', whereas this bottled equivalent – a touch of 'cyfareddol du' (black magic), as the label used to claim – is labelled a 'stout'.

TASTING NOTES

A ruby beer with a creamy aroma of dark malt. On the palate it is dry and moreish, with fruit, bitterness and roasted malt well restrained, before a gently bitter, toasty, dry finish that is also lightly fruity.

Draig Aur

● ABV 4.2% ● BOTTLE SIZE 500 ml ● SERVE cool
● INGREDIENTS Maris Otter pale malt/crystal malt/amber malt/ Challenger and Fuggle hops

Launched in cask at CAMRA's Cardiff Beer Festival in 1998, and in bottle soon after. Draig Aur means Gold Dragon.

TASTING NOTES

An orange-gold ale with a fruit salad aroma. The taste is hoppy and bitter, with blackcurrant and other fruitiness. Dry, bitter finish.

Barcud Coch

● ABV 4.3% ● BOTTLE SIZE 500 ml ● SERVE cool
● INGREDIENTS Maris Otter pale malt/crystal malt/amber malt/ Challenger and Golding hops

The name of this bitter, introduced in 1998, means 'Red Kite'. The beer was once described on the label as being 'coch', 'prin' and 'prydferth'– red, rare and beautiful, just like the bird it is named after.

TASTING NOTES

Reddish-bronze with a fruity hop aroma. The taste is smooth and quite bitter, and features fruity flavours. Dry, gently bitter, fruity-hop finish.

Blodeuwedd

● ABV 4.5% ● BOTTLE SIZE 500 ml ● SERVE cool
● INGREDIENTS Pale malt/Hallertau hops

This Soil Association-accredited organic beer was launched in 2000 and takes its name from Welsh legend. Blodeuwedd, it is said, was a beautiful maiden created out of flowers by two powerful magicians. Tragedy befell the girl when she plotted with her lover to kill her husband. As a punishment for her sins, she was transformed into an owl, 'a creature of the night'. 'Blodeuwedd' is Welsh for owl but literally translates as 'flower face'.

TASTING NOTES
A golden ale with a fruity nose. The taste features spicy, peppery hops, bitterness and underlying light fruit, before a very hoppy, bitter finish.

Cwrw 2000

● **ABV 5%** ● **BOTTLE SIZE 500 ml** ● **SERVE cool**
● **INGREDIENTS Maris Otter pale malt/crystal malt/amber malt/pale chocolate malt/Challenger and Fuggle hops**
Brewed originally for the new millennium celebrations, Cwrw 2000 ('Ale 2000') owes its longevity to the picture of seaside Llangranog on the label, which makes it a good seller among summer visitors.
TASTING NOTES
A ruby ale with a full, biscuity malt aroma. The taste is soft and malty with suggestions of dark fruit and a light citrus edge. Bitter, malty finish with a touch of roasted malt and a lingering hint of fruit.

Nadolig

● **ABV 6.2%** ● **BOTTLE SIZE 500 ml** ● **SERVE cool**
● **INGREDIENTS Maris Otter pale malt/crystal malt/amber malt/pale chocolate malt/Challenger, Fuggle and Golding hops/spices**
Laced with spices – including cinnamon and nutmeg – for a festive feel, Nadolig (literally 'Christmas') is only available from October to January.
TASTING NOTES
A red beer with mixed spices in the aroma and malt and perfumed spice in the taste. Bittersweet, scented, increasingly bitter finish.

Yr Hen Darw Du

● **ABV 6.2%** ● **BOTTLE SIZE 500 ml** ● **SERVE cool**
● **INGREDIENTS Maris Otter pale malt/crystal malt/amber malt/dark chocolate malt/black malt/Challenger hops**
'The Old Black Bull', for those not versed in the language of Heaven. This complex winter warmer takes its name from the brewery's bovine neighbours on the Pentregat farm. It also recalls a Welsh legend of the Green Lady of the Lake, who, it is said, gifted the Welsh Black cattle to the people in return for saving her magical white cow from slaughter.
TASTING NOTES
A deep ruby-coloured beer with a slightly leathery, 'fruit cocktail' aroma. The taste is smooth, bitter, fruity and a touch warming. Dry, bitter, lightly roasted, fruity aftertaste.

Chiltern

The Chiltern Brewery, Nash Lee Road, Terrick,
Aylesbury, Buckinghamshire HP17 0TQ.
Tel. (01296) 613647 Fax (01296) 612419
E-mail: info@chilternbrewery.co.uk
Website: www.chilternbrewery.co.uk
Mail order service

Chiltern Brewery was set up in 1980 on a small farm and is the oldest microbrewery in Buckinghamshire. The Jenkinson family who run it specialize in beer-related foods (cheeses, sausages, mustards, etc.), as well as traditional ales. On site is a well-stocked visitors' centre-cum-shop and a small but interesting collection of local breweriana. Only two of Chiltern's bottled beers are bottle conditioned.

Glad Tidings

● **ABV 4.6%** ● **BOTTLE SIZE 500 ml** ● **SERVE cool**
● **INGREDIENTS Maris Otter pale malt/chocolate malt/roasted barley/ Bramling Cross hops/nutmeg/coriander/orange peel**

The name reveals the timing of this Christmas beer, first brewed in 2003. The brewery describes it as a spiced milk stout, and takes pride in using only authentic ingredients – no extracts, oils, juices or flavourings – to create a seasonal accent. The beer is bottled after four weeks' maturation. It is left unfined and unfiltered and then kräusened. Drink it – within six months – with after-dinner chocolates, the family says.

TASTING NOTES

A ruby ale with dark malt overlaid by spices (nutmeg and a whiff of orange) in the nose. The mildly warming taste is also spicy but soft, with a mellow maltiness and smooth sweetness nicely balanced by a persistent orange-lemon tang. Bittersweet, spicy finish with hops building and gentle roasted grain lingering.

Bodgers Barley Wine ★

● **ABV 8.5%** ● **BOTTLE SIZE 500 ml** ● **SERVE cool**
● **INGREDIENTS Maris Otter pale malt/Challenger, Fuggle and Golding hops**

Brewed first in 1990, to commemorate the tenth anniversary of the founding of the brewery, Bodgers recalls the tradition of the Chiltern Bodger (a craftsman-chairmaker who worked in the surrounding beechwoods) in its name, and the year of the brewery's birth in its original gravity (1080). It is a fine accompaniment to the Chiltern range of beer-related foods, although the Jenkinsons also suggest it could be served lightly chilled as an aperitif or at room temperature instead of a dessert wine. Bottled by hand in house, the beer is conditioned in tank for a month first, then filtered and re-pitched with new yeast. The individually-numbered bottles are kept at the brewery to mature for four weeks and best before dates are set at two years. New sepia-tinged labels have been introduced since the last edition of this book. They include a photograph of the Bodger at work in 1929.

TASTING NOTES

A dark golden beer, with lemon at first, then nutty malt and finally vinous fruit in the aroma. The taste is creamy and sweet, with plenty of vinous fruit and only light hop resins. Dry, warming, gum-tingling finish, with hops and lingering malty/fruity sweetness.

Church End

Church End Brewery Ltd., Ridge Lane, Nuneaton, Warwickshire CV10 0RD. Tel. (01827) 713080 Fax (01827) 717328
E-mail: stewart.elliott@btconnect.com
Website: www.churchendbrewery.co.uk

Church End Brewery was founded in 1994, in an old coffin workshop next to The Griffin Inn in Shustoke, Warwickshire. In 2001 it moved to new premises, five miles away in Ridge Lane, near Atherstone. It introduced its first bottled beer with Rugby Ale (5%) in 1998. Since then two further bottles have been added, although the beers are now being relaunched after a short absence from the shelves. Bottling takes place at Hobson's Brewery in Shropshire, where the beer is filtered and re-seeded with fresh yeast. A one-year best before date is applied. Nuns Ale was the first to be brought back, followed by Arthur's Wit. Rugby Ale is also set to return, but with a different recipe.

Nuns Ale

● **ABV 4.5%** ● **BOTTLE SIZE 500 ml** ● **SERVE cool**
● **INGREDIENTS Pale malt/crystal malt/Green Bullet, Cascade and Amarillo hops**

Brewed to raise money for St Mary Abbey in Nuneaton (which once had its own brewery and was responsible in part for the town's name),

Nuns Ale first appeared in 2002 and is now produced several times a year. The choice of hops is interesting to say the least, with Green Bullet from New Zealand teamed up with Cascade and Amarillo from America.

TASTING NOTES

Pale golden, with hops over delicate malt in the faintly honeyed aroma. The taste is crisp, floral-hoppy and bitter, backed by soft honeyed malt, with a hint of lemon on the swallow. Dry, notably hoppy, bitter finish.

Arthur's Wit

● ABV 6% ● BOTTLE SIZE 500 ml ● SERVE cool

● INGREDIENTS Pale malt/torrefied wheat/Mount Hood and Cascade hops

Introduced as a cask beer six years ago, Arthur's Wit was bottled for the first time in 2002. Despite its Belgian sounding name, this is not a spiced wheat beer, but a strong golden ale – and a good bread and cheese accompaniment, according to the brewers.

TASTING NOTES

A big malty aroma heralds this powerful, bittersweet mix of malt and orangey hops, the hops taking over, along with bitterness, in the finish.

City of Cambridge

City of Cambridge Brewery Co. Ltd., Ely Road, Chittering, Cambridge CB5 9PH. Tel. (01223) 864864

E-mail: sales@cambridge-brewery.co.uk

Website: www.cambridge-brewery.co.uk

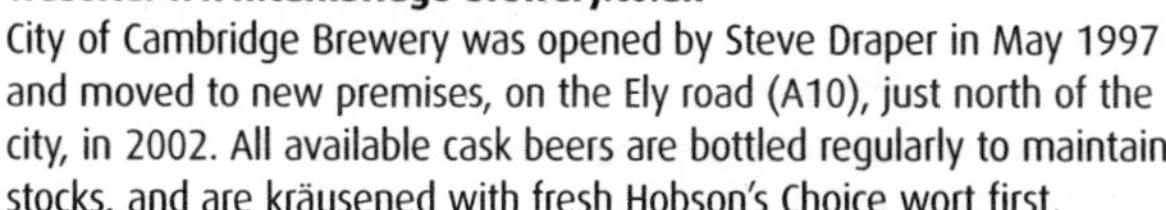

City of Cambridge Brewery was opened by Steve Draper in May 1997 and moved to new premises, on the Ely road (A10), just north of the city, in 2002. All available cask beers are bottled regularly to maintain stocks, and are kräusened with fresh Hobson's Choice wort first.

Jet Black

● ABV 3.7% ● BOTTLE SIZE 500 ml ● SERVE cool

● INGREDIENTS Maris Otter pale malt/crystal malt/caramalt/roasted barley/First Gold hops

A Cambridge Beer Festival champion from 1998.

TASTING NOTES

Subtle chocolate features in the aroma of this softly malty, light-bodied beer which has a gentle fruit edge, and roasted malt in the easy finish.

Boathouse Bitter/Easter Bunny

● ABV 3.8% ● BOTTLE SIZE 500 ml ● SERVE cool
● INGREDIENTS Maris Otter pale malt/crystal malt/First Gold and Cascade hops

Most of the brewery's bottled beers reflect the life and culture of the university city of Cambridge in their names, this one majoring on the rowing heritage. The beer is also bottled as Easter Bunny at Eastertime.

TASTING NOTES

A deep amber beer with a rich, chocolaty nose, supported by a little citrus hoppiness. The taste is malty and fruity (pineapple notes from the Cascade hops), with hints of chocolate, but quite dry. Very dry, mostly bitter, malt and fruit aftertaste. Plenty of depth for its strength.

Hobson's Choice

● ABV 4.1% ● BOTTLE SIZE 500 ml ● SERVE cool
● INGREDIENTS Maris Otter pale malt/caramalt/First Gold hops

This brew, launched in 1997, is based on the story of Mr Hobson, a Cambridge horse-merchant who, legend has it, allowed only the particular horse he specified to be hired – hence 'Hobson's Choice'.

TASTING NOTES

A bronze beer with a fresh, fruity, spritzy nose, backed by malt. On the palate, it is crisp and generally bitter but delicately fruity, too, although it is clearly less malty to taste than some of the brewery's other ales. Very dry, bitter finish with lingering fruit.

Major stockists Local Asda, Tesco and Waitrose

Trinity

● ABV 4.3% ● BOTTLE SIZE 500 ml ● SERVE cool
● INGREDIENTS Maris Otter pale malt/crystal malt/caramalt/roasted barley/First Gold and Cascade hops

A blend of Boathouse Bitter and Atom Splitter (see opposite), available on draught in summer months (Trinity is the university's summer term).

Sunset Square

● ABV 4.4% ● BOTTLE SIZE 500 ml ● SERVE cool
● INGREDIENTS Maris Otter pale malt/crystal malt/caramalt/roasted barley/First Gold hops

Now named after one of Cambridge's squares – a suntrap on summer evenings – this beer was formerly known as Blend 42 and is a mix of two of City of Cambridge's other brews – Hobson's Choice and Atom Splitter. The '42' referred to the answer to the Ultimate Question to Life, the Universe and Everything, as posed by the late Douglas Adams in *The Hitch-hiker's Guide to the Galaxy* (Adams was born in Cambridge).

TASTING NOTES

An amber ale with a juicy, citrus nose. Juicy, fruity and peppery hops dominate the taste and also bring a crisp, firm bitterness. Long, dry, bitter and hoppy aftertaste.

Atom Splitter/Atomic Ale/Patron Saint

● **ABV 4.7%** ● **BOTTLE SIZE 500 ml** ● **SERVE cool**

● **INGREDIENTS Maris Otter pale malt/crystal malt/caramalt/roasted barley/First Gold hops**

It was in Cambridge that scientist Ernest Rutherford did much of his research into splitting the atom and this beer, introduced in bottle in 1998, recalls those days. (The working title for the beer was Rutherford IPA – which is now a different, draught-only session ale.) The beer is now also sold as Atomic Ale and, for St George's Day, as Patron Saint.

TASTING NOTES

An amber beer with a rich, malty, chocolaty nose, backed by a hint of orange. Mouthfilling malt and lemon/orange fruitiness feature in the well-rounded taste, which leans towards sweetness but never quite gets there as hop bitterness blends in. Clean, dry, pleasantly bitter finish, with lingering malt and orange notes.

Major stockists Local Asda and Waitrose

Mich'aelmas

● **ABV 4.6%** ● **BOTTLE SIZE 500 ml** ● **SERVE cool**

● **INGREDIENTS Maris Otter pale malt/crystal malt/caramalt/roasted barley/First Gold and Cascade hops**

The brewery's original Christmas ale, in fact a blend of porter and a best bitter. Available autumn to Christmas.

New Model Ale

● **ABV 4.6%** ● **BOTTLE SIZE 500 ml** ● **SERVE cool**

● **INGREDIENTS Maris Otter pale malt/crystal malt/caramalt/roasted barley/First Gold and Bramling Cross hops**

The latest addition to the range, a red beer with connections to Oliver Cromwell, who was born in Huntingdon and studied at Cambridge.

Darwin's Downfall

● **ABV 5%** ● **BOTTLE SIZE 500 ml** ● **SERVE cool**
● **INGREDIENTS Maris Otter pale malt/crystal malt/caramalt/roasted barley/First Gold hops**

Darwin's Downfall is another of City of Cambridge's blends, this time a ruby beer successfully combining Atom Splitter and Parkers Porter. Its name recalls Charles Darwin's links with the university city and the label shows the various stages of human/ape evolution.

TASTING NOTES

Luscious tropical fruit fills the aroma. The taste is bitter and fruity, with some roasted grain behind. Dry, roasted, bitter finish.

Holly Heaven

● **ABV 5.1%** ● **BOTTLE SIZE 500 ml** ● **SERVE cool**
● **INGREDIENTS Maris Otter pale malt/crystal malt/caramalt/roasted barley/First Gold hops**

Another Christmas beer, available on draught October–December.

Parkers Porter

● **ABV 5.3%** ● **BOTTLE SIZE 500 ml** ● **SERVE cool**
● **INGREDIENTS Maris Otter pale malt/crystal malt/caramalt/roasted barley/First Gold hops**

The central area of greenbelt in Cambridge is a meadow known as Parkers Piece, as recalled in the name of this dark ruby porter.

TASTING NOTES

Nutty, roasted malt in the aroma leads to a malty, lightly chocolaty taste which is fairly fruity with a good bitter balance. Dry, fruity, gently bitter finish, with a suggestion of liquorice.

Major stockist Local Waitrose

Bramling Traditional

● **ABV 5.5%** ● **BOTTLE SIZE 500 ml** ● **SERVE cool**
● **INGREDIENTS Maris Otter pale malt/crystal malt/caramalt/roasted barley/First Gold and Bramling Cross hops**

Distinctive Bramling Cross hops dominate the taste as well as the name.

TASTING NOTES

Strong blackcurrant notes fill the aroma of this reddish-amber bitter and emerge again in the fruity taste. Not as sweet as many beers of this strength, it has good balancing bitterness and a dry, bitter, fruity finish.

Cobra

Cobra Beer Ltd., Alexander House, 14–16 Peterborough Road, London SW6 3BN. Tel. (020) 7731 6200 Fax (020) 7731 6201
E-mail: cobrabeer@cobrabeer.com
Website: www.cobrabeer.com

Cobra as a curry lager brand seems to have been around for decades. The truth is it was only set up in 1989 when Karan Bilimoria, son of an Indian Army general, spotted a gap in the market for what he described as a less bloating beer for drinking with curry. With the help of a Czech brewer, Karan devised a beer that was initially brewed for him in India. When production problems began to affect the supply, he switched production to Charles Wells in Bedford. The original Cobra lager is still brewed there, as well as under contract in Poland. Cobra has now expanded its range and in 2005 introduced the unusual King Cobra.

King Cobra ★

● **ABV 8%** ● **BOTTLE SIZE 750 ml** ● **SERVE cool**
● **INGREDIENTS Not declared**

Although Cobra is a British company, and therefore warrants a listing in this book, King Cobra is an Indian lager, brewed in Poland and bottled in Belgium. Production takes places at the state-of-the-art Browar Belgia plant, between Warsaw and Krakow, which is owned by Belgian brewer Palm. Palm also owns Rodenbach in Belgium, a brewery famous for its sour red beers. King Cobra is brewed to the standard Cobra recipe, but is beefed up for the higher strength. Although the ingredients are not disclosed, the recipe contains maize and rice, as well as barley, and the hops are German. The beer is fermented in shallow, horizontal vessels, to encourage fruity flavours to develop. When it reaches 7.8%, it is filtered, primed with sugar and tankered from Poland to Rodenbach for bottling. Here it is flash pasteurized and re-seeded with fresh yeast, a Belgian ale strain that works well in the bottle. The beer is bottled flat but warm conditioned for two weeks to start the secondary fermentation. The beer is elegantly packaged in near-black, Champagne-style bottles. It's not cheap, but makes a welcome change from the usual curry beers.

TASTING NOTES

A golden beer with grainy cereal and a hint of sour lemon that gradually gives way to melon in the nose. Melon juiciness continues in

the mouth, along with grainy cereals and gently spicy, bitter hops. There's some alcoholic warmth, and pleasant, bittersweet fruit at all times. Dry, a little chewy, bitter and fruity aftertaste.
Major stockist Sainsbury's

Combe Martin

Combe Martin Brewery, 4 Springfield Terrace, High Street, Combe Martin, Devon EX34 0EE. Tel. (01271) 883507
Website: combemartinbrewery.prizaar.com
This tiny brewery produces bottled beer in small quantities for the North Devon tourist trade.

Past-Times

● ABV 3.9% ● BOTTLE SIZE 500 ml ● SERVE cool
● INGREDIENTS Pale malt/crystal malt/demerara sugar/Jeanette and Admiral hops
This dark golden bitter was first produced in 2004 and includes a new dwarf hop called Jeanette. Bottles are simply filled with cask beer primed with sugar. The best before date is set at six months.
TASTING NOTES
A hoppy, malty aroma leads to a sharp, bittersweet taste of malt, hops and toasted grain. Dry, bittersweet, malty finish with toasted notes.

Coniston

Coniston Brewing Co. Ltd., Coppermines Road, Coniston, Cumbria LA21 8HL.
Tel. (01539 4) 41133 Fax (01539 4) 41177
E-mail: coniston.brewery@kencomp.net
Website: www.conistonbrewery.com
Mail order service
This little brewery was set up in 1994 behind Coniston's Black Bull pub and achieved a minor miracle in turning out CAMRA's *Champion Beer of Britain* in 1998, in Bluebird Bitter. With orders flooding in, and capacity way surpassed by demand, Coniston contracted out the brewing of this bottled version to Brakspear, who also produced the bottles of Old Man Ale that were introduced in 2000. Since the demise of the Henley brewery, the contract to brew Coniston beers for the bottle has stayed

with former Brakspear head brewer Peter Scholey. He now produces the beers himself, using equipment at Hepworth & Co. in Horsham.

Bluebird Bitter ★

● ABV 4.2% ● BOTTLE SIZE 500 ml ● SERVE cool
● INGREDIENTS Maris Otter pale malt/crystal malt/Challenger hops

Hot on the heels of the success of cask Bluebird (3.6%), this stronger version soon began to win accolades of its own, with gold medals at London's International Food Exhibition and the *Beauty of Hops* competition. In 2001, the beer picked up yet another *Beauty of Hops* gold, this time judged by a panel of female experts as *The Ultimate Fem'ale in a Bottle*, and in 2003 it earned a silver in the *International Beer Competition*. Before bottling, the beer is filtered and re-seeded with the same primary yeast. The best before date is set at 12 months after bottling. The beer – which Coniston's Ian Bradley sees as an ideal partner for fish and curry dishes, because of the spicy hop character – takes its name from the famous *Bluebird* land and water speed machines used by Donald Campbell, who was tragically killed on Coniston Water in 1967. The beer is imported into the US by Shelton Brothers of New York.

TASTING NOTES

A copper beer with a fruity hop nose. Pepper, spice and the zest of citrus continue in the clean, crisp taste and the dry, bitter, hoppy finish.

Major stockists Asda, Booths, Co-op, Sainsbury's, Waitrose

Bluebird XB

● ABV 4.4% ● BOTTLE SIZE 500 ml ● SERVE cool
● INGREDIENTS Maris Otter pale malt/crystal malt/torrefied wheat Challenger and Mount Hood hops

The latest addition to the Coniston range of bottled beers is this version of Bluebird, with a pronounced American accent. Pitched just a touch stronger than the original bottled Bluebird, this beer also includes Mount Hood hops from the USA in a coals-to-Newcastle bid to capture a slice of the American beer business.

TASTING NOTES

Copper-coloured, with piney hops at first in the nose, then a lime and grapefruit accent. The taste is nicely balanced with gentle, toffeeish malt in the background and a prevailing citrus sharpness. Dry, bitter citrus fruit leads the way in the aftertaste.

Old Man Ale

● **ABV 4.8%** ● **BOTTLE SIZE 500 ml** ● **SERVE cool**

● **INGREDIENTS Maris Otter pale malt/crystal malt/roasted barley/ Challenger hops**

Named after the mountain overlooking Coniston, Old Man – described as 'an old style bitter' – was first produced in cask in 1995, although at a lower ABV (4.4%) than this bottled version. The inclusion of roasted barley helps the beer to nicely complement beef and venison dishes, Ian reckons, and he says Old Man also goes well with black pudding.

TASTING NOTES

A strong ruby ale with a malty aroma featuring a little orange fruit. The crisp taste also features dark malt and spicy, orangey hops, with a suggestion of creamy toffee. Dry, bitter, malty finish with roasted barley.

Major stockists Booths, Co-op

Conwy

Conwy Brewery Ltd., Unit 17, Conwy Morfa Business Park, Ffordd Sam Pari, Conwy LL32 8HB. Tel. (01492) 585287

E-mail: enquiries@conwybrewery.co.uk

Website: www.conwybrewery.co.uk

Mail order service

Small brewery set up in autumn 2003 after two years of planning and now serving around 30 pubs in North Wales. The beers below are now bottled in house direct from casks and primed with a little sugar. Best before dates are kept sensibly short at four months. The beers are sold under both Welsh and English names.

Castle Bitter/Cwrw Castell

● **ABV 3.8%** ● **BOTTLE SIZE 500 ml** ● **SERVE cool**

● **INGREDIENTS Maris Otter pale malt/crystal malt/chocolate malt/ wheat malt/Pioneer and Cascade hops**

A session bitter named after Conwy's most famous landmark. It's the brewery's biggest selling beer in cask form.

TASTING NOTES

An amber brew with a malty, toffeeish aroma. The taste is also malty and toffeeish, but not particularly sweet, thanks to a resin-like hop balance. Hops gradually build in the drying, malty finish.

Sun Dance/Dawns Haul

● ABV 4% ● BOTTLE SIZE 500 ml ● SERVE cool
● INGREDIENTS Maris Otter low colour malt/wheat malt/Styrian Golding hops

This summer ale with a citrus accent was first produced in 2005.

Celebration Ale/Cwrw Gwledd

● ABV 4.2% ● BOTTLE SIZE 500 ml ● SERVE cool
● INGREDIENTS Maris Otter pale malt/crystal malt/chocolate malt/ wheat malt/Cascade and Styrian Golding hops

Featuring Conwy Castle on the label, this was the first beer off the production line. The distinctive hoppy aroma comes from American Cascades which are allowed to stand in the copper after the boil has finished to impart their citrus qualities. The Welsh name is not a literal translation of the English. Cwrw Gwledd actually means 'feast ale'.

TASTING NOTES

An amber beer with juicy grapefruit in the aroma, backed by good maltiness. In the mouth, a smooth malty base is enlivened by a burst of grapefruit from the hops. The finish is dry and malty with developing bitter grapefruit notes.

Welsh Pride/Balchder Cymru

● ABV 4.4% ● BOTTLE SIZE 500 ml ● SERVE cool
● INGREDIENTS Maris Otter pale malt/crystal malt/Challenger and Golding hops

A new beer brewed to coincide with St David's Day and the Six Nations rugby championship, when Welsh pride is at its most exuberant.

Honey Fayre/Cwrw Mêl

● ABV 4.5% ● BOTTLE SIZE 500 ml ● SERVE cool
● INGREDIENTS Maris Otter pale malt/crystal malt/wheat malt/ Challenger and Pioneer hops/honey

Welsh honey is added to this brew after the copper boil but before fermentation begins, the aim being a dry-tasting beer with honeyed aromas. It's named after Conwy's Honey Fayre, a street market dating back to medieval times that gave Welsh people the right to sell local produce inside the English walled town. Brewer Gwynne Thomas recommends drinking it with Conwy mussels.

Special/Arbennig

● ABV 4.5% ● BOTTLE SIZE 500 ml ● SERVE cool
● INGREDIENTS Maris Otter pale malt/crystal malt/roasted barley/ wheat malt/Challenger and Pioneer hops

A new dark premium ale, added to the range in autumn 2005.

TASTING NOTES

A bronze beer with gently biscuity and toffeeish malt in the aroma, and a malty taste with hints of nut and toffee. Hops ensure it's not too sweet. Dry, malty, increasingly hoppy and bitter aftertaste.

Telford Porter

● ABV 5.6% ● BOTTLE SIZE 500 ml ● SERVE cool
● INGREDIENTS Maris Otter pale malt/crystal malt/roasted barley/ Pioneer, Challenger and Golding hops

Commemorating the opening of Thomas Telford's suspension bridge to the Isle of Anglesey in 1826, this porter was introduced for Conwy's Feast food and drink festival in 2005.

Coors

Coors Brewers Ltd., PO Box 217, High Street, Burton upon Trent, Staffordshire DE14 1BG. Tel. (01283) 511000 Fax (01283) 513873

The White Shield Brewery, Coors Visitor Centre, Horninglow Street, Burton upon Trent, Staffordshire DE14 1YQ.
Tel. (01283) 513507 Fax (01283) 513613
E-mail: steve.wellington@coorsbrewers.com
Website: www.coorsvisitorcentre.com

Proof that large-scale brewing is now an international affair was provided by the sale of Bass. The historic brewer was purchased in 2000 by Interbrew, which, because it also owned Whitbread, was then forced to sell off part of its new acquisition. In stepped Coors, one of America's major brewers, to take over most of the Bass breweries and some of its brands, including the Worthington's range. Thus a high-tech Colorado company became owners of the Bass Museum, a shrine to the halcyon days of traditional ale production, and with it its vibrant Museum Brewing Company. This has now been re-named Coors Visitor Centre.

The Museum Brewery began life as a static display. It is housed in a former engine room, in a corner of what used to be the Bass tradesmen's yard, amidst former cobblers', coppersmiths' and tailors' units. The equipment was recovered from M&B's Cape Hill brewery in Birmingham, with parts of the kit dating from 1850 and 1920. Although pieced together in 1976, the equipment only became fully operational again in 1994 and, with long-term Bass employee Steve Wellington installed as brewer, began to specialize in reviving lost beer brands from the company's archives. A new bottling line, capable of filling 900 bottles per hour, was introduced to cope with demand for Worthington's White Shield, which was acquired following the closure of King & Barnes in Horsham. The beer had suffered a chequered recent past. At the end of 1997 Bass had announced that the beer, one of the world's classic bottle-conditioned ales, was to be discontinued. After a wave of protest, Bass relented and sold the brewing and marketing rights to King & Barnes, who made a success of the beer, taking gold in the 2000 *Champion Beer of Britain* competition. However, the brewery was closed shortly after, leaving White Shield looking for another new home. Steve Wellington was keen to accept the challenge. Under Coors, rebranding of the Worthington's range has taken place, including for White Shield, which Coors has added to its general portfolio. The Museum Brewing Company is now known as The White Shield Brewery.

Worthington's White Shield ★

● ABV 5.6% ● BOTTLE SIZE 275/500 ml ● SERVE cool
● INGREDIENTS Pale malt/crystal malt/Fuggle, Challenger and Northdown hops

For years Worthington's White Shield, along with Guinness Extra Stout, was the welcome standby for beer lovers who found themselves marooned in a keg-only pub. In many ways, it's the archetypal Burton pale ale, so it's pleasing to see it back home, after short stopovers at Bass plants in Sheffield and Birmingham, and later at King & Barnes. The beer is now brewed five times a week and has been given a new label, underlining the history of India pale ales. After reaching an all-time low of just 300 barrels a year in the mid-1990s, the beer has bounced back, with output now in excess of 1,000 barrels and growing. The one-millionth bottle from the new production line rolled off in 2005. In the copper, Fuggle and Challenger (now replacing Golding) hops provide the bitterness, with Northdowns added for aroma.

Following primary fermentation, the beer is conditioned for three weeks in tanks, then filtered and re-seeded with new 'sticky' yeast (a different strain to that used earlier in the brewing process). No finings are used, so White Shield is a vegetarian/vegan beer. Primings may be added to ensure fermentability in the bottle. Bottles are then matured for one month before release and should improve with keeping up to the best before date of three years, although White Shield fans often tuck bottles away for much longer. The beer was judged top bottle-conditioned beer in the 2003 *International Beer Competition*, run by *Off Licence News.*

TASTING NOTES

An amber beer with a malty, fruity nose, including hints of tropical fruit and aniseed. The full taste features silky, nutty malt sweetness, sound hop bitterness and a light undercurrent of tropical fruit and almond. Bitter hops lead over moreish, nutty malt in the finish.

Major stockists Booths, Sainsbury's, Tesco, Waitrose

P2

● **ABV 8%** ● **BOTTLE SIZE 275 ml** ● **SERVE cool**
● **INGREDIENTS Pale malt/crystal malt/black malt/Fuggle and Golding hops**

P2 is a strong, Baltic-style stout, of the sort once shipped to the imperial court of Russia in the 19th century. The beer is allowed eight or nine days' primary fermentation, then cooled to 10°C in tanks for two weeks. The temperature is then lowered further for another couple of weeks of conditioning before the beer is primed with sucrose and bottled. Although a six-month best before date is applied, the strength of the beer ensures it survives and matures well beyond this period. This and No. 1 (below) are likely to be brewed only at Christmastime.

TASTING NOTES

A very dark brown beer with a powerful aroma combining fruit with the scent of polished leather. In the mouth, it is smooth and sweetish with good roast malt and fruit flavours. The dry finish features mellow, sweetish roast malt with pleasant hop bitterness to balance.

No.1 Barley Wine

● **ABV 10.5%** ● **BOTTLE SIZE 275 ml** ● **SERVE cool**
● **INGREDIENTS Pale malt/Fuggle and Golding hops**

No.1 is a re-creation of the famous Bass barley wine of the same name which was consigned to the archives years ago. In its latter days, that beer was pasteurized but it had been enjoyed by many drinkers in its natural, bottle-conditioned form for decades. No.1 is an intriguing beer. Its hue is dark red yet the colour is only derived from pale malt that caramelizes during the extra-long, 12-hour boil. This evaporates the wort down from an initial five barrels to three. With three separate hop charges at various stages, however, this is no sweet, cloying mixture. The beer is matured in cask for more than 12 months before bottling.

TASTING NOTES

A dark ruby beer with a powerful, sherry-like nose. The taste is mouth-filling, warming and fruity, with some liquorice character and bitterness. Ultra-long, creamy, bitter fruit finish.

Corvedale

Corvedale Brewery, The Sun Inn, Corfton, Craven Arms, Shropshire SY7 9DF. Tel. (01584) 861503
E-mail: normanspride@aol.com
Website: www.suninncorfton.co.uk

Publican Norman Pearce is the brewer in the tiny brewery housed behind The Sun Inn in rural Shropshire. He now bottles the beers himself, filling glassware with unfiltered, unfined beer from a cask. The beers are therefore acceptable to vegetarians. Best before dates are set at nine months. Special/commemorative brews are also bottled from time to time and own label beers are sold to local restaurants.

Katie's Pride

● ABV 4.3% ● BOTTLE SIZE 500 ml ● SERVE cool
● INGREDIENTS Maris Otter pale malt/crystal malt/chocolate malt/ wheat malt/Jenny hops

This mild is the latest addition to the Corvedale bottled beer range. In its cask-conditioned form, it won gold medals in the SIBA (Society of Independent Brewers) West beer competition in 2004 and 2005. A pride of lions features on the label and the beer was named after Norman's daughter who helps run the pub. The hop quoted was a trial hop and will need replacing now that it is now longer available.

TASTING NOTES

A dark gold/amber beer with an aroma that starts malty and spicy and becomes citrus-fruity and floral. The taste is dry and fairly bitter, yet malty, with light floral and fruity notes. Dry, hoppy and bitter finish.

Norman's Pride

● ABV 4.3% ● BOTTLE SIZE 500 ml ● SERVE cool
● INGREDIENTS Maris Otter pale malt/crystal malt/wheat malt/ Northdown hops

Norman's own beer, his first commercial brew, introduced in 1999.

TASTING NOTES

A dark golden/amber ale with a soft, fruity, bubblegum-like aroma. The taste is dry, bitter and fruity with lingering bubblegum, while the finish is bitter and malty.

Teresa's Birthday

● ABV 4.5% ● BOTTLE SIZE 500 ml ● SERVE cool
● INGREDIENTS Maris Otter pale malt/crystal malt/wheat malt/ Northdown and Pilgrim hops

A tawny beer devised by Norman for his wife's birthday: the strength is raised by 0.1% every January.

Secret Hop

● ABV 4.5% ● BOTTLE SIZE 500 ml ● SERVE cool
● INGREDIENTS Maris Otter pale malt/crystal malt/wheat malt/ Susan hops

As its name suggests, this premium ale began life using an undisclosed hop strain. Initially given only a number (93/50), the hop – grown near Ledbury – was later available under the name of Susan. However, as this is no longer available, the hops will need to change.

TASTING NOTES

An amber bitter with a blackcurrant nose. Blackcurrants and bitterness fill the mouth before a slightly toasted, bitter, blackcurrant finish.

Dark and Delicious

● ABV 4.6% ● BOTTLE SIZE 500 ml ● SERVE cool
● INGREDIENTS Maris Otter pale malt/crystal malt/chocolate malt/ wheat malt/Northdown and Susan hops

Described by Norman as a 'black bitter', this beer was introduced as a one-off for Christmas 2000 but has proved popular enough to become a regular brew. Silver medallist in the SIBA West bottled beer contest in 2005. See Secret Hop for a note about the Susan hops.

TASTING NOTES

A deep red beer with an aroma that is biscuity and malty, with a little chocolate and a suggestion of cinnamon. Biscuity dark chocolate features in the fairly bitter taste, with just a little hop fruit throughout. Dry, bitter, nutty, roasted finish.

Cotleigh

Cotleigh Brewery, Ford Road, Wiveliscombe, Somerset TA4 2RE. Tel. (01984) 624086 Fax (01984) 624365
E-mail: sales@cotleighbrewery.com
Website: www.cotleighbrewery.co.uk
Mail order service

Cotleigh was founded way back in 1979 and has moved home a number of times as trade has developed. New owners took over in 2003 and the first bottle-conditioned beer rolled out in the same year. That was a version of the Christmas ale, Red Nose Reinbeer, but this is now a filtered product. However, two new bottled real ales have been introduced. These are brewed at Cotleigh and bottled by O'Hanlon's in Devon, keeping the same yeast used in the primary fermentation.

Buzzard

● ABV 4.8% ● BOTTLE SIZE 500 ml ● SERVE cool
● INGREDIENTS Pale malt/crystal malt/chocolate malt/Golding, Fuggle and Northdown hops

Cotleigh has always been associated with birds of prey (its charitable partner is the Hawk and Owl Trust) and Buzzard – a dark ale – has been sold on draught for more than 20 years.

TASTING NOTES

Dark malts with coffee and liquorice notes fill the aroma of this red beer. Coffeeish dark malt and more liquorice come through in the taste and finish, which is increasingly bitter and smoky, with a hint of tropical fruit on the swallow.

Peregrine Porter

● ABV 5% ● BOTTLE SIZE 500 ml ● SERVE cool
● INGREDIENTS Pale malt/crystal malt/chocolate malt/brown malt/ black malt/Golding, Fuggle and Challenger hops

First brewed for the guest beer market in 1995, Peregrine Porter was not bottled until 2005. The eye-catching labels for both Cotleigh's beers have won technical printing awards.

TASTING NOTES

A ruby beer with a soft, chocolaty and peppery aroma. There are traces of pear in the light fruitiness of the bittersweet taste, with smooth, silky chocolate behind and roasted grains and a hint of liquorice poking through. Full, creamy, coffeeish finish.

Country Life

Country Life Brewery, The Big Sheep, Abbotsham, Devon EX39 5AP. Tel. (01237) 420808
E-mail: countrylifebrewery@tiscali.co.uk
Website: www.countrylifebrewery.co.uk

This small brewery was acquired from Lundy Island in 1999 and set up at the Pig on the Hill pub, near Westward Ho! The plant was then moved in 2002 to The Big Sheep farm attraction, where the beers are offered in daily tastings to visitors and brewery tours are available in summer. The beers are transferred to a bottling tank from the fermenter, allowed to settle and then bottled in house. A 4–6-month shelf life is predicted for most of the beers and all are said to be acceptable to vegetarians. Monthly special cask brews may also find their way into bottles from time to time.

Old Appledore

● **ABV 3.7%** ● **BOTTLE SIZE 500 ml** ● **SERVE cool**
● **INGREDIENTS Maris Otter pale malt/roasted barley/Fuggle and Golding hops**

Formerly brewed to a higher ABV (4.2%) than the draught equivalent, this beer now matches the award-winning cask version in its strength.

TASTING NOTES

An amber ale with a bittersweet, apple-fruity taste. Spicy malt and liquorice feature in the aroma, while the finish is dry and bitter, also with a suggestion of liquorice.

Baa Tenders Best

● **ABV 4.2%** ● **BOTTLE SIZE 500 ml** ● **SERVE cool**
● **INGREDIENTS Maris Otter pale malt/roasted malt/Challenger hops**

On draught this best bitter is sold under the name of Lacey's Best, or sometimes badged as a pub's house beer. The bottle is packaged as being from The Big Sheep Brewery.

TASTING NOTES
Amber in colour, this best bitter has a spicy, creamy malt aroma, with hints of liquorice and fruit. The taste is bittersweet and apple-fruity with spicy malt. Dry, bitter, almost liquorice-like finish.

Pot Wallop

● **ABV 4.4%** ● **BOTTLE SIZE 500 ml** ● **SERVE cool**
● **INGREDIENTS Maris Otter pale malt/Fuggle and Golding hops**
First brewed for the Westward Ho! Potwalloping Festival in 2000 and now available all year-round. The festival celebrates the ancient ritual of replacing washed-up pebbles on the town's famous pebble ridge.
TASTING NOTES
A golden ale with spicy, light malt in the aroma along with a little tart fruit and herbal hop. The taste is bitter, with more tart fruit and floral notes. Dry, bitter and notably hoppy finish.

Golden Pig

● **ABV 4.7%** ● **BOTTLE SIZE 500 ml** ● **SERVE cool**
● **INGREDIENTS Maris Otter pale malt/crystal malt/Challenger hops**
Golden Pig was the first of Country Life's bottled beers and is good with fish, according to Simon.
TASTING NOTES
A dark golden bitter with a malty, spicy and fruity aroma. Tart fruit, lots of hops and full, delicate malt feature on the palate, followed by a dry, hoppy and tangy finish with decent malt support.

Country Bumpkin

● **ABV 6%** ● **BOTTLE SIZE 500 ml** ● **SERVE cool**
● **INGREDIENTS Maris Otter pale malt/chocolate malt/Challenger and Golding hops**
A strong amber ale, also sold in cask form.
TASTING NOTES
A spicy, malty aroma leads to earthy, spicy malt in the dry, bitter taste, with a little tart fruit. Malt lingers in the bitter, hoppy, drying aftertaste.

HB

● **ABV 8–10%** ● **BOTTLE SIZE 500 ml** ● **SERVE cool**
● **INGREDIENTS Vary**
HB stands for Head Banger, a one-off winter brew, with a recipe that

changes as Simon thinks fit. He bottles 1,500 bottles and sells the excess beer to beer festivals the following summer.

TASTING NOTES

2005 brew (8%): An amber ale with spicy malt, fruit and a touch of alcohol in the aroma. The taste is sweet and malty, spicy and warming, with light tropical fruit and a touch of astringency. Dry, bittersweet, malty and increasingly hoppy finish with almost liquorice notes.

Cropton

Cropton Brewery Co., The New Inn, Cropton, Pickering, North Yorkshire YO18 8HH. Tel. (01751) 417330 Fax (01751) 417582
E-mail: info@croptonbrewery.co.uk
Website: www.croptonbrewery.co.uk
Mail order service

Cropton Brewery was set up in 1984 in the cellar of the New Inn, initially just to supply that pub. By 1994 it had outgrown the cellar and a purpose-built brewery was installed behind the pub. The beers all bear logos declaring that they are Vegetarian Society accredited. They are matured in conditioning tanks, filtered and then re-seeded with fresh yeast before bottling, and carry a 12-month best before stamp. The US importer is Shelton Brothers.

Endeavour

● **ABV 3.6%** ● **BOTTLE SIZE 500 ml** ● **SERVE cool**
● **INGREDIENTS Pale malt/Challenger and Golding hops**

Named after Captain Cook's famous ship, that originally sailed from nearby Whitby, Endeavour is a bitter aimed at the tourist market in the seaside resort (a replica of *Endeavour* sails into Whitby every year and draws in the crowds).

TASTING NOTES

A dark golden/orange ale with bitter oranges and hop resins in the nose and taste, and a dry, hoppy finish.

Major stockists (all beers) Local Asda and Tesco

King Billy Bitter

● **ABV 3.6%** ● **BOTTLE SIZE 500 ml** ● **SERVE cool**
● **INGREDIENTS Pale malt/Challenger and Golding hops**

This golden ale takes its name from the statue of King William III outside the King William pub in Hull. In 1993, the landlord of the pub asked Cropton for a brew which his regulars could 'drink all day and not become excitable', hence this popular quaffing brew.

TASTING NOTES

Zesty bitter oranges and a light creaminess in the aroma lead to a dry, hoppy taste of bitter oranges, before a dry, bitter and hoppy finish.

Two Pints Bitter

● ABV 4% ● BOTTLE SIZE 500 ml ● SERVE cool

● INGREDIENTS Pale malt/crystal malt/Challenger and Golding hops

A pint of Two Pints was first served at the New Inn in 1984, the brewery's first year, but the beer did not find its way into a bottle until 1996. It's now the brewery's biggest selling beer, taking its name from the idea that one pint of Two Pints 'is worth two of any other'.

TASTING NOTES

An amber-coloured ale with bitter, orangey hops in the taste, preceded by an orange marmalade nose. The dry finish is bitter and hoppy.

Honey Gold

● ABV 4.2% ● BOTTLE SIZE 500 ml ● SERVE cool

● INGREDIENTS Pale malt/honey/First Gold hops

This beer (for a time known as Honey Farm Bitter) was introduced in cask form for Cropton's first beer festival in 1998, and is now a summer supplement to the brewery's range. It is a single-varietal hop brew, using only First Gold, along with a dose of local Yorkshire honey.

TASTING NOTES

A golden beer with a honeyed nose. The crisp, bitter taste has a light hop edge, with soft honey evident particularly on the swallow. Bitter, hoppy finish with more than a hint of honey.

Scoresby Stout

● ABV 4.2% ● BOTTLE SIZE 500 ml ● SERVE cool

● INGREDIENTS Pale malt/crystal malt/roasted barley/Challenger and Golding hops

This dark brew takes its name from William Scoresby, a whaling captain who hailed from Cropton. Among his various achievements, Scoresby is said to have invented the crow's nest. He is now commemorated with a plaque at Whitby harbour. The cask equivalent of this beer made its debut in 1988 and this bottled option was first produced in 1996.

TASTING NOTES
This ruby beer has a grainy coffee aroma with a suggestion of liquorice. The taste is malty and bitter, enhanced by roasted grain notes. Roasted grain dominates the dry, bitter finish.

Uncle Sams Bitter

● **ABV 4.4%** ● **BOTTLE SIZE 500 ml** ● **SERVE cool**
● **INGREDIENTS Pale malt/crystal malt/Cascade hops**
Certainly the most distinctive of Cropton's bottled ales, Uncle Sams is a homage to the American microbrewer revolution and is chock-full of the perfumed aroma and taste of American Cascade hops. Both this and the original cask version were introduced in 1997.
TASTING NOTES
An orange-golden beer with a bitter grapefruit aroma. This is reflected in the taste, which features tart, bitter orange, lemon and grapefruit notes. The aftertaste is dry, citrus and full of scented hops.

Rudolph's Revenge

● **ABV 4.6%** ● **BOTTLE SIZE 500 ml** ● **SERVE cool**
● **INGREDIENTS Pale malt/crystal malt/roasted barley/Cascade and Styrian Golding hops**
This is Cropton's Christmas beer and shares with Uncle Sams an American nuance, thanks to the use of Cascade hops. At 4.6%, it is one of the UK's less potent Christmas ales, and is also sold in cask.
TASTING NOTES
A red ale with a malty, lightly citrus aroma. Citrus fruit continues in the malty taste, as the aromatic hops take hold and roasted barley drifts well into the background. The long aftertaste is hoppy, tangy and roasty.

Yorkshire Moors

● **ABV 4.6%** ● **BOTTLE SIZE 500 ml** ● **SERVE cool**
● **INGREDIENTS Pale malt/crystal malt/roasted malt/Fuggle and Progress hops**
An amber ale, created to commemorate 50 years of the National Park service in 2002 and now a permanent member of the Cropton range.
TASTING NOTES
An amber-red ale with a malty, spicy nose with bitter orange emerging. The taste is bitter with a sharp hoppiness edging out dark malt flavours. The finish is dry and bitter with roasted grain notes.

Monkman's Slaughter

● ABV 6% ● BOTTLE SIZE 500 ml ● SERVE cool
● INGREDIENTS Pale malt/crystal malt/roasted malt/Challenger and Golding hops

Originally known by the name 'Special Strong', this powerful beer takes its unusual, and rather macabre, title from two quite innocent sources. These are Colin Monkman and Colin Slaughter, the brewery's barley farmer and head brewer, respectively.

TASTING NOTES

Red-amber with citrus hops and smooth malt in the nose. Citrus fruits continue in the taste, over a full malty base that includes darker malt elements. Roasted malt adds bitterness and dryness to the finish.

Darwin

Darwin Brewery Ltd., 63 Back Tatham Street,
Sunderland, Tyne & Wear SR1 3SD.
Tel. (0191) 515 2535 Fax (0191) 515 2531
E-mail: info@darwinbrewery.com
Website: www.darwinbrewery.com

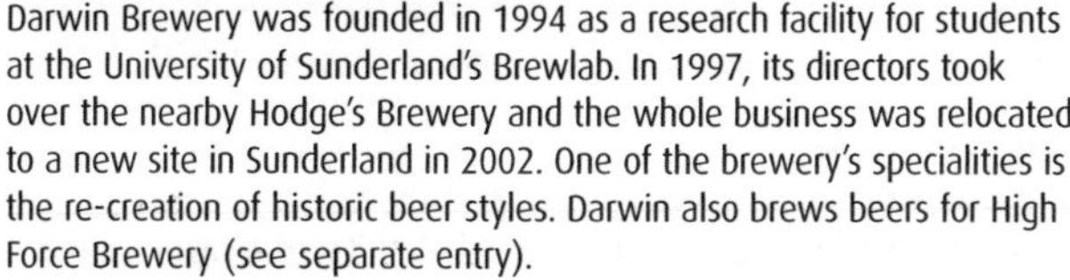

Darwin Brewery was founded in 1994 as a research facility for students at the University of Sunderland's Brewlab. In 1997, its directors took over the nearby Hodge's Brewery and the whole business was relocated to a new site in Sunderland in 2002. One of the brewery's specialities is the re-creation of historic beer styles. Darwin also brews beers for High Force Brewery (see separate entry).

Richmond Ale

● ABV 4.5% ● BOTTLE SIZE 500 ml ● SERVE cool
● INGREDIENTS Pale malt/crystal malt/brown malt/black malt/ Fuggle and Golding hops

Showing Richmond Castle on its 'stained-glass'-style label, Richmond Ale is described as a 'double brown ale' and is brewed using North Yorkshire malt and a northern yeast strain. A recipe from a Ripon brewery gave Brewlab director Dr Keith Thomas a feeling for the malt character of a beer that might have been sold in the late 1800s and records from a maltings near Richmond showed what brewers were ordering at the time. For the yeast, Keith turned to local fruit. He felt that the brewers of the time would have thrown their yeast around without much thought and he considered that yeast living wild on fruit in the area today would have been related to the brewers' yeast of the time. Richmond Ale is also available as a filtered beer, so look for this tastier bottle-conditioned version, which is kräusened prior to filling.

TASTING NOTES

Red/brown with an aroma of malt and toffee. The taste is malty, nutty and fruity, with balancing hop bitterness. Dry, bitter, malty finish.

Doghouse

Doghouse Brewery, Scorrier, Redruth, Cornwall TR16 5BN.
Tel./Fax (01209) 822022
E-mail: starhawk@dsl.pipex.com

Doghouse Brewery was set up in 2001 in a former canine rescue centre. Its bottled ales are all treated with priming sugars and filled directly from the cask, with six months allowed in the best before dates.

Biter

● **ABV 4%** ● **BOTTLE SIZE 500 ml** ● **SERVE cool**
● **INGREDIENTS Optic pale malt/crystal malt/Northdown and Styrian Golding hops**

One of the brewery's original beers, a play on the term 'bitter'.

Dozey Dawg

● **ABV 4.4%** ● **BOTTLE SIZE 500 ml** ● **SERVE cool**
● **INGREDIENTS Optic pale malt/crystal malt/Pilot and Cascade hops**

First brewed as a summer beer in 2003 and retained as a regular brew.

TASTING NOTES

A golden bitter, with light malt and fruit in the nose, sharp hops and malt in the mouth and a little toasted grain with the same flavours in the finish.

Cornish Corgi

● **ABV 4.5%** ● **BOTTLE SIZE 500 ml** ● **SERVE cool**
● **INGREDIENTS Optic pale malt/crystal malt/Pilot and Styrian Golding hops**

Originally the Golden Jubilee beer (then called Loyal Corgi), this beer, like other Doghouse brews, originally included the new Pilot variety of dwarf hops. This has been discontinued so the hops will change.

Dogfight

● **ABV 4.7%** ● **BOTTLE SIZE 500 ml** ● **SERVE cool**

● **INGREDIENTS Optic pale malt/crystal malt/chocolate malt/roasted barley/Pilot and Cascade hops**

This dark, malty ale is in fact a blend of two other beers, Dozey Dawg and Bow Wow.

TASTING NOTES

A tawny ale with a malty aroma, a sharp, malty, nutty taste with citrus notes, and roasted grain in the aftertaste.

Staffi Stout

● **ABV 4.7%** ● **BOTTLE SIZE 500 ml** ● **SERVE cool**

● **INGREDIENTS Optic pale malt/black malt/roasted barley/Fuggle and Golding hops**

'A Staffordshire bull terrier has a strong bite and so does this stout', says brewer Steve Willmott. This dark beer is usually only brewed in springtime.

TASTING NOTES

A ruby beer with light fruit and creamy malt in the nose. Nutty, roasted malt in the taste is rounded off by a malty, roasted finish.

Bow Wow

● **ABV 5%** ● **BOTTLE SIZE 500 ml** ● **SERVE cool**

● **INGREDIENTS Optic pale malt/crystal malt/chocolate malt/roasted barley/torrefied wheat/Challenger hops**

A strong ale continuing the 'doggie' theme.

TASTING NOTES

A tawny ale with an estery, pear drop and treacly malt nose. Malty to taste, with a tart fruitiness, it finishes malty and bittersweet.

Dingo Lager

● **ABV 5%** ● **BOTTLE SIZE 500 ml** ● **SERVE cold**

● **INGREDIENTS Lager malt/Hallertau hops**

Brewed with a lager yeast, this is the brewery's wild dog response to ubiquitous Aussie beer brands. The beer is lagered for two–three months prior to bottling.

TASTING NOTES

A pale golden beer with a light, malty aroma. Light, sweet malt in the taste is offset by sharp, fruity hops. Bittersweet finish.

Colliewobbles/Christmas Tail

● **ABV 5.8%** ● **BOTTLE SIZE 500 ml** ● **SERVE cool**
● **INGREDIENTS Optic pale malt/crystal malt/chocolate malt/roasted barley/torrefied wheat/Fuggle and Golding hops**
A winter brew called Christmas Tail that is re-branded as Colliewobbles for sale at other times of the year.

Dow Bridge

Dow Bridge Brewery, 2–3 Rugby Road, Catthorpe, Lutterworth, Leicestershire LE17 6DA.
Tel./Fax (01788) 869121
E-mail: dowbridge.brewery@virgin.net
Dow Bridge Brewery was founded in 2002 by Russell Webb and has already been forced to extend its capacity. Bottled beers were added in early summer 2006 and these are packaged for Dow Bridge by Bells Brewery in Ullesthorpe.

Bonum Mild

● **ABV 3.6%** ● **BOTTLE SIZE 500 ml** ● **SERVE cool**
● **INGREDIENTS Maris Otter pale malt/crystal malt/chocolate malt/black malt/Fuggle and Golding hops**
The names of Dow Bridge's beers are all loosely themed around Leicestershire's Roman past. *Bonum*, in Latin, means good.

Ratae'd

● **ABV 4.3%** ● **BOTTLE SIZE 500 ml** ● **SERVE cool**
● **INGREDIENTS Maris Otter pale malt/crystal malt/Fuggle and Golding hops**
The name of this best bitter is a play on words: Ratae Coritanorum was the Roman name for Leicester.

Fosse

● **ABV 4.8%** ● **BOTTLE SIZE 500 ml** ● **SERVE cool**
● **INGREDIENTS Maris Otter pale malt/crystal malt/chocolate malt/Fuggle and Golding hops**
Named after the famous Fosse Way, the straight Roman road that ran from Exeter to Leicester. Like the other bottled beers, this strong bitter is also sold in cask-conditioned form.

Downton

Downton Brewery Co. Ltd., Unit 11, Batten Road,
Downton Business Centre, Downton, Salisbury,
Wiltshire SP5 3HU. Tel. (01722) 322890 Fax (01725) 513513
E-mail: martins@downtonbrewery.com

Downton Brewery was founded in 2003 with equipment leased from near-neighbour Hop Back. For a while it brewed an own-label bottle-conditioned ale called Firebrand Great British Beer for Thresher, but sadly this has been discontinued. Downton's other beers all share the Chimera name, drawing inspiration from the mythical beast made up of a lion, a goat and a snake. Only one beer is bottled at present.

Chimera India Pale Ale

● **ABV 7%** ● **BOTTLE SIZE 500 ml** ● **SERVE cool**
● **INGREDIENTS Pale malt/maize/Golding and Pioneer hops**

This strong IPA has won several awards in its draught version since it was introduced in 2004. For the bottle, which is brewed at Downton and packaged at Hop Back, the beer is kräusened after primary fermentation, cold filtered and then re-seeded with fresh yeast. The best before date is set at 18 months. The strong, hoppy flavours marry wonderfully with strong cheeses, say the brewers.

TASTING NOTES

A bright golden IPA with a full but delicate malt and 'sherbet lemons' aroma. The taste is powerfully hoppy and perfumed, with light lemon notes and alcohol-related spice and warmth. Dry, very hoppy finish.

Durham

The Durham Brewery, Unit 5A,
Bowburn North Industrial Estate,
Bowburn, Co. Durham DH6 5PF.
Tel. (0191) 377 1991 Fax (0191) 377 0768
E-mail: gibbs@durham-brewery.co.uk
Website: www.durham-brewery.co.uk

Mail order service

Durham Brewery was set up by music teachers Steve and Christine Gibbs who foresaw redundancy heading their way as cuts in their local education budget loomed. That was back in 1994 and the brewery now produces a wide range of cask beers and several highly-regarded bottle-conditioned beers, including a past CAMRA *Champion Bottled Beer*. All are brewed and bottled on site, with beers passing from fermenters into conditioning tanks, where gravity is allowed to drop out most of the yeast. This ensures that all the bottled beers are acceptable to vegetarians and vegans. There is no filtration and primings are added only if deemed necessary. Steve is no advocate of filtering beer for bottling and re-pitching with new yeast. 'Our only application of modern methods is in scrupulous hygiene and cleanliness,' declares the brewery's literature. Best before dates are fixed at one year after bottling for the weaker beers, with longer allowed for the stronger examples.

Cloister

● ABV 4.5% ● BOTTLE SIZE 500 ml ● SERVE cool
● INGREDIENTS Maris Otter pale malt/lager malt/crystal malt/ wheat malt/Saaz, Target, Cascade and Columbus hops

All the brewery's beer names have connections with the spiritual roots of Durham city and in particular the spellbinding cathedral. In its cask form, the beer is known as Prior's Gold.

TASTING NOTES

A full-flavoured, golden bitter with a citrus hop aroma (grapefruit and a little pineapple). The taste is a crisply bitter mix of citrus fruits, with grapefruit well to the fore, while the drying finish also has a bitter grapefruit hop character.

Evensong ★

● ABV 5% ● BOTTLE SIZE 500 ml ● SERVE cool
● INGREDIENTS Maris Otter pale malt/crystal malt/amber malt/ Munich malt/wheat malt/Golding, Challenger and Fuggle hops

Introduced in 2001 and based on a recipe dating from 1937 from the long-defunct Whitaker's Brewery in Halifax. Although the spirit of the original remains, says Steve Gibbs, this is now a completely Durham creation. CAMRA's *Champion Bottled Beer* of Britain in 2005.

TASTING NOTES

A rich ruby ale with a white head and mellow fruit (tinned peaches?) in the aroma, along with gentle dark malt. There's more mellow fruit and smooth dark malt in the taste, offset by a crisp bitter edge. Toasted malt emerges in the lightly fruity, dry, bitter finish.

St Cuthbert

● ABV 6.5% ● BOTTLE SIZE 500 ml ● SERVE cool
● INGREDIENTS Maris Otter pale malt/crystal malt/wheat malt/ Challenger, Target, Columbus, Golding and Saaz hops

St Cuthbert was Durham's first bottle-conditioned beer and was initially called Millennium City – a reference to the fact that Durham was celebrating its 1,000th year as a city at the turn of the millennium. In 2000 Durham re-christened the beer in honour of the saint whose relics were brought to Durham from Lindisfarne by monks. Inspired by a vision, the monks' decision to settle here heralded the foundation of the city and St Cuthbert still lies in the magnificent cathedral.

TASTING NOTES

This strong amber IPA has an orange aroma and a smooth, toffeeish malt taste, balanced by citrus fruits. Hints of pear drops expose the strength, but the beer falls on the bitter side of bittersweet. Soft, bitter finish of malt and fruit.

Benedictus ★

● ABV 8.4% ● BOTTLE SIZE 500 ml ● SERVE cool
● INGREDIENTS Maris Otter pale malt/crystal malt/wheat malt/ Golding, Target, Saaz, Styrian Golding and Columbus hops

Based on St Cuthbert, but with a deeper golden colour, Benedictus, a barley wine, was added to the range in 2001.

TASTING NOTES

An orange-amber barley wine that drinks like a Belgian tripel. Tropical and citrus fruits share the aroma with lightly piney hops. The taste is full and malty, with big, spicy, citrus hops and a warming alcoholic base, while the equally warming finish is dry yet still with a thick maltiness and lots of hoppy, spicy fruit notes.

Temptation ★

● ABV 10% ● BOTTLE SIZE 500 ml ● SERVE cool
● INGREDIENTS Maris Otter pale malt/brown malt/amber malt/ roasted barley/wheat malt/Target and Golding hops

We all know the Biblical perils of succumbing to temptation, but many drinkers think it's worth making an exception for this brew. The name it was first sold under reveals the style: it was simply called Imperial Russian Stout. The beer has a 'best between' window of six months to five years, but Steve reckons it could age well up to 20 years.

TASTING NOTES
Black as sin. Hints of pear drop and banana enhance biscuity dark malts in the heady, winey aroma. In the mouth, the beer is silky smooth and offers sweet malt ahead of coffee, caramel, liquorice and plain chocolate. Spicy alcohol wafts around and banana is everywhere. Soft liquorice and coffee emerge in the lip-tingling, drying finish.

Earl Soham

Earl Soham Brewery, The Street, Earl Soham, Suffolk IP13 7RT.
Tel. (01728) 684097
E-mail: info@earlsohambrewery.co.uk
Website: www.earlsohambrewery.co.uk
Founded behind The Victoria pub in the village of Earl Soham in 1984, this brewery moved along the road to larger premises in a converted garage in 2001. Next door stands Tastebuds, a well-stocked post-office/delicatessen that sells Earl Soham's beers.

Gannet Mild

● **ABV 3.3%** ● **BOTTLE SIZE 500/750 ml** ● **SERVE cool**
● **INGREDIENTS Maris Otter pale malt/crystal malt/black malt/Fuggle and Golding hops**
Like other Earl Soham's beers, Gannet Mild – one of the brewery's earliest offerings – is allowed 14 days in cask before bottling. The same yeast used in primary fermentation is carried over into the bottle.
TASTING NOTES
A light ruby mild with a malty, nutty, fruity aroma. The taste is bittersweet and malty yet with a little hop adding dryness. Gently bitter, drying finish with nutty roasted grain behind.

Victoria Bitter

● **ABV 3.6%** ● **BOTTLE SIZE 500/750 ml** ● **SERVE cool**
● **INGREDIENTS Maris Otter pale malt/crystal malt/Whitbread Golding Variety, Fuggle and Golding hops**
A golden ale named after the pub which was Earl Soham's first home.
TASTING NOTES
A light bitter with a good aroma for its strength – fruity, hoppy and malty. Grassy hops overlay a smooth, malty base in the bittersweet taste, before a hoppy finish.

Sir Roger's Porter

● ABV 4% ● BOTTLE SIZE 500/750 ml ● SERVE cool
● INGREDIENTS Maris Otter pale malt/crystal malt/black malt/ roasted barley/Fuggle, Styrian Golding and Golding hops
A dark, malty porter, first brewed for Christmas 1999 and now usually produced about once a year.

Gold

● ABV 4% ● BOTTLE SIZE 500 ml ● SERVE cool
● INGREDIENTS Maris Otter pale malt/crystal malt/Brewer's Gold hops
A single-varietal hop beer brewed every six months. The name is likely to change to Brandeston Gold as the range is repackaged.
TASTING NOTES
This copper beer has a hoppy, orange-zesty nose, a perfumed, bitter orange taste with sweet, smooth malt, and a dry, hoppy aftertaste.

Albert Ale

● ABV 4.4% ● BOTTLE SIZE 500/750 ml ● SERVE cool
● INGREDIENTS Maris Otter pale malt/crystal malt/black malt/ roasted barley/Whitbread Golding Variety and Golding hops
Albert Ale is mainly hopped with Whitbread Golding Variety (WGV) but is given a charge of Goldings after the boil for extra aroma. Goldings are also used to dry hop the beers. It was first brewed in 1985.
TASTING NOTES
A copper beer with a malty, hoppy aroma. The taste is malty but not sweet, with nutty, roasted grain prominent and a strong hop balance. Nutty, dark malt and hops finish.

Elveden

Elveden Ales, by Walled Garden, Elveden Courtyard, Elveden, Thetford, Norfolk IP24 3TQ. Tel. (01842) 878922
This five-barrel brewery was opened in early 2004 by Iceni Brewery's Brendan Moore and his daughter, Frances. It is housed on the Elveden estate, the home of the Guinness family, who encourage the production and sale of local crafts and food and drink on the site. As well as brewing, Frances (when not at university) also demonstrates the skill of malting here, and hops are allowed to grow alongside the brewery.

Stout

● **ABV 5%** ● **BOTTLE SIZE 500/750 ml** ● **SERVE cool**
● **INGREDIENTS Maris Otter pale malt/roasted barley/wheat/Boadicea hops/molasses**

Aged in oak casks when it is sold on draught, this traditional stout is laced with black strap molasses in the copper.

TASTING NOTES

A very dark brown beer with dark malt but also floral, fruity notes in the nose. The taste is bitter, with a light malty sweetness and plenty of roasted grain, plus a hint of peachy fruit. Dry, bitter, roasted finish.

Elveden Ale

● **ABV 5.2%** ● **BOTTLE SIZE 500/750 ml** ● **SERVE cool**
● **INGREDIENTS Maris Otter pale malt/wheat/Boadicea hops**

Like the Stout, Elveden Ale is bottled in stone-effect jugs.

TASTING NOTES

Orange-gold, this strong ale has a floral, peachy aroma and a bitter taste with a peachy fruitiness. The finish is hoppy and bitter.

English Wines

English Wines Group, Chapel Down Winery, Tenterden Vineyard, Small Hythe, Tenterden, Kent TN30 7NG.
Tel. (01580) 763033 Fax. (01580) 765333
E-mail: sales@englishwinesgroup.com
Website: www.englishwinesgroup.com
Mail order service

This well-established Sussex vineyard, whose wines are sold under the Chapel Down label, entered the world of beer production in late 2005, joining forces with Hepworth & Co. in Horsham, which brews and bottles the beer. There are three beers in the range, an IPA, a premium lager and a porter, all sold under the Curious Brew name, but only the porter is bottle conditioned. The best before date is set at 12 months. The US importer is GK Skaggs of Irvine, California.

Curious Brew Admiral Porter

● **ABV 5%** ● **BOTTLE SIZE 330 ml** ● **SERVE cool**
● **INGREDIENTS Pale malt/crystal malt/amber malt/chocolate malt/black malt/Admiral and Golding hops**

Taking its name from the hop that provides much of the bitterness, this porter also uses Sussex barley and is conditioned with oak. A special goblet has been designed to enhance the drinking pleasure.

TASTING NOTES

A deep ruby porter with an oaky-woody, vinous aroma with creamy dark malts. Creamy, oaky-sour notes lead in the taste, with dark malt and a little tart fruit. Increasingly bitter, oaky, dry, dark malt finish.

Exe Valley

Exe Valley Brewery, Silverton, Exeter, Devon EX5 4HF.
Tel. (01392) 860406 Fax (01392) 861001
E-mail: exevalley@supanet.com
Website: www.siba-southwest.co.uk/breweries/exevalley

Exe Valley Brewery, formerly known as Barron's Brewery, moved into bottled beer production in 2001, and now uses Country Life Brewery for bottling. Green beer is racked into casks ready for bottling, then the bottled beer is allowed to mature at the brewery before going on sale.

Devon Glory

● **ABV 4.7%** ● **BOTTLE SIZE 500 ml** ● **SERVE cool**
● **INGREDIENTS Optic pale malt/crystal malt/chocolate malt/wheat malt/Challenger hops**

Devon Glory has been in bottle for several years but its recipe has been tinkered with over the past year or so, with Fuggle and Golding hops taken out and leaving Challenger as the sole seasoning. Best before dates are fixed at seven months post-bottling.

Fallen Angel

Fallen Angel Microbrewery, PO Box 95, Battle, East Sussex TN33 0XF.
Tel. (01424) 777996 Fax (01424) 777976
E-mail: custservice@fallenangelbrewery.com
Website: www.fallenangelbrewery.com
Mail order service

Small, family brewery that produces no draught beer, only bottle-conditioned ales. The distinguishing feature of the packaging is original artwork, drawn by erotic artist Lynn Paula Russell. Unfortunately, the brewery is not very forthcoming about ingredients or the bottling procedure, except to say that no finings are used, thus making all beers acceptable to vegetarians. Best before dates are set at six months.

St Patrick's Irish Stout

● **ABV 3.1%** ● **BOTTLE SIZE 500 ml** ● **SERVE cool**
● **INGREDIENTS Pale malt/chocolate malt/roasted barley/other ingredients not declared**

A dark-coloured but light-bodied stout, first brewed in 2004.

TASTING NOTES

A deep ruby beer with dark malt in the aroma and taste, which is also lightly bitter and chocolaty. Dry, bitter chocolate finish.

Fire in the Hole Chili Beer

● **ABV 3.3%** ● **BOTTLE SIZE 500 ml** ● **SERVE cold**
● **INGREDIENTS Not declared**

First brewed in 2004 and containing hot chillies. The brewers suggest that it is served ice cold in shot glasses. Good with barbecues, they say.

TASTING NOTES

Yellow-gold with chillis and a little tart citrus fruit in the aroma. Initial malt sweetness is swept aside by an onslaught of fiery chilli, which burns long into the finish. Not so much a beer as a test of endurance.

Cowgirl Lite

● **ABV 3.7%** ● **BOTTLE SIZE 500 ml** ● **SERVE cool**
● **INGREDIENTS Not declared**

First brewed in 2004, with Cascade hops for an American flavour.

TASTING NOTES

A golden ale with a hoppy, citrus aroma. Soft malt is overlaid with spicy, citrus hops in the taste, with a hint of elderflower. Dry, bitter and hoppy finish. Full flavours for the strength.

New Zealand Bitter

● **ABV 3.9%** ● **BOTTLE SIZE 500 ml** ● **SERVE cool**
● **INGREDIENTS Not declared**

An adventurous bronze ale brewed with New Zealand hops.

TASTING NOTES

Perfumed, spicy and floral notes combine with bitter citrus in the complex aroma. The taste is also perfumed, hoppy and mostly bitter, with just a little malt for balance. Dry, hoppy, perfumed finish.

Shepherdess Draught

● **ABV 3.9%** ● **BOTTLE SIZE 500 ml** ● **SERVE cool**
● **INGREDIENTS Not declared**

A light ale, first brewed towards the end of 2005.

TASTING NOTES

An orange-golden beer with a slightly perfumed aroma of apricots, citrus and a little malt. Juicy tropical fruits dominate the palate, which is initially fairly sweet but then balanced by light hops. Bitter, juicy fruits lead in the finish, eventually giving way to hops.

Tawny Honey Rose

● **ABV 3.9%** ● **BOTTLE SIZE 500 ml** ● **SERVE cool**
● **INGREDIENTS Not declared**

A fruit beer, first brewed in 2004, and including black cherries.

TASTING NOTES

Tawny, as its name implies, this beer has an aroma of candied fruit and a little orange. The taste is sweetish, with light lemon and dried fruits, but also a dry backdrop. Dry, fruity, bittersweet finish.

Kama Sumatra

● **ABV 4%** ● **BOTTLE SIZE 500 ml** ● **SERVE cool**
● **INGREDIENTS Not declared**

An unusual porter, first brewed in 2005, featuring Sumatran coffee.

TASTING NOTES

A garnet-coloured beer with an aroma of coffee, spice and zesty citrus. Coffee is immediately obvious in the taste but not overpowering. Perfumed, juicy citrus notes also feature and there's some bitter chocolate, too. Dry, coffee finish.

Hickory Switch Porter

● **ABV 4.3%** ● **BOTTLE SIZE 500 ml** ● **SERVE cool**
● **INGREDIENTS Not declared**

First brewed in 2004 and featuring both honey and hickory smoke. Try adding some to chillis or barbecue sauces, say the brewers.

TASTING NOTES

Smoky, hickory flavours dominate this well-balanced, interesting ruby beer. The taste also has both sweet and dark malt characters, with a light lemony edge from the hops, and there's a touch of liquorice on the swallow. More dark and roasted malts emerge in the bitter finish.

Howlin' Red Ale

● **ABV 4.4%** ● **BOTTLE SIZE 500 ml** ● **SERVE cool**
● **INGREDIENTS Not declared**

Like some other Fallen Angel beers, Howlin' Red contains honey, which is fine for vegetarians but not for vegans.

TASTING NOTES

Amber-red, with a fruity aroma (light oranges and peaches). The taste is also full and fruity, with sweet tinned fruit balanced by a firm, bitter, drying edge. The mellow finish is increasingly bitter, with lingering fruit.

Lemon Weissbier

● **ABV 4.5%** ● **BOTTLE SIZE 500 ml** ● **SERVE cold**
● **INGREDIENTS Not declared**

First brewed in 2004. Brewed to be served cloudy, Bavarian fashion.

TASTING NOTES

A yellow beer with lemon throughout. The taste is refreshingly sharp but well balanced with sweetness. There are light gingery notes, too, before a dry, lemony, gently bitter aftertaste.

Angry Ox Bitter

● **ABV 4.8%** ● **BOTTLE SIZE 500 ml** ● **SERVE cool**
● **INGREDIENTS Not declared**

This red-coloured premium ale was first brewed in 2004.

TASTING NOTES

Hop resins, dark malt and bitter citrus fruit compete in the aroma. The taste is full bodied, with sweet, smooth malt, big dried fruit flavours and a gentle hop note for crispness and balance. The fruity and sweet finish dries and becomes bitter as hops and roasted malt kick in.

Black Cat Ale

● **ABV 4.8%** ● **BOTTLE SIZE 500 ml** ● **SERVE cool**
● **INGREDIENTS Not declared**

First brewed in 2004, this deep ruby beer includes honey as well as Willamette hops from the USA.

TASTING NOTES

The zesty oranges in the aroma are unexpected from the colour, with dark malts only softly in the background. Juicy orange flavours continue in the bittersweet taste, again leaving dark malt behind. Only a modest finish, however, with mildly bitter dark malt and faint oranges.

Farmer's

Farmer's Ales, Maldon Brewing Co. Ltd., The Stable Brewery, Silver Street, Maldon, Essex CM9 4QE. Tel. (01621) 851000
E-mail: info@maldonbrewing.co.uk
Website: www.maldonbrewing.co.uk

Maldon Brewing Co. was set up in 2002 by Nigel and Christine Farmer and now trades as Farmer's Ales. It is based next to the Blue Boar Hotel in Mauldon, which takes most of the brewery's beers.

A Drop of Nelson's Blood

● **ABV 3.8%** ● **BOTTLE SIZE 500 ml** ● **SERVE cool**
● **INGREDIENTS Maris Otter pale malt/crystal malt/black malt/ Cascade and First Gold hops/brandy**

There's a shot of brandy in every cask of this session beer – a reference to the fact that Nelson's body was brought back to Britain in a cask of brandy, which the sailors reportedly drank on their return. First brewed for Trafalgar Day a few years ago.

Sweet Farmer's Ale

● **ABV 4%** ● **BOTTLE SIZE 500 ml** ● **SERVE cool**
● **INGREDIENTS Maris Otter pale malt/crystal malt/chocolate malt/ Fuggle hops/honey**

Inevitably abbreviated to Sweet FA, this lightly-hopped ale is dosed with Maldon honey produced across the road from the brewery.

The Hotel Porter

● **ABV 4.1%** ● **BOTTLE SIZE 500 ml** ● **SERVE cool**
● **INGREDIENTS Maris Otter pale malt/roasted barley/rolled oats/ Challenger and Golding hops**

Originally a brew for the Blue Boar Hotel, next to the brewery.

Puck's Folly

● **ABV 4.2%** ● **BOTTLE SIZE 500 ml** ● **SERVE cool**
● **INGREDIENTS Lager malt/Golding hops**

A local production of *A Midsummer Night's Dream* was the inspiration for this pale beer. Nigel had been enjoying a pint of Buffy Brewery's Polly's Folly just before watching the play, and, seeing the character of Puck, put the two ideas together.

Edward Bright Stout

● ABV 4.8% ● BOTTLE SIZE 500 ml ● SERVE cool
● INGREDIENTS Maris Otter pale malt/chocolate malt/Golding hops
Edward Bright was a famously large (44 stones), 18th-century Maldon grocer. It was once bet that 700 men could fit inside his waistcoat. One crafty villager fetched seven men from the district known as Dengie Hundred. They squeezed into the waistcoat and the bet was won.

Felstar

The Felstar Brewery, Felsted Vineyard, Crix Green,
Felsted, Essex CM6 3JT. Tel./Fax (01245) 361504
E-mail: felstarbrewery@supanet.com
Website: www.felstarbrewery.co.uk
Mail order service
Felstar Brewery was built in 2001 in the old bonded stores of Felsted Vineyard, the first commercial vineyard in East Anglia. Production of its own beers neatly filled a space in the site's own shop, between English wines and ciders. The brewery is run by former graphic designer Marcello Davanzo (known to everyone as Franco), who has chosen the rooster as his brewery logo. If you ever call into Franco's shop, you'll know why. Try driving out again without running over one of his free-ranging poultry stock. His beers are bottled on site, being racked bright after conditioning in the cask and seeded with the same yeast as used in primary fermentation. Bottom-fermenting beers are kräusened and/or primed with unrefined molasses. Best before dates are generally fixed at 12 months. Franco is one of the most inventive brewers around, tearing up the rulebooks and mixing and matching ale recipes with lager production methods. He has now built a new shop on the site and expanded the brewery's fermentation capacity. One of his latest projects is producing 100 different, limited edition bottle-conditioned beers named after Essex towns and villages.

Crix Gold

● ABV 4% ● BOTTLE SIZE 500 ml ● SERVE cool
● INGREDIENTS Lager malt/caramalt/wheat malt/First Gold, Jenny and Brewer's Gold hops
The sprawling settlement of Felsted is actually made up of several smaller villages, most with names ending in 'Green'. Crix Green is

where the brewery is located (follow the brown vineyard signs) – hence the name of this and other beers. An unusual selection of hops includes the trial dwarf hop named Jenny. This and Ruth, another triallist used in other Felstar beers, have now been discontinued, but Franco still has supplies vacuum-packed and in his freezer for use in the near future.

TASTING NOTES

A golden ale with a fresh, citrus hop nose backed by biscuity malt. Tart lemon dominates the crisp taste; dry, bitter finish.

Hops & Glory

● ABV 4% ● BOTTLE SIZE 500 ml ● SERVE cool

● INGREDIENTS Maris Otter pale malt/crystal malt/chocolate malt/ wheat malt/Brewer's Gold and Fuggle hops

'Fruity when young, complex when mature', is how Franco describes this best bitter, brewed a couple of times a year.

Chick Chat

● ABV 4.1% ● BOTTLE SIZE 500 ml ● SERVE cool

● INGREDIENTS Maris Otter and Pearl pale malt/chocolate malt/ torrefied wheat/Bramling Cross and Fuggle hops

Taking its inspiration from the free-range fowl that wander the brewery grounds, this beer is also sold in cask form.

Grand Crix

● ABV 4.1% ● BOTTLE SIZE 500 ml ● SERVE cool

● INGREDIENTS Maris Otter pale malt/caramalt/crystal malt/ unmalted barley/Bramling Cross and Ruth hops

Maturity is the name of the game here, with Grand Crix given a long conditioning in oak casks that have been seasoned with fresh root ginger and coriander. The beer is brewed just once a year.

TASTING NOTES

A copper beer with a perfumed aroma of ginger and other spices. Tangy spice also leads in the bitter taste and features in the dry, bitter finish.

Lord Kulmbach

● ABV 4.4% ● BOTTLE SIZE 500 ml ● SERVE cold

● INGREDIENTS Maris Otter pale malt/lager malt/crystal malt/black malt/wheat malt/Brewer's Gold and Fuggle hops

Franco describes this as a bottom-fermented stout, in other words a stout that brewed like a lager. Primary cold fermentation takes ten days, five more days are permitted to allow diacetyl (butterscotch notes) to round out and then the beer is cold-matured for eight weeks.

TASTING NOTES

A near-black beer with light roasted malt and a blackberry fruitiness in the nose. The same fruit emerges in the crisp, clean taste before being passed by roasted malt. The dry aftertaste is also bitter and roasted.

Hoppin' Hen

● ABV 4.5% ● BOTTLE SIZE 500 ml ● SERVE cool

● INGREDIENTS Maris Otter and Pearl pale malt/crystal malt/wheat malt/roasted barley/First Gold, Jenny and Hersbrucker hops

A beer that is best drunk young, according to Franco. This premium ale features dwarf and German hops and is primed with maple syrup.

TASTING NOTES

A copper beer with a fruity, malt and hops aroma, underscored by soft melon and pineapple notes. The taste is a crisp mix of malt and fruity hops, with the same tropical fruit notes. Dry, hoppy, lightly fruity finish.

Old Crix

● ABV 4.5% ● BOTTLE SIZE 500 ml ● SERVE cool

● INGREDIENTS Maris Otter pale malt/crystal malt/chocolate malt/ wheat malt/First Gold and Perle hops

Again Franco has pulled out all the stops to produce a beer that is different. This time he takes an ale recipe and brews it in continental fashion, using a double-decoction system (the wort is pumped from vessel to vessel and exposed to higher temperatures to extract brewing sugars). He then dry hops the beer with more Perle hops.

TASTING NOTES

Rich orange notes emerge in the otherwise malty aroma of this robust amber beer. The taste is nutty and malty with a good hop overlay and hints of fruit. The 'mature oak' signposted on the label also comes through. Bitter fruit and hops fill the aftertaste.

Wheat

● ABV 4.8% ● BOTTLE SIZE 500 ml ● SERVE cold

● INGREDIENTS Pearl pale malt/crystal malt/wheat malt/roasted barley/Mount Hood hops

This weissbier-styled brew is lightly hopped and nicely acidic, making it,

according to Franco, a good drink to enjoy with crisp fish and chips.
TASTING NOTES
Golden, with a light orangey aroma spiked with a pinch of pepper. Orange/lemon notes lead in the mouth, supported by a strong peppery spiciness. Orange and lemon continue in the spicy, warming finish.

Good Knight

● ABV 5% ● BOTTLE SIZE 500 ml ● SERVE cool
● INGREDIENTS Maris Otter pale malt/crystal malt/chocolate malt/caramalt/roasted barley/Bramling Cross, First Gold and Perle hops
Another double-decoction beer, Good Knight is a strong mild/porter with lager connections. It matures well in the bottle, declares Franco.

Peckin' Order

● ABV 5% ● BOTTLE SIZE 500 ml ● SERVE cold
● INGREDIENTS Lager malt/crystal malt/wheat malt/Brewer's Gold and Perle hops
Taking three months from brewing to bottling, Peckin' Order enjoys a primary fermentation with a gradually-reduced temperature and ten days' rest before long cold conditioning.
TASTING NOTES
Malt, fruit and floral hop notes mark out the aroma of this dark golden brew. Its taste is lightly fruity, with a buttery maltiness plus lemon notes on the swallow. Creamy malt finish with bitterness and hop emerging.

Peckin' Python

● ABV 5% ● BOTTLE SIZE 500 ml ● SERVE cold
● INGREDIENTS Lager malt/crystal malt/wheat malt/Brewer's Gold and Perle hops/nettles
Brewed as for Peckin' Order, this lager also includes fresh nettles for a golden-green colour and more bittersweetness.

Red Wheat Lager

● ABV 5% ● BOTTLE SIZE 500 ml ● SERVE cold
● INGREDIENTS Lager malt/wheat malt/Horizon and Hersbrucker hops/maple syrup
Fermented for a total of 12 weeks, this new beer contains a 60/40 mix of lager malt and wheat malt. It is hopped three times, twice with

Horizon (a relatively new American hop) for bitterness and once with Hersbrucker for aroma. As this beer is not fined, but naturally sedimented and racked, it is acceptable to vegans. Maple syrup is employed along with fresh yeast for kräusening.

Roosters Rest

● **ABV 5%** ● **BOTTLE SIZE 500 ml** ● **SERVE cool**
● **INGREDIENTS Maris Otter pale malt/caramalt/torrefied wheat/torrefied barley/Bramling Cross, Jenny and Hersbrucker hops**
Roosters Rest is a strong bitter. It is the bottled version of a cask beer that was cheekily called Betty's Best, when it was introduced to commemorate The Queen's Golden Jubilee in 2002.

Jet-Lager

● **ABV 5.2%** ● **BOTTLE SIZE 500 ml** ● **SERVE cool**
● **INGREDIENTS Lager malt/crystal malt/chocolate malt/invert sugar/Brewer's Gold and Mount Hood hops**
A black lager, mashed by double decoction. After fermentation (during which the Mount Hood hops are added) and a rest period, the beer is kräusened and lagered for four weeks before being racked for bottling.

Dark Wheat

● **ABV 5.4%** ● **BOTTLE SIZE 500 ml** ● **SERVE cool**
● **INGREDIENTS Pearl pale malt/black malt/wheat malt/chocolate wheat malt/Mount Hood hops**
A medium-hopped, slowly-fermented wheat beer brewed twice a year.

Lord Essex

● **ABV 5.4%** ● **BOTTLE SIZE 500 ml** ● **SERVE cool**
● **INGREDIENTS Maris Otter pale malt/caramalt/chocolate wheat malt/roasted barley/Mount Hood and Phoenix hops**
This strong old ale is the result of a long mashing, double decoction, a vigorous lengthy boil – and a brewing accident. The ever-experimental Franco initially used American Galena hops in the brew, not appreciating that they would shed a large quantity of seeds. The seeds blocked the filters on his copper, leading to a long, laborious run-off of wort, which meant that the beer was sitting on the hops for two hours longer than planned. It didn't do the brew any harm. That edition, in cask, was winner of the 2004 Chelmsford Winter Beer Festival competition.

Haunted Hen

● ABV 6% ● BOTTLE SIZE 500 ml ● SERVE cool
● INGREDIENTS Maris Otter pale malt/caramalt/chocolate malt/ chocolate wheat malt/torrefied wheat/Golding, Jenny and Hersbrucker hops

Brewed every October and ripened in heavily toasted oak rum casks, Haunted Hen is a stout brewed for maturity and is claimed to be at its best when over a year old. A Chelmsford Winter Beer Festival award-winner in 2003 in its cask form.

TASTING NOTES

A near-black beer with a rich, biscuity, malt and coffee nose. Liquorice notes feature in the bittersweet, nutty, roasted taste, with a suggestion of fruit throughout, though perhaps not as much body as expected. Bittersweet, roasted malt finish.

Howlin' Hen

● ABV 6.5% ● BOTTLE SIZE 330 ml ● SERVE cool
● INGREDIENTS Maris Otter and Pearl pale malt/wheat malt/roasted barley/Golding, Jenny and Hersbrucker hops

Brewed in September, ideally for drinking at Christmas the following year, this rich beer is conditioned in oak casks for a vanilla accent, making it, says Franco, 'justifiably expensive'. He also claims it goes excellently with fruit cakes and puddings.

TASTING NOTES

A very deep ruby stout with a moussey brown foam. Light fruit notes give way to mellow, creamy, sweet coffee in the aroma, while the creamy, sweetish, coffeeish taste has a warmth that indicates its strength. Strong, bitter coffee finish.

Fenland

Fenland Brewery Ltd., Unit 2, Fieldview, Cowbridge Hall Road, Little Downham, Cambridgeshire CB6 2UQ.
Tel. (01353) 699966 Fax (01353) 699967
E-mail: enquiries@elybeer.co.uk
Website: www.elybeer.co.uk
Mail order service

Fenland Brewery was set up in 1997 but came into the hands of new owner David Griffiths at the end of 2003. David has inherited some beer names and recipes, but also made changes and added new beers himself. The bottled beers bear the dual name of Fenland/Isle of Ely, as David tries to reposition the business. In addition to the beers featured below, Fenland's seasonal cask beers are often bottled.

St Audrey's Ale

● ABV 3.9% ● BOTTLE SIZE 500 ml ● SERVE cool
● INGREDIENTS Maris Otter pale malt/crystal malt/Fuggle and First Gold hops

A session bitter named after Ely's patron saint.

Babylon Banks

● ABV 4.1% ● BOTTLE SIZE 500 ml ● SERVE cool
● INGREDIENTS Maris Otter pale malt/Munich malt/chocolate malt/ black malt/Pilot and Golding hops

Babylon Banks is an area on the river in the city of Ely.

Osier Cutter

● ABV 4.2% ● BOTTLE SIZE 500 ml ● SERVE cool
● INGREDIENTS Maris Otter pale malt/lager malt/Challenger and Styrian Golding hops

An osier cutter is a traditional Fenland job. It involves cutting down the supple branches of the osier tree (a kind of willow) for basket making.

Smokestack Lightning

● ABV 4.2% ● BOTTLE SIZE 500 ml ● SERVE cool
● INGREDIENTS Maris Otter pale malt/crystal malt/caramalt/ chocolate malt/black malt/First Gold, Golding and Fuggle hops

David inherited this mild along with the brewery. He's kept the name (derived from a blues song) but changed the recipe.

Sparkling Wit

● ABV 4.5% ● BOTTLE SIZE 500 ml ● SERVE cool
● INGREDIENTS Maris Otter pale malt/wheat malt/First Gold hops/ coriander seeds/honey

Sparkling Wit, along with Doctor's Orders opposite, appeared in early editions of this book but have been absent in recent years. David has revived the beers, slightly adjusting the recipe for this Belgian-style witbier. The coriander and honey are added during the copper boil.

TASTING NOTES
Golden, with a perfumed, slightly earthy and peppery aroma of lemon. The taste is bittersweet, slightly earthy and perfumed once again, with gentle lemon. The same flavours continue in the drying, bitter finish.

Doctor's Orders

● ABV 5% ● BOTTLE SIZE 500 ml ● SERVE cool
● INGREDIENTS Maris Otter pale malt/crystal malt/caramalt/ First Gold hops
Fenland's strong ale, only a seasonal beer in its cask form.
TASTING NOTES
Light amber, with a malty aroma overlaid with hops. The taste is also full and malty, sweetish but crisp, with a little hop dryness. Nutty, dark malt flavours emerge in the finish, which dries as bitterness increases.

Fox

Fox Brewery, Fox & Hounds, 22 Station Road, Heacham, Norfolk PE31 7EX. Tel. (01485) 570345 Fax (01485) 579491
E-mail: info@foxbrewery.co.uk
Website: www.foxbrewery.com
This pub brewery opened in 2002 and brews not just for the pub but other outlets, too. Sales of bottles (added in 2003) have really taken off. Both pub and brewery have been extended as a result.

Branthill Best

● ABV 3.8% ● BOTTLE SIZE 500 ml ● SERVE cool
● INGREDIENTS Maris Otter pale malt/amber malt/pale chocolate malt/torrefied wheat/Phoenix, Cascade and First Gold hops
A beer using barley from Branthill Farm at Wells-next-the-Sea, Norfolk.
TASTING NOTES
Red-amber, with a malty, lightly chocolaty, nutty aroma. The taste and finish are also nutty and malty, with some bitterness and hints of roast.

Drop of Real Norfolk

● ABV 3.8% ● BOTTLE SIZE 500 ml ● SERVE cool
● INGREDIENTS Maris Otter pale malt/torrefied wheat/Fuggle and Styrian Golding hops
A pale, citrus bitter, introduced in the last couple of years.

Heacham Gold

● ABV 3.9% ● BOTTLE SIZE 500 ml ● SERVE cool
● INGREDIENTS Lager malt/wheat malt/Cascade, Phoenix and First Gold hops

A fruity bitter named after the brewery's home town.

TASTING NOTES

A pale yellow beer with a surprisingly malty nose. The sweetish taste is also malty yet quickly becomes crisp and lightly citrus. Bittersweet, lemony, lingering malt finish.

Nina's Mild

● ABV 3.9% ● BOTTLE SIZE 500 ml ● SERVE cool
● INGREDIENTS Maris Otter pale malt/crystal malt/chocolate malt/ black malt/torrefied wheat/Fuggle and Challenger hops

A dark mild, added to the range since the last edition of this book.

TASTING NOTES

Bourneville chocolate and tobacco feature in the aroma of this deep red mild. Dark, nutty malt, rather than hop, provides bitterness in the mouth, with a light drying character from the grain. Bitter chocolate continues, too, right through to the drying finish. Not a sweet mild.

LJB

● ABV 4% ● BOTTLE SIZE 500 ml ● SERVE cool
● INGREDIENTS Maris Otter pale malt/crystal malt/chocolate malt/ Challenger, Fuggle and Target hops

LJB stands for Little John Bristow – brewer Mark Bristow's young son (the beer celebrated his birth in 2002).

TASTING NOTES

A dark amber ale with a hoppy nose. The taste is hoppy and quenching, with a light, malty sweetness. Dry, hoppy finish.

Red Knocker

● ABV 4.2% ● BOTTLE SIZE 500 ml ● SERVE cool
● INGREDIENTS Maris Otter pale malt/crystal malt/Cascade, Fuggle and First Gold hops

A copper bitter, bottled, like the others, by allowing cask beer to drop bright, transferring it to a new cask and kräusening before filling.

TASTING NOTES

Another red-amber beer, this time with a hoppy aroma backed by a little malt. It's a full-flavoured, hoppy, malty best bitter to taste, with a mellow, moreish, pleasantly bitter and hoppy finish.

Branthill Norfolk Nectar

● ABV 4.3% ● BOTTLE SIZE 500 ml ● SERVE cool
● INGREDIENTS Maris Otter pale malt/torrefied wheat/Bramling Cross and Fuggle hops

A fairly sweet beer, hence the name Norfolk Nectar.

TASTING NOTES

A yellow beer featuring a bready aroma and a gently bitter taste, with fruity sweetness. Drying, hoppy finish.

Cerberus Norfolk Stout

● ABV 4.5% ● BOTTLE SIZE 500 ml ● SERVE cool
● INGREDIENTS Maris Otter pale malt/crystal malt/torrefied wheat/crushed wheat/roasted barley/Fuggle hops

A ruby stout recalling the three-headed dog of Hell from mythology.

TASTING NOTES

An aroma of mellow, creamy, coffee, plus a hint of blackberry, leads to a creamy, mellow, coffeeish, bittersweet taste, with blackberry fruit emerging. Drying, bittersweet, creamy, roasted malt finish.

Heacham Kriek

● ABV 5.1% ● BOTTLE SIZE 500 ml ● SERVE cool
● INGREDIENTS Maris Otter pale malt/crystal malt/chocolate malt/black malt/Target, Fuggle, Cascade and Bramling Cross hops/cherries

A new variation on the theme of Nelson's Blood (below), but without the rum and replacing the cloves with whole cherries in the copper. That's not how kriek is made in Belgium, of course, but it does add a rich fruitcake character to the beer, according to Mark.

Nelson's Blood

● ABV 5.1% ● BOTTLE SIZE 500 ml ● SERVE cool
● INGREDIENTS Maris Otter pale malt/crystal malt/chocolate malt/black malt/Target, Fuggle, Cascade and Bramling Cross hops/cloves/Nelson's Blood rum

First brewed for the 200th anniversary of the Battle of Trafalgar, this commemorative brew contains a shot of Nelson's Blood rum. This rum is exclusive to The Lord Nelson pub in Nelson's home village of Burnham

Thorpe and has been produced since Trafalgar time. About 150 ml is added to every nine-gallon cask prior to bottling. Earlier, the beer is seasoned with cloves, which are added to the copper boil.

IPA

● ABV 5.2% ● BOTTLE SIZE 500 ml ● SERVE cool
● INGREDIENTS Maris Otter pale malt/crystal malt/Target and First Gold hops

A traditional India pale ale, re-created by Mark after researching beer recipes from the 19th century.

TASTING NOTES

A golden ale with a sharp, fruity hop aroma, a robustly hoppy, pleasantly fruity, drying taste, and a dry, hoppy finish.

Punt Gun

● ABV 5.9% ● BOTTLE SIZE 500 ml ● SERVE cool
● INGREDIENTS Maris Otter pale malt/crystal malt/black malt/ torrefied wheat/Fuggle and Bramling Cross hops

A strong old ale in the mould of Theakston's Old Peculier.

TASTING NOTES

A very dark ruby beer with a malty, lightly fruity aroma that is a little creamy and grainy. The taste is malty, lightly sweet and alcoholic, with hints of almonds and gentle fruit. Bittersweet, dark malt finish.

Freeminer

Freeminer Brewery Ltd., Whimsey Road,
Steam Mills, Cinderford, Gloucestershire GL14 3JA.
Tel. (01594) 827989 Fax (01594) 829464
Website: www.freeminer.com

Established in 1992, the only brewery in the Royal Forest of Dean moved to new, larger premises in 2002. Bottling on a major scale resumed in 2003, with the launch of the Co-op own-label beer, Gold Miner, and continued with the re-launch in stylish new packaging of three old favourites, Trafalgar, Speculation and Waterloo. These beers, like other Freeminer ales, despite suggesting otherwise, recall the Forest's mining heritage in their titles. (For the record, a 'freeminer' is a male born within the hundred of St Briavels who has claimed his birthright to mine the area without charge by reaching the age of 21 and working a year and a day in a local mine.) Bottling is now handled by Meantime Brewing and new to the range is an acclaimed 'own-label' product for Morrisons. Green beer is trucked from Freeminer to Greenwich, where it is matured, chilled, fined, sterile filtered and then re-pitched with a special bottling yeast before filling. Rogue Ales imports Freeminer beers into the USA.

Waterloo

● ABV 4.5% ● BOTTLE SIZE 500 ml ● SERVE cool
● INGREDIENTS Optic pale malt/crystal malt/Cascade, First Gold and Golding hops

Based on a Freeminer cask beer called Iron Brew, but with less bitterness, this red-amber ale is a good partner for barbecue food, roast pork and cheeses, according to brewer Don Burgess.

TASTING NOTES

There's plenty of malt in the aroma, along with hints of orange and a light milk-chocolate sweetness. The taste is smooth, milky and malty, with traces of bitter orange and a notable hop character that develops strongly without being aggressive. Bitter, hoppy, drying finish.

Speculation

● ABV 4.8% ● BOTTLE SIZE 500 ml ● SERVE cool
● INGREDIENTS Optic pale malt/crystal malt/chocolate malt/Fuggle and Golding hops

Speculation is a premium ale named after a long-closed Forest of Dean mine that is now used as a popular picnic area.

TASTING NOTES

A deep amber beer with a spicy, malty aroma. Robust and bitter in the mouth, it also features a spicy maltiness for balance and a light fruit tang. Bitter, hoppy, drying finish.

Gold Miner ★

● ABV 5% ● BOTTLE SIZE 500 ml ● SERVE cool
● INGREDIENTS Optic pale malt/pale crystal malt/First Gold hops

Exclusive to the Co-op, Gold Miner was launched in 2003, although the beer had previously enjoyed success as a cask beer called Gold Standard, winner of a *Beauty of Hops* award for its use of First Gold.

TASTING NOTES

A golden beer with lots of fruity hop resins in the nose, with almost

pineapple notes. Fruity hops dominate the taste, but there's also a fine malty-sweet balance. Hoppy, dry, tangy finish.
Major stockist Co-op

Morrisons The Best ★

● **ABV 6%** ● **BOTTLE SIZE 500 ml** ● **SERVE cool**
● **INGREDIENTS Optic pale malt/other malts not declared/First Gold, Golding and Fuggle hops**

After success with Gold Miner for the Co-op, Freeminer further mined the own-label sector with this new beer for Morrisons' *The Best* range of quality foods and drinks. The beer draws on other Freeminer ales for inspiration. Chiefly, it is modelled on Speculation, but Don Burgess refuses to be drawn on the exact make-up, except to say that it includes six different malts in all.

TASTING NOTES
A big toffeeish, malty aroma, laced with peppery, fruity hops, offers a good indication of what is to follow on the tongue – namely full, deep malt balanced by tangy hops. The finish is dry, bitter and lip-smackingly hoppy with a toasted malt note.
Major stockist Morrisons

Trafalgar

● **ABV 6%** ● **BOTTLE SIZE 500 ml** ● **SERVE cool**
● **INGREDIENTS Optic pale malt/crystal malt/Golding hops**

The heavy hop character of this potent brew recalls the days of the British Empire when strong, hoppy IPAs were stashed aboard sailing ships for the long journey to the Indian subcontinent. Trafalgar is reputedly based on a formula for a 9% beer but the restraints of excise duties prohibit the recipe from being followed to the letter. As if there weren't enough hops in the brew to start with, Freeminer also dry hops to embellish the nose and finish. This clearly impressed judges at the 1997 *Beauty of Hops* awards who accorded the beer the title of *Best Bottled Single Varietal*. Trafalgar was a Forest of Dean mine, the first in the world to be electrically lit.

TASTING NOTES
A dark golden beer with estery fruits – pineapple, melon and orange – in the nose, with toffee notes emerging. The full-bodied taste is fairly sweet and toffee-malty, with lots of estery fruit and a developing hop presence. The big, long, hoppy finish is dry and lip-smacking.

Frog Island

Frog Island Brewery, The Maltings, Westbridge, St James Road, Northampton NN4 8DU. Tel. (01604) 587772
E-mail: beer@frogislandbrewery.co.uk
Website: www.frogislandbrewery.co.uk
Mail order service

Taking its name from an area of Northampton that is prone to flooding, Frog Island hopped into the brewing world in 1994. It set up shop in an old malthouse once owned by the Thomas Manning brewery. The beers are bottled on site, unprimed, from a conditioning tank, without the use of isinglass finings (rendering all three acceptable to vegetarians).

Natterjack

● ABV 4.8% ● BOTTLE SIZE 500 ml ● SERVE cool
● INGREDIENTS Maris Otter pale malt/wheat malt/Target and Golding hops

Natterjack, previously a cask beer, was introduced in bottle in 2000.

TASTING NOTES

A copper ale with a rich, orangey, hoppy aroma. The bittersweet taste is powerfully fruity and hoppy (smoky orange notes), while the finish is bitter and fruity with a strong, lingering hoppiness.

Fire-Bellied Toad

● ABV 5% ● BOTTLE SIZE 500 ml ● SERVE cool
● INGREDIENTS Pale malt/crystal malt/wheat malt/Phoenix hops

This single-varietal hop beer was introduced in 1998 and comes wrapped in a dramatic label showing a mythical bird-creature attacking the eponymous toad. The best before date is set at around six months.

TASTING NOTES

A dark golden, hoppy ale. The aroma features orangey citrus notes from the hops, whilst the taste is fruity but bitter, again with citrus notes and tangy hop. Long-lasting, dry, bitter, tangy hop-fruit finish.

Croak & Stagger

● ABV 5.6% ● BOTTLE SIZE 500 ml ● SERVE cool
● INGREDIENTS Pale malt/crystal malt/chocolate malt/wheat malt/ Target and Cascade hops

Dark amber Croak & Stagger was Frog Island's first foray into the bottled beer world. It is a variation of a cask winter ale of the same name. Brewers Bruce Littler and Graham Cherry toned down the ABV (to provide a little less croak and a smaller chance of a stagger) and began bottling in 1996. Eight months' best before date.

TASTING NOTES

Dark, chocolaty malt and hop fruit feature in the aroma. The full, sweet taste is packed with orange and pineapple hop flavours on a smooth, chocolaty malt base. Dry, bittersweet, chocolaty finish, with tangy hops.

Fuller's

Fuller, Smith and Turner PLC, Griffin Brewery,
Chiswick Lane South, Chiswick, London W4 2QB.
Tel. (020) 8996 2000 Fax (020) 8995 0230
E-mail: info@fullers.co.uk
Website: www.fullers.co.uk

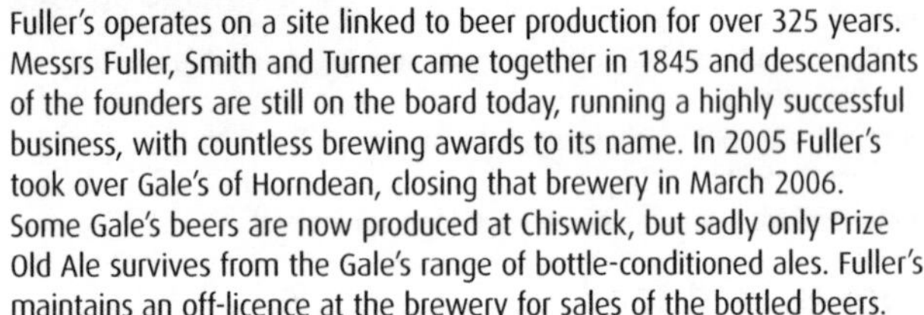

Fuller's operates on a site linked to beer production for over 325 years. Messrs Fuller, Smith and Turner came together in 1845 and descendants of the founders are still on the board today, running a highly successful business, with countless brewing awards to its name. In 2005 Fuller's took over Gale's of Horndean, closing that brewery in March 2006. Some Gale's beers are now produced at Chiswick, but sadly only Prize Old Ale survives from the Gale's range of bottle-conditioned ales. Fuller's maintains an off-licence at the brewery for sales of the bottled beers.

1845 ★

● **ABV 6.3%** ● **BOTTLE SIZE 500 ml** ● **SERVE cool**
● **INGREDIENTS Pale malt/crystal malt/amber malt/Golding hops**

1845 was first brewed in February 1995, with the Prince of Wales doing the honours and adding the hops to the copper. It was a new ale to commemorate the 150th anniversary of the founding of the company and was designed to reflect the type of brew available during the 1840s, hence the use of only Golding hops, the inclusion of amber malt for some biscuity character and the decision to bottle condition it. Its success (twice CAMRA's *Champion Bottle-conditioned Beer*) has made it a permanent member of the Fuller's range, with brews taking place monthly. After primary fermentation, the beer enjoys two weeks in conditioning tanks and is then filtered, re-seeded with fresh primary fermentation yeast and bottled, with no primings. Two weeks of conditioning follow before the bottles are released. Once this two-week period has been observed, Fuller's reckons that the beer is at its best and will remain so at least up to the two-year best before date.

TASTING NOTES

A rich, dark amber beer with a fruity, malty nose, balanced by hints of sherry and Golding hop. The very full, smooth, malty and fruity taste is quickly tempered by hop bitterness. Hops and a liquorice-like bitterness feature in the lingering dry, malty finish.

Major stockists Asda, Sainsbury's, Tesco, Waitrose

Vintage Ale ★

● **ABV 8.5%** ● **BOTTLE SIZE 550 ml** ● **SERVE cool**

● **INGREDIENTS (*2005 vintage*) Optic pale malt/Fuggle hops**

Fuller's Vintage Ale is usually brewed in a one-off batch (initially 85,000 bottles, now 50,000) in September each year. The packaging is high quality, allowing the brewery to charge around £3.50 per bottle. For that, you get an individually numbered item in a presentation box, with a best before date set three years on. More importantly, you get a rather special beer. Fuller's aficionados will probably gather that the ale is in fact a version of the brewery's excellent Golden Pride, a rich barley wine which is parti-gyled (brewed from the same mash) with ESB and London Pride. But, by giving this beer the bottle conditioning treatment (including four weeks in conditioning tanks before filtering and re-seeding with fresh Fuller's yeast), the result is a noticeably lighter, fresher beer, quite different to the original Golden Pride, which is supplied in pasteurized bottles. Some brews have used annual champion strains of barley and hops, although now there has been a return to standard floor-malted barley and regular hops. In 2005, just Fuggle hops were used and for 2006 the beer includes Fuggle and Super Styrians from Slovenia. Fuller's has organized occasional 'vertical tastings' of all Vintage Ales to date, showcasing how the beers have matured and the flavours ripened over the years.

TASTING NOTES

Vintage Ale 1997 (tasted after six years): Red in colour, with a raisin aroma and a silky, warming, fruity taste.

Vintage Ale 1998 (tasted young): Chestnut, with pronounced orangey, hop-resin notes in the aroma, alongside thick, treacly malt and a little sherry. Very full on the palate, it is rather sweet but also tangy and hop-fruity. Sugary sweet notes just win over fresh, fruity hops in the finish.

Soft, creamy raisin notes emerge with time as the sugary notes fade.
Vintage Ale 1999 (tasted after 18 months): Amber, with a slightly savoury aroma of bitter, orangey hops. The taste is malty, sweet, fruity and warming, with a hint of almond. Malt, hops and bittersweet fruit fill the aftertaste. Becomes winey with maturity.
Vintage Ale 2000 (tasted young): Bright amber, with a luscious Seville orange aroma. The taste bursts with orange fruit and thick, malty sweetness, countered by zesty, orange peel bitterness. Bitter orange finish. Still sweetish when tasted two years on but with a Cointreau-like quality and a lip-smacking hop dryness in the aftertaste.
Vintage Ale 2001 (tasted young): Deep amber, with raspberryish notes in the nose before a tangy, bittersweet, warming taste of orange and a liquorice-like bitterness. Fruit, bitter hops and sweetness run into the finish. Cherry and marzipan notes come through with age, along with more bitterness in the aftertaste.
Vintage Ale 2002 (tasted young): Dark copper, with an orangey, hoppy, tobacco-ish aroma. Cherries and marzipan in the sweet, peppery taste.
Vintage Ale 2003 (tasted young): Red-amber, with light hop aromas, backed with orange fruit and malt. The rich, malty taste is sweetish but excellently balanced by tangy hop notes, bitter fruit and hints of cherry and marzipan. Bitter, hoppy finish with lingering malt and fruit.
Vintage Ale 2004 (tasted young): Amber, with hop resins first on the nose, followed by light tangerines and subtle malt. The taste has a perfumed, tangerine accent from the start, backed up by marzipan. Drying, gum-tingling, hoppy and mostly bitter aftertaste.
Vintage Ale 2005 (tasted young): Bronze, with an aroma of sweet red apples, bitter oranges and faint chocolate, plus liquorice-like hop resins. The creamy, moussey taste is sweet and filled with juicy oranges, glacé cherries, sultanas and a trace of marzipan. The firm hoppiness verges on liquorice and there's light chocolate behind it all. The finish takes time to build but eventually offers bitter fruits, almonds and tangy hops.
Major stockist Waitrose

Prize Old Ale ★

● **ABV 9%** ● **BOTTLE SIZE 275 ml** ● **SERVE at room temperature** ● **INGREDIENTS Maris Otter pale malt/crystal malt/black malt/ Fuggle, Golding and Challenger hops**

Famous for its corked bottle, Prize Old Ale was introduced to Gale's in the 1920s, when a new head brewer brought the recipe with him from

Yorkshire. The recipe remained largely unchanged in the subsequent 80 years up to the brewery's closure, except for switching whole hops for pellets and the replacement of wooden hogsheads, which were used for conditioning the beer, with metal tanks. This was where the beer was allowed to mature for six–12 months. At Gale's, more of the Gale's yeast used for primary fermentation was added before bottling, to ensure a secondary fermentation. As the beer was not fined, it was acceptable to vegetarians. Prize Old Ale was also aged in bottle for three months at the brewery before release. Thereafter, it was said to improve for up to at least five years (although the best before date was set at two years). All bottles are now individually numbered and, being corked, should be stored horizontally, to keep the cork moist. The 2006 vintage had already been bottled before Gale's was closed, and the 2007 was already maturing in tanks. This will be bottled in due course at Fuller's. POA is the sort of beer to enjoy with cheese after dinner – better than any port, the Gale's brewers used to insist – or to sip by a roaring fire in winter. It is a classic and it will be a great shame if it has no long-term future.

TASTING NOTES

(*Based on young samples*) A dark ruby beer with a deep, vinous, fruity aroma with hints of vanilla. The taste is a powerful, mouth-filling combination of fruit (dates and raisins), bitterness and alcohol. The finish is dry, with bitter fruit and hops shading out sweetness.

The hunt for vegetarian beers... The ingredients of beer are, by definition, acceptable to vegetarians and vegans. Malt and other cereals, hops, yeast and water hold no fears. However, often in the processing of a beer, a product called isinglass or finings is added, which sets alarm bells ringing in vegetarian circles. Isinglass is made from the swim bladder of a tropical fish and has magical properties in attracting yeast sediment and dragging it to the bottom before bottling, so rendering the beer clear. Not all breweries now use finings, so vegetarians should check the listings for truly animal-free beer.

Fulstow

Fulstow Brewery, 6 Northway, Fulstow, Louth, Lincolnshire LN11 0XH. Tel. (01507) 363642
E-mail: fulstow.brewery@virgin.net
Website: www.fulstowbrewery.co.uk
Mail order service

This small Lincolnshire brewery was set up in 2004. Its beers also carry the name Fugelestou Ales, after the ancient name of its home village. For bottling, the beer is dropped bright, primed with dried malt extract and re-seeded with fresh yeast. Best before dates are set at 12 months.

Fulstow Common

● **ABV 3.8%** ● **BOTTLE SIZE 500 ml** ● **SERVE cool**
● **INGREDIENTS Pearl pale malt/crystal malt/torrefied wheat/ Northdown, Phoenix and Saaz hops**

Named after the village common land, this copper-hued ale was first brewed in 2004. Like the other bottled beers, it's also sold in cask form.

TASTING NOTES

Hop resins feature along with malt and a little fruit in the nose. The taste is crisply bitter and fairly dry with hops, a little fruit and a base of malty sweetness. Bitter, dry finish with hops and a toasted maltiness.

Marsh Mild

● **ABV 3.8%** ● **BOTTLE SIZE 500 ml** ● **SERVE cool**
● **INGREDIENTS Pearl pale malt/crystal malt/dark chocolate malt/ Northdown and Golding hops**

Fulstow is known as a 'marsh' village, thanks to the proximity of the Lincolnshire marshes. Hence the name of this ruby-coloured mild.

TASTING NOTES

Biscuity dark malts and fruit in the aroma are followed by more dark malt in the dryish taste, with faint toffee and fruit on the swallow. Malty, biscuity finish with dark chocolate and an increasing bitterness.

Northway IPA

● **ABV 4.2%** ● **BOTTLE SIZE 500 ml** ● **SERVE cool**
● **INGREDIENTS Pearl pale malt/crystal malt/torrefied wheat/ Phoenix and Saaz hops**

The name coming from the brewery's location on a road called

Northway, this golden ale was silver medallist in the 2005 *Champion Beer of Lincolnshire* contest in its draught form.

TASTING NOTES

Slightly earthy malt and citrus fruit give way to a firm hoppiness in the aroma. There's more citrus fruit in the taste, with hops in the finish.

Pride of Fulstow

● ABV 4.5% ● BOTTLE SIZE 500 ml ● SERVE cool

● INGREDIENTS Pearl pale malt/crystal malt/torrefied wheat/ Challenger and Golding hops

This copper-coloured premium bitter takes its name from the village's own steam traction engine.

TASTING NOTES

A full, tropical fruit aroma is followed by pear drops and dryish malt in the bitter taste. Bitter, malty, increasingly hoppy aftertaste.

Sledge Hammer Stout

● ABV 8% ● BOTTLE SIZE 500 ml ● SERVE cool

● INGREDIENTS Pearl pale malt/crystal malt/chocolate malt/brown malt/roasted barley/Phoenix and Golding hops

Originally brewed as a one-off, this strong dark brown stout has now acquired a cult following. No finings are used, as it's too dark for a haze to affect the appearance, and it's therefore okay for vegetarians.

TASTING NOTES

Smoky dark malts and liquorice fill the nose, and there's more smoky malt in the taste, but balanced by sweetness, sultana flavours and spicy alcohol notes. The finish is drying and features roasted grain along with some sweetness, but coffee lingers longest.

Grainstore

Davis'es Brewing Co. Ltd., The Grainstore Brewery,
Station Approach, Oakham, Rutland LE15 6RE.
Tel. (01572) 770065 Fax (01572) 770068
E-mail: grainstorebry@aol.com
Website: www.grainstorebrewery.com

Rutland beers were once famous, thanks to the presence of Ruddles Brewery, now sadly defunct. Rutland beers live on, however, chiefly through Grainstore. The company name is actually Davis'es Brewing, after the names of its founders, Mike Davies and Tony Davis, the latter a former Ruddles employee. Their brewery was established in an old railway grainstore. Just one bottled beer is produced, and this is filled by hand from casks after kräusening.

Ten Fifty

● ABV 5% ● BOTTLE SIZE 500 ml ● SERVE cool
● INGREDIENTS Maris Otter pale malt/Fuggle and Northdown hops
The brewery's second ever draught beer, first brewed in 1994 and taking its name from its original gravity (1050). The best before date is set at six months. Good with local produce like Stilton cheese and Melton Mowbray pork pies, says Tony Davis.

TASTING NOTES
An amber-red beer with a malty, fruity aroma. Citrus-sharp at first, the taste is generally malty, however, with a hint of almonds. The dry, bitter and hoppy aftertaste features lingering malt.

Great Gable

Great Gable Brewing Co. Ltd., Wasdale Head Inn,
Wasdale, Gosforth, Cumbria CA20 1EX.
Tel. (01946 7) 26229 Fax (01946 7) 26334
E-mail: info@greatgablebrewing.co.uk
Website: www.greatgablebrewing.co.uk
The Wasdale Head Inn stands remote and welcoming at the heart of Lakeland climbing and walking country. Since 2002, it has been home to the Great Gable microbrewery. Spring water from the fellside is used in each brew. The first bottled beer, Yewbarrow, arrived in 2004, filled from casks – after three months' conditioning – by Brewlab at the University of Sunderland, without filtration, re-pitching of yeast or kräusening. Scawfell (4.8%) and Illgill IPA (5%) were also available in bottle for a while. Now the brewery is looking to start bottling in house and these beers are likely to be among the first off the production line.

Yewbarrow

● ABV 5.5% ● BOTTLE SIZE 500 ml ● SERVE cool
● INGREDIENTS Pale malt/crystal malt/amber malt/chocolate malt/oat malt/Northdown hops/honey/fruit syrup
First brewed at Christmas 2002 under the name of Yulebarrow – a pun

on Yewbarrow, the fell on which the brewery's spring is located – this strong mild proved so popular that it was kept on and is now sold under the simpler Yewbarrow name (except in December).

TASTING NOTES

A ruby beer with coffee and plain-chocolate biscuits in the aroma. The taste is a beautifully balanced, quite grainy combination of biscuity malt, coffee and bittersweetness, while the aftertaste is dry and bitter with mellow roasted malt.

Green Tye

Green Tye Brewery, Green Tye, Much Hadham, Hertfordshire SG10 6JP. Tel./Fax (01279) 841041
E-mail: bottled@gtbrewery.co.uk
Website: www.gtbrewery.co.uk
Mail order service

Established in 1999, Green Tye is a small brewery in the village of Green Tye. Brewer William Compton turns out a wide range of cask ales, many of which find their way into bottle. He has bottled since late 2002, allowing the beer to drop bright in the cask and then kräusening. Twelve-month best before dates are applied.

Shot in the Dark

● ABV 3.6% ● BOTTLE SIZE 500 ml ● SERVE cool
● INGREDIENTS Maris Otter pale malt/crystal malt/dark chocolate malt/wheat malt/Challenger and Golding hops

This red quaffing ale was Green Tye's first beer and was very much a trial – hence the name. It is now generally brewed once a year.

Union Jack

● ABV 3.6% ● BOTTLE SIZE 500 ml ● SERVE cool
● INGREDIENTS Maris Otter pale malt/crystal malt/amber malt/ flaked maize/Challenger and Bramling Cross hops

In its cask form, Union Jack replaced Green Tye's IPA in 2002. This bottled version arrived later the same year and is now a regular brew.

TASTING NOTES

A dark golden session ale with plenty of hops and floral notes in the aroma. The taste is mostly bitter and dry, with hop character but also some background sweetness. Light, dry and hoppy finish.

Mustang Mild

● ABV 3.7% ● BOTTLE SIZE 500 ml ● SERVE cool

● INGREDIENTS Maris Otter pale malt/crystal malt/chocolate malt/ brown malt/flaked maize/Fuggle hops

First brewed in 2000, Mustang Mild takes its name from the P-51 Mustang aircraft that flew, under British colours, from a World War II airfield not far from the brewery. The beer is usually only brewed on request these days.

TASTING NOTES

A light ruby ale with an aroma of fruit and toffeeish malt. The same flavours continue in the taste and in the dry finish.

Snowdrop

● ABV 3.9% ● BOTTLE SIZE 500 ml ● SERVE cool

● INGREDIENTS Maris Otter pale malt/crystal malt/Golding hops

A golden, winter beer, as its name implies, first bottled in 2002 after being introduced in its cask version in 2000.

Smile for the Camera!

● ABV 4% ● BOTTLE SIZE 500/750 ml ● SERVE cool

● INGREDIENTS Maris Otter pale malt/wheat malt/flaked maize/ Northdown, Golding and Styrian Golding hops/honey/elderflowers

This summer brew originally featured a new hop known as Susan, and was conceived as an entry for the *Beauty of Hops* competition to find the *Ultimate Wedding Beer* in 2002. It has since, reportedly, been drunk in place of Champagne at two weddings known to William, including one in France. To complete the sparkling wine concept, the larger, 750 ml bottles are stoppered with a cork and caged. With Susan hops being discontinued, William has now had to change the hop selection.

XBF

● ABV 4% ● BOTTLE SIZE 500 ml ● SERVE cool

● INGREDIENTS Maris Otter pale malt/crystal malt/amber malt/ flaked barley/Pilgrim hops

First brewed and bottled in April 2003 to celebrate the tenth annual beer festival (hence XBF) at the adjacent Prince of Wales pub.

TASTING NOTES

A copper-hued ale with blackcurrant and a little spice in the nose. The same spicy fruitiness runs into the taste and the dry, bitter aftertaste.

Autumn Rose

ABV 4.2% BOTTLE SIZE 500 ml SERVE cool
INGREDIENTS Maris Otter pale malt/crystal malt/chocolate malt/ wheat malt/flaked maize/First Gold hops
This tawny/brown seasonal beer originally showcased another new hop called Ros, and now includes the popular dwarf hop First Gold.

Ditch Diver

ABV 4.2% BOTTLE SIZE 500 ml SERVE cool
INGREDIENTS Maris Otter pale malt/dark crystal malt/amber malt/ Challenger and Bramling Cross hops
A deep amber best bitter introduced in cask form in 2001.
TASTING NOTES
A malty, nutty aroma leads to a malty and nutty taste with an overriding sharp lime fruitiness. Malty, nutty, toasted aftertaste.

East Anglian Gold

ABV 4.2% BOTTLE SIZE 500 ml SERVE cool
INGREDIENTS Maris Otter pale malt/flaked maize/TA 200 hops
A new golden ale for 2006, brewed with trial hops.

Green Tiger

ABV 4.2% BOTTLE SIZE 500 ml SERVE cool
INGREDIENTS Maris Otter pale malt/crystal malt/flaked maize/ Golding hops/ginger
An amber ale designed as a summer quencher when created in 2000.

Mad Morris

ABV 4.2% BOTTLE SIZE 500 ml SERVE cool
INGREDIENTS Maris Otter pale malt/wheat malt/Northdown, Golding and Styrian Golding hops
A straw-coloured May Day beer (available for a few months thereafter).

Wheelbarrow

ABV 4.3% BOTTLE SIZE 500 ml SERVE cool
INGREDIENTS Maris Otter pale malt/crystal malt/wheat malt/ Challenger hops
This amber beer takes its name from the two partners in the brewery: 'Will' Compton and Gary 'Barra' Whelan.

TASTING NOTES
An orange-gold beer with fruity, grassy hops in the nose. The taste is sharp and fruity, with a dry, fruity finish.

Bowled Over!

● **ABV 4.5%** ● **BOTTLE SIZE 500 ml** ● **SERVE cool**
● **INGREDIENTS Maris Otter pale malt/crystal malt/wheat malt/ Northdown and Golding hops**
A beer introduced in bottle in 2004, although available on draught since 2001. The label shows the game of bowls, rather than cricket.
TASTING NOTES
A copper-coloured brew with a nice mix of malt and hops in the nose. Nutty malt and sharpish, fruity hops feature in the taste, rounded off by a modest, nutty, gently bitter, toasted malt finish.

Coal Porter

● **ABV 4.5%** ● **BOTTLE SIZE 500 ml** ● **SERVE cool**
● **INGREDIENTS Maris Otter pale malt/dark chocolate malt/wheat malt/Bramling Cross hops**
Winner of several beer festival awards since it arrived in cask in 2000.
TASTING NOTES
Deep, deep ruby (almost black) in colour, this porter has a biscuity aroma of roasted malt and coffee, a nicely balanced taste of sweet malt, bitterness and mellow coffee, and a coffeeish finish.

Conkerer

● **ABV 4.7%** ● **BOTTLE SIZE 500 ml** ● **SERVE cool**
● **INGREDIENTS Maris Otter pale malt/crystal malt/wheat malt/ Northdown, Golding and Styrian Golding hops**
The name of this robust autumn ale reflects the horse chestnut debris that covers the brewery car park at this time of year.

Greene King

Greene King PLC, Westgate Brewery, Bury St Edmunds, Suffolk IP33 1QT. Tel. (01284) 763222 Fax (01284) 706502
Website: www.greeneking.co.uk
Founded in 1799, Greene King is now one of Britain's 'super-regional' breweries, having expanded by acquiring pub groups and other

breweries in recent years. From Morland (now closed) Greene King acquired its only bottle-conditioned ale (although it does produce a range of pasteurized beers, including the notable Strong Suffolk, a complex blend of matured and young ales).

Hen's Tooth

● ABV 6.5% ● BOTTLE SIZE 500 ml ● SERVE cool
● INGREDIENTS Pipkin pale malt/crystal malt/maltose syrup/ Challenger and Golding hops

Hen's Tooth was launched in 1998, its name suggesting a resemblance to Old Speckled Hen in its make up. The other relevance of the name is to convey how rare it is to find a beer of this strength which is not too heavy or chewy – as rare, as Morland put it at the time, 'as a hen's tooth'. The beer is now brewed at Bury St Edmunds to the same Morland recipe, and cool conditioned for a week before being tankered to Hepworth & Co. in Horsham for bottling. There the yeast count and fermentability of the remaining sugars are checked and, if required, corrected with new yeast and primings. The yeast used throughout is the old Morland yeast. The best before date is set at 12 months.

TASTING NOTES

Dark amber, with a fruity, malty, almost liquorice-like nose. Sweet and a little nutty in the mouth, it features ripe malt and plenty of hop, with hints of liquorice, pear drops and pineapple. Dry, hoppy, bitter finish.
Major stockists Asda, Booths, Sainsbury's, Tesco

Hammerpot

Hammerpot Brewery Ltd., Unit 30, The Vinery, Arundel Road, Poling, West Sussex BN18 9PY. Tel. (01903) 883338
E-mail: info@hammerpot-brewery.co.uk
Website: www.hammerpot-brewery.co.uk

This tiny brewery opened in 2005, near Hammerpot village, to serve pubs in Sussex and surrounding counties. Bottling followed soon after.

Red Hunter

● ABV 4.3% ● BOTTLE SIZE 500 ml ● SERVE cool
● INGREDIENTS Pale malt/crystal malt/chocolate malt/roasted barley/Progress and Golding hops

Red Hunter was the aircraft (a Hawker Hunter Mark III) that broke the world airspeed record on 7 September 1953 by reaching 727 mph in the skies above Sussex. The plane took off from Tangmere, a few miles from the brewery, piloted by Squadron Leader Neville Duke. This commemorative, suitably red, beer was first brewed in 2005.

TASTING NOTES

Malt, hints of liquorice and spicy hop resins fill the aroma. Creamy, sweetish malt leads in the taste, with a little chocolate, nut, liquorice and spicy hops. There's more sweet, creamy malt in the finish, which dries as gentle roasted grains and hoppy bitterness emerge.

Hampshire

Hampshire Brewery Ltd., 6–8 Romsey Industrial Estate, Greatbridge Road, Romsey, Hampshire SO51 0HR.
Tel. (01794) 830529 Fax (01794) 830528
E-mail: online@hampshirebrewery.com
Website: www.hampshirebrewery.com

Founded in Andover in 1992, Hampshire moved to Romsey in 1997, filling a void left in the town by the closure of Strong's Brewery by Whitbread in 1981. The brewery has now built up a core range of eight bottle-conditioned beers, which are supplemented by short runs in bottle of seasonal cask beers. These have included: They Think It's All Over (3.5%, a single-hop ale – Target); Mayhem (4.1%, a ruby mild); Indian Summer (4.2%, a pale bronze ale); T'ale of the Dragon (4.2%, a light golden ale); Wild Thing (4.2%, an IPA); Trappist Monkey (4.3%, a Belgian-style ale); Grim Reaper (4.4%, an old ale); Bewitched (4.5%, an oat-infused brown beer for Hallowe'en); Laughing Leprechaun (4.5%, an Irish stout); Penny Black Porter (4.5%); Porky & Best (4.5%, a best bitter); Seduction (4.5%, a brown bitter); Thunderbolt (4.5%, a hoppy bitter); Tinsel Tickler (4.5%, a citrus beer for Christmas); The Bee's Knees (4.6%, a honeyed wheat beer); Heaven Can Wait (4.8%, a dark wheat beer); St Clements (4.8%, a citrus wheat beer); Bohemian Rhapsody (5%, a pilsener-style beer); Good King Censlas (5%, a winter ale); Hampshire Hare (5%, a golden ale); Merlins Magic (5%, a ruby ale); Not Tonight Josephine (5%, a German helles); Uncle Sams (5%, a US-style pale ale) and Fallover (6%, a mahogany autumn ale). The beers are both warm- and cold-conditioned after fermentation, then filtered and re-seeded with new bottling yeast. A 12-month best before date is stamped on each bottle.

King Alfred's

● ABV 3.8% ● BOTTLE SIZE 500 ml ● SERVE cool
● INGREDIENTS Maris Otter pale malt/crystal malt/Challenger, First Gold and Golding hops

Building on the county's association with King Alfred, this copper-coloured bitter was the brewery's first regular cask beer.

TASTING NOTES

Light fruit and malt in the nose. The taste is hoppy, but not without malt or sweetness, and gentle fruit runs throughout. Hoppy, dry finish.

Strongs Best Bitter

● ABV 3.8% ● BOTTLE SIZE 500 ml ● SERVE cool
● INGREDIENTS Maris Otter pale malt/crystal malt/black malt/ Challenger, Progress and Golding hops

Once, billboards advertising Strong's beers were commonplace in the South. Hampshire has revived the lost brewery's popular bitter and in doing so has underlined its own identity as today's Romsey brewery.

TASTING NOTES

A dark copper bitter with malt leading in the aroma but with plenty of hop fruitiness. On the palate, fruity spritziness lightens a rich, malty base. Hops take over in the initially bittersweet finish.

Ironside Best

● ABV 4.2% ● BOTTLE SIZE 500 ml ● SERVE cool
● INGREDIENTS Maris Otter pale malt/crystal malt/Progress, Golding and Styrian Golding hops

A premium ale named after Edmund II, 11th-century king of England. Part of Hampshire's ancient kings range.

TASTING NOTES

A dark golden ale dominated by citrus hops (orange and grapefruit) in the nose. Mouthfilling grapefruit and orange peel in the taste winds up with a dry, bitter, citrus finish.

Major stockist Local Asda

Lionheart

● ABV 4.5% ● BOTTLE SIZE 500 ml ● SERVE cool
● INGREDIENTS Maris Otter pale malt/lager malt/Northdown, First Gold and Perle hops

A well-established golden ale with King Richard I connections.

TASTING NOTES
Toffeeish malt and floral hop notes lead in the nose, while the same maltiness is crisped up by sharp hop in the mouth for an almost 'lemon toffee' taste. Dry, hoppy finish with lingering malt.

King's Ransom

● ABV 4.8% ● BOTTLE SIZE 500 ml ● SERVE cool
● INGREDIENTS Lager malt/caramalt/First Gold, Golding and Styrian Golding hops
Once known as Gold Reserve, a name that reflected its brilliant colour.
TASTING NOTES
Lemon fruitiness in the aroma is enhanced by a suggestion of tropical fruit. The crisp, fruity, slightly perfumed, hop-spicy taste has a clean, moreish, light malt base. Hop dryness emerges in the finish.

Pendragon

● ABV 4.8% ● BOTTLE SIZE 500 ml ● SERVE cool
● INGREDIENTS Maris Otter pale malt/crystal malt/black malt/ Challenger, Progress and Golding hops
Named after the father of King Arthur, this strong, reddish ale was first produced in cask form in 1993.
TASTING NOTES
Light banana notes feature in the malty aroma. The taste is complex but well balanced, with light banana, malt and hops. Dry, bitter, malt and hops finish, with a little banana character still in evidence.

Pride of Romsey

● ABV 5% ● BOTTLE SIZE 500 ml ● SERVE cool
● INGREDIENTS Maris Otter pale malt/crystal malt/Challenger, Golding and Cascade hops
Pride of Romsey – declared on the label to be an IPA – is a 'thank you' beer, brewed in appreciation of the welcome the people of Romsey gave to the arrival of the brewery, and also to commemorate the revival of brewing in the town. It first appeared in cask form and instantly scooped a bronze medal at the 1998 *Brewing Industry International Awards*. This bottled version followed in the same year.
TASTING NOTES
A copper-coloured beer with a slightly spicy, malty nose with hints of citrus fruits (grapefruit). The taste is a strong, bitter, mouth-filling

combination of the same fruit, malt and hop, which carries on to dominate the dry finish.
Major stockists Asda and local Waitrose

1066

● ABV 6% ● BOTTLE SIZE 500 ml ● SERVE cool
● INGREDIENTS Maris Otter pale malt/lager malt/caramalt/ Northdown, First Gold and Perle hops
William the Conqueror 1066, as it is fully named on the label, was first brewed as a cask beer in 1994, although the recipe has now changed.
TASTING NOTES
A dark golden ale with lemon-citrus notes and a touch of pear drop in the malty aroma. Light-textured for its gravity, it is sweet and lemony to taste, with malt, hops and an alcoholic warmth in the background. Citrus hops feature in the dry, bittersweet finish.

Hardys & Hansons

Hardys & Hansons plc, The Brewery, Kimberley, Nottingham NG16 2NS. Tel. (0115) 938 3611 Fax (0115) 945 9055
E-mail: info@hardysandhansons.plc.uk
Website: www.hardysandhansons.plc.uk
A merger in 1930 brought together Hardys (established 1832) and Hansons (1847), two Nottingham breweries. Members of the original families still ran the business until it was acquired by Greene King in summer 2006. The future of the brewery, as a result, is now uncertain.

Olde Trip

● ABV 4.3% ● BOTTLE SIZE 500 ml ● SERVE cool
● INGREDIENTS Maris Otter pale malt/Target, Challenger and Golding hops
First brewed and bottled in 2004, Olde Trip celebrates one of Britain's oldest pubs. The Olde Trip to Jerusalem – its name linked to the Crusades – was partly carved out of the rock on which Nottingham Castle stands in 1189 and is now part of the Hardys & Hansons estate. The beer is hopped early with a mix of Target and Challenger, and then late hopped with Goldings. More Challengers are added during the two-week maturation the beer enjoys before it is shipped to Thwaites for bottling, where it is filtered and re-seeded with fresh yeast.

Harveys

Harvey and Son (Lewes) Ltd., The Bridge Wharf Brewery, 6 Cliffe High Street, Lewes, East Sussex BN7 2AH. Tel. (01273) 480209 Fax (01273) 483706 E-mail: maj@harveys.org.uk Website: www.harveys.org.uk

This popular, family-run brewery, established in the 18th century, has an excellent reputation for its bottle-conditioned 1859 Porter (4.8%). The only problem is that the beer is now only bottle conditioned in small runs on special request (usually around March, when the cask version is available), and most bottles of the porter are pasteurized. However, Harveys did take the bold step of introducing the intriguing, award-winning bottled beer mentioned below in 1999.

Imperial Extra Double Stout ★

● ABV 9% ● BOTTLE SIZE 330 ml ● SERVE cool

● INGREDIENTS Maris Otter pale malt/amber malt/brown malt/black malt/Fuggle and Golding hops

A tribute to Albert Le Coq, a Belgian who successfully marketed Courage's renowned Imperial Russian Stout to the Baltic region, and particularly the Russian Empire, in the early 1800s. This beer's label re-tells the Le Coq story, including how the brewery his company set up to produce his own powerful beer in Estonia was nationalised by the Bolsheviks in 1917. This beer is inspired by Le Coq's original recipe and has been bottled up to now with a cork stopper for Harveys by Gale's. Despite the closure of the Horndean brewery, stocks are sufficient to meet demand for the next few years. B United are the US importers.

TASTING NOTES

A deep, deep ruby beer with a smoky, fruity, vinous aroma with hints of polished leather. This complex brew is vinously fruity, creamy, bittersweet, spicy, roasted and warming in the mouth, with a lingering, bitter, coffee-roast finish and a touch of winey fruit to the end.

High Force

High Force Hotel Brewery, Forest-in-Teesdale, Barnard Castle, Co. Durham DL12 0XH. Tel. (01833) 622222 Fax (01833) 622264

High Force Hotel is a whitewashed, 19th-century pub close to the 70-

foot High Force waterfall in an area of outstanding natural beauty, near the Pennine Way. A small brewery opened here in 1995 and claimed to be the highest in Britain, at 1,060 feet above sea level. However, since 2001, all beer production has been handled by Darwin Brewery.

Forest XB

● ABV 4.2% ● BOTTLE SIZE 500 ml ● SERVE cool
● INGREDIENTS Pale malt/crystal malt/chocolate malt/torrefied wheat/Willamette hops

The newer of the two High Force bottled beers, Forest XB was added in 1999 and reflects the pub's setting at Forest-in-Teesdale in its name.

TASTING NOTES

An interesting dark amber beer with a fruity, malty, lightly chocolaty aroma. A little salty on the palate, it has good bitterness and fruity hop notes over a rich malty base. Dry, bitter hop finish.

Cauldron Snout

● ABV 5.6% ● BOTTLE SIZE 500 ml ● SERVE cool
● INGREDIENTS Pale malt/crystal malt/black malt/Challenger hops

Cauldron Snout is named after a waterfall five miles from the hotel in Upper Teesdale. The label depicts a prehistoric water stone, used to indicate sources of water on the Pennine moors.

TASTING NOTES

A dark ruby beer with a clean, leathery aroma of dark malt. Full and bittersweet in the mouth, it has decent hop character, pruney fruit and smooth, mellow malt on the swallow. Bitter, dry, roasted malt finish.

Hilden

Hilden Brewing Co., Hilden House, Grand Street, Lisburn, Co. Antrim BT27 4TY. Tel. (028 92) 663863 Fax (028 92) 603511
E-mail: james@hildenbrewery.co.uk
Mail order service

Hilden, founded in 1981, was, for some years, the only cask ale brewery in Northern Ireland, albeit a very small one with limited outlets. Access to the beers is still difficult, but the installation of a bottling line in 1999 now allows more people to sample Hilden's ales. Four-pack 'Hilden Ale Sacks' form part of the marketing exercise. The beers are bottled at the brewery, with a three-month best before date.

Original Ale

● **ABV 4.6%** ● **BOTTLE SIZE 500 ml** ● **SERVE cool**

● **INGREDIENTS Halcyon pale malt/crystal malt/chocolate malt/black malt/First Gold, Northdown and Golding hops**

The big brother of the popular cask beer Hilden Ale (4%), Hilden Original Ale was introduced in 1998.

TASTING NOTES

A copper beer with a fruity, malty nose. Smooth, slightly sweet and very fruity to taste, it has plenty of malt flavour and a light bitter edge. Bitterness builds to overshadow malt and fruit in the dry finish.

Molly Malone Single X

● **ABV 4.6%** ● **BOTTLE SIZE 500 ml** ● **SERVE cool**

● **INGREDIENTS Halcyon pale malt/chocolate malt/black malt/ Northdown, Golding and Hallertau hops**

A porter introduced in 2000 and including Hallertau hops from New Zealand.

TASTING NOTES

A ruby-red porter with a slightly vinous, fruity aroma supported by roasted malt. The dry, vinous taste mostly features gentle roasted malt which continues on into the dry, bitter aftertaste.

Hillside

Hillside Brewery, Corse, Lumphanan, Aberdeenshire AB31 4RY.
Tel. (013398) 83506
E-mail: brewery@hillsidecroft.eclipse.co.uk
Website: www.hillsidecroft.eclipse.co.uk

Small brewery that began production in January 2006. Ex-archaeologist Rob James is the man in charge, a former home brewer with 20 years' experience. The bottled beer is allowed a couple of weeks' conditioning after fermentation and then bottled with primings. Four more weeks of conditioning then follow, before the bottles go on sale.

Macbeth

● **ABV 4.2%** ● **BOTTLE SIZE 500 ml** ● **SERVE cool**

● **INGREDIENTS Pale malt/crystal malt/wheat malt/ Fuggle and Cascade hops**

The famous Scottish king was killed just over the hill from the brewery at the Battle of Lumphanan (1057) – hence this commemorative golden beer, which is stylishly packaged in slender German swing-top bottles. Its bold hopping makes it a good choice for drinking with curries and other spicy foods. The brewery declares it suitable for vegetarians.

TASTING NOTES

Hop resins dominate the aroma, with floral and citrus notes. The taste is notably hoppy with nods towards citrus fruits. Dry, very hoppy finish.

Hobsons

Hobsons Brewery & Co. Ltd., Newhouse Farm, Tenbury Road, Cleobury Mortimer, Kidderminster, Worcestershire DY14 8RD.
Tel. (01299) 270837
E-mail: beer@hobsons-brewery.co.uk
Website: www.hobsons-brewery.co.uk
Mail order service

This family-run brewery was set up in 1993 but moved to its current premises (an attractive old farm building) in 1996. An extension to the property in 2001 provided space for a bottling plant. The bottles are very nicely presented and all are declared acceptable to vegetarians.

Manor Ale

● ABV 4.2% ● BOTTLE SIZE 500 ml ● SERVE cool
● INGREDIENTS Maris Otter pale malt/Cascade, Challenger and Golding hops

Brewed and bottled on behalf of Severn Valley Railway, Manor Ale is also sold in cask form under the name of Steam No.9. In the same way as other Hobsons beers, it is filtered and re-seeded with fresh yeast prior to bottling. Best before dates are fixed at 12 months.

TASTING NOTES

An unusual golden beer, surprisingly nutty and malty in the aroma. A nutty bitterness comes to the fore in the mouth, backed by light citrus notes. Dry, bitter, nutty finish.

Town Crier

● ABV 4.5% ● BOTTLE SIZE 500 ml ● SERVE cold
● INGREDIENTS Maris Otter pale malt/crystal malt/wheat/Progress and Golding hops

Intriguingly described by the brewers as a 'pale Bavarian ale', Town

Crier is recommended for drinking younger and cooler than their other bottled offerings. It was first brewed for a town crier competition in 1995.

TASTING NOTES

A pale golden beer with light lemon notes in the malt-and-hop nose. Earthy malt is overlaid by lemony, spicy, bitter hops in the mouth, leaving a dry, malty finish with hops building.

Major stockists Local Co-op and Spar

Old Henry

● **ABV 5.2%** ● **BOTTLE SIZE 500 ml** ● **SERVE cool**
● **INGREDIENTS Maris Otter pale malt/crystal malt/Challenger and Golding hops**

Although largely the same brew as the draught beer of the same name, Old Henry is a touch more heavily hopped for the bottle, to compensate for the absence of dry hops in the cask. The label describes this full-flavoured amber ale as a beer 'best served with mature Shropshire Blue cheese'.

TASTING NOTES

The malty, spicy nose has a little toffee and liquorice. The taste is malty yet dry and mostly bitter, with toffee, liquorice and a savoury note. Dry, malty, bitter and hoppy aftertaste.

Major stockist Local Spar

Hoggleys

Hoggleys Brewery, 30 Mill Lane, Kislingbury, Northamptonshire NN7 4BD. Tel. (01604) 831762
E-mail: hoggleys@hotmail.com
Website: www. hoggleys.co.uk

Starting tiny, as a part-time operation in 2003, Hoggleys is now looking to grow a little, with capacity increasing to an eight-barrel run and full-time working introduced. The business name is drawn from a merger of the surnames of the two founders, Julie Hogg and Roy Crutchley. In addition to the two beers featured below, Northamptonshire Bitter and Mill Lane Mild (both 4%) have also been bottled and are likely to be available more frequently with the brewery's expansion. The beers are not fined, making them acceptable to vegetarians. They are filled directly from a conditioning tank and primed with sugar.

Kislingbury Bitter

● ABV 4% ● BOTTLE SIZE 500 ml ● SERVE cool
● INGREDIENTS Pale malt/chocolate malt/torrefied wheat/Fuggle, Challenger and Golding hops

Named after the brewery's home village, Kislingbury Bitter was the second ever Hoggleys brew, described by Roy as a 'traditional English pint'. A stronger bottled version may be forthcoming.

TASTING NOTES

An amber-brown ale with a full, clean malt, hop and fruit mix in the aroma. Rich malty flavours fill the mouth but it's not sweet thanks to a good hop balance. A touch of astringency also helps offset the malt. Dry, bitter, malty finish with hops building.

Solstice Stout

● ABV 5% ● BOTTLE SIZE 500 ml ● SERVE cool
● INGREDIENTS Pale malt/chocolate malt/roasted barley/torrefied wheat/Fuggle and Challenger hops/cinnamon/nutmeg/molasses

Brewed originally to mark an annual boating trip Roy makes over the winter solstice, this spiced beer is now more readily available.

TASTING NOTES

A dark ruby stout with a biscuity, malty, smoky nose. The same smoky notes lead in the taste, supported by lots of sweet, dark malt and hints of coffee, chocolate and a little tropical fruit. Roasted grain arrives quickly in the dry, bitter finish.

Hogs Back

Hogs Back Brewery Ltd., Manor Farm,
The Street, Tongham, Surrey GU10 1DE.
Tel. (01252) 783000 Fax (01252) 782328
E-mail: info@hogsback.co.uk
Website: www.hogsback.co.uk
Mail order service

This purpose-built brewery was set up in restored farm buildings (circa 1768) in 1992. All the brewery's bottled beers are handled in house. The brews are filtered and then injected with fresh yeast prior to filling with, occasionally, priming sugars added to ensure a good fermentation in the bottle. Best before dates are set at 14 months. The elaborate, gold-embossed labels are the work of brewery partner Tony Stanton-

Precious, a former draughtsman. Hogs Back also has a fine shop/off-licence on site, offering a wide range of bottled beers from other breweries. Hogs Back beers are imported into the USA through Aiko LLC.

TEA (Traditional English Ale)/Gardeners Tipple

● ABV 4.2% ● BOTTLE SIZE 500 ml ● SERVE cool
● INGREDIENTS Maris Otter pale malt/crystal malt/ Fuggle and Golding hops

TEA is one of Hogs Back's longest established brews and was launched in bottle in 1997. The beer is now brewed weekly. The cask version claimed the *Best Bitter* title at the 2000 *Champion Beer of Britain* contest. The beer is also sold under the name of Gardeners Tipple at the Royal Horticultural Society in Wisley, Surrey, and various farm shops.

TASTING NOTES

An amber beer with nutty malt supported by smoky orange in the nose. Lightly nutty malt and smoky, fruity hops feature in the well-balanced, bittersweet taste. Pleasantly bitter, drying finish.

Major stockists Budgens, Harrods, Sainsbury's, Tesco, Waitrose

BSA (Burma Star Ale)

● ABV 4.5% ● BOTTLE SIZE 500 ml ● SERVE cool
● INGREDIENTS Maris Otter pale malt/crystal malt/chocolate malt/ Fuggle and Golding hops

Introduced in 1995 to commemorate the 50th anniversary of VJ Day, and as a tribute to members of the Burma Star Association and prisoners of war in the Far East, BSA was re-labelled to mark the 50th anniversary of the founding of the Association in 1951. The beer is available in cask- as well as bottled-form. The label depicts servicemen of the day (actually the partners' parents – one of whom served in the Burma Star movement) and recalls the famous and poignant quotation:

'When you go home tell them of us and say –
For your tomorrow we gave our today'.

The Imperial War Museum has taken stocks for its visitors and, for every bottle sold, Hogs Back pledges a donation to the BSA's welfare fund.

TASTING NOTES

A copper-red ale with an earthy, spicy malt aroma. The taste is malty, spicy, hoppy, lightly fruity and quite earthy, while the finish is dry, lightly roasted and hoppy, with a touch of liquorice.

Major stockists Harrods, local Sainsbury's

OTT (Old Tongham Tasty or Over the Top)

● ABV 6% ● BOTTLE SIZE 500 ml ● SERVE cool
● INGREDIENTS Maris Otter pale malt/crystal malt/chocolate malt/ Fuggle and Golding hops

A cask beer introduced in bottle in 2000. The label features pigs flying 'over the top' of the Tongham brewery.

TASTING NOTES

A dark ruby beer with biscuity roasted malt, winey fruit, an oat-like creaminess and a touch of liquorice in the nose. The taste is sweet, lightly fruity and filled with dark, nutty malt. The finish is also nutty and dry, with roasted malt, developing hop notes and persistent sweetness.

Major stockist Harrods

Brewster's Bundle

● ABV 7.4% ● BOTTLE SIZE 275 ml ● SERVE cool
● INGREDIENTS Maris Otter pale malt/crystal malt/ Fuggle and Golding hops

Another commemorative brew, this ale was initially produced each February, but is now bottled every two months. The 'Bundle' in question is Charley, the first baby daughter of Hogs Back's lady brewster, Maureen Zieher. Charley was born in February 1994 at the weight of 7lb 4oz (hence the 7.4% ABV).

TASTING NOTES

A copper-coloured beer with a malty, lightly hoppy, vinous-fruity aroma (hints of raspberry). The taste is smooth, sweetish, malty and fruity (with some tropical notes), before a mellow, warming finish of bittersweet fruit.

Major stockist Harrods

Wobble in a Bottle/Santa's Wobble

● ABV 7.5% ● BOTTLE SIZE 275 ml ● SERVE cool
● INGREDIENTS Maris Otter pale malt/crystal malt/chocolate malt/ Fuggle and Golding hops

Hogs Back's Christmas cask beer is called Santa's Wobble. It is bottled under that name at Christmas but for the rest of the year it goes by the name of Wobble in a Bottle. It was first produced in 1996.

TASTING NOTES

A red beer with a malty, raspberry-ish aroma with hints of liquorice. The taste is malty and fruity, with light almond notes and liquorice, and a

pleasant bitter edge, but without much alcoholic heaviness or cloying sweetness. Bitterness dominates hop and fruit in the tingling finish.
Major stockist Harrods

A over T (Aromas over Tongham) ★

● ABV 9% ● BOTTLE SIZE 275 ml ● SERVE cool
● INGREDIENTS Maris Otter pale malt/crystal malt/chocolate malt/ Fuggle and Golding hops

One of Hogs Back's earliest brews, A over T (named after its unfortunate side-effect but diplomatically explained as standing for 'Aromas over Tongham') first tempted drinkers in 1993, when it appeared in cask form. In 2006 it was judged CAMRA's *Champion Winter Beer of Britain.*

TASTING NOTES

A red-amber beer with a malty, surprisingly juicy, citrus aroma. Full-flavoured, it is sweet, creamy and citrus to taste, featuring tangy fruit and hop before a warming aftertaste that is tangy-fruity and bitter.
Major stockist Harrods

Hop Back

Hop Back Brewery PLC, Units 22–24,
Downton Business Centre, Downton,
Salisbury, Wiltshire SP5 3HU.
Tel. (01725) 510986 Fax (01725) 513116
E-mail: info@hopback.co.uk
Website: www.hopback.co.uk
Mail order service (01725) 511331

Originally based at a Salisbury brew pub, The Wyndham Arms, Hop Back was set up in 1986. It moved to a unit on an industrial area at Downton in 1992 and continues to expand. It stepped up its bottled beer production in 1997 with the installation of a new bottling line. All bottled beers are cold conditioned at 3°C, filtered and kräusened prior to bottling. Best before dates are set at 12 months after bottling.

Crop Circle

● ABV 4.2% ● BOTTLE SIZE 500 ml ● SERVE cool
● INGREDIENTS Optic pale malt/flaked maize/wheat malt/Golding, Pioneer and Tettnang hops/coriander

Winner of the small brewer category in the Spring/Summer 2000 *Tesco*

Beer Challenge, Crop Circle was designed as a light beer for the warmer months, with bitterness playing second fiddle to aroma when it came to the choice of hops. Goldings and Pioneer do most of the hop work, with German Tettnangs added late in the copper. Coriander is added at this stage, too, to enhance the summery fruitiness.

TASTING NOTES

A light-bodied, watery-golden-coloured beer with an aroma full of zesty, lemon and orange notes and an earthy coriander spiciness. The taste is rich in fresh, lightly perfumed and spicy, summery flavours – orange, lemon juice and a growing hoppy bitterness. Dry, hoppy, bitter, orange-lemon finish.

Major stockists Booths, local Waitrose

Taiphoon

● **ABV 4.2%** ● **BOTTLE SIZE 500 ml** ● **SERVE cool**
● **INGREDIENTS Optic pale malt/Golding and Pioneer hops/coriander/lemongrass**

Introduced in 1999, Taiphoon is designed as a partner for Asian cuisine. The key ingredient, lemongrass, imparts an exotic spiciness.

TASTING NOTES

A pale golden beer with a malty, yet peppery, spicy and perfumed nose. It is also peppery and scented in the mouth, with malt sweetness in the background for balance. The finish is spicy, bitter and scented.

Major stockists Booths, local Waitrose

Entire Stout ★

● **ABV 4.5%** ● **BOTTLE SIZE 500 ml** ● **SERVE cool**
● **INGREDIENTS Optic pale malt/chocolate malt/roasted barley/wheat crystal malt/Challenger and Golding hops**

A cask beer for over ten years, Entire Stout finally made it into bottle in December 2001. Produced without isinglass finings, the beer is good news for vegetarians and vegans (the beer is simply transferred from the fermenting vessel to the tank from which it is bottled). Winner of the *Tucker's Maltings Bottled Beer Competition* in 2004 and 2006.

TASTING NOTES

A dark red beer with a coffee and caramel aroma preceding a crisp, bitter, dark malt taste with a caramel-like sweetness and a dry, bitter, coffeeish roasted finish.

Major stockists Booths, local Waitrose

Summer Lightning ★

● **ABV 5%** ● **BOTTLE SIZE 500 ml** ● **SERVE cool**
● **INGREDIENTS Optic pale malt/Golding hops**

The Summer Lightning story begins in 1988. Brewery founder John Gilbert came up with the recipe for this pale, crisp and hoppy, yet strong, beer to contrast with other 5% beers of the time, which were nearly all dark, sweet and sickly. For a name, he stole the title of a PG Wodehouse novel. In cask form the beer has been a trend-setter. Since winning the *Best New Brewery Beer* award at the *Champion Beer of Britain* contest in 1989, it has inspired brewers up and down the land to create strong but pale beers which have appeal beyond the traditional ale drinker. The bottle-conditioned version is now a single-hop brew, dropping the Challenger hops it used to include in favour of East Kent Goldings only. The draught version maintains both hops. The brewery recommends serving this and its other bottled beers on the cold side of cool. CAMRA's *Best Bottle-Conditioned Beer* in 1997.

TASTING NOTES

A pale, easy-drinking, strong bitter, quenching but dry. The citrus, hoppy nose leads to a crisp, clean hoppiness with light lemon in the taste and a dry, hoppy, bitter finish.

Major stockists Asda, Booths, Co-op, Morrisons, Oddbins, Tesco, Waitrose

Hopdaemon

Hopdaemon Brewery Co. Ltd., Unit 1,
Parsonage Farm, Seed Road, Newnham, Kent ME9 0NA.
Tel. (01795) 892078

E-mail: hopdaemon@supanet.com

New Zealander Tonie Prins founded Hopdaemon on the edge of Canterbury in 2001. However, demand for his beers led to a move to new premises in Newnham in 2005. Tonie describes his beers as 'traditional ales with a slight New World twist' and, to market them, has combined the medieval traditions of Canterbury and its cathedral with a sprinkling of legend and a touch of home-spun folklore based around the local hopgardens. He bottles the beers by hand himself, chilling them for up to a week before filling to allow proteins to drop out and then re-seeding with dried bottling yeast. Tonie also supplies own-label beers for major London museums and arts centres.

Skrimshander IPA

● ABV 4.5% ● BOTTLE SIZE 500 ml ● SERVE cool

● INGREDIENTS Pale malt/crystal malt/caramalt/Fuggle, Golding and Bramling Cross hops

Inspired by Herman Melville's classic novel, Moby Dick, and its references to skrimshander (the craft of carving whale ivory), this beer, like the other bottled beers, is also sold in cask form.

TASTING NOTES

Spicy, citrus hop aromas emerge from this copper ale. The taste is fruity but delicate, with grapefruit notes alongside spicy hops. The dry, hoppy finish has more lingering fruit as bitterness grows.

Major stockists (all beers) Local Sainsbury's, Tesco and Thresher

Green Daemon

● ABV 5% ● BOTTLE SIZE 330 ml ● SERVE cold

● INGREDIENTS Pale malt/lager malt/New Zealand hops

Tonie has yet to apply for accreditation for this organic beer, so he has to settle for calling it 'natural' instead. However, the ingredients are all organic, including hops from back home which are not, Tonie is quick to point out, the organic Hallertau hops for which New Zealand is well known. Green Daemon is lagered for three weeks before bottling.

TASTING NOTES

Golden, with lots of juicy citrus (grapefruit and orange) and tropical fruit in the aroma. Zesty, bittersweet grapefruit leads in the mouth, with yet more tropical fruit. Dry, gently bitter, fruity and hoppy aftertaste.

Leviathan

● ABV 6% ● BOTTLE SIZE 500 ml ● SERVE cool

● INGREDIENTS Pale malt/crystal malt/chocolate malt/caramalt/ wheat malt/Fuggle and Bramling Cross hops

'A beast of a beer', laughs Tonie, referring to the giant sea monster from the pages of the Bible that gives its name to his strong, but subtle, ale.

TASTING NOTES

A red beer with hints of pineapple and lemon in the hoppy nose, along with gentle dark malts. Easy-drinking for its strength, its taste is full of juicy, fruity hops, with pineapple to the fore, plus a peppery bitterness, over a smooth malty sweetness. The dry, fruity and hoppy finish lasts well, with malt sweetness in evidence, too.

Humpty Dumpty

Humpty Dumpty Brewery, Church Road, Reedham, Norfolk NR13 3TZ.
Tel. (01493) 701818 Fax (01493) 700727
E-mail: sales@humptydumptybrewery.co.uk
Website: www.humptydumptybrewery.co.uk

Opened by brewer Mick Cottrell in 1998 next to The Railway Tavern pub in Reedham, Humpty Dumpty moved in 2001 to a new site alongside Pettitts Animal Park (a popular family attraction) in the same attractive riverside village. The new premises have allowed brewery expansion and also offer a spacious gift shop/off-licence, where Humpty Dumpty's bottled beers (in gift packs and individually), plus other souvenirs, can be purchased. In May 2006, the brewery was sold to a new company, Norfolk Broads Brewing, but still trades as Humpty Dumpty.

Nord Atlantic

● **ABV 3.7%** ● **BOTTLE SIZE 500 ml** ● **SERVE cool**
● **INGREDIENTS Maris Otter pale malt/crystal malt/caramalt/wheat malt/Challenger and Fuggle hops**

Humpty Dumpty's beers generally recall the names of famous steam engines, such as *Nord Atlantic*, on their labels. Like the other bottled beers, this session ale is brewed and bottled on site after conditioning in cask. Each beer is kräusened to ensure a good secondary fermentation. Twelve months are allowed in the best before date.

Lemon & Ginger

● **ABV 4%** ● **BOTTLE SIZE 500 ml** ● **SERVE cool**
● **INGREDIENTS Maris Otter pale malt/caramalt/wheat malt/Bramling Cross and Cascade hops/lemons/stem ginger**

It took Mick a couple of years to perfect this beer. The way he devised to add fresh lemons and stem ginger to the brew remains a secret.

Humpty Dumpty

● **ABV 4.1%** ● **BOTTLE SIZE 500 ml** ● **SERVE cool**
● **INGREDIENTS Maris Otter pale malt/crystal malt/caramalt/wheat malt/Challenger and Fuggle hops**

Humpty Dumpty was a class of steam locomotive that ran locally.

TASTING NOTES

An orange-gold beer with fruity and floral notes in the nose. Bold flavours hog the palate – hops, bitterness and fruit primarily, over a sweet base – before a dry, bitter, hoppy and fruity aftertaste.

Brief Encounter

● ABV 4.3% ● BOTTLE SIZE 500 ml ● SERVE cool
● INGREDIENTS Maris Otter pale malt/wheat malt/Golding hops

First brewed in 2000, this best bitter pays homage to the classic 1945 movie starring Trevor Howard and Celia Johnson, the most famous scenes of which were set at a railway station. The beer is also sold at the Brief Encounter restaurant at the station, Wymondham, Norfolk.

Reed Cutter

● ABV 4.4% ● BOTTLE SIZE 500 ml ● SERVE cool
● INGREDIENTS Maris Otter pale malt/wheat malt/Fuggle and First Gold hops

A pale ale named after local reed beds and in turn giving its name to the brewery's first pub, four miles away at Cantley.

TASTING NOTES

A golden ale with a softly fruity aroma of oranges, pineapple and hop. The bittersweet taste has more soft fruit, this time peachy and floral, as well as a hop edge. Dry, hoppy, bitter finish with lingering fruit.

Peto's Porter

● ABV 5% ● BOTTLE SIZE 500 ml ● SERVE cool
● INGREDIENTS Maris Otter pale malt/crystal malt/amber malt/chocolate malt/wheat malt/First Gold hops

A porter named in honour of one Samuel Peto, 19th-century Lord Mayor of Lowestoft. Peto was a pioneer of railways in East Anglia and his statue can be seen at Norwich station.

Railway Sleeper

● ABV 5% ● BOTTLE SIZE 500 ml ● SERVE cool
● INGREDIENTS Maris Otter pale malt/crystal malt/amber malt/wheat malt/First Gold hops

A single-varietal hop beer using the popular dwarf hop, First Gold. First brewed back in 1998.

TASTING NOTES

Spicy, creamy malt leads in the aroma of this red-amber ale, with lots of creamy malt overlaid by a light lemony hoppiness in the mostly bitter taste. Hop eventually wins through over malt in the finish, but lemon notes linger on.

Iceni

The Iceni Brewery, 3 Foulden Road, Ickburgh, Mundford, Norfolk IP26 5BJ. Tel. (01842) 878922 Fax (01842) 879216

Iceni was founded by Ulsterman Brendan Moore in 1995 and some of his beers are named after Celtic queens and/or the Iceni tribe, which once inhabited this part of England. The beers, left to drop bright, are kräusened with a wort and yeast mixture before bottling from casks. Best before dates are set at one year. Brendan – a driving force in the local microbrewing movement – also bottles for other small producers and is a partner with his daughter, Frances, in Elveden Ales (see entry).

Honey Mild

- **ABV 3.6%** ● **BOTTLE SIZE 500 ml** ● **SERVE cool**
- **INGREDIENTS Maris Otter pale malt/crystal malt/roasted barley/flaked barley/Fuggle and Challenger hops/honey**

This ruby beer is the same brew as Thetford Forest Mild (see below), except for the addition of honey. It was first produced in 2000.

TASTING NOTES

A complex beer with a honey-caramel nose with roasted bits – like liquid Crunchie bars. The taste begins malty sweet and honeyish but turns dry and gently bitter. Dry, honeyed finish with dark malt.

Thetford Forest Mild

- **ABV 3.6%** ● **BOTTLE SIZE 500 ml** ● **SERVE cool**
- **INGREDIENTS Maris Otter pale malt/crystal malt/roasted barley/flaked barley/Fuggle and Challenger hops**

Introduced in spring 2000, this mild is named after the large tract of forest that runs up to the brewery's home.

TASTING NOTES

A dark ruby mild with a coffee and biscuity malt aroma. The taste is sweetish and malty, but well balanced. Bittersweet, malty finish.

Boadicea Chariot Ale

- **ABV 3.8%** ● **BOTTLE SIZE 500 ml** ● **SERVE cool**
- **INGREDIENTS Maris Otter pale malt/Fuggle and Challenger hops**

Iceni's original beer, Boadicea first tempted Norfolk drinkers back in 1995. It was re-introduced in 2000.

TASTING NOTES

Amber, with a slightly piney, nutty, fruity nose. Piney, spicy, perfumed hops lead in the mouth. The finish is bitter and increasingly hoppy.

Elveden Forest Gold

● ABV 3.9% ● BOTTLE SIZE 500 ml ● SERVE cool

● INGREDIENTS Maris Otter pale malt/caramalt/Fuggle, Challenger and Brewer's Gold hops

Elveden Forest, close to the brewery's home, is probably best known as the site of one of the Centre Parks holiday villages.

TASTING NOTES

A golden ale with a floral hop nose, a crisp, fruity, spicy and hoppy taste, and a light, hoppy finish with lingering fruit.

Celtic Queen

● ABV 4% ● BOTTLE SIZE 500 ml ● SERVE cool

● INGREDIENTS Maris Otter pale malt/caramalt/Fuggle and Challenger hops

Most of Iceni's labels look like the open pages of a book, displaying the name of the beer on the left and a picture, plus a legend or quotation, on the right. This beer's image is of the Celtic Queen herself, pondering her duty 'to be a fierce warrior, leader of her people'.

TASTING NOTES

Amber with a mixed fruit aroma. On the palate, there is full fruitiness and malt, but the beer is dry, not too sweet and nicely restrained, with a gentle, clean hop bitterness. Dry, fruity, moreish, bitter aftertaste.

Fine Soft Day

● ABV 4% ● BOTTLE SIZE 500 ml ● SERVE cool

● INGREDIENTS Maris Otter pale malt/caramalt/Fuggle and Challenger hops/maple syrup

Maple syrup is the unusual ingredient. It is added when the beer is racked into casks after primary fermentation.

TASTING NOTES

An attractive bronze beer with an aroma of ripe, sweet malt and citrus fruit. The full, bittersweet taste is grainy, malty, dry and very fruity (citrus and melon), while the aftertaste is dry and increasingly bitter.

Lovely Day

● ABV 4% ● BOTTLE SIZE 500 ml ● SERVE cool

● INGREDIENTS Maris Otter pale malt/caramalt/Challenger, Fuggle and Boadicea hops

An addition to the range since the last edition of this book, late hopped with the new floral hop strain, Boadicea.

Red, White & Blueberry

● ABV 4% ● BOTTLE SIZE 500 ml ● SERVE cool

● INGREDIENTS Maris Otter pale malt/caramalt/Cascade hops/ blueberries

As suggested by the US flag on the label, this is a beer devised to catch the eye of American servicemen on duty at East Anglia's airbases. Originally blueberries fresh from a local farm were used, but these are not always available. The fruit is crushed and added as a priming in a cask prior to bottling.

TASTING NOTES

A light amber beer with an aroma of sweet, ripe fruit. There's a lightly tart edge to the perfumed fruitiness in the taste, which is bittersweet with a touch of astringency as found in the skins of fruit. Dry, bitter finish with lingering perfumed fruit.

Swaffham Pride

● ABV 4% ● BOTTLE SIZE 500 ml ● SERVE cool

● INGREDIENTS Maris Otter pale malt/caramalt/fruit sugar/Fuggle and Challenger hops

Swaffham Pride was first brewed in 1999 to commemorate the opening of the Ecotech Centre (shown on the label) in nearby Swaffham.

TASTING NOTES

A lovely 'fruit cocktail' – tinned pears and peaches – aroma introduces this amber ale. Juicy fruit also dominates crisp bitterness and a light background sweetness in the taste, before a dry, bitter, hoppy finish.

Cranberry Wheat

● ABV 4.1% ● BOTTLE SIZE 500 ml ● SERVE cool

● INGREDIENTS Lager malt/caramalt/wheat malt/Cascade hops/ cranberries

Cranberries offer brewers a different angle when considering fruit beers. Being rather bitter, they provide fruit character without too much sweetness, as Fuller's discovered when introducing its Organic Honey Dew with Cranberry. Iceni's cranberry beer dates from 2000.

TASTING NOTES

A peachy-golden beer with a fruity, hoppy nose. The taste is a mostly bitter mix of hop, malt and light cranberry, with bitterness gradually taking over. Dry, bitter cranberry finish.

Snowdrop

● **ABV 4.1%** ● **BOTTLE SIZE 500 ml** ● **SERVE cool**
● **INGREDIENTS Lager malt/crushed wheat/Fuggle, Challenger and Cascade hops**

An annual brew, Snowdrop appears in spring, and is a beer to try with puddings, according to Iceni.

TASTING NOTES

A pale golden beer with a crisp, fruity (peaches and oranges) nose. The clean taste is a pleasant mix of peachy fruit and crisp, lightly-scented hop bitterness. The finish has a gentle smack of bitter, peachy fruit.

Fen Tiger

● **ABV 4.2%** ● **BOTTLE SIZE 500 ml** ● **SERVE cool**
● **INGREDIENTS Maris Otter pale malt/caramalt/Fuggle and Challenger hops/coriander**

Coriander, one of the many herbs and spices used to flavour beer before hops were introduced, is recalled in this bitter.

TASTING NOTES

An amber ale with a balanced aroma of light orange fruit and sweet malt. The taste is a crisp, clean mix of lightly spicy, gently bitter fruits, while the finish is dry, moreish and slightly perfumed, with bitter fruit and emerging hop character.

On Target

● **ABV 4.2%** ● **BOTTLE SIZE 500 ml** ● **SERVE cool**
● **INGREDIENTS Maris Otter pale malt/caramalt/Target, Fuggle and Challenger hops**

Target hops provide the inspiration for the name of this best bitter. It 'always hits the mark', if you believe the label.

TASTING NOTES

Amber in colour, this best bitter has toffeeish malt and an earthy hop fruitiness in the aroma. The taste is predominantly bitter and hoppy, but with good malt support. Plenty of body for its strength. Very dry, bitter and hoppy finish.

Thomas Paine Porter

● ABV 4.2% ● BOTTLE SIZE 500 ml ● SERVE cool
● INGREDIENTS Maris Otter pale malt/crystal malt/flaked wheat/torrefied wheat/roasted barley/Fuggle and Challenger hops
Named after local hero Thomas Paine, a philosopher, theologian and activist in the American War of Independence – 'Born in Thetford in 1737: a noted author, revolutionary and man of reason', according to the label. This ruby porter was added in 1999.

Honey Stout

● ABV 4.3% ● BOTTLE SIZE 500 ml ● SERVE cool
● INGREDIENTS Maris Otter pale malt/crystal malt/caramalt/roasted barley/Fuggle and Challenger hops/honey
A near-black beer, based on the brewery's cask Celtic Stout, with Irish honey added for a new dimension.

Phoenix

● ABV 4.3% ● BOTTLE SIZE 500 ml ● SERVE cool
● INGREDIENTS Lager malt/crushed wheat/Phoenix hops
A single-varietal beer introduced in 2002, showcasing the not-widely-used Phoenix hops, with the fire-regenerated, mythological bird of the same name depicted on the label.

TASTING NOTES
A golden ale with a sharp, hoppy, lemon aroma. Piney hops dominate, leaving light lemon in the hoppy, bitter finish.

Deirdre of the Sorrows

● ABV 4.4% ● BOTTLE SIZE 500 ml ● SERVE cool
● INGREDIENTS Maris Otter pale malt/roasted barley/Fuggle and Challenger hops
A beer dedicated to 'the fairest and most beautiful of all the daughters of Ulster', destined to 'bring sorrow and pain to all the heroes of Ulster', according to the label.

TASTING NOTES
Orange-gold, with a malty nose. Fruit, malt and hops combine in the gently bitter taste; dry, fruity, pleasantly bitter finish.

Ported Porter

● **ABV 4.4%** ● **BOTTLE SIZE 500 ml** ● **SERVE cool**
● **INGREDIENTS Maris Otter pale malt/torrefied wheat/flaked barley/roasted barley/Fuggle and Challenger hops/port**

Brendan Moore grew up with the Irish tradition of adding fortified wines to stout and in 2000 created his own all-in-one equivalent, adding a bottle of port to each firkin.

TASTING NOTES

Dark ruby, with soft roasted grain, a little fruit and some caramel in the aroma. The taste is also soft, nutty, gently roasted and bittersweet, with a hint of winey fruit. Dry, bitter finish, with a little sweet fruit.

Roísín Dubh

● **ABV 4.4%** ● **BOTTLE SIZE 500 ml** ● **SERVE cool**
● **INGREDIENTS Maris Otter pale malt/torrefied wheat/roasted barley/Fuggle and Challenger hops**

Inspired by a sweet, dark beer from the Midlands, Roísín Dubh is Gaelic for 'dark rose'. The beer first appeared back in 1996.

TASTING NOTES

A deep red ale with a fruity, floral nose. Smooth, clean fruity flavours fill the mouth, with a solid balancing bitterness and a little nut. The finish is dry, very moreish, soft and fruity, yet bitter, with a hint of toffee.

Good Night Out

● **ABV 4.5%** ● **BOTTLE SIZE 500 ml** ● **SERVE cool**
● **INGREDIENTS Maris Otter pale malt/roasted barley/Fuggle and Challenger hops/port**

First brewed for a brewers' get-together in 1998, hence the name, and based on Deirdre of the Sorrows, with a bottle of port added per firkin.

TASTING NOTES

Another amber beer with a mellow fruity nose, but this time the added port provides a 'crushed raspberry' aroma. The taste is fruity, with raspberries and melons, but fairly dry and not sweet. Dry, bitter finish.

It's a Grand Day

● **ABV 4.5%** ● **BOTTLE SIZE 500 ml** ● **SERVE cool**
● **INGREDIENTS Maris Otter pale malt/Fuggle and Challenger hops/ginger**

Designed as a refreshing summer ale, It's a Grand Day ('for a great ale') is a stronger version of Iceni's Fen Tiger, but with the addition of stem ginger instead of coriander.

TASTING NOTES

An amber beer with an aroma of fruit and ginger spice. The crisp, refreshing taste features plenty of ginger, but without the accustomed 'burn', and is well balanced to allow malt and hop flavour through. Ginger and hops compete in the finish.

Norfolk Lager

● ABV 5% ● BOTTLE SIZE 500 ml ● SERVE cold

● INGREDIENTS Lager malt/wheat malt/Hersbrucker hops

This beer was initially brewed in 1998 under the name of L.A.D. Lager. The first batch was a keg product (chilled and filtered but not pasteurized), the initials L.A.D. conveniently standing – apparently – for 'Lager Awareness Day'. Laddish marketing, complete with poses by a blonde model, attracted the attentions of the tabloid press. The beer has since been sold in cask form and this bottle-conditioned version first arrived in 1999. The former image has been quietly dropped in recent years as the new name of Norfolk Lager has been adopted.

TASTING NOTES

A pale golden beer with a floral hop nose. It is malty and sweet to taste, with clean, lightly perfumed hop notes. Dry, bittersweet, malt and hops finish. Tasty and well rounded.

Norfolk Gold

● ABV 5% ● BOTTLE SIZE 500 ml ● SERVE cool

● INGREDIENTS Maris Otter pale malt/caramalt/Fuggle and Challenger hops

Aimed at the tourist trade on the popular Norfolk coast, this beer was first bottled in 1998.

TASTING NOTES

A golden beer with a slightly toffeeish, spicy, fruity nose. There are distinct pineapple notes in the taste, a little spice and a hint of tartness. Dry, fruity, spicy finish.

Raspberry Wheat

● ABV 5% ● BOTTLE SIZE 500 ml ● SERVE cool

● INGREDIENTS Maris Otter pale malt/lager malt/wheat malt/Hersbrucker hops/raspberries

Although pulped raspberries are added after primary fermentation in the Belgian style, this is not a sour framboise-like fruit beer. It is more of a summer quencher, brought to Norfolk from the USA by an itinerant brewer who worked at Iceni for a while.

TASTING NOTES

Pale gold, with raspberries and bubblegum in the aroma. Delicate and bittersweet on the palate, it is refreshingly understated, with gentle raspberries edging out light hops. Moreish, hop and raspberry finish.

Swaffham Gold

● ABV 5% ● BOTTLE SIZE 500 ml ● SERVE cool

● INGREDIENTS Maris Otter pale malt/caramalt/Fuggle and Challenger hops/maple syrup

Another tourist-orientated beer, Swaffham Gold is the brewery's cask Iceni Gold with added maple syrup.

TASTING NOTES

A smooth and tasty, dark golden beer with fruit, spice and butterscotch in the nose. Butterscotch, malt and fruit linger in the mouth, alongside a crisp, but mellow bitterness. Dry malty, gently bitter aftertaste.

Winter Lightning

● ABV 5% ● BOTTLE SIZE 500 ml ● SERVE cool

● INGREDIENTS Lager malt/wheat malt/Hersbrucker hops

Hersbrucker hops add a continental touch to this winter beer.

TASTING NOTES

Pale golden, with a 'fruit cocktail' aroma. The fruity, bittersweet taste is full and well rounded. Nicely bitter, very fruity, gently warming finish.

Men of Norfolk

● ABV 6.2% ● BOTTLE SIZE 500/750 ml ● SERVE cool

● INGREDIENTS Maris Otter pale malt/crystal malt/torrefied wheat/ flaked barley/roasted barley/Fuggle and Challenger hops

Aimed at the hardy winter tourists to this lovely part of the world, this strong, rich stout is only brewed for bottling.

TASTING NOTES

A very dark brown beer with dark malt and a little pineapple and pear drop in the aroma. The taste is smooth, malty and sweetish, but nicely balanced and not cloying. Liquorice notes, roasted grain and estery fruit play in the background, before a lingering, roasted, liquorice finish.

Islay

Islay Ales Company Ltd., The Brewery, Islay House Square, Bridgend, Isle of Islay PA44 7NZ. Tel./Fax (01496) 810014
E-mail: info@islayales.com
Website: www.islayales.com
Mail order service

Using the slogan 'Ales from the Isle of Malts', Islay Ales was founded in 2003, at last offering a little variation on an island that had seven, world-famous distilleries, but no brewery. The beers are all bottled by hand after the beer has been kräusened, and are also sold in cask form.

Finlaggan Ale

● ABV 3.7% ● BOTTLE SIZE 500 ml ● SERVE cool
● INGREDIENTS Pale malt/crystal malt/Golding, Mount Hood and Styrian Golding hops

Named after Loch Finlaggan, a lake at the northern end of the island.

TASTING NOTES

A light amber beer with fruity, citrus hops in the aroma over gentle malt. The taste is crisp, dry and nicely bitter with a pleasant citrus hop character, while the finish is dry, bitter and hoppy.

Black Rock Ale

● ABV 4.2% ● BOTTLE SIZE 500 ml ● SERVE cool
● INGREDIENTS Pale malt/crystal malt/roasted barley/Golding, Mount Hood and Fuggle hops

Black Rock is a landmark in Loch Indaal, close to the brewery.

TASTING NOTES

Another amber beer, with fruit, malt and hop mixing in the aroma. There are unusual fruity flavours in the mouth, with bitter citrus notes to the fore. Hops and dark cereals also feature. Dry, bitter, hoppy finish.

Dun Hogs Head Ale

● ABV 4.4% ● BOTTLE SIZE 500 ml ● SERVE cool
● INGREDIENTS Pale malt/crystal malt/chocolate malt/wheat malt/roasted barley/Fuggle and Bramling Cross hops

This dark ruby stout takes its name not from a type of beer cask but from a coastal landmark on the eastern shore of the island. The brewers suggest you try it with sweet, creamy puddings or dark chocolate.

TASTING NOTES
The biscuity dark grains in the aroma continue in the taste, with plain chocolate notes and a hint of liquorice as bitterness kicks in. The finish is dry and roasted, with bitter chocolate and coffee lingering.

Saligo Ale

● ABV 4.4% ● BOTTLE SIZE 500 ml ● SERVE cool
● INGREDIENTS Pale malt/lager malt/wheat malt/Golding and Bramling Cross hops
Saligo is a bay on the west coast of Islay. The beer named after it is available on draught in summer but more regularly in bottle.
TASTING NOTES
A golden ale with a big peachy aroma. There's more peach in the taste, which is also floral and bittersweet. Dry, bitter, peachy finish.

Angus Og Ale

● ABV 4.5% ● BOTTLE SIZE 500 ml ● SERVE cool
● INGREDIENTS Pale malt/crystal malt/Golding, Mount Hood and Styrian Golding hops
Angus Og was Lord of the Isles in the 14th century and resided on the Isle of Islay. He was an ally of Robert the Bruce.

Ardnave Ale

● ABV 4.6% ● BOTTLE SIZE 500 ml ● SERVE cool
● INGREDIENTS Pale malt/crystal malt/Golding, Mount Hood, Fuggle and Styrian Golding hops
This golden bitter is named after Ardnave Point, at the northern end of Loch Gruinart on Islay, where you can often see seals at play.
TASTING NOTES
A dark golden beer with a spicy, fruity aroma and taste (oranges, lemons and tinned peaches). Tangy hop resins come through in the mouth and the aftertaste is bitter, drying and hoppy.

Nerabus Ale

● ABV 4.8% ● BOTTLE SIZE 500 ml ● SERVE cool
● INGREDIENTS Pale malt/dark crystal malt/caramalt/chocolate malt/wheat malt/Amarillo and Bramling Cross hops
This winter ale commemorates the ancient settlement of Nerabus (or Nerabolis) where various members of the Donald clan are buried.

TASTING NOTES
This red beer features toffee and malt in the aroma, backed by light fruit. The taste is full and malty, with more toffee balanced out by lemon, orange and blackberry fruitiness from the hops. Dry, pleasantly bitter, malty finish with roasted grain notes emerging.

Single Malt Ale

● **ABV 5%** ● **BOTTLE SIZE 500 ml** ● **SERVE cool**
● **INGREDIENTS Pale malt/Amarillo and Bramling Cross hops**
First brewed in 2005 for the Festival of Islay Malt and Music, and now an annual brew for the event, which is held at the end of May.

Ballinaby Ale

● **ABV 7.1%** ● **BOTTLE SIZE 500 ml** ● **SERVE cool**
● **INGREDIENTS Pale malt/crystal malt/caramalt/chocolate malt/ Challenger, Northdown and Bramling Cross hops**
Ballinaby is a village near Loch Gorm, on the western side of Islay. The ruby-hued beer sharing its name is brewed in small batches (280 bottles only in 2006), again for the Festival of Islay Malt and Music.
TASTING NOTES
Biscuity dark malts lead in the aroma, with hints of polished leather and a little vinous fruit (blackcurrants and pineapple). Dark chocolate features on the tongue with lemony fruit and an alcoholic spiciness. The finish is modest, however, with bitter chocolate eventually taking over.

Isle of Purbeck

Isle of Purbeck Brewery, Bankes Arms Hotel, Manor Road, Studland, Swanage, Dorset BH19 3AU.
Tel. (01929) 450227 Fax (01929) 450307
Small brewery that has been operating from the Bankes Arms Hotel since 2003. The bottled beers are a new addition to the range and are filled from tanks for the brewery by Branded Drinks in Gloucestershire.

IPA

● **ABV 4.8%** ● **BOTTLE SIZE 500 ml** ● **SERVE cool**
● **INGREDIENTS Maris Otter pale malt/crystal malt/Bramling Cross, Whitbread Golding Variety and Pioneer hops**
A new, hoppy, citrus-flavoured India pale ale.

Solar Power

● ABV 5% ● BOTTLE SIZE 500 ml ● SERVE cool
● INGREDIENTS Lager malt/caramalt/wheat malt/Northdown, First Gold and Perle hops

This glass of liquid sunshine provides a neat counter to a draught beer in the Isle of Purbeck range called Fossil Fuel.

TASTING NOTES

A golden ale with a spicy, softly citrus-fruity aroma. The taste is bittersweet and fruity, with citrus notes and a full, smooth, malty body. Dry, hoppy, fruity and bitter aftertaste.

Isle of Skye

**The Isle of Skye Brewing Co. (Leann an Eilein) Ltd.,
The Pier, Uig, Isle of Skye IV51 9XP.
Tel. (01470) 542477 Fax (01470) 542488
E-mail: info@skyebrewery.co.uk
Website: www.skyebrewery.co.uk**

Founded in 1995, to bring real ale relief to an otherwise discerning drinkers' desert, Isle of Skye has now expanded its brewing capacity and added two bottle-conditioned beers to its range. The beers are conditioned in tank and then filled on site without finings or filtration, making them acceptable to vegetarians. Best before dates are set nine months after bottling.

Misty Isle

● ABV 4.3% ● BOTTLE SIZE 660 ml ● SERVE cold
● INGREDIENTS Maris Otter pale malt/carapils malt/wheat malt/ Hersbrucker hops/organic lemon juice

Delivered in outsize, clear-glass bottles, this hazy orange beer is a striking discovery. It's brewed as a summer quencher (also in cask), taking its lead from Belgian witbiers, and is recommended by the brewers as an ideal accompaniment for salads and cold dishes. The Isle of Skye is often called the Misty Isle and, given the cloudy appearance of this brew, that seemed a good name for the beer too.

TASTING NOTES

A cloudy orange beer with a tart, spicy nose. The taste is also tart, spicy and fruity (hints of orange and lemon), before a drying, tart, spicy, increasingly bitter aftertaste.

Am Basteir

● ABV 7% ● BOTTLE SIZE 500 ml ● SERVE cool
● INGREDIENTS Maris Otter pale malt/crystal malt/amber malt/torrefied wheat/organic demerara sugar/Fuggle hops

The name means 'The Executioner' in Gaelic and is taken from one of the mountains on the Isle of Skye's Cuillin Ridge. The beer itself is a bottled version of the draught Cuillin Beast (same ABV).

TASTING NOTES

A hazy orange ale with a malty, slightly nutty, heady aroma of dark berries. Tart berry fruit, sweet malt and hop notes mingle in the mouth, along with a suggestion of coconut. The thickish finish is dry and malty with tart fruit, before hops take over.

Itchen Valley

Itchen Valley Brewery Ltd., Unit B, Prospect Commercial Park, Prospect Road, New Alresford, Hampshire SO24 9QF.
Tel. (01962) 735111 Fax (01962) 735678
E-mail: info@itchenvalley.com
Website: www.itchenvalley.com

Itchen Valley Brewery was founded in 1997 but changed hands a year later. The new owners launched into bottle-conditioned beers in a big way and bottling now accounts for around 15% of the business. All the beers now are bottled under contract at Arkell's in Swindon. They are filtered and fresh yeast is added prior to bottling. Itchen Valley's parent company specializes in pub signage, hence the colourful bottle labels. Many bottles are sold at farmers' markets. A move to new, larger premises, close to the original site, took place in June 2006. An on-site shop is now planned and the 4.2% cask best bitter, Hampshire Rose, may be added to the bottled range in the near future.

Fagins

● ABV 4.1% ● BOTTLE SIZE 500 ml ● SERVE cool
● INGREDIENTS Maris Otter pale malt/crystal malt/wheat malt/First Gold, Golding and Fuggle hops

Depicting the Dickensian villain on the label, Fagins is an early Itchen Valley brew that has been retained by the current ownership.

TASTING NOTES

An amber ale with malt and grapefruit dominant in the nose. Grapefruit hoppiness and pleasant bitterness feature in the taste, on a silky malt bed. Dry, bitter, lightly fruity finish.

Wykehams Glory

● ABV 4.3% ● BOTTLE SIZE 500 ml ● SERVE cool
● INGREDIENTS Maris Otter pale malt/crystal malt/chocolate malt/ First Gold hops

Wykehams Glory, with its striking green label, is named after William of Wykeham, who founded nearby Winchester College in the 14th century.

TASTING NOTES

This red-brown ale has a fruity aroma (both tropical and citrus notes), a mostly bitter, fruity-hop taste, and a dry, bitter finish with lingering fruit.

Treacle Stout

● ABV 4.4% ● BOTTLE SIZE 500 ml ● SERVE cool
● INGREDIENTS Maris Otter pale malt/crystal malt/chocolate malt/ roasted barley/Progress hops/treacle/liquorice

The first of two new beers, this time unusually flavoured with liquorice and treacle. The liquorice is added to the copper boil, while the treacle primes the finished beer before it is bottled.

TASTING NOTES

A ruby/brown beer with a creamy collar. Coffeeish dark malt and treacle feature in the aroma before more dark malts, treacle and light liquorice combine in the smooth taste. The same flavours lead in the mostly bitter finish, with liquorice more pronounced.

Hambledon Bitter

● ABV 4.5% ● BOTTLE SIZE 500 ml ● SERVE cool
● INGREDIENTS Maris Otter pale malt/Cascade hops/honey/ elderflower

A new beer celebrating the village that is widely recognized as the home of cricket. Hambledon, with its famous Bat & Ball pub, and cricket club established in 1760, is just 15 miles away from the brewery. Honey and elderflower spice up the finished beer before it heads for bottling.

TASTING NOTES

A dark golden ale with a big fruity aroma (elderflower and grapefruit). The same fruitiness dominates the taste, with hops emerging to lead elderflower in the finish.

Major stockist Local Tesco

Pure Gold

● **ABV 4.8%** ● **BOTTLE SIZE 500 ml** ● **SERVE cool**
● **INGREDIENTS Maris Otter pale malt/lager malt/Saaz and Cascade hops**

Pure Gold is an ale/lager cross, bursting with hop flavour. The secret is the addition of Cascade hops in the fermenter, to complement the gentler Saaz hops which make their presence known in the copper.

TASTING NOTES

A bright golden beer with a stunning aroma of pineapple, grapefruit and resin-like hop. The hop flavours are full and juicy, with pineapple, grapefruit and a rounded bitterness drowning out an initial sweetish note. The finish is dry, strongly hoppy and fruity.

Father Christmas

● **ABV 5%** ● **BOTTLE SIZE 500 ml** ● **SERVE cool**
● **INGREDIENTS Maris Otter pale malt/crystal malt/Challenger hops**

Despite its seasonal name, Father Christmas is actually sold all year.

TASTING NOTES

Amber-red, with a pleasantly fruity, perfumed nose. The taste is well balanced and has a restrained sweetness, gentle fruit, a hint of spice and a mild bitterness. Moreish malt and hops linger in the dry finish.

Wat Tyler

● **ABV 5%** ● **BOTTLE SIZE 500 ml** ● **SERVE cool**
● **INGREDIENTS Maris Otter pale malt/crystal malt/Progress hops**

Recalling, in its name, the famous leader of the Peasants' Revolt of 1381, Wat Tyler is described on the dark red label as 'a rebel of a beer' and 'a strong real ale winter warmer'.

TASTING NOTES

This red-brown ale has a fruity, malty nose, a bitter but balanced taste of smooth malt and hops, and a dry, bitter, hoppy finish.

Jolly Brewer

The Jolly Brewer, Kingston Villa, 27 Poplar Road,
Wrexham LL13 7DG. Tel. (01978) 261884
E-mail: pene@jollybrewer.co.uk
Website: www. jollybrewer.co.uk

Since 2000, Penelope Coles has branched out from the off-licence and craft brewing shop she runs in Wrexham and opened her own commercial brewery, building on 25 years of brewing experience. No finings are used in the beers, making them acceptable to vegans.

Benno's

● **ABV 4%** ● **BOTTLE SIZE 500 ml** ● **SERVE cold**
● **INGREDIENTS Lager malt/Hallertau hops**

A lager brewed for the Wrexham FC Supporters Trust, with 1990s striker Gary Bennett honoured in the name. The town of Wrexham has a distinguished lager-brewing heritage, dating back to the 19th century. This and Tommy's (overleaf) are sold in tall, distinctive, 500 ml bottles.

TASTING NOTES

A golden lager with an aroma of gentle, herbal hops. The taste is a good balance of sweet malt and the same, tangy, herbal hops, rounded off by a dry, herbal hop aftertaste.

Suzanne's Stout

● **ABV 4%** ● **BOTTLE SIZE 500 ml** ● **SERVE cool**
● **INGREDIENTS Maris Otter pale malt/roasted barley/flaked barley/ Challenger and Target hops**

A dark beer named after one of Pene's daughters.

Taid's Garden

● **ABV 4.2%** ● **BOTTLE SIZE 500 ml** ● **SERVE cool**
● **INGREDIENTS Maris Otter pale malt/pilsener malt/wheat malt/ Golding, Fuggle and Hallertau hops**

The aroma and taste of this floral ale reminded Pene of her childhood days in her grandad's garden (that's what the name means). A variation of the same beer, using Cascade and Golding hops and known as Taid's Fragrant Garden, is also sometimes available.

TASTING NOTES

A red-amber ale with a malty but floral aroma. The taste is also malty, yet mostly bitter and nicely balanced, with light toffee and floral hops. The finish is dry, malty, bitter and hoppy.

Diod y Gymraef

● **ABV 4.5%** ● **BOTTLE SIZE 500 ml** ● **SERVE cool**
● **INGREDIENTS Maris Otter pale malt/Golding and Fuggle hops**

A drink for Welsh ladies, if the name is to be believed.

Lucinda's Lager

● ABV 4.5% ● BOTTLE SIZE 500 ml ● SERVE cold
● INGREDIENTS Pilsner malt/wheat malt/Golding, Fuggle and Hallertau hops

Another of Pene's daughters features in the title of this lager.

Taffy's Tipple

● ABV 4.5% ● BOTTLE SIZE 500 ml ● SERVE cool
● INGREDIENTS Maris Otter pale malt/amber malt/chocolate malt/ Target, Golding, Challenger and Northern Brewer hops

A dark bitter, which, like all the other beers, is bottled by hand direct from the fermenting vessel, with glucose added for priming.

Y Ddraig Goch

● ABV 4.5% ● BOTTLE SIZE 500 ml ● SERVE cool
● INGREDIENTS Maris Otter pale malt/chocolate malt/flaked barley/ Golding, Challenger and Northern Brewer hops

The name of this dark ale simply translates as The Red Dragon.

Tommy's

● ABV 5.5% ● BOTTLE SIZE 500 ml ● SERVE cold
● INGREDIENTS Maris Otter pale malt/chocolate malt/Hallertau hops

The second Wrexham Supporters Trust beer, a dark lager marking the career of the late Tommy Bamford, the club's greatest ever striker.

TASTING NOTES

A dark red beer with biscuity dark chocolate notes in the aroma. The taste is sweet, with dark malt counter bitterness and more chocolate. The finish is dry, with the bitterness of dark malt taking over.

Keltek

Keltek Brewery, Candela House, Cardrew Industrial Estate, Redruth, Cornwall TR15 1SS. Tel. (01209) 313620 Fax (01209) 215197
E-mail: sales@keltekbrewery.co.uk
Website: www.keltekbrewery.co.uk

Founded in Tregony in 1997, to supply beers to the Roseland peninsula of Cornwall, Keltek was later moved to Lostwithiel. It has since been moved, yet again, to new premises in Redruth and is now a subsidiary of OMC (UK) Ltd., a business that specializes in fibre optics and lighting.

Kornish Nektar

● ABV 4.2% ● BOTTLE SIZE 500 ml ● SERVE cool
● INGREDIENTS Not declared

A new beer, with honey added towards the end of the brewing process.

TASTING NOTES

A ruby ale with creamy dark malts and liquorice in the otherwise floral aroma. There are more sweet, dark malts in the nutty, peppery taste, which has a light tartness and faint honey. Dry, malty, bittersweet finish.

Magik

● ABV 4.2% ● BOTTLE SIZE 500 ml ● SERVE cool
● INGREDIENTS Not declared

A best bitter with citrus notes. Like Keltek's other beers, it is bottled from a cask, without the use of finings, making it acceptable to vegans.

TASTING NOTES

A red-amber beer with a malty, citrus-fruity, lightly spicy aroma. The taste is malty and sharp, with some citrus fruit. Dry, malty finish with hops coming through.

King

● ABV 5.1% ● BOTTLE SIZE 500 ml ● SERVE cool
● INGREDIENTS Pale malt/crystal malt/Cascade and Hallertau hops

Featuring the 'sword in the stone' on its colourful label, King was first produced in 1998 and has been twice winner of the *Tucker's Maltings Bottled Beer Competition*. It was also winner of the SIBA (Society of Independent Brewers) *National Brewing Competition*'s bottled beer category in 2001. Both awards came under the previous management.

TASTING NOTES

Golden, with hop resins and orange-citrus in the aroma. Bittersweet orange-citrus notes feature in the taste before a dry, bitter fruit finish.

Uncle Stu's Famous Steak Pie Stout

● ABV 6.5% ● BOTTLE SIZE 275 ml ● SERVE cool
● INGREDIENTS Not declared

Another new addition to the range. Uncle Stu is Stuart Heath, the man who founded the brewery and who was responsible for its recipes.

TASTING NOTES

A deep ruby, strong stout with vinous sweet fruit, dark malt and a little liquorice in the aroma. Dark malts, along with plain chocolate, feature in the creamy, mildly bitter, slightly earthy and alcoholic taste. The bitter finish has dry, roasted grain and a touch of liquorice.

Kripple Dick

● ABV 7% ● BOTTLE SIZE 275 ml ● SERVE cool
● INGREDIENTS Pale malt/crystal malt/chocolate malt/amber malt/ First Gold and Hallertau hops

There are echoes of a beer once produced by St Austell Brewery in the name and style of this barley wine, which was introduced in 2001, but which has now been reduced in strength from the original 8.5%.

TASTING NOTES

A ruby beer with a malty-sweet, fruity, alcoholic aroma. Tart fruit and sweet malt appear in the taste, with a touch of liquorice. Dry, malty, fruity and bittersweet aftertaste.

Beheaded '76'

● ABV 7.6% ● BOTTLE SIZE 275 ml ● SERVE cool
● INGREDIENTS Pale malt/crystal malt/chocolate malt/wheat malt/ First Gold and Cluster hops

Beheaded was developed in 2003 at a dizzy 10% ABV. The beer is now a more manageable 7.6% – hence the small addition to the name.

TASTING NOTES

An amber-red beer with a spicy, malty, lightly vinous aroma with faint strawberry notes. The taste is creamy, malty and sweetish, with a vinous catch, some berry fruit and warming alcohol. The drying, warming, bittersweet finish is increasingly hoppy.

King

WJ King & Co. (Brewers), 3–5 Jubilee Estate, Foundry Lane, Horsham, West Sussex RH13 5UE. Tel. (01403) 272102 Fax (01403) 754455
E-mail: sales@kingfamilybrewers.co.uk
Website: www.kingfamilybrewers.co.uk
Mail order service

Bill King, latterly managing director of the late King & Barnes, returned to brewing on a much smaller scale in 2001. Setting up this small brewery in the same town of Horsham, Bill was swiftly brewing up to capacity and bottled beers were soon added to the cask range. All beers are filled directly from the fermenter, without filtering or the use of isinglass finings, making them acceptable to vegetarians. The brewery shop is open Saturdays, 10am–2pm.

Five Generations

● **ABV 4.4%** ● **BOTTLE SIZE 500 ml** ● **SERVE cool**

● **INGREDIENTS Maris Otter pale malt/crystal malt/chocolate malt/ wheat malt/Golding and Cascade hops**

A new beer, brewed to celebrate five generations of brewing in Horsham. The label depicts early family brewer James King (1808–79).

TASTING NOTES

Amber-red, with a fruity, hoppy aroma, backed by a little chocolate and toffee from the malt. The taste is a full-flavoured mix of sharp, fruity hops and malt, with some dark, roasted notes. Dry, hoppy, bitter finish.

King's Old Ale

● **ABV 4.5%** ● **BOTTLE SIZE 500 ml** ● **SERVE cool**

● **INGREDIENTS Maris Otter pale malt/crystal malt/chocolate malt/ wheat malt/Whitbread Golding Variety and Challenger hops**

A bottled version of the brewery's beer festival award-winning, dark winter ale that was first brewed in 2002.

TASTING NOTES

Deep ruby, with chocolate in the nose. The taste is a silky smooth, mild mix of burnt malt, chocolate, coffee and a little winey fruit, rounded off by a pleasant burnt/roasted flavour and a light toffee-malt edge.

Mallard Ale

● **ABV 5%** ● **BOTTLE SIZE 500 ml** ● **SERVE cool**

● **INGREDIENTS Maris Otter pale malt/Golding hops**

A golden beer, a stronger, bottled version of King's draught Summer Ale.

TASTING NOTES

An aroma of orangey hops leads to a bittersweet taste where delicate malt is overlaid with sharp, tangy hop fruit (pineapple notes). Dry finish.

Red River Ale

● **ABV 5%** ● **BOTTLE SIZE 500 ml** ● **SERVE cool**

● **INGREDIENTS Maris Otter pale malt/crystal malt/chocolate malt/ enzymic malt/Golding, Whitbread Golding Variety and Challenger hops**

This strong beer takes its name from a tributary that runs from a mill pond in Horsham and is one of a few such 'red rivers' coloured by rust from the region's old iron workings.

TASTING NOTES

A light ruby beer with a white head. There is plenty of fruit on the rich malt in the nose, with a hint of chocolate behind. The smooth taste is nutty and has sweet, fruity notes, plus bits of roasted malt poking through. Nutty, roasted, bitter and slightly estery finish.

Cereal Thriller

● ABV 6.3% ● BOTTLE SIZE 500 ml ● SERVE cool ● INGREDIENTS Maris Otter pale malt/crystal malt/chocolate malt/ enzymic malt/flaked maize/Whitbread Golding Variety hops

When Bill was at King & Barnes, they produced a beer with a high percentage of maize called Cornucopia. This is Bill's latest variation on the theme, the name chosen through a local competition when it was first bottled in 2004.

TASTING NOTES

Hazy orange, with light pear drop, subtle malt and grain in the nose. The taste is sweet, rich and lightly fruity, with a burnt grain edge. Toasted grain and hop bitterness take over from sweetness in the finish.

Merry Ale

● ABV 6.5% ● BOTTLE SIZE 500 ml ● SERVE cool ● INGREDIENTS Maris Otter pale malt/crystal malt/chocolate malt/ enzymic malt/Golding and Whitbread Golding Variety hops

A stronger version of Red River, this is King's Christmas ale in bottle, introduced in 2003.

TASTING NOTES

A red-amber ale with a deeply malty, treacle-toffee aroma. The sweet, full-bodied taste is also rich and full of toffee-malt, with a touch of warmth. A bittersweet, toffeeish aftertaste rounds off.

Kingstone

Kingstone Brewery, Kinsons Farm, Whitebrook, Monmouth NP25 4TX. Tel./Fax (01600) 860778

Small farm brewery that opened in 2005. The beers are matured for a month before release, having been filled directly from a conditioning tank, with no primings. Best before dates are set at six months.

Classic Bitter

● **ABV 4.5%** ● **BOTTLE SIZE 500 ml** ● **SERVE cool**

● **INGREDIENTS Maris Otter pale malt/crystal malt/Northern Brewer, Cascade and Bramling Cross hops**

'A classic farmhouse brew', according to brewer Brian Austwick, hence the name. This was Kingstone's first ever beer, introduced in October 2005.

TASTING NOTES

There's a pungently hoppy, orangey, spicy aroma to this orange-coloured beer, and the taste is also robustly hoppy, filled with tangy resins and flashes of orange and lemon. The finish is dry and notably hoppy with bitter fruit.

Millers Ale

● **ABV 4.9%** ● **BOTTLE SIZE 500 ml** ● **SERVE cool**

● **INGREDIENTS Maris Otter pale malt/crystal malt/wheat malt/ Fuggle and First Gold hops**

There's a high proportion of wheat malt in this premium beer that celebrates in its name the watermills that once powered the industries of the Wye Valley.

TASTING NOTES

A pale amber beer with a softly fruity aroma of melons, tinned peaches and pears, with a little hop resin. There are more gentle fruits and soft malt in the taste, which also has some alcoholic warmth and a little astringency. The tart finish becomes bitter and dry.

Gatehouse Ale

● **ABV 5.1%** ● **BOTTLE SIZE 500 ml** ● **SERVE cool**

● **INGREDIENTS Maris Otter pale malt/crystal malt/Challenger and Northern Brewer hops**

Also sold on draught as Brew III or Three Castles Ale, this orange-coloured beer takes its name from Monmouth's Monnow Gate, a 14th-century fortification that dominates the town's famous 13th-century bridge over the River Monnow.

TASTING NOTES

Hops and juicy fruit are well to the fore in the nose (oranges, pineapple and tinned pears). The same fruit leads in the mouth, backed by tangy hop bitterness and some alcoholic warmth. Dry, bitter and hoppy aftertaste. A very full flavoured beer.

Leatherbritches

Leatherbritches Brewery, The Bentley Brook Inn, Fenny Bentley, Ashbourne, Derbyshire DE6 1LF. Tel. (07976) 279253
Website: www.leatherbritches.co.uk

The Bentley Brook Inn is a Peak District pub run by the Allingham family from 1977 until 2005. Although the pub has been sold now, the small brewery at the rear is still owned and run by Edward Allingham. All four beers are bottled on site direct from a conditioning tank.

Hairy Helmet

● **ABV 4.9%** ● **BOTTLE SIZE 500 ml** ● **SERVE cool**
● **INGREDIENTS Maris Otter pale malt/Progress and Styrian Golding hops**

Formerly sold in bottle as Ale Conner's Tipple.

TASTING NOTES

A very pale, yellow-gold beer with a big grapefruit aroma. The taste is sweetish, with more grapefruit and scented floral notes. Floral hops persist in the finish, but bitterness just takes over.

Ale Conner's Bespoke

● **ABV 5.2%** ● **BOTTLE SIZE 500 ml** ● **SERVE cool**
● **INGREDIENTS Maris Otter pale malt/crystal malt/Progress and Styrian Golding hops**

The name of the brewery is derived from the garments worn by ale conners in centuries past. The job of these officials was to test the quality and strength of beers. They did so – it is said – by sitting on a small pool of beer. Their assessment of it was based on how sticky their leather britches became. Bespoke was Leatherbritches' first cask beer.

TASTING NOTES

A dark golden ale with citrus hops in the nose. Floral, fruity notes lead in the mouth, including a hint of pear drop and a waft of orange blossom. Dry, floral-fruity, gently bitter aftertaste.

Ale Conner's Porter

● **ABV 5.4%** ● **BOTTLE SIZE 500 ml** ● **SERVE cool**
● **INGREDIENTS Maris Otter pale malt/crystal malt/dark chocolate malt/Progress hops**

The label of this and the other beers depicts two ale conners 'sitting down on the job'. It is reported that only leather britches were tough enough to stand the wear and tear of the profession.

TASTING NOTES

A ruby beer with a dense, creamy head. A lightly roasted, biscuity malt aroma leads to a sweetish, biscuity taste, with a gentle creaminess and soft roasted malt. Bittersweet, malty finish with roasted flavours.

Blue

● **ABV 9%** ● **BOTTLE SIZE 330 ml** ● **SERVE cool**

● **INGREDIENTS Maris Otter pale malt/crystal malt/torrefied wheat/ berries/cinnamon/hops vary**

Inspired by Belgian fruit beers. Berries are added to the copper boil and the hop back. The fruits used vary, but have included blackberries and the more exotic aronia berries. The hops also vary from brew to brew.

Leek

Staffordshire Brewery Ltd. (t/a Leek Brewing Company), Units 11 and 12, Churnet Side, Cheddleton, Leek, Staffordshire ST13 7EF. Tel./Fax (01538) 361919

E-mail: leekbrewery@hotmail.com

Brewery established in 2002 that moved to a new home in summer 2004. In addition to being part of a business that produces hand-made cheeses, Leek turns out a wide range of bottled beers, which are declared to be safe for vegans as they contain no finings.

Staffordshire Gold

● **ABV 3.8%** ● **BOTTLE SIZE 500 ml** ● **SERVE cool**

● **INGREDIENTS Maris Otter pale malt/lager malt/wheat malt/ Cascade hops**

A pale, hoppy beer that, like the other ales, is mostly sold in local off-licences and at farmers' markets.

Dovd Ale

● **ABV 4%** ● **BOTTLE SIZE 500 ml** ● **SERVE cool**

● **INGREDIENTS Pale malt/crystal malt/wheat malt/Cascade hops**

A copper beer featuring American hops. The name celebrates beautiful Dovedale, which, brewer Adrian Corke reveals, is partly in Staffordshire as well as Derbyshire – a fact that is all too often ignored, he says.

Danebridge IPA

● **ABV 4.1%** ● **BOTTLE SIZE 500 ml** ● **SERVE cool**
● **INGREDIENTS Maris Otter pale malt/Fuggle and Cascade hops**

A golden ale named after a bridge in the Peak District National Park, near the village of Winkle.

TASTING NOTES

A pale golden beer with a sherbety, hoppy aroma laced with tropical fruit notes. The taste is sharp, hoppy and fruity, while the finish is also hoppy, but dry.

Staffordshire Bitter

● **ABV 4.2%** ● **BOTTLE SIZE 500 ml** ● **SERVE cool**
● **INGREDIENTS Maris Otter pale malt/crystal malt/Challenger hops**

An amber best bitter.

Black Grouse

● **ABV 4.5%** ● **BOTTLE SIZE 500 ml** ● **SERVE cool**
● **INGREDIENTS Maris Otter pale malt/crystal malt/chocolate malt/wheat malt/roasted barley/Fuggle and Bramling Cross hops**

A porter named after a rare bird that has been re-introduced recently to the local moorland.

TASTING NOTES

A very dark ruby/brown porter with a mellow coffee aroma. There's plenty of roasted grain bitterness in the taste but also a nice balance from a surprising amount of hops. Moderate, bitter, roasted finish.

Hen Cloud

● **ABV 4.5%** ● **BOTTLE SIZE 500 ml** ● **SERVE cool**
● **INGREDIENTS Maris Otter pale malt/lager malt/wheat malt/Golding hops**

A beer introduced in summer 2004 and named after a local hill.

St Edward's

● **ABV 4.7%** ● **BOTTLE SIZE 500 ml** ● **SERVE cool**
● **INGREDIENTS Maris Otter pale malt/crystal malt/wheat malt/Target and First Gold hops**

St Edward Street in Leek is home to the brewery tap, The Bull's Head.

TASTING NOTES

A red-amber ale with fruity hops and a hint of nut in the nose. The taste is bittersweet, nutty and fruity, and the finish is hoppy and bitter with some dark malt flavour persisting.

Rudyard Ruby

● ABV 4.8% ● BOTTLE SIZE 500 ml ● SERVE cool
● INGREDIENTS Maris Otter pale malt/crystal malt/chocolate malt/ Fuggle and First Gold hops
This brew takes its name from a local lake, which, apparently, gave its name to author Rudyard Kipling, too.

Leekenbrau

● ABV 5% ● BOTTLE SIZE 500 ml ● SERVE cool
● INGREDIENTS Lager malt/First Gold and Golding hops
A strong golden beer with German connections.

Strawberry/Peach Sunset

● ABV 5% ● BOTTLE SIZE 500 ml ● SERVE cool
● INGREDIENTS Maris Otter pale malt/wheat malt/Fuggle hops/ strawberries or peaches
Two golden, fruit-flavoured beers with the fruit added between the copper boil and fermentation.

Double Sunset

● ABV 5.2% ● BOTTLE SIZE 500 ml ● SERVE cool
● INGREDIENTS Maris Otter pale malt/wheat malt/Fuggle and First Gold hops
In summer, you can see two sunsets from Leek, as the sun disappears, and re-appears, behind the Bosley Cloud hills.

Leek Abbey Ale

● ABV 5.5% ● BOTTLE SIZE 500 ml ● SERVE cool
● INGREDIENTS Maris Otter pale malt/chocolate malt/wheat malt/ Fuggle and Challenger hops
A dark ruby beer for winter, named after the long-gone local abbey.

Cheddleton Steamer

● ABV 6% ● BOTTLE SIZE 500 ml ● SERVE cool
● INGREDIENTS Pale malt/wheat malt/hops not declared
A wheat beer in the German style. The name reflects the proximity of

the Cheddleton Steam Railway and the cloudy, steam-like appearance of the beer when sold in cask form (it tends to drop clear in the bottle).

Tittesworth Tipple

● ABV 6.5% ● BOTTLE SIZE 500 ml ● SERVE cool
● INGREDIENTS Maris Otter pale malt/wheat malt/Fuggle and Cascade hops

A golden wheat ale inspired by a local reservoir.

Little Valley

Little Valley Brewery Ltd., Turkey Lodge, New Road, Cragg Vale, Hebden Bridge, West Yorkshire HX7 5TT.
Tel. (01422) 883888 Fax (01422) 883222
E-mail: info@littlevalleybrewery.co.uk
Website: www.littlevalleybrewery.co.uk

Little Valley was opened in 2005 by Dutch brewer Wim van der Spek, previously of Black Isle Brewery and breweries in Germany and The Netherlands. His beers are all organic and approved by the Soil Association, as well as vegan, backed by Vegan Society accreditation. The attractively packaged bottles carry a 100% guarantee that, if they are found below standard within the best before period, they will be replaced. Prior to bottling, Wim kräusens the beers.

Withens IPA

● ABV 3.9% ● BOTTLE SIZE 500 ml ● SERVE cool
● INGREDIENTS Cellar pale malt/caramalt/wheat malt/Cascade and First Gold hops

Withens is the name of a reservoir a couple of miles from the brewery, from which Little Valley takes its water. A golden ale.

TASTING NOTES

The aroma is spicy and hoppy, with an orange note. There's more citrus in the crisp, hoppy taste, with bitterness and gentle malty sweetness. Soft, understated finish, until drying hops force their way through.

Cragg Vale Bitter

● ABV 4.2% ● BOTTLE SIZE 500 ml ● SERVE cool
● INGREDIENTS Cellar pale malt/crystal malt/wheat malt/Challenger and Golding hops

Cragg Vale is the peaceful corner of the Pennines that Little Valley calls home. Back in the 18th century, it was famous for its band of coin counterfeiters, who sneakily chipped bits of gold off legal coins for use in making forgeries.

TASTING NOTES

A refreshing and spritzy, golden beer with hop resins giving way to grapefruit notes in the aroma. The taste is also fresh and citrus-accented, with grapefruit-like hop notes providing bitterness and sweetness for balance coming from the malt. Citrus notes fade into a pithy hop bitterness in the dry finish.

Hebden's Wheat

● ABV 4.5% ● BOTTLE SIZE 500 ml ● SERVE cool

● INGREDIENTS Cellar pale malt/wheat malt/Hallertau and Hersbrucker hops/coriander seeds/lemon peel

Wim's Dutch roots show through in this variation on the theme of a witbier. The grist is half-and-half barley malt and wheat malt. Coriander seeds and lemon peel are added to the brew after it has passed through the whirlpool and before fermentation begins.

TASTING NOTES

A hazy yellow beer with a pleasant, lightly bready aroma of bubblegum, pepper and juicy lemons. The battle in the mouth is between tart citrus fruit and sweet cereals, with a keen bitter, hoppy edge and a gingery, peppery spiciness for good measure. Dry, bitter, hoppy finish with lingering tart lemon and spices.

Stoodley Stout

● ABV 4.8% ● BOTTLE SIZE 500 ml ● SERVE cool

● INGREDIENTS Cellar pale malt/crystal malt/chocolate malt/oats/ Pacific Gem and First Gold hops

This full-bodied stout takes its name from Stoodley Pike, a local hill crowned with an obelisk that can be seen for miles. The monument was placed there in 1856, at the end of the Crimean War, and is a well-known landmark.

TASTING NOTES

Dark ruby in colour, with biscuity coffee and a little plain chocolate in the nose. The taste is also biscuity and bittersweet, with coffee and dark chocolate flavours, a hint of iron and a little tart fruit. Heavily roasted grains come to the fore in the enjoyably bitter finish.

Tod's Blonde

● ABV 5% ● BOTTLE SIZE 500 ml ● SERVE cool
● INGREDIENTS Cellar lager malt/wheat malt/Pacific Gem and Hersbrucker hops

Todmorden is the next town along from the brewery, some five miles away. This is Wim's recreation of a Belgian blonde, but toned down in strength for the UK market.

TASTING NOTES

A yellow beer with a malty aroma tinged with tart fruit. The taste is unusual: malty, nutty and creamy-sweet, offset by sappy hops and warming alcohol notes. There's a little tart lemon on the swallow, before a drying, bitter, fairly thick finish.

Moor Ale

● ABV 5.5% ● BOTTLE SIZE 500 ml ● SERVE cool
● INGREDIENTS Cellar pale malt/Munich malt/peated malt/Pacific Gem and First Gold hops/heather

Designed to reflect the colour of local moorland in winter, this strong ale includes smoked peated malt. A few heather flowers are added after the whirlpool stage to emulate the aromas of the countryside.

TASTING NOTES

Dark golden, with a hint of red, this full-bodied ale features grassy hops, tart fruit and malt in the nose. Sweet, nutty malt continues in the mouth, balanced by tangy, grassy hop resins, some citrus sharpness and earthy spice. The finish is dry, bitter and hoppy, with lingering malt.

Lizard

Lizard Ales Ltd., Unit 2A, Treskewes Industrial Estate, St Keverne, Helston, Cornwall TR12 6PE. Tel. (01326) 281135

Small brewery which opened on the Lizard peninsula in 2004 and is run by former lawyer Mark Nattrass.

Kernow Gold

● ABV 3.7% ● BOTTLE SIZE 500 ml ● SERVE cool
● INGREDIENTS Not declared

Kernow is the Cornish name for Cornwall. The beer is also sold in cask form. Like the other two bottled beers, it is declared by the brewery to be acceptable to vegetarians.

TASTING NOTES
A dark golden beer with malt, toffee and grassy hop resins in the nose. Malt and assertive hops feature in the bittersweet taste with a spicy note and gentle toffee. Dry, bitter and hoppy aftertaste.

Bitter

● **ABV 4.2%** ● **BOTTLE SIZE 500 ml** ● **SERVE cool**
● **INGREDIENTS Not declared**

While the brewery refuses to disclose how the beers are bottled, or the ingredients of each beer, the label for Lizard Bitter does declare the use of Fuggle hops.

TASTING NOTES
A red best bitter with creamy, toffee-malt in the aroma, with a spicy note. The unusual taste is malty but savoury, with more toffee and hops. Dry, malty and increasingly hoppy finish.

An Gof

● **ABV 5.2%** ● **BOTTLE SIZE 500 ml** ● **SERVE cool**
● **INGREDIENTS Not declared**

From the label we know that An Gof is made using wood-smoked malts. It is named after Mychel Josef, a blacksmith from St Keverne ('an Gof' is Cornish for blacksmith) who led a Cornish rebellion against unfair taxes imposed by King Henry VII in 1497. He was defeated in London and brutally executed at Tyburn.

TASTING NOTES
Another red ale, with a malty nose, a full, bittersweet, malty taste with a keen, lightly fruity hop edge, and a drying, malty, increasingly hoppy and bitter aftertaste.

Loddon

The Loddon Brewery Ltd., Dunsden Green Farm, Church Lane, Dunsden, Oxfordshire RG4 9QD.
Tel. (0118) 948 1111 Fax (0118) 948 1010
E-mail: sales@loddonbrewery.com
Website: www.loddonbrewery.com

A 240-year-old brick and flint barn between Reading and Henley-on-Thames was extensively renovated to house Loddon Brewery when it was established in 2003. Chris and Vanessa Hearn run the business,

Chris using the sales skills he previously exercised at Batemans, Morrells and other companies. The brewery is large by microbrewing standards, with a capacity of 90 barrels. Its first bottle-conditioned beer arrived in 2005 and now there are plans to bottle two more draught brews: the sweet, nutty Hullabaloo and the chocolaty old ale, Hocus Pocus.

Ferryman's Gold

● ABV 4.8% ● BOTTLE SIZE 500 ml ● SERVE cool
● INGREDIENTS Maris Otter pale malt/caramalt/wheat malt/torrefied wheat/Fuggle and Styrian Golding hops

The brewery's flagship golden ale, Ferryman's had already won beer festival awards as a cask beer before Chris decided to bottle it. The beer is brewed to a higher original gravity than the cask version, but with the fermentation halted early, to leave plenty of unfermented sugars for bottle conditioning. It is then drawn off the fermenter without fining or filtration and shipped down the M4 to Swindon, where Arkell's conditions it for ten days and then bottles it with a fresh dose of an old Whitbread yeast. With fermentation resuming in the bottle, the finished product pours at around 4.8% (compared to the cask's 4.4%). Best before dates are set nine months post-bottling.

TASTING NOTES

A golden orange beer with bitter oranges and hop resins in the nose. The taste is bittersweet, with lots of citrus hop over a smooth, malty base. Drying, hoppy finish, with lingering orange and syrupy malt.

Major stockist Local Wetherspoon pubs

Mauldons

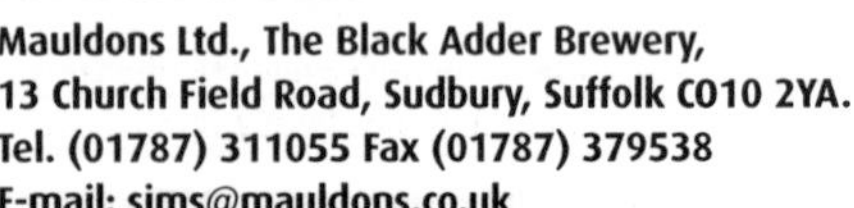

Mauldons Ltd., The Black Adder Brewery,
13 Church Field Road, Sudbury, Suffolk CO10 2YA.
Tel. (01787) 311055 Fax (01787) 379538
E-mail: sims@mauldons.co.uk
Website: www.mauldons.co.uk
Mail order service

Founded in 1982, Mauldons was set up by former Watney's brewer Peter Mauldon, who was keen to re-establish the family brewing name. Mauldons had brewed in Suffolk since the 1790s when the Sudbury premises was closed by its new owners, Greene King, at the turn of the 1960s. Peter's story is one of success, his most famous beer, Black

Adder, winning CAMRA's *Champion Beer of Britain* contest in 1991. He retired in 2000, selling the business to former Adnams salesman Steve Sims. Steve has sought to capitalize on the fame of Black Adder, adding the subtitle 'The Black Adder Brewery' to the Mauldons name and launching the beer in bottle. Three further bottle-conditioned beers have been added since. The beers are held for a week in conditioning tanks prior to bottling by an outside contractor, with 12-month best before dates applied. The brewery moved to larger premises in the same town in 2005.

May Bee

● ABV 3.9% ● BOTTLE SIZE 500 ml ● SERVE cool
● INGREDIENTS Maris Otter pale malt/Fuggle and Styrian Golding hops/honey

The latest addition to the bottled range, a honey-infused beer introduced in 2006, although the draught version dates back to 1990.

TASTING NOTES

A golden beer with a spicy, citrus, floral aroma and a honey accent. The taste is crisp and notably bitter for a honey beer, with a pronounced citrus/floral edge and just a little honey softness in the background. The finish is bitter, hoppy and dry.

Suffolk Pride

● ABV 4.8% ● BOTTLE SIZE 500 ml ● SERVE cool
● INGREDIENTS Maris Otter and Pearl pale malt/crystal malt/Golding and Fuggle hops

Suffolk Pride dates back even earlier than Black Adder, first rolling out in cask form in 1984. Great for washing down a curry, suggests Steve.

TASTING NOTES

The hoppy aroma of this golden beer leads to a pleasantly malty taste with a crisp, lightly fruity hop overlay. Bitter, malty, hoppy finish.
Major stockist Local Waitrose

Bah Humbug

● ABV 4.9% ● BOTTLE SIZE 500 ml ● SERVE cool
● INGREDIENTS Maris Otter and Pearl pale malt/Fuggle and Styrian Golding hops

The Christmas beer, first brewed for cask in 1991. It's a strong bitter to complement a cheese board, reckons Steve.

Black Adder ★

● ABV 5.3% ● BOTTLE SIZE 500 ml ● SERVE cool
● INGREDIENTS Maris Otter and Pearl pale malt/crystal malt/black malt/Fuggle hops

First brewed in 1988, when the *Blackadder* TV series was in its prime, this multi-award-winning beer was apparently named after a local vicar.

TASTING NOTES

Near-black, with ruby tints, Black Adder has coffeeish dark malt in the nose and follows this with a complex taste of mellow dark malt, chocolate and a pleasant bitterness that increases in the nutty, roasted malt finish. Easy to drink for its strength.

Major stockist Local Waitrose

Meantime

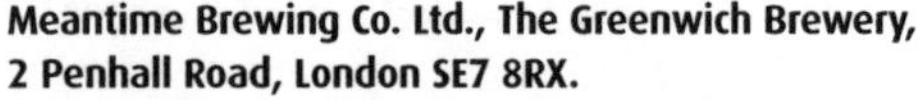

Meantime Brewing Co. Ltd., The Greenwich Brewery, 2 Penhall Road, London SE7 8RX.
Tel. (020) 8293 1111 Fax (020) 8293 4004
E-mail: info@meantimebrewing.co.uk
Website: www.meantimebrewing.co.uk

Meantime Brewing was set up by continental beer specialist Alastair Hook, who re-creates classic European beer styles (Belgian ales, kölsch, Viennese lagers, wheat beers, etc.) at his Greenwich base. Courtesy of Sainsbury's supermarkets, several of his bottled beers now grace the national stage, and the following are bottle conditioned. Some of these beers are imported to the USA by Artisanal Imports.

Taste the Difference Bavarian Style Wheat Beer

● ABV 5% ● BOTTLE SIZE 330 ml ● SERVE cold
● INGREDIENTS Pale malt/wheat malt/Perle and Northern Brewer hops

Taste the Difference Wheat Beer – which includes a hefty 65% wheat malt in its grist – is traditionally decoction mashed, fermented with a German wheat beer yeast and kräusened before bottling. To emphasise the fact that wheat beers are best drunk young, the best before date is set at just six months.

TASTING NOTES

A cloudy yellow beer with banana, hints of pineapple, apple and clove

in the nose. Sweet fruit leads the way in the mouth, with banana and tropical fruits up front and sharp lemon and lime behind, then a clove-like bitterness adds balance. The dry finish is increasingly bitter and clove-like but with lingering fruit and a touch of sourness.
Major stockist Sainsbury's

Taste the Difference Raspberry Wheat Beer

● **ABV 5%** ● **BOTTLE SIZE 330 ml** ● **SERVE cold**
● **INGREDIENTS Pale malt/wheat malt/raspberries/Perle and Northern Brewer hops**

Part of Sainsbury's *Taste the Difference* collection, Meantime's Raspberry Wheat Beer was launched in 2003, following the success of the brewery's other beers for the supermarket chain (most of these are filtered, but not pasteurized). The malt grist is split 50/50 between low-colour malt and wheat malt, and crushed raspberries are used for flavouring and to help the bottle fermentation. The best before date is set at nine months. A treat with a bar of chocolate, claims Alastair.

TASTING NOTES

A hazy red-gold beer with raspberries, a little nut and a vanilla creaminess in the nose. Raspberry sharpness in the mouth is tempered by just enough sweetness to make this a tart, but quenching, drink. Dry, increasingly bitter, raspberry finish.
Major stockist Sainsbury's

Coffee Beer ★

● **ABV 6%** ● **BOTTLE SIZE 330 ml** ● **SERVE cool**
● **INGREDIENTS Pale malt/brown malt/chocolate malt/black malt/other malts/Fuggle hops/coffee**

Alastair conceived this beer while attending the *World Beer Cup* in the USA. He was judging the category for coffee beers and realized that most beers added coffee to a stout base, whereas, in his mind, a softer, less astringent porter base would be more compatible. Initially brewed to only 4%, Meantime's Coffee Beer has now been boosted to 6% and brought things back full circle when it won the gold medal itself in the *World Beer Cup* in 2006. Although the full list of ingredients is not declared, we do know that Fairtrade coffee from Rwanda is added to the porter to create this distinctive beer. Try it instead of coffee after a meal, but bear in mind that it does contain caffeine. The best before date is fixed at 12 months after bottling.

TASTING NOTES
A deep garnet-coloured beer with a rich fresh coffee bean and chocolate aroma (like walking past Starbuck's). Good roasted coffee flavours dominate the taste, but without overwhelming the creaminess in the background and the fine balance of bitterness and sweetness. Coffee fills the finish, too, but this is only gentle bitter.
Major stockist Sainsbury's

Wheat Grand Cru

● ABV 6.3% ● BOTTLE SIZE 330/750 ml ● SERVE cold
● INGREDIENTS Pale malt/wheat malt/Perle and Northern Brewer hops
First brewed in spring 2005 as a premium version of Meantime's popular wheat beer. Choose a small bottle for one, or a larger one to share, and drink it with shellfish, salads or white meats. The best before date is set at six months.
TASTING NOTES
A golden beer with bubblegum, banana and cloves in the nose. More banana follows in the mouth, with warming, spicy alcohol, sharp apple, faint vanilla, a spike of clove and a touch of sourness. Dry banana finish with a clove bitterness.

Chocolate

● ABV 6.5% ● BOTTLE SIZE 330 ml ● SERVE cool
● INGREDIENTS Pale malt/chocolate malt/other dark malts/Fuggle hops/chocolate
A rich beer containing real chocolate, to enhance and complement the dark malty flavours of the mash. Like other Meantime beers, this is acceptable to vegetarians. Six months' best before date.
TASTING NOTES
A ruby ale with chocolate and vanilla in the aroma. Creamy chocolate flavours lead in the taste, but bitter roasted notes see off the initial sweetness. Roasted malts linger in the dry, bitter chocolate finish.
Major stockist Sainsbury's

London Porter ★

● ABV 6.5% ● BOTTLE SIZE 750 ml ● SERVE cool
● INGREDIENTS Pale malt/brown malt/chocolate malt/black malt/other malts/Fuggle hops

Porter, in the 18th century, was a blend of three types of beer. This authentic reproduction similarly blends young and aged beer and in total employs seven varieties of malt to re-create, using modern materials, a drop of London's history. Like the India Pale Ale below, London Porter is packaged in 750 ml Champagne-style bottles, topped with a cork and wire cage.

TASTING NOTES

A deep ruby porter with a biscuity, dark chocolate aroma. Biscuity, sweet malt continues on the palate, along with dark chocolate, coffee, gentle liquorice and a light spiciness. Good airy body. The finish is dry, chocolaty and biscuity, with a touch of liquorice and lasting bitter coffee.

Major stockist Sainsbury's

Raspberry Grand Cru

● **ABV 6.5%** ● **BOTTLE SIZE 330 ml** ● **SERVE cold**
● **INGREDIENTS Pale malt/wheat malt/raspberry fruit extract/Perle and Northern Brewer hops**

A beefed-up version of the beer Meantime sells very successfully on draught. It comes in the distinctive mini-Champagne bottles that Meantime uses for all its beers. One to try with chocolate puddings or soft cheeses, perhaps. Six months' best before date.

TASTING NOTES

Gold with a blush of red. Raspberries dominate the nose, taste and finish, but there's more sweetness here than in Meantime's other raspberry beer. Bitterness builds in the dry aftertaste.

India Pale Ale ★

● **ABV 7.5%** ● **BOTTLE SIZE 330 ml** ● **SERVE cool**
● **INGREDIENTS Maris Otter pale malt/Fuggle and Golding hops**

First brewed in spring 2005, after lengthy research into the origins of the first India pale ales, this is another painstaking historical re-creation. The beer is matured prior to bottling, a dry hopping procedure takes place and then the beer is filled, without re-seeding with new yeast or priming with sugars. The best before date is set at five years and you are advised to allow it to mature awhile in the bottle. The brewers describe it as 'the original curry beer'.

TASTING NOTES

A dark golden IPA with an aroma packed with enticing hop resins and the zest of orange peel. The taste is equally loaded, bursting with

tangy, peppery hops and bitter citrus fruit with full malt support. The dry finish is lip-smackingly hoppy and long lasting.
Major stockist Sainsbury's

Mersea Island

Mersea Island Brewery, Rewsalls Lane, East Mersea, Colchester, Essex CO5 8SX. Tel. (01206) 385900
E-mail: roger.barber@merseawine.com
Website: www.merseawine.com

This brewery was set up on a family-owned vineyard in 2005. They also offer bed & breakfast accommodation and holiday lets, if you fancy learning more about the beers and wines while exploring the Essex coast. All the beers are sterile filtered, primed with sugar syrup and re-seeded with fresh, bottom-fermenting yeast for bottling, with six-month best before dates applied.

Island Pale Ale

● **ABV 3.9%** ● **BOTTLE SIZE 500 ml** ● **SERVE cool**
● **INGREDIENTS Maris Otter pale malt/caramalt/black malt/Fuggle, Challenger, Phoenix and Cascade hops**

Based on the brewery's cask bitter, Yo Boy, this beer was, like the other bottled ales, introduced in January 2006.

TASTING NOTES

A dark golden ale with a Horlicks maltiness giving way to fruity hop in the aroma. The taste is hoppy and gently perfumed, with sweet malt support. Dry, hoppy aftertaste.

Island Gold

● **ABV 4.5%** ● **BOTTLE SIZE 500 ml** ● **SERVE cool**
● **INGREDIENTS Lager malt/crystal malt/wheat malt/Perle and Hersbrucker hops**

An ale that's been made to resemble a lager, through its selection of malts and hops. The brewers say it goes down a treat with summer barbecues.

TASTING NOTES

A quaffable golden bitter featuring a lightly malty aroma with gentle lemon notes. Lemony hops continue in the rather delicate, bittersweet taste and in the dry finish.

Island Monkeys

● ABV 4.5% ● BOTTLE SIZE 500 ml ● SERVE cool
● INGREDIENTS Maris Otter pale malt/crystal malt/caramalt/wheat malt/roasted barley/Fuggle and Golding hops
Described by the brewery as 'a strong stout/porter style with a good liquorice flavour'.
TASTING NOTES
A deep ruby stout with biscuity, creamy dark malts, plain chocolate and liquorice in the aroma. Bitter dark malts continue in the mouth, along with plain chocolate, before a very dry, bitter chocolate finish. There's very little sweetness, making this an unusual, uncompromising drink.

Island Stout

● ABV 5% ● BOTTLE SIZE 500 ml ● SERVE cool
● INGREDIENTS Maris Otter pale malt/crystal malt/caramalt/chocolate malt/black malt/Fuggle hops
Described as 'a mild stout'. In contrast to Island Monkeys, it certainly is.
TASTING NOTES
A soft ruby stout with a lightly fruity then creamy, chocolaty nose. More light, creamy chocolate leads in the taste, which is mostly bitter but rather mellow. Dry, chocolaty finish.

Millstone

Millstone Brewery Ltd., Unit 4 Vale Mill, Micklehurst Road, Mossley, Lancashire OL5 9JL. Tel./Fax (01457) 835835
E-mail: info@millstonebrewery.co.uk
Website: www.millstonebrewery.co.uk
Millstone Brewery was set up in 2003 in a former textile mill by friends Nick Boughton and Jon Hunt. They now sell beer to more than 100 outlets and started bottling in autumn 2004. The bottled beers are generally only sold in local outlets. In addition to the beers listed, Millstone may also bottle its Christmas Ruby (4.7%) in winter.

Three Shires Bitter

● ABV 4% ● BOTTLE SIZE 500 ml ● SERVE cool
● INGREDIENTS Golden Promise pale malt/First Gold, Golding and Liberty hops
The brewery stands at the junction of three counties – Yorkshire,

Lancashire and Cheshire – hence the name of this pale, hoppy bitter, the first beer ever produced by Millstone.

Windy Miller

● ABV 4.1% ● BOTTLE SIZE 500 ml ● SERVE cool
● INGREDIENTS Golden Promise pale malt/pale rye malt/Green Bullet and Pilot hops

Originally brewed to celebrate Saddleworth's Whit Friday Brass Band Contest. The unusual ingredients include Green Bullet hops from New Zealand and also Pilot, a dwarf hop which has now been discontinued. First Gold may be used as a replacement in future.

Grain Storm

● ABV 4.2% ● BOTTLE SIZE 500 ml ● SERVE cool
● INGREDIENTS Golden Promise pale malt/crystal wheat malt/Green Bullet and Pacific Hallertau hops

There are more New Zealand hops in this golden bitter, which, like the other beers, is bottled in house after being primed with cane sugar.

Autumn Leaves

● ABV 4.3% ● BOTTLE SIZE 500 ml ● SERVE cool
● INGREDIENTS Golden Promise pale malt/dark crystal malt/Hilary and Cascade hops

This seasonal brew will also need a replacement hop as the dwarf hop Hilary, like Pilot mentioned above, has been discontinued. A copper-coloured ale with a name inspired by the jazz standard.

Millstone Edge

● ABV 4.4% ● BOTTLE SIZE 500 ml ● SERVE cool
● INGREDIENTS Golden Promise pale malt/crystal malt/First Gold, Golding and Fuggle hops

Millstone Edge is a rocky outcrop about three miles from the brewery. The beer that shares its name is an amber premium bitter.

True Grit

● ABV 5% ● BOTTLE SIZE 500 ml ● SERVE cool
● INGREDIENTS Golden Promise pale malt/Chinook hops

The hops this time are American and the beer name refers to rock found in the nearby Pennines (rather than the John Wayne film).

Moor

Moor Beer Company, Whitley Farm, Ashcott, Somerset TA7 9QW.
Tel./Fax (01458) 210050
E-mail: arthur@moorbeer.co.uk
Website: www.moorbeer.co.uk
Mail order service

Moor Beer Company was founded on a dairy farm (now a pig farm) by Arthur Frampton in 1996. Brewing ceased temporarily in 2005 when the equipment was sold to the Otley Brewery in South Wales, which then produced Moor's beers for a while. However, a new ten-barrel brewery was due to be installed at Moor in summer 2006. The three beers listed here are bottled by Leek Brewery, with best before dates set at six months.

Merlins Magic

● **ABV 4.3%** ● **BOTTLE SIZE 500 ml** ● **SERVE cool**
● **INGREDIENTS Maris Otter pale malt/crystal malt/amber malt/ Fuggle and Liberty hops**

Conjuring up dreamy images of the myths and legends of the South West, Merlins Magic, already an established cask ale, was first bottle conditioned back in spring 1999.

TASTING NOTES

A red beer with a malty, appley aroma. Dryish, fruity and malty to taste, it ends in a dry, bitter, malty finish.

Peat Porter

● **ABV 4.5%** ● **BOTTLE SIZE 500 ml** ● **SERVE cool**
● **INGREDIENTS Maris Otter pale malt/crystal malt/amber malt/ chocolate malt/Bramling Cross and Fuggle hops**

First brewed in 1997, this beer remembers the 'peat porters', the labourers who carried peat from the local moorland in years gone by and stacked it ready for use. Despite the name, there is no peated malt included in the recipe, so don't expect any smoky or whisky-like flavours.

TASTING NOTES

A ruby beer with a biscuity, dark malt nose. The bittersweet taste has a light fruitiness, backed by dark, coffeeish malt flavours. Dry, bitter, roasted malt finish, featuring plain chocolate and gentle coffee.

Old Freddy Walker

● ABV 7.3% ● BOTTLE SIZE 500 ml ● SERVE cool
● INGREDIENTS Maris Otter pale malt/crystal malt/black malt/ Nugget and Liberty hops

Old Freddy Walker, Moor's first bottled beer, appeared in 1998 and is named after an old seaman who used to live in the brewery's village. It is also available in cask form and is one of the more unusual and novel beers in this book, being brewed with Nugget hops, which are known for their high alpha acid content. Alpha acids are responsible for bitterness, so, generally speaking, you don't need so many of them to make an impact. Blended with Liberty hops into a mash produced from a complex dark malt grist, they produce a dangerously drinkable, deceptively strong brew with a full fruitiness. These attributes helped Old Freddy collect the silver medal at the *Tucker's Maltings Bottled Beer Competition* (for beers brewed in the South West) in 1999. The cask version was voted CAMRA's *Champion Winter Beer of Britain* in 2004.

TASTING NOTES

A ruby ale with a coffee-coloured head. The berry-fruity, toffeeish, malty aroma is followed by a full, complex taste in which sweet dark malt flavours are topped with juicy, vinous, citrus and berry fruits. The aftertaste is dry, bittersweet and fruity with dark malts.

Moulin

Moulin Brewery, 2 Baledmund Road, Moulin, by Pitlochry, Perthshire & Kinross PH16 5EH.
Tel. (01796) 472196 Fax (01796) 474098
E-mail: enquiries@moulinhotel.co.uk
Website: www.moulinhotel.co.uk

Moulin Brewery was opened in 1995 at the Moulin Hotel in Pitlochry, during celebrations for the hotel's 300th anniversary (the hotel housed a brewery when it opened in 1695, so it was deemed fitting to recommence brewing on the site). Brewing has been relocated since to the Old Coach House opposite the main building.

Ale of Atholl

● ABV 4.5% ● BOTTLE SIZE 500 ml ● SERVE cool
● INGREDIENTS Maris Otter pale malt/crystal malt/chocolate malt/ roasted malt/Fuggle hops

Ale of Atholl (taking its name from the brewery's location in the Vale of Atholl, an area in which it is more common to find whisky distilleries than breweries) was first bottle conditioned in late 1996. The beer is allowed to settle in tank and then bottled, with more yeast and sugar added, in glassware overprinted with the history of Moulin village.

TASTING NOTES

A ruby beer with a fruity, malty, lightly chocolaty nose with hop resin notes. Fruity, citrus hops and dark malt are well balanced in the dry taste. Dark malt and hops emerge again in the dry, gently bitter finish.

North Cotswold

North Cotswold Brewery, Ditchford Farm, Moreton-in-Marsh, Gloucestershire GL56 9RD. Tel. (01608) 663947
E-mail: ncb@pillingweb.co.uk
Website: www.northcotswoldbrewery.co.uk

North Cotswold Brewery was founded in 1999 but was taken over by former Firkin and other company brewer Jon Pilling in 2005. His ten-barrel brewkit turns out cask beers for the local trade, as well as the four bottle-conditioned beers featured below, which are filtered and re-seeded with fresh yeast prior to bottling. Long (two-year) best before dates are applied.

Summer Solstice

● **ABV 4.5%** ● **BOTTLE SIZE 500 ml** ● **SERVE cool**
● **INGREDIENTS Lager malt/wheat/Saaz and Hersbrucker hops/ coriander**

Summer Solstice is Jon's wheat beer, an English take on the genre.

TASTING NOTES

A very pale golden beer with a hoppy, lemony sharpness in the aroma. The taste is bittersweet and lemony, too, with a tartness drying the palate all the time. Very dry, bitter finish.

Hung Drawn n'Portered

● **ABV 5%** ● **BOTTLE SIZE 500 ml** ● **SERVE cool**
● **INGREDIENTS Maris Otter pale malt/crystal malt/chocolate malt/ black malt/wheat/Bramling Cross and Fuggle hops/black treacle**

First brewed in January 2005, Hung Drawn n'Portered has already picked up beer festival awards in its cask version.

Stour Stout

● ABV 5% ● BOTTLE SIZE 500 ml ● SERVE cool
● INGREDIENTS Maris Otter pale malt/crystal malt/chocolate malt/dark roasted malt/wheat/Golding and Fuggle hops

An Irish-style stout, named after the nearby River Stour.

TASTING NOTES

An attractive ruby beer with a biscuity, chocolaty aroma. There's more biscuity malt in the taste, along with bitter roasted grain, while the finish is dry, malty and roasted, with coffee taking over. Light bodied.

Blitzen

● ABV 6% ● BOTTLE SIZE 500 ml ● SERVE cool
● INGREDIENTS Maris Otter pale malt/crystal malt/roasted malt/wheat/Golding and Fuggle hops/dried fruit/treacle/cloves/nutmeg/cinnamon sticks/root ginger/all spice

First brewed in November 2005 and still only produced once a year, in time for Christmas, this is a beer Jon describes as 'liquid Christmas pudding'. It goes well with rich meats and game, he adds.

TASTING NOTES

An amber-red ale with Christmas spices in the nose – nutmeg and cinnamon particularly – over toffeeish malt. The same maltiness and spices continue in the mouth, before a dry, chewy, bitter finish.

North Yorkshire

North Yorkshire Brewing Company Ltd., Pinchinthorpe Hall, Guisborough, North Yorkshire TS14 8HG. Tel./Fax (01287) 630200
E-mail: nyb@pinchinthorpe.freeserve.co.uk
Website: www.pinchinthorpehall.co.uk
Mail order service

North Yorkshire was founded in Middlesbrough in 1989 and moved in 1998 to Pinchinthorpe Hall, a moated, listed house that was home to the noble Lee family and their descendants for centuries until 1957. The house now also includes a hotel and restaurant, and its own spring water is used for brewing. All the beers are registered as organic. In addition to the beers featured, the following draught beers are also bottled at times: Golden Ginseng (3.6%), Crystal Tips (4%), Love Muscle (4%), Honey Bunny (4.2%), Xmas Herbert (4.4%), Blonde (4.6%), White Lady (4.7%), Cosmic Glow (4.8%), Northern Star (4.8%), Shooting

Star (4.8%), Southern Cross (4.8%) and Rocket Fuel (5%). New labels have been introduced in recent years.

Best Bitter

● **ABV 3.6%** ● **BOTTLE SIZE 500 ml** ● **SERVE cool**
● **INGREDIENTS Maris Otter pale malt/First Gold hops**

A pale bitter, bottled, like the other beers, on site directly from casks, after the beer has been matured. Best before dates are set at one year.

TASTING NOTES

A golden beer with a lightly hoppy, bubblegum aroma. In the mouth it is clean, bittersweet and fruity, with a crisp, but light, hop edge. Hops and bitterness grow, but fruit lingers, in the drying finish.

Prior's Ale

● **ABV 3.6%** ● **BOTTLE SIZE 500 ml** ● **SERVE cool**
● **INGREDIENTS Maris Otter pale malt/First Gold hops**

A beer commemorating the fact that one of the Lee family, Walter de Thorpe, was Prior of Guisborough (1393–1408), where the hall stands.

TASTING NOTES

Light malt and hop compete with bubblegum in the nose of this golden session ale. The taste balances malt and tangy hop, giving a hint of tart fruit. Tangy hop lingers in the finish.

Archbishop Lee's Ruby Ale

● **ABV 4%** ● **BOTTLE SIZE 500 ml** ● **SERVE cool**
● **INGREDIENTS Maris Otter pale malt/chocolate malt/First Gold hops**

There was not only a prior in the family, but an Archbishop of York, too (1531–44).

TASTING NOTES

An amber ale with a spicy malt nose. Malt also leads in the bittersweet taste, supported by citrus hop, before a dry, bittersweet, hoppy finish.

Boro Best

● **ABV 4%** ● **BOTTLE SIZE 500 ml** ● **SERVE cool**
● **INGREDIENTS Maris Otter pale malt/chocolate malt/First Gold hops**

'A northern, rounded, full-bodied beer', according to the new label. Its name refers back to the brewery's first home over on Teesside.

TASTING NOTES

Amber in colour, this best bitter has a malt and bubblegum nose and a sweetish, gentle taste of malt and hops. More hop adds some bitterness to the aftertaste.

Cereal Killer

● ABV 4.5% ● BOTTLE SIZE 500 ml ● SERVE cool
● INGREDIENTS Maris Otter pale malt/wheat malt/First Gold hops
A wheaty addition to the range.
TASTING NOTES
A golden beer, with a bready aroma of light banana and clove. The taste is bittersweet and gently bready, with a hop sharpness and soft lemon and clove flavours. Dry, bitter, slightly chewy aftertaste.

Fools Gold

● ABV 4.6% ● BOTTLE SIZE 500 ml ● SERVE cool
● INGREDIENTS Maris Otter pale malt/First Gold hops
The name of this premium ale combines the historic setting of the brewery and the use of organic First Gold hops. A medieval jester ('a fool') features on the label.
TASTING NOTES
Suggestions of bubblegum feature in the aroma of this golden beer, which also has a light, hoppy, melon-fruity fragrance. The taste is mostly bitter with soft fruit and malt. Bitter hops dominate the finish.

Golden Ale

● ABV 4.6% ● BOTTLE SIZE 500 ml ● SERVE cool
● INGREDIENTS Maris Otter pale malt/First Gold hops
As for all the other beers, this strong pale ale carries a certification stamp from the Organic Food Federation.
TASTING NOTES
Light tart fruit features in the nose, while sweetish malt is countered by fruity hop in the taste but retains the upper hand. Bittersweet, fruity finish, with increasing hop.

Flying Herbert

● ABV 4.7% ● BOTTLE SIZE 500 ml ● SERVE cool
● INGREDIENTS Maris Otter pale malt/chocolate malt/First Gold hops
One of North Yorkshire's earliest brews, with a daft name plucked out of the air by brewer George Tinsley's sister. The airborne hero in the name is depicted in cartoon form on the label.

TASTING NOTES
A red beer with malt and a little hop in the aroma. There's a good hop counter to sweet, nutty malt in the taste, and a hoppy, nutty, dry aftertaste.

Lord Lee's

● **ABV 4.7%** ● **BOTTLE SIZE 500 ml** ● **SERVE cool**
● **INGREDIENTS Maris Otter pale malt/chocolate malt/First Gold hops**
Named after Sir Richard Lee, a family member who became Lord Mayor of London (1460 and 1469).
TASTING NOTES
Amber, with a dense, creamy head, Lord Lee's is spicy and malty to the nose, with a fine balance of malt and hops in the mouth. Bitterness grows in the malty finish.

Dizzy Dick

● **ABV 4.8%** ● **BOTTLE SIZE 500 ml** ● **SERVE cool**
● **INGREDIENTS Maris Otter pale malt/chocolate malt/First Gold hops**
A strong, dark beer, long in North Yorkshire's brewing portfolio.
TASTING NOTES
A bronze beer with a soft malty, lightly chocolaty aroma. Smooth malt leads in the mouth, with light chocolate and a good, spicy, peppery hop balance. Bitter, malty, nutty aftertaste.

O'Hanlon's

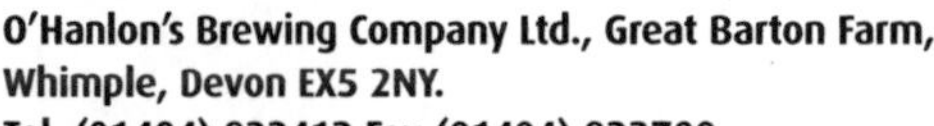

O'Hanlon's Brewing Company Ltd., Great Barton Farm, Whimple, Devon EX5 2NY.
Tel. (01404) 822412 Fax (01404) 823700
E-mail: info@ohanlonsbrewery.com
Website: www.ohanlons.co.uk
Mail order service
O'Hanlon's was set up in 1996 to serve John O'Hanlon's pub in Clerkenwell, London, but quickly expanded to supply other outlets. In 2000, he sold the pub and moved the brewery to Devon. The bottling operation has expanded considerably and the brewery has now secured the contract to brew and market the revered Thomas Hardy's Ale, as well as its old stablemate, Royal Oak. Beers are imported into the US by Phoenix Imports and O'Hanlon's is active in other export markets, too.

Double Champion Wheat Beer

● ABV 4% ● BOTTLE SIZE 500 ml ● SERVE cool
● INGREDIENTS Optic pale malt/wheat malt/caramalt/Challenger, First Gold and Cascade hops/coriander seeds

A wheat beer in the Belgian style, low on bitterness but laced with aromatic hops (First Gold and Cascade are the late hops) and spiced with coriander seeds. Prior to bottling, the beer is filtered and re-seeded with dried bottling yeast. Winner of SIBA's *Wheat Beer Challenge* 1999 and 2002, hence the addition of 'Double Champion' to the beer's name. Drink with oriental foods or even good old fish and chips, suggest the brewers.

TASTING NOTES

A golden beer with a lightly spiced, lemon-orange peel aroma. The taste is orange peel bitter, lightly perfumed and dry, and the finish is dry, bitter and slightly bready, with lingering orange and perfume notes.
Major stockists Booths, Thresher, local Majestic

Yellowhammer

● ABV 4.2% ● BOTTLE SIZE 500 ml ● SERVE cool
● INGREDIENTS Optic pale malt/caramalt/First Gold and Cascade hops

A golden beer with a complex hopping regime: First Gold hops are used for bitterness, Cascades are the late hop and then the beer is dry hopped with more First Gold. Runner-up at the *Tucker's Maltings Bottled Beer Competition* in 2003.

TASTING NOTES

A soft, malty beer with a light 'sherbet lemons' fruitiness. Well-balanced and clean.

Original Port Stout ★

● ABV 4.8% ● BOTTLE SIZE 500 ml ● SERVE cool
● INGREDIENTS Optic pale malt/crystal malt/caramalt/roasted barley/flaked barley/Phoenix and Styrian Golding hops/port

A 'corpse reviver', in the Irish tradition of hang-over cures, this dry stout is enhanced by the addition of Ferreira port prior to bottling, at a ratio of two bottles per brewer's barrel (36 gallons), which raises the strength from 4.6 to 4.8%. The cask version was one of O'Hanlon's early beers – the port was added to mark out the cask beer from a popular keg stout John's pub also sold – and this bottled equivalent was introduced in 2000. In 2001, it claimed the gold medal at *Tucker's*

Maltings Bottled Beer Competition. The draught version then took the top stout prize in CAMRA's *Champion Winter Beer of Britain* awards for 2002, while this bottled version was CAMRA's *Champion Bottled Beer* in 2003. Phoenix is the main bittering hop, with Styrian Goldings added late for aroma. The beer is lightly fined prior to bottling.

TASTING NOTES

A ruby-brown beer with fruit in the biscuity, roasted barley nose. This is a classic, dry, bitter stout in the mouth, with more than a trace of winey fruit. Dry, roasted, bitter finish.

Major stockists Booths, local Majestic, Sainsbury's and Waitrose

Good Will

● ABV 5% ● BOTTLE SIZE 500 ml ● SERVE cool

● INGREDIENTS Optic pale malt/crystal malt/torrefied wheat/ Challenger, Northdown, Styrian Golding and Amarillo hops

The brewery's Christmas ale, now also in bottle in and around the festive season. Note the use of American Amarillo hops.

Royal Oak

● ABV 5% ● BOTTLE SIZE 500 ml ● SERVE cool

● INGREDIENTS Optic pale malt/crystal malt/torrefied wheat/ Challenger, Northdown and Golding hops

Like the celebrated Hardy's Ale featured below, Royal Oak – first brewed in 1896 – was another great beer that Eldridge Pope threw away when it left brewing. O'Hanlon's has revived the brew and made it bottle conditioned for the first time. The label recommends it with grilled meats or a cheeseboard.

TASTING NOTES

An amber beer with pleasant sweet esters at first on the nose, followed by malt and apricots. The taste is robust, hoppy and malty, with apricot notes, although perhaps not quite as sweet and fruity as the Royal Oak of old. Big, hoppy finish.

Major stockists Booths, local Asda, Majestic, Morrisons and Sainsbury's

Thomas Hardy's Ale ★

● ABV 11.7% ● BOTTLE SIZE 330 ml ● SERVE cool

● INGREDIENTS Low-colour pale malt/crystal malt/Northdown, Challenger, Styrian Golding and Golding hops

A bottled classic, Hardy's Ale was created by Dorchester brewer Eldridge

Pope in 1968 to commemorate the 40th anniversary of the death of Wessex writer Thomas Hardy. Its inspiration was a passage in Hardy's novel *The Trumpet-Major*, which described Dorchester's strong beer thus:

'It was of the most beautiful colour that the eye of an artist in beer could desire; full in body, yet brisk as a volcano; piquant, yet without a twang; luminous as an autumn sunset; free from streakiness of taste but, finally, rather heady.'

This famous quote was recalled on the label of each individually numbered bottle of Hardy's Ale. The beer seemed lost forever when Eldridge Pope (now no longer in brewing) lost interest in the beer after the 1999 vintage. However, following an absence of four years, Hardy's was brought back to life by O'Hanlon's, in conjunction with Phoenix Imports, which bought the brand and sees a future for it in the US. The beer enjoys two-and-a-half weeks of primary fermentation, three months of secondary fermentation, and a month of cold conditioning and dry hopping, before being fined and bottled. O'Hanlon's recommends ageing the beer for at least nine months before sampling.

TASTING NOTES

From the red hue of its 'autumn sunset luminosity' to its sweet, fruity finish and lingering hop tang, this re-creation is as complex and absorbing as the original Hardy. The big taste has pronounced melon flavours and loads of warm, malty sweetness, and hints of cherry poke through the estery fruit that emerges. Probably needs more time in the bottle and should mature nicely.

Major stockists Booths, local Majestic

Oakleaf

Oakleaf Brewing Company Ltd., 7 Clarence Wharf Industrial Estate, Mumby Road, Gosport, Hampshire PO12 1AJ.
Tel. (023 92) 513222 Fax (023 92) 510148
E-mail: info@oakleafbrewing.co.uk
Website: www.oakleafbrewing.co.uk

Ed Anderson, a former Firkin brew pub brewer, set up Oakleaf with his father-in-law, Dave Pickersgill, in 2000. Their industrial unit home stands on the side of Gosport harbour. They brew and bottle the following beers in house, with each beer filtered, re-seeded with fresh yeast and given a best before date 12 months after bottling.

Maypole Mild

ABV 3.8% • BOTTLE SIZE 500 ml • SERVE cool
• INGREDIENTS Optic pale malt/crystal malt/chocolate malt/roasted barley/Fuggle and Golding hops
A traditional dark mild. The cask version picked up a gold medal at the SIBA (Society of Independent Brewers) national championship in 2004.

Bitter

• ABV 3.8% • BOTTLE SIZE 500 ml • SERVE cool
• INGREDIENTS Optic pale malt/crystal malt/Fuggle, First Gold and Styrian Golding hops
The brewery's standard bitter was introduced in bottled form in 2004.

Heart of Oak

• ABV 4.5% • BOTTLE SIZE 500 ml • SERVE cool
• INGREDIENTS Optic pale malt/crystal malt/chocolate malt/Golding, Cascade, Brewer's Gold and Bramling Cross hops
Brewed initially to mark the 200th anniversary of the Battle of Trafalgar, Heart of Oak is named after the old sailors' song.

It's Not Bitter

• ABV 4.9% • BOTTLE SIZE 500 ml • SERVE cold
• INGREDIENTS Lager malt/Saaz hops
Originally known by its full name of I Can't Believe It's Not Bitter, making a play on the name of well-known spreading margarine, this is Oakleaf's lager.

Hole Hearted

• ABV 4.7% • BOTTLE SIZE 500 ml • SERVE cool
• INGREDIENTS Optic pale malt/caramalt/torrefied wheat/ Cascade hops
This golden ale (good with spicy foods, white meats and fish, it is claimed) takes its name from the fact that it was originally brewed for sale at the Hole in the Wall pub in Southsea. The cask version was CAMRA's *Champion Beer of Hampshire* in 2002 and 2003, while this bottled companion was a SIBA regional champion in 2003.

TASTING NOTES
An explosion of grapefruit notes awaits you in the aroma and taste of this premium ale, with a light malty sweetness in the background. The

bitter, tangy Cascade hops linger on in the finish.
Major stockist Local Waitrose

Blake's Gosport Bitter

● ABV 5.2% ● BOTTLE SIZE 500 ml ● SERVE cool
● INGREDIENTS Optic pale malt/crystal malt/chocolate malt/flaked barley/Fuggle and Golding hops

This dark ale commemorates the old Blake's Brewery in Gosport, which was taken over in 1926 and eventually closed. A beer to go with steaks and other red meats, the brewers suggest.

TASTING NOTES

A ruby ale with a malty, chocolaty nose. Dark malt leads in the bittersweet taste with persistent, fruity hops in the background. Roasted malt takes over in the bitter finish, but hop-fruit lingers.

Eichenblatt Bitte

● ABV 5.4% ● BOTTLE SIZE 500 ml ● SERVE cool
● INGREDIENTS Smoked malt/wheat malt/Styrian Golding and Saaz hops

Here's an unusual offering: a smoked wheat beer. The name translates as 'An oakleaf, please'.

Blake's Heaven

● ABV 7% ● BOTTLE SIZE 500 ml ● SERVE cool
● INGREDIENTS Optic pale malt/crystal malt/chocolate malt/flaked barley/Fuggle and Golding hops

This is a stronger version of Blake's Gosport Bitter, but is only available in winter months.

Old Bear

Old Bear Brewery, Unit 4B, Atlas Works, Pitt Street, Keighley, West Yorkshire BD21 4YL. Tel./Fax (01535) 601222
Website: www.oldbearbrewery.com
Mail order service

Small brewery founded in 1993 as Old White Bear Brewery, and later undergoing a change of ownership as well as name. A move to new, custom-designed premises took place in 2004. The beers featured opposite are now bottled by hand in house.

Original

● **ABV 3.9%** ● **BOTTLE SIZE 500 ml** ● **SERVE cool**
● **INGREDIENTS Maris Otter pale malt/crystal malt/pale chocolate malt/black malt/torrefied wheat/flaked barley/Fuggle, Golding, Saaz and Progress hops**

Originally called Best Bitter, when brewed at the old brewery and re-named when the brewery moved. As for all three beers, Original is racked bright and then primed with corn sugar, powdered glucose and dried malt prior to bottling. A one-year best before date is applied. The label describes it as 'The "no codswallop" bitter'.

TASTING NOTES

A copper ale with a sulphurous, malty aroma. The taste is dry and hoppy, with a little malt sweetness for balance. Bitter, hoppy, dry finish.

Goldilocks

● **ABV 4.5%** ● **BOTTLE SIZE 500 ml** ● **SERVE cool**
● **INGREDIENTS Lager malt/wheat malt/torrefied wheat/roasted barley/Golding, Northern Brewer, Fuggle and Crystal hops**

A blond beer, described on the label as 'Yorkshire Lager'.

Hibernator

● **ABV 5%** ● **BOTTLE SIZE 500 ml** ● **SERVE cool**
● **INGREDIENTS Maris Otter pale malt/crystal malt/dark chocolate malt/black malt/torrefied wheat/flaked barley/Pioneer and Northern Brewer hops**

An obvious name for a winter beer from a bear brewery: brewed since October 2002 and a beer festival award-winner.

TASTING NOTES

A big, tasty, ruby beer with a malty, roasted, lightly smoked aroma. Roasted malt lies over a bed of sweeter malt in the mouth, followed by a dry, roasted, bitter finish.

Old Chimneys

Old Chimneys Brewery,
Hopton End Farm, Church Road,
Market Weston, Diss, Norfolk IP22 2NX.
Tel. (01359) 221013 Office: (01359) 221411

Suffolk brewery, despite the postal address, founded by former Greene

King and Broughton brewer Alan Thomson in 1995. His first bottles came out in autumn 2000, majoring on strong beers for sipping, but more quaffable brews have found their way into bottle in recent years. All the beers are matured in cask and sometimes kräusened or primed prior to bottling. Bottles are then given three weeks' secondary fermentation at the brewery before they go on sale. All beers are declared suitable for vegetarians, but Black Rat and Hairy Canary, with their milk-derived lactose, do not conform to vegan standards. Best before dates are generally set at 12 months after bottling (18 months for Good King Henry Special Reserve). The beers are now also sold direct from the brewery shop, which is open Friday, 2–7pm, and Saturday, 10am–1pm.

Meadow Brown Ale

● ABV 3.4% ● BOTTLE SIZE 500 ml ● SERVE cool
● INGREDIENTS Pale malt/crystal malt/wheat malt/roasted barley/ Fuggle and Challenger hops

Meadow Brown Ale takes its name from a rare type of butterfly but is in fact a bottled version of Old Chimneys' cask Military Mild. The beer is usually parti-gyled (brewed as part of the same batch) with Black Rat Stout. A little wheat malt has been added to this and some other beers since the last edition of this book, to help with head retention.

TASTING NOTES

A thinnish, but clean beer, with various shades of maltiness, from sweetness to hints of chocolate. Malty, chocolaty aroma; malty, bittersweet finish with light roasted notes.

Great Raft Bitter

● ABV 4.1% ● BOTTLE SIZE 500 ml ● SERVE cool
● INGREDIENTS Pale malt/crystal malt/caramalt/Challenger and Target hops

One of the brewery's three original draught beers, Great Raft has been available in bottled form since 2002. The beer takes its name from Britain's rarest and largest spider, which inhabits a local fen. Also sold as Brockford Bitter at the Mid-Suffolk Light Railway, Wetheringsett.

TASTING NOTES

A copper-coloured ale with a gently toffeeish malt aroma. Malt and toffee lead again in the taste, balanced by a light hoppy sharpness. Dry, toffeeish, malty finish with hops building.

Hairy Canary

● ABV 4.2% ● BOTTLE SIZE 500 ml ● SERVE cold
● INGREDIENTS Lager malt/wheat malt/sugar/Hallertau hops/lactose/stem ginger/lemon

The brewery's fruit beer, designed as a thirst quencher for hot days. Wort is drawn from a brew of Brimstone (see overleaf) 24 hours into fermentation and mixed with sucrose, lactose, stem ginger and lemon. The name is borrowed from a rare yellow fly.

TASTING NOTES

A very pale golden beer with an aroma of fresh ginger and lemon. The taste is light, spritzy and refreshing, with more ginger and lemon in evidence. Ginger warmth develops slowly in the dry finish while lemon lingers.

Black Rat Stout ★

● ABV 4.5% ● BOTTLE SIZE 500 ml ● SERVE cool
● INGREDIENTS Pale malt/crystal malt/wheat malt/roasted barley/lactose/Fuggle and Challenger hops

Although Black Rat is brewed alongside Meadow Brown Ale, it differs considerably in strength and also in the inclusion of lactose. Lactose is not fermentable by standard brewers' yeast and so the sugars remain in the brew adding body (the best known beer to include lactose is Mackeson, the classic milk stout). Also sold as Leading Porter at the Mid-Suffolk Light Railway.

TASTING NOTES

A deep ruby stout with a biscuity, gently sour, bitter chocolate aroma, a mellow, chocolaty, slightly sour taste, and a dry, creamy, coffeeish aftertaste.

Golden Pheasant

● ABV 4.7% ● BOTTLE SIZE 500 ml ● SERVE cool
● INGREDIENTS Pale malt/caramalt/Challenger and Target hops

Named after the oriental bird which lives in a nearby forest, Golden Pheasant is also sold in cask form in spring and summer, and has been bottled since 2002.

TASTING NOTES

A dark golden ale that pours with a white collar of foam. The aroma is fruity and floral, with malt support, while the crisp taste offers malt, hops, citrus fruit and nuts. Nutty, bitter and dry finish, with a hop tang.

Natterjack

● ABV 5.2% ● BOTTLE SIZE 500 ml ● SERVE cool
● INGREDIENTS Pale malt/crystal malt/caramalt/Fuggle and Challenger hops

Inspired by the heathland toad, Natterjack is another of Old Chimneys' original cask brews. Bottling started in 2002.

TASTING NOTES

Red-brown in colour, Natterjack has a nose of chocolate, malt and a touch of spice. Fairly sweet, nutty malt and spicy bitterness lead in the taste, with some light estery notes. Toasted malt, chocolate, nut, hops and bitterness combine in the aftertaste.

India Pale Ale ★

● ABV 5.6% ● BOTTLE SIZE 500 ml ● SERVE cool
● INGREDIENTS Pale malt/amber malt/caramalt/Target and Challenger hops

Known as Lord Kitchener's India Pale Ale, when sold at the Mid-Suffolk Light Railway (Lord Kitchener opened the old railway line and was Commander-in-Chief in India, 1902–9). This authentic IPA is strong and well hopped, as beers intended for the long sea journey to India needed to be in the 19th century. Only Target hops are boiled in the copper, but Alan allows Challenger hops to sit in the hop back as the wort is run off, infusing their own character into the brew and enhancing the aroma. Kitchener still appears on the label, in familiar 'Your country needs you' pose. The best before date is set at 15 months.

TASTING NOTES

A dark golden IPA with plenty of body. The taste is filled with sweet, fruity hops and malt. Rich, fruity, jammy aroma; hoppy, fruity, bitter finish with lingering sweet malt.

Brimstone

● ABV 6.5% ● BOTTLE SIZE 275 ml ● SERVE cold
● INGREDIENTS Lager malt/wheat malt/sugar/Hallertau hops

This strong lager is named after a yellow butterfly. It was first brewed in 2000.

TASTING NOTES

A golden lager with a herbal, almost minty nose. The full-bodied taste features herbal, lightly citrus hops over full, lightly toffeeish malt. Dry, bittersweet aftertaste with herbal hop notes.

Redshank ★

● **ABV 8.7%** ● **BOTTLE SIZE 275 ml** ● **SERVE cool**
● **INGREDIENTS Pale malt/crystal malt/caramalt/Fuggle and Challenger hops**

This strong, fruity ale shares its name with a wading bird.

TASTING NOTES

A red beer with a big vinous aroma of strawberries. Strawberry and other fruits are balanced by a touch of liquorice and warming alcohol in the taste before a mellow, bittersweet, fruity aftertaste.

Good King Henry Special Reserve ★

● **ABV 11%** ● **BOTTLE SIZE 275 ml** ● **SERVE cool**
● **INGREDIENTS Pale malt/crystal malt/wheat malt/roasted barley/ Fuggle and Challenger hops**

Good King Henry was an imperial Russian stout, brewed to 9.6% ABV. In 2005, however, Old Chimneys celebrated its tenth anniversary with a stronger version, stored in cask with oak granules for six months. The beer was then given a further 18 months to mature in the bottle before going on sale. This new Special Reserve has now taken over entirely, and the original Good King Henry has been usurped. However, contrary to first impressions, this beer takes its name not from a monarch but from an unusual, rarely-grown vegetable. Only limited numbers of each vintage are available, each bottle given a three-year best before date.

TASTING NOTES

A near black beer with a rich, treacly, molasses aroma with light vanilla, oaky notes. The smooth, creamy taste is full, sweet and nourishing, malty, vinous and warming, with a fine bitter balance. Mellow caramel and roasted barley linger in the warming, bittersweet finish.

Old Luxters

Old Luxters Vineyard, Winery & Brewery, Hambleden, Henley-on-Thames, Oxfordshire RG9 6JW.
Tel. (01491) 638330 Fax (01491) 638645
E-mail: enquiries@chilternvalley.co.uk
Website: www.chilternvalley.co.uk
Mail order service

Old Luxters was set up in 1990 in a 17th-century barn by David Ealand, owner of Chiltern Valley Wines. A new bottling line was installed in spring 1998 and the brewery has since expanded its contract brewing and bottling services for other producers. In total, conditioning and maturation for bottled beers at the brewery take five weeks, with beers filtered and re-seeded with primary fermentation yeast. Best before dates are generally set one-year from bottling. In addition to the beers listed below, a pack of three, variously spiced Winter Warmers (5%) has been available in recent years.

Fortnum & Mason Summer Ale

● ABV 4.5% ● BOTTLE SIZE 330 ml ● SERVE cool
● INGREDIENTS Maris Otter pale malt/crystal malt/chocolate malt/ Fuggle and Golding hops/elderflowers

In 1999 Old Luxters began bottling beer for exclusive London store Fortnum & Mason (see Fortnum's Ale opposite). In 2002 this seasonal brew was added, given a summery fragrance with elderflowers. A good accompaniment for fish or poultry, thinks brewery founder David Ealand.

TASTING NOTES

A golden beer with a strong, herbal aroma (slightly earthy and perfumed). The taste matches the aroma, although with sweet elderflower flavour emerging, while the finish is drying, with a touch more bitterness.

Major stockist Fortnum & Mason

Old Windsor Gold Ale

● ABV 4.5% ● BOTTLE SIZE 500 ml ● SERVE cool
● INGREDIENTS Maris Otter pale malt/crystal malt/Fuggle and Golding hops

Added to the range in 2001, this is one of two beers prepared for Royal Farms, for sale at Windsor Farm Shop.

TASTING NOTES

A smooth, copper-gold beer with a creamy, nutty aroma. Creamy malt, a little nut and a light, citrus hoppiness follow in the mouth, finished by a creamy, bitter, malty aftertaste.

Dark Roast

● ABV 5% ● BOTTLE SIZE 500 ml ● SERVE cool
● INGREDIENTS Maris Otter pale malt/crystal malt/chocolate malt/ Fuggle and Golding hops

This cask and bottled brew arrived in 1997.

TASTING NOTES
A dark chestnut-coloured beer with a malty aroma tinged with cocoa and citrus hops. Crisp, malty and gently roasted in the mouth, it is well balanced and has orangey citrus notes. The aftertaste is dry and bittersweet, with mellow roasted grain. Not as strong in roast flavour as its name implies.

Fortnum's Ale

● **ABV 5%** ● **BOTTLE SIZE 330 ml** ● **SERVE cool**
● **INGREDIENTS Maris Otter pale malt/crystal malt/chocolate malt/ Fuggle and Golding hops**
Another beer exclusively for Fortnum & Mason. The royal grocers approached Old Luxters for this special brew, having already sold Chiltern Valley's wines.
TASTING NOTES
A copper beer with orange and malt in the aroma. Silky, nutty malt and fruity hops combine in the clean, bittersweet taste, while the aftertaste is hoppy, toasty, nutty and gently bitter.
Major stockist Fortnum & Mason

Luxters Gold

● **ABV 5%** ● **BOTTLE SIZE 330 ml** ● **SERVE cool**
● **INGREDIENTS Maris Otter pale malt/Fuggle and Golding hops**
In 1997, Old Luxters secured a contract with the Gilbey's wine importer/restaurateur company, to produce Gilbey's Gold (ABV 5%), a 'farmhouse ale' in dark green 330 ml bottles. The beer proved so successful that it was added to the permanent range, with the name changed accordingly.
TASTING NOTES
A golden beer with spicy hops edging out malt in the aroma. The taste nicely balances malt and spicy hops, and there is a hint of grapefruit, too. Hoppy, dry finish.

Old Windsor Dark Ale

● **ABV 5%** ● **BOTTLE SIZE 500 ml** ● **SERVE cool**
● **INGREDIENTS Maris Otter pale malt/crystal malt/chocolate malt/ Fuggle and Golding hops**
The second beer brewed for the Royal Farms. As its name implies, it is darker than the first and just a touch stronger.

Barn Ale

● ABV 5.4% ● BOTTLE SIZE 500 ml ● SERVE cool
● INGREDIENTS Maris Otter pale malt/crystal malt/chocolate malt/ Fuggle and Golding hops

Taking its name from the brewery's rustic location, Barn Ale, first brewed in 1993, is considerably stronger than the cask Barn Ale Special (4.5%) on which it is based.

TASTING NOTES

Dark copper, combining fruit, silky, chocolaty malt and hops in a good body. Malty, chocolaty, orange fruit nose; dry, fruity, bittersweet finish.

Major stockist Local Waitrose

Damson Ale

● ABV 7% ● BOTTLE SIZE 500 ml ● SERVE cool
● INGREDIENTS Maris Otter pale malt/crystal malt/chocolate malt/ damson juice/Fuggle and Golding hops

Old Luxters used to bottle Damson Beer for Strawberry Bank Brewery (now closed) in Cumbria. This is its successor. Cumbrian damson juice is added to the beer 24 hours after primary fermentation has begun.

TASTING NOTES

Damsons feature strongly in the otherwise musty, spicy aroma of this red-amber brew, and dominate in the same way in the warming, bittersweet taste. Drying, bittersweet, damson finish.

Thinking green, drinking green... **The term 'green beer' is not one you normally want to hear, as it refers to beer that is not yet ready to drink. However, with the rapid increase in the number of organic beers on sale, at least one sort of green beer is now very welcome. More and more breweries are producing beer made from organically-grown malts and hops. In some cases, the whole of the brewery's output is organic. Dozens of organic beers are now identified in the pages of this book. They may cost a few pennies more than other beers, but at least they offer drinkers the chance to do their bit for the environment.**

Oldershaw

Oldershaw Brewery, 12 Harrowby Hall Estate, Harrowby, Grantham, Lincolnshire NG31 9HB. Tel. (01476) 572135 Fax (01476) 572193
E-mail: oldershawbrewery@btconnect.com
Website: www.oldershawbrewery.com

Brewery founded by Gary and Diane Oldershaw next to the family home in 1997, the first brewery in Grantham for 30 years. The bottled beers are produced very much on an *ad hoc* basis, to use up surplus beer after all required casks have been filled. Any of the Oldershaw range may therefore be bottled, although the ones below are the most likely to be found. They may not all be available at any one time.

Caskade

● ABV 4.2% ● BOTTLE SIZE 500 ml ● SERVE cool
● INGREDIENTS Optic pale malt/crystal malt/Cascade hops

The name's a play on words, reflecting the choice of American hops for what is primarily a golden cask-conditioned ale.

Grantham Stout

● ABV 4.3% ● BOTTLE SIZE 500 ml ● SERVE cool
● INGREDIENTS Optic pale malt/crystal malt/chocolate malt/roasted barley/wheat malt/First Gold, Willamette and Golding hops

Brewed to 'an original Lincolnshire recipe', according to the brewery's literature, this dark stout, like the other beers, is bottled from a cask, using a small, four-head manual filler. 'There's nothing added and nothing taken away', says Gary Oldershaw.

Regal Blonde

● ABV 4.4% ● BOTTLE SIZE 500 ml ● SERVE cool
● INGREDIENTS Lager malt/wheat malt/Hersbrucker, Saaz and Cascade hops

A lager-style beer. Spell the word lager backwards and you get 'Regal'.

Isaac's Gold

● ABV 4.5% ● BOTTLE SIZE 500 ml ● SERVE cool
● INGREDIENTS Optic pale malt/First Gold hops

A golden ale celebrating Grantham's association with the great Sir Isaac Newton, who was educated at King's School in the town.

Old Boy

- **ABV 4.8%** • **BOTTLE SIZE 500 ml** • **SERVE cool**
- **INGREDIENTS Optic pale malt/crystal malt/chocolate malt/wheat malt/First Gold, Fuggle, Cascade and Willamette hops**

There's a top-hatted toff on the label of this chestnut-coloured ale.

Alchemy

- **ABV 5.3%** • **BOTTLE SIZE 500 ml** • **SERVE cool**
- **INGREDIENTS Optic pale malt/First Gold hops**

A strong golden ale, dwelling on Newton's scientific experiments.

Organic

The Organic Brewhouse, Unit 1, Higher Bochym Workshops, Cury Cross Lanes, Mullion, Helston, Cornwall TR12 7AZ.
Tel. (01326) 241555
E-mail: orgbrewandy@tiscali.co.uk

This entirely organic brewery was set up by Andy Hamer in 2000 in a former slaughterhouse in the shadow of Goonhilly Downs radio station in Cornwall. It is the southernmost brewery in mainland Britain. The first bottle-conditioned beer was brewed in 2001. The vegan-friendly beers are filled from a cask or conditioning tank and may be kräusened if necessary. Ten-month best before dates are set (a year for Wolf Rock).

Lizard Point

- **ABV 4%** • **BOTTLE SIZE 500 ml** • **SERVE cool**
- **INGREDIENTS Pale malt/crystal malt/Hallertau hops**

Named after the most southerly point on the British mainland (close to the brewery), Lizard Point was one of Andy's first cask brews.

Serpentine

- **ABV 4.5%** • **BOTTLE SIZE 500 ml** • **SERVE cool**
- **INGREDIENTS Pale malt/crystal malt/chocolate malt/wheat malt/Hallertau hops**

Taking its name from the local bedrock, which is often shaped into decorative tourist souvenirs, Organic's first bottled beer.

TASTING NOTES

Tawny, with a malty, chocolaty, biscuity nose and a malty, sweet taste with light roasted grain and chocolate. Bitter, roasted, malty finish.

Black Rock Stout

● ABV 4.7% ● BOTTLE SIZE 500 ml ● SERVE cool
● INGREDIENTS Pale malt/crystal malt/chocolate malt/wheat malt/ Hallertau hops
A stout introduced in December 2001 and named after an island at the entrance to Falmouth harbour. The hops used, as in the other beers, are imported from New Zealand.

Wolf Rock

● ABV 5% ● BOTTLE SIZE 500 ml ● SERVE cool
● INGREDIENTS Pale malt/crystal malt/wheat malt/Hallertau hops
Another beer from late 2001, named after the famous Wolf Rock lighthouse that can be seen from the brewery.

TASTING NOTES
A copper beer with a soft fruity aroma (sweet apple and strawberry). Although the taste is fruity and sweetish, there are enough hop resins and bitterness for balance, and a little warmth to expose the strength. Bitter, hoppy, fruity finish.

Oulton

Oulton Ales Ltd., Unit 2, Harbour Road, Oulton Broad, Suffolk NR32 3LZ. Tel. (01502) 587905
E-mail: waynemoore@oultonales.co.uk
Website: www.oultonales.co.uk
Mail order service
Oulton Ales brews on the site formerly used by Green Jack Brewery (former partner Tim Dunford left in 2002 and now owns the Green Jack name). All the beers are presented in swing-topped bottles, although different glassware may be employed in future.

Sunrise

● ABV 4% ● BOTTLE SIZE 500 ml ● SERVE cool
● INGREDIENTS Maris Otter pale malt/crystal malt/caramalt/maize/ Challenger and Styrian Golding hops/elderflower
A cask-conditioned beer for summer months, first put into bottle in 2003. Like the other beers, this is hand filled on site, after kräusening. The beer is named Sunrise as the brewery stands on the fringe of Lowestoft, the most easterly point in the United Kingdom.

Nautilus

● **ABV 4.2%** ● **BOTTLE SIZE 500 ml** ● **SERVE cool**
● **INGREDIENTS Maris Otter pale malt/crystal malt/chocolate malt/caramalt/Challenger and Styrian Golding hops**

Formerly Green Jack's Grasshopper, introduced in 1997, and now adopting a name more in keeping with the seafaring industries of Lowestoft.

TASTING NOTES

An amber-red beer with a hoppy nose, a fresh, hoppy taste, well balanced with malt, and a dry, hoppy, moreish finish.

Gone Fishing

● **ABV 5%** ● **BOTTLE SIZE 500 ml** ● **SERVE cool**
● **INGREDIENTS Maris Otter pale malt/crystal malt/chocolate malt/caramalt/Fuggle hops**

A strong, single-varietal hop bitter, in bottle since 2002. Apparently, it goes very well with a slice of banana cake.

Cormorant Porter

● **ABV 5.2%** ● **BOTTLE SIZE 500 ml** ● **SERVE cool**
● **INGREDIENTS Optic pale malt/crystal malt/caramalt/chocolate malt/roasted chocolate malt/Challenger and Styrian Golding hops**

This porter has been available in cask-conditioned form for about four years but has been offered in bottle-conditioned form only for the last couple of years.

Roaring Boy

● **ABV 8.5%** ● **BOTTLE SIZE 500 ml** ● **SERVE cool**
● **INGREDIENTS Maris Otter pale malt/caramalt/maize/candy sugar/Challenger and Cascade hops**

This the beer Green Jack used to call Ripper, which was first produced in 1995. Its current name refers to the fishermen of Pakefield, known as the Roaring Boys (Oulton Ales took over The Ship Inn, which acted as their HQ). Prior to bottling, the ale is matured for at least 12 months in casks.

TASTING NOTES

An amber beer with a hoppy nose with hints of bitter orange. The robust flavour is sweetish, malty and full of tangy, fruity hops. Hoppy, tangy, warming aftertaste with a little nut.

Paradise

Paradise Brewing Co., Ty Tan-y-Mynydd, Moelfre, Abergele, Conwy LL22 9RF. Tel./Fax (01352) 762822
E-mail: paradisebrewery@uwclub.net

Beers bottled under the name of The Old Creamery Bottling Company originate from Paradise Brewery, a business set up by John Wood in 2000 and operating originally from an old creamery in Wrenbury, Cheshire. In 2006, the Wrenbury site was closed and a move to the North Wales address above was scheduled. However, planning permission was initially refused, leaving John to brew his beers for the time being at Three Rivers Brewing in Stockport. The first regular bottles rolled out in 2004 and are sold at farmers' markets in the North-West.

Old Creamery Mild

● **ABV 3.6%** ● **BOTTLE SIZE 500 ml** ● **SERVE cool**
● **INGREDIENTS Maris Otter pale malt/chocolate malt/Golding hops**

A beer first sold in cask in 2000 for CAMRA's May Mild Month. Like the other bottled beers, this mild is filled direct from the conditioning tank.

Farmers Favourite

● **ABV 4%** ● **BOTTLE SIZE 500 ml** ● **SERVE cool**
● **INGREDIENTS Maris Otter pale malt/crystal malt/Northdown hops**

A beer brewed specifically for farmers' markets, initially in 2002.

TASTING NOTES

A golden ale with a spicy, yeasty aroma and a sharp, bitter taste with a little malty sweetness. Dry, bitter finish.

Dabbers

● **ABV 5%** ● **BOTTLE SIZE 500 ml** ● **SERVE cool**
● **INGREDIENTS Maris Otter pale malt/wheat malt/Styrian Golding hops**

A Dabber, in local terms, is a person who originates in Nantwich, the nearest major town to the brewery. Another of the earliest brews, this wheat beer was first on sale as a cask beer in 2000.

TASTING NOTES

Another golden beer, with piney hop resins in the nose and taste. There's also some nutty malt sweetness in the mouth and a citrus acidity. Dry, nutty, softly bitter aftertaste.

Nantwich Ale

● ABV 5.6% ● BOTTLE SIZE 500 ml ● SERVE cool
● INGREDIENTS Maris Otter pale malt/crystal malt/Fuggle hops

A new beer, introduced on draught for a Christmas beer festival in 2003 and first bottled in March 2004.

TASTING NOTES

A red beer with a malty aroma, backed by a little fruit. The taste is also malty and sweet, with a rye-like nuttiness, just a little hop and some alcohol. Dry, nutty, malty finish.

Parish

Parish Brewery, 6 Main Street, Burrough-on-the-Hill, Leicestershire LE14 2JQ. Tel. (01664) 454801

Parish Brewery is one of Britain's great survivors among microbreweries. Founded in 1983 in Burrough-on-the-Hill, it then moved to Somerby in the same county of Leicestershire, but now has returned home. Owner Barrie Parish now just produces one bottled beer.

Baz's Bonce Blower

● ABV 12% ● BOTTLE SIZE 500 ml ● SERVE cool
● INGREDIENTS Maris Otter pale malt/crystal malt/black malt/ Golding, Fuggle and Willamette hops

The beer that made Barrie Parish famous. When the brewery was established at The Stag & Hounds pub (making it the first brew pub of the modern era in Leicestershire), Barrie needed something a little out of the ordinary to draw the punters out to the country. He found it in this notorious beer, which requires a double fermentation to achieve its giddy, 12% strength (sometimes even a touch stronger). After Parish's yeast has given up the ghost during the first fermentation, fresh yeast is pitched and kept alive by the addition of a secret 'yeast food' to enable it to venture into territory where beer yeasts normally fear to tread. A good mix of hops provides a counterbalance to all the alcohol. But if you think this is a strong beer, you should have tried Baz's Super Brew. In 1995 it featured in the *Guinness Book of Records* as the strongest beer in the world (23%). Barrie extols the virtues of Bonce Blower as a fine accompaniment to some of the excellent local Stiltons.

TASTING NOTES

A ruby beer with a malty, alcoholic aroma with a whiff of almonds. The taste is sweetish, almondy, malty and alcoholic, with a sherry-like fruitiness. Warm, sweetish, malty and fruity aftertaste.

Peelwalls

Peelwalls Ltd., Peelwalls Steading, Peelwalls Farmhouse, Ayton, Borders TD14 5RL. Tel. (01890) 781048
E-mail: peelwallsltd@aol.com

Peelwalls is an unusual enterprise. It was founded in 2004 on a former farm and, in addition to beer, makes wines from imported grape juices and cider and perry from both local apples and brought-in juice. Although the brewery was set up with the conventional mash tun and copper arrangement, these vessels have now been taken away and all the beers are produced from hopped malt extracts that are prepared by an outside company, following Peelwalls' own specifications and recipes.

Bitter

- **ABV 4%** - **BOTTLE SIZE 500 ml** - **SERVE cool**
- **INGREDIENTS Hopped malt extract**

Like the other beers, this bitter is bottled in house directly from the fermenting vessel, retaining original primary fermentation yeast.

Golden Harvest

- **ABV 4.2%** - **BOTTLE SIZE 500 ml** - **SERVE cool**
- **INGREDIENTS Hopped malt extract**

First brewed at harvest-time, hence the name.

IPA

- **ABV 4.8%** - **BOTTLE SIZE 500 ml** - **SERVE cool**
- **INGREDIENTS Hopped malt extract**

The IPA, together with Peelwalls' other beers, is largely sold at farmers' markets in the Scottish Borders.

Pipe Major Stout

- **ABV 5%** - **BOTTLE SIZE 500 ml** - **SERVE cool**
- **INGREDIENTS Hopped malt extract**

A number of Peelwalls' original recipes were donated by a former piper. They've been changed since but this stout recognizes his contribution.

Pen-lon

Pen-lon Cottage Brewery, Pen-lon Cottage Trading Ltd., Pen-lon Farm, Llanarth, Ceredigion SA47 0QN. Tel. (01545) 580022
E-mail: beer@penlon.biz
Website: www.penlon.biz

Sheep are the inspiration behind the beers from this small West Wales producer, which describes itself as 'not just a microbrewery but a cottage industry where hand-crafted brewing complements the natural farm cycle'. To this end they even grow some of their own hops, and feed the spent malt grains to their own pigs. The first beers arrived in shops in 2004, with attractive labels drawn by Penny Samociuk who runs the brewery with husband Stefan. Best before dates for the weaker beers are set at six months, with longer advised for those with more clout. A couple of seasonal beers may also be bottled: Autumn Harvest Golden Ale and Shepherd's Delight Christmas Ale. No cask ales are currently produced.

Lambs Gold

● **ABV 3.2%** ● **BOTTLE SIZE 500 ml** ● **SERVE cool**
● **INGREDIENTS Maris Otter pale malt/light crystal malt/Target, Tettnanger and Willamette hops**

A gold award-winner in the Wales *True Taste* competition for 2005–6, and one of the weakest bottle-conditioned beers in production.

TASTING NOTES

A dark golden beer with malt, gentle, spicy hops and apricots and oranges in the aroma. There's plenty of taste for the strength, with hop resins leading over sweet malt and orange fruitiness building. The drying finish becomes more bitter as hops fight through.

Tipsy Tup

● **ABV 3.8%** ● **BOTTLE SIZE 500 ml** ● **SERVE cool**
● **INGREDIENTS Maris Otter pale malt/light crystal malt/Target, Tettnanger and Willamette hops**

Like the other beers, this pale ale is bottled by hand straight from the fermenter, with the addition of a small amount of priming sugar.

TASTING NOTES

Amber, with bitter oranges in the light aroma. The bitter and hoppy taste has a light maltiness for balance. Dry, bitter, hoppy finish.

Stock Ram

● **ABV 4.5%** ● **BOTTLE SIZE 500 ml** ● **SERVE cool**
● **INGREDIENTS Optic pale lager malt/roasted barley/flaked barley/ Target, Tettnanger and Nugget hops**

A dry and bitter stout, brewed for local preferences, says Stefan.

TASTING NOTES

A deep ruby-coloured beer with dark malts and biscuity grain featuring in the slightly sour, creamy aroma. There's full, smooth malt, with hints of coffee, chocolate and liquorice, in the taste, and also a touch of citrus fruit. Bitterness builds nicely in the drying, biscuity, dark chocolate aftertaste.

Twin Ram

● **ABV 4.8%** ● **BOTTLE SIZE 500 ml** ● **SERVE cool**
● **INGREDIENTS Maris Otter pale malt/light crystal malt/Target, Tettnanger and Willamette hops**

This is the beer the brewer drinks, which is as good a recommendation as any. Twin Ram is Stefan's favourite evening tipple and marries perfectly with thick-cut ham, granary bread and mustard, he reckons. This strong ale earned a commendation at the Wales *True Taste* awards for 2005–6.

TASTING NOTES

An orange-amber-coloured strong ale. Hop resins and fruit, with a little liquorice and toffee, fill the aroma. Toffeeish malt leads on the palate, with spicy hop for contrast, before a drying, malty and pleasantly bitter finish.

Ewes Frolic

● **ABV 5.2%** ● **BOTTLE SIZE 500 ml** ● **SERVE cold**
● **INGREDIENTS Optic pale lager malt/light crystal malt/Target, Tettnanger and Sterling hops**

Ewes Frolic is a lager, made with floor-malted lager malt and hops that include home-grown Sterling, a Saaz hybrid.

TASTING NOTES

Juicy citrus fruits and pineapple, along with sweet malt, feature in the nose of this golden beer. There's plenty of malty body in the mouth, countered by a firm hoppy balance. Strong herbal notes and a little citrus sharpness emerge later. The smooth aftertaste nicely balances malt and hops.

Ramnesia

● **ABV 5.6%** ● **BOTTLE SIZE 500 ml** ● **SERVE cool**
● **INGREDIENTS Maris Otter pale malt/light crystal malt/Target, Tettnanger and Willamette hops**

'It just gets better as it gets older,' says Stefan about this strong ale. He also produces bacon that has been cured in this particular beer.

TASTING NOTES

A tawny, strong ale with a little blackcurrant in the fruity nose. Pleasant, toffeeish malt flavours feature in the taste, along with more blackcurrants, before a soft, smooth, drying finish with hops building and light blackcurrant and liquorice notes.

Pitfield

Pitfield Brewery, The Nurseries, London Road,
Great Horkesley, Colchester, Essex CO6 4AJ.
Tel. (08458) 331492
E-mail: sales@pitfieldbeershop.co.uk
Website: www.pitfieldbeershop.co.uk
Mail order service

Pitfield was founded way back in 1981 and, after several years out of production, was revived in 1996, next to Hoxton's well-known Beer Shop. The shop closed, after more than 20 years of pioneering work in fine beer sales, in 2006, but the business goes on as a mail order operation. Pitfield has now re-opened its brewery in a garden/craft centre in Essex, where a vineyard already operates. In 2000 the brewery was certified to be an organic producer, and now has Soil Association accreditation, but the range of historic re-creation beers, with the exception of 1850 London Porter, is not organic, although there are plans to make them organic soon. These historic beers are listed separately at the end of the Pitfield entry. The beers are matured in cask for two–three weeks before being racked mostly bright. New yeast is added as required, with maltose syrup primings used to encourage a good secondary fermentation. The bottles are then kept at the brewery for at least two weeks before release. Six months are specified as a best before date. Because finings have been omitted, the beers hold no fears for vegetarians or vegans, but they may be a little hazy as a result. Special one-off brews are occasionally produced, such as St George's Ale (4.3%) in April and Pumpkin Porter (5%) for Hallowe'en.

Original Bitter

ABV 3.7% • BOTTLE SIZE 500 ml • SERVE cool

• INGREDIENTS Maris Otter pale malt/crystal malt/wheat malt/ Fuggle, Challenger and Golding hops

Pitfield's standard session bitter was one of its first ever brews. It was renamed Pitfield Original Bitter in 1999.

TASTING NOTES

An orange/gold-coloured beer with a hoppy nose. The taste is dry and hoppy with gentle malt behind. Very dry, hoppy finish.

Shoreditch Stout

• ABV 4% • BOTTLE SIZE 500 ml • SERVE cool

• INGREDIENTS Maris Otter pale malt/roasted barley/flaked barley/ Fuggle, Challenger and Target hops

Not as 'stout' as some, this brew was added in 1997.

TASTING NOTES

A very dark brown beer with a smoky aroma. It is a little sour in the mouth but also fruity and malty. Gently roasted, bitter malt finish.

East Kent Goldings

• ABV 4.2% • BOTTLE SIZE 500 ml • SERVE cool

• INGREDIENTS Maris Otter pale malt/crystal malt/wheat malt/ flaked maize/Golding hops

This single-varietal hop beer was first produced in 1999.

TASTING NOTES

An orange-gold ale with a fruity, peppery hop nose. Fruity hop is well balanced by smooth malt in the taste, which is not too bitter. Dry, gently bitter finish.

Eco Warrior

• ABV 4.5% • BOTTLE SIZE 500 ml • SERVE cool

• INGREDIENTS Chariot pale malt/sugar/Hallertau hops

This beer, launched in 1998, set the Pitfield organic ball rolling. It quickly found itself a niche and has been stocked by health food shops.

TASTING NOTES

A hazy golden beer with a fruity hop bouquet (hints of tinned peaches). In the mouth, the initially sweetish taste is balanced by delicate, soft, orangey-peachy hops which provide slowly increasing bitterness. The aftertaste is dry, with fruity hop lingering.

Hoxton Best Bitter

● **ABV 4.8%** ● **BOTTLE SIZE 500 ml** ● **SERVE cool**
● **INGREDIENTS Maris Otter pale malt/crystal malt/dried pale malt/roasted barley/Northdown, Challenger and Golding hops**

Designed as a pseudo-Scottish brew, with typically strong malty characteristics, this beer was formerly known as Hoxton Heavy. The use of a little dried malt adds a touch of sweetness and balances out the roasted barley flavours.

TASTING NOTES

A dark copper beer with a malty, chocolaty nose, a malty but citrus taste, with balancing bitterness, and a bitter malt finish.

Black Eagle

● **ABV 5%** ● **BOTTLE SIZE 500 ml** ● **SERVE cool**
● **INGREDIENTS Maris Otter pale malt/crystal malt/black malt/wheat malt/Fuggle, Challenger and Styrian Golding hops**

Black Eagle may ring bells with drinkers acquainted with Pitfield beers of old. It is reminiscent of the brewery's famous Dark Star, *Champion Beer of Britain* in 1987, which is now produced by Dark Star Brewing.

TASTING NOTES

A dark ruby beer, with an aroma of ripe red berry fruits. The taste is smooth and fruity but with some dark malt flavour and good hop balance. Dry, mostly bitter, lingering finish.

N1

● **ABV 5%** ● **BOTTLE SIZE 330 ml** ● **SERVE cool**
● **INGREDIENTS Pale malt/wheat malt/Hallertau hops/coriander**

Brewed with a genuine wheat beer yeast, this is Pitfield's version of a Belgian witbier, complete with coriander spicing.

TASTING NOTES

A hazy yellow beer with a bready, lemon juice aroma. Lemon tartness, sweetness, spice and a touch of warmth combine in the mouth, before a drying, lemony, slightly chewy finish.

1850 London Porter ★

● **ABV 5%** ● **BOTTLE SIZE 500 ml** ● **SERVE cool**
● **INGREDIENTS Maris Otter pale malt/brown malt/roasted barley/Golding hops**

Pitfield had been producing this porter off and on for a few years before it decided to include it in the new range of beers based on historic beer styles. The recipes for these brews have been inspired by the work of the Durden Park Beer Circle, a dedicated and enthusiastic group of private brewers (one reluctantly uses the titles 'amateur' or 'home brewers', such is their proficiency and attention to detail). The Circle goes to extreme lengths to re-create beers that have long ceased to be part of the portfolio of brewers today, unearthing the truth about how beers used to taste.

TASTING NOTES

A deep ruby beer with a coffeeish aroma. The taste is nutty and bittersweet with light roasted notes amidst the malt. Dry, nutty, coffeeish, gently bitter finish.

1830 Amber Ale

● ABV 6% ● BOTTLE SIZE 500 ml ● SERVE cool

● INGREDIENTS Maris Otter pale malt/amber malt/chocolate malt/ Fuggle, Golding and Styrian Golding hops

In Victorian times, amber malt was widely used in brewing but it died out in the 20th century. It is now proving popular among brewers keen to resurrect old-fashioned beers.

TASTING NOTES

Actually ruby in colour, this strong ale has soft, juicy pineapple and malt in the nose. Pineapple again features in the taste, overlaying plenty of malt, with nutty, toasted notes emerging on the swallow. Dry, roasted malt aftertaste.

1824 Mild Ale

● ABV 6.5% ● BOTTLE SIZE 500 ml ● SERVE cool

● INGREDIENTS Maris Otter pale malt/black malt/wheat malt/ Golding hops

Mild – an endangered species among beer styles – is most commonly found as a weak beer, around 3–3.5% alcohol, these days. There are some stronger milds around, as this book illustrates, and this particular beer serves as a reminder that, in days gone by, mild was not only Britain's most popular brew but a rather potent drink, too.

TASTING NOTES

Another ruby beer with some light fruit in the creamy, malty nose. Smooth malt leads in the mouth, with hints of darker malt and some fruit. Dry, bitter, roasted malt finish.

1837 India Pale Ale ★

ABV 7% • BOTTLE SIZE 500 ml • SERVE cool

• INGREDIENTS Maris Otter pale malt/roasted barley/Northdown and Golding hops

A powerful IPA in the traditional style, emulating the sort of beer that was strong and hoppy enough to withstand the rough sea crossing to India in the 19th century.

TASTING NOTES

An amber beer, with a big, hoppy and fruity aroma, with malt in support. The taste is full and sweetish, with lots of hops and fruit (including tropical). Drying, bittersweet, hoppy, warming finish, with lingering tropical fruit.

1792 Imperial Stout ★

ABV 9.3% • BOTTLE SIZE 330 ml • SERVE cool

• INGREDIENTS Maris Otter pale malt/roasted barley/wheat malt/ Northdown hops

Helping to fill a gap vacated by Courage's renowned Imperial Russian Stout, this strong, complex brew is typical of the beers that crossed the Baltic to warm the hearts of the imperial Russian court at the turn of the 19th century.

TASTING NOTES

This potent black brew has a clean, slightly savoury aroma, with a hint of liquorice in its roasted notes and a light whiff of fruit. Smooth, oily malt leads in the taste, which is sweetish, with raisin and coffee notes. Rather easy to drink for its strength. A mellow, sweetish, dark malt finish rounds off.

1896 XXXX Stock Ale ★

ABV 10% • BOTTLE SIZE 500 ml • SERVE cool

• INGREDIENTS Maris Otter pale malt/crystal malt/Northdown hops

A beer to lay down and enjoy in a couple of years' time. Stock ales were designed for such keeping, having the alcohol and body to mature long after brewing.

TASTING NOTES

A dark golden beer with a rich, vinously fruity, malty nose. The big, warming taste is sweet and fruity, yet complex and spicy, before a long, bittersweet, fruity aftertaste. Another deceptive and dangerously drinkable beer for its mighty strength.

Poachers

Poachers Brewery, 439 Newark Road, North Hykeham, Lincolnshire LN6 9SP. Tel. (01522) 807404
Website: www.poachersbrewery.co.uk

Poachers was opened in May 2001 and is run by ex-RAF man George Batterbee, who now brews in a converted barn behind his house. The range of bottled beers are all matured in cask before being racked bright and kräusened for bottling.

Trembling Rabbit Mild

● ABV 3.4% ● BOTTLE SIZE 500 ml ● SERVE cool
● INGREDIENTS Maris Otter pale malt/crystal malt/chocolate malt/ Cascade and Mount Hood hops

Stuck for a name for this mild, George threw it open to regulars at The Eight Jolly Brewers pub in Gainsborough, who took part in a competition to devise a suitable title.

TASTING NOTES

A red beer with a malty, sharply fruity nose, a malty taste, with roasted grain on the swallow, and a bitter, roasted malt aftertaste.

Shy Talk Bitter

● ABV 3.7% ● BOTTLE SIZE 500 ml ● SERVE cool
● INGREDIENTS Maris Otter pale malt/crystal malt/Challenger, Cascade and Mount Hood hops

A pale golden beer, named after a boat spotted in Whitby harbour.

Poachers Pride

● ABV 4% ● BOTTLE SIZE 500 ml ● SERVE cool
● INGREDIENTS Maris Otter pale malt/crystal malt/Cascade and Mount Hood hops

An amber ale, inspired by the Chris Rea song 'Too Much Pride'.

Poachers Trail

● ABV 4.2% ● BOTTLE SIZE 500 ml ● SERVE cool
● INGREDIENTS Maris Otter pale malt/roasted barley/Golding and Styrian Golding hops

This was the brewery's first commercial brew. At the time it didn't have a name and was just listed as 'Trial', which later evolved into Trail.

TASTING NOTES
A copper beer with an orangey, malty aroma. The taste is full of juicy fruit (slightly tart lemon), with good malt balance and a touch of roast. Dry, roasted, pleasantly bitter aftertaste.

Billy Boy

● **ABV 4.4%** ● **BOTTLE SIZE 500 ml** ● **SERVE cool**
● **INGREDIENTS Maris Otter pale malt/crystal malt/Mount Hood and Fuggle hops**
A dark brown beer that George has named after his pet border collie.

Black Crow Stout

● **ABV 4.5%** ● **BOTTLE SIZE 500 ml** ● **SERVE cool**
● **INGREDIENTS Maris Otter pale malt/roasted barley/Challenger, Chinook and Styrian Golding hops**
Named after the birds in the small wood behind the original brewery, although it has been revealed since that they were actually rooks.
TASTING NOTES
Ruby, with a mellow, biscuity, dark malt nose, a soft, almost burnt, grainy, bitter flavour and a bitter, roasted grain finish.

Poachers Dick

● **ABV 4.5%** ● **BOTTLE SIZE 500 ml** ● **SERVE cool**
● **INGREDIENTS Maris Otter pale malt/crystal malt/Golding, Cascade, Mount Hood, Challenger and Styrian Golding hops**
A premium ale named after George's dad, Richard Batterbee.
TASTING NOTES
A tawny/amber ale with a fruit aroma (rhubarb and gooseberries) and a bittersweet, fruity taste. Dry, hoppy, increasingly bitter finish.

Jock's Trap

● **ABV 5%** ● **BOTTLE SIZE 500 ml** ● **SERVE cool**
● **INGREDIENTS Maris Otter pale malt/roasted barley/Cascade and Mount Hood hops**
A Scottish pun for a beer featuring American hops.
TASTING NOTES
An amber beer with an aroma of malt and fruity hops. The same hoppy flavours continue in the sweetish, fruity taste, while the finish is dry, bitter and hoppy with lingering fruit.

Trout Tickler

● ABV 5.5% ● BOTTLE SIZE 500 ml ● SERVE cool
● INGREDIENTS Maris Otter pale malt/crystal malt/chocolate malt/ Mount Hood and Cascade hops
A dark, malty ale said to have liquorice undertones.

Potton

The Potton Brewery Co., 10 Shannon Place, Potton, Bedfordshire SG19 2SP. Tel. (01767) 261042
E-mail: info@potton-brewery.co.uk
Website: www.potton-brewery.co.uk
Reviving the Potton Brewery Co. name after it disappeared following a take-over in 1922, this business was set up in 1999, by two former Greene King employees. Their beers are conditioned first in casks, decanted, kräusened and then bottled. Some own-label beers are also produced for other businesses.

John Cunningham Night Fighter

● ABV 4% ● BOTTLE SIZE 500 ml ● SERVE cool
● INGREDIENTS Pearl pale malt/crystal malt/caramalt/roasted barley/Target and First Gold hops
This new, dark, malty beer is brewed in honour of John 'Cat's Eyes' Cunningham, one of Britain's most famous wartime pilots of night fighter aircraft, who died in 2002. The bottles are sold at the RAF Museum at Hendon and the Imperial War Museum at Duxford, among other places.

Butlers' Ale

● ABV 4.3% ● BOTTLE SIZE 330 ml ● SERVE cool
● INGREDIENTS Pearl pale malt/crystal malt/Target and First Gold hops
Brewed for Wimpole Hall, a National Trust property in Cambridgeshire, this best bitter is dedicated to the loyal butler, who traditionally savoured a glass of home brew downstairs after a hard day's service upstairs.

TASTING NOTES
An amber ale with malt and fruit in the nose, a pleasant, mostly bitter and nutty taste, and a dry, bitter aftertaste.

Shambles Bitter

ABV 4.3% BOTTLE SIZE 500 ml SERVE cool
INGREDIENTS Pearl pale malt/crystal malt/Target and Styrian Golding hops

The Shambles – a series of trading stalls – in Potton's market place were reconstructed in the late 18th century by the Lord of the Manor, one Samuel Whitbread. As the label of this beer reports, the stalls were used by farmers and other merchants until the end of the 19th century and were eventually demolished in 1954.

TASTING NOTES

An amber bitter with a 'fruit cocktail' aroma. There's a hint of pear drop in the taste, countered by crisp bitterness and malt sweetness. Dry, bitter finish with some lingering fruit.

No-ale Spiced

ABV 4.8% BOTTLE SIZE 500 ml SERVE cool
INGREDIENTS Pearl pale malt/crystal malt/carapils malt/roasted barley/Target and First Gold hops/seasonal spices

This beer is based on the brewery's Christmas cask ale, but with added seasonal spices (including ginger, cinnamon, mace and cloves).

Princetown

Princetown Breweries Ltd., The Brewery, Station Road, Princetown, Devon PL20 6QX. Tel. (01822) 890789 Fax (01822) 890798
E-mail: ale@princetownbreweries.co.uk
Website: www.princetownbreweries.co.uk

Princetown Brewery was established in 1994 by former Gibbs Mew and Hop Back brewer Simon Loveless. The brewery moved to a new site, a few hundred yards from its original base, in 2004. Bottling stopped following the move but was due to recommence in summer 2006.

Jail Ale

ABV 4.8% BOTTLE SIZE 500 ml SERVE cool
INGREDIENTS Pipkin pale malt/crystal malt/wheat malt/Challenger and Progress hops

Based, as it is, just a short tunnelling distance from the famous prison, what else could the brewery call its premium beer? This bottled version of an award-winning cask ale is racked bright and re-seeded with yeast and fresh wort before bottling. Winner of the *Tucker's Maltings Bottled Beer Competition* in 1999.

TASTING NOTES

An amber beer with a floral, fruity aroma with light pear drops. The taste is malty, sweetish, fruity and flower-scented but has good hop balance. Bittersweet, malty finish.

Purple Moose

Bragdy Mws Piws Cyf, Madoc Street, Porthmadog, Gwynedd LL49 9DB. Tel./Fax (01766) 515571
E-mail: beer@purplemoose.co.uk
Website: www.purplemoose.co.uk

Purple Moose was opened in 2005 by brewer Lawrence Washington in a former sawmill and farmers' warehouse in the coastal town of Porthmadog. His bottled beers are filled from conditioning tanks, without filtration, re-seeding of yeast or priming, and are matured at the brewery for about a month before going on sale. The best before dates are set at one year. All beers are declared safe for vegans.

Cwrw Eryri/Snowdonia Ale

● **ABV 3.6%** ● **BOTTLE SIZE 500 ml** ● **SERVE cool**
● **INGREDIENTS Maris Otter pale malt/crystal malt/torrefied wheat/ Pioneer, Golding and Hallertau hops**

This summer beer, first brewed in 2006, celebrates the glory of the Snowdonia National Park, which is on the brewery's doorstep.

TASTING NOTES

A golden ale with piney hops in the nose, followed by a bitter, lightly citrus, piney hop taste. Sweet malt is stronger on the swallow, before a dry, hoppy, bitter aftertaste.

Cwrw Madog/Madog's Ale

● **ABV 3.7%** ● **BOTTLE SIZE 500 ml** ● **SERVE cool**
● **INGREDIENTS Maris Otter pale malt/crystal malt/dark crystal malt/torrefied wheat/Pioneer and Golding hops**

First brewed in 2005, Madog's Ale is named after one William Madocks (1773–1828), who built the harbour at Porthmadog and facilitated the export of slate from the nearby mountains. From 'Port Madog' comes the present name of the town.

TASTING NOTES
Amber in colour, with malt, fruit, light toffee and tea-like hop resins in the aroma. The taste is sharply hoppy at first, but there's toffeeish malt behind and a little citrus washing around. The finish is dry, bitter and hoppy with a hint of roasted malt.

Cwrw Glaslyn/Glaslyn Ale

● ABV 4.2% ● BOTTLE SIZE 500 ml ● SERVE cool
● INGREDIENTS Maris Otter pale malt/crystal malt/torrefied wheat/ Pioneer, Golding and Hallertau hops
The River Glaslyn flows down from Snowdon and into the sea at Porthmadog, hence the name of this golden ale.
TASTING NOTES
Gentle grapefruit and a little grassy hop feature in the nose. The taste is hoppy and tea-like, with grapefruit notes and a tannin astringency that overpowers light, malty sweetness. Dry, very hoppy aftertaste.

Ochr Tywylly y Mws/Dark Side of the Moose

● ABV 4.6% ● BOTTLE SIZE 500 ml ● SERVE cool
● INGREDIENTS Maris Otter pale malt/crystal malt/dark crystal malt/ roasted barley/Pioneer and Bramling Cross hops
A winter ale first brewed in 2005. All Purple Moose bottled beers are also available in cask form.
TASTING NOTES
Ruby, with nutty malt, perfumed citrus notes and gentle chocolate in the aroma. More perfumed citrus leads in the mouth, with good, nutty malt support. Roasted malt takes over in the dry, nicely bitter finish.

RCH

RCH Brewery, West Hewish, Weston-super-Mare, Somerset BS24 6RR.
Tel. (01934) 834447 Fax (01934) 834167
E-mail: rchbrew@aol.com
Website: www.rchbrewery.com
This brewery was originally installed behind the Royal Clarence Hotel at Burnham-on-Sea in the early 1980s (hence the name), but since 1993 brewing has taken place on a rural site, a couple of fields away from the rumble of the M5 motorway. The beers are shipped in conditioning tanks to Branded Drinks in Gloucestershire for bottling, with the best

before date for all brews set at six months. Pitchfork, Old Slug Porter and Ale Mary are distributed in the USA by B United.

On the Tiles

● ABV 3.9% ● BOTTLE SIZE 500 ml ● SERVE cool
● INGREDIENTS Pale malt/crystal malt/Fuggle and Progress hops

On the Tiles is a bottled version of RCH's draught bitter, PG Steam, and was launched initially as part of a pack for sale in BHS in 1998.

TASTING NOTES

A pale brown beer with a fine hoppy nose, backed with fruit and a little toffee. The taste is hoppy, with plenty of fruit. Hoppy, bitter finish.

Pitchfork

● ABV 4.3% ● BOTTLE SIZE 500 ml ● SERVE cool
● INGREDIENTS Pale malt/Fuggle and Golding hops

First produced in 1993, this beer's name was derived from the unsuccessful Pitchfork Rebellion against King James II by the followers of the Duke of Monmouth. They challenged the King's forces at nearby Sedgemoor in July 1685. The beer is also available in cask (*Champion Best Bitter* at CAMRA's *Champion Beer of Britain* awards in 1998).

TASTING NOTES

A golden beer with a mouth-wateringly fruity nose. Initially soft and fruity to taste, it soon gains a solid, slightly perfumed, orangey hop edge. Hoppy, bitter and dry finish.

Major stockists Local Tesco and Thresher

Old Slug Porter ★

● ABV 4.5% ● BOTTLE SIZE 500 ml ● SERVE cool
● INGREDIENTS Pale malt/crystal malt/black malt/Fuggle and Golding hops

Old Slug was named after the pesky little creatures that enjoyed the sandy soil around RCH's old brewery. The slugs are now a thing of the past, but the beer still has a dedicated following. Winner of the *Tucker's Maltings Bottled Beer Competition* in 1998.

TASTING NOTES

A ruby porter with biscuity malt and mellow coffee in the nose. Not too full-bodied, it nonetheless has bags of taste – good, bitter coffee with some sweetness, nuttiness and hops behind. Bitter coffee and plain chocolate feature in the big, dry aftertaste.

Double Header

ABV 5.3% **BOTTLE SIZE 500 ml** **SERVE cool**
INGREDIENTS Pale malt/Golding hops

The winner of Asda's first bottled beer contest, Double Header is named after a train pulled by two engines (as depicted on the label, which also says the ale is 'ideal with roast meats, casseroles or cheese').

TASTING NOTES

A strong, golden ale with smoky orange hops in the nose, plus a little chocolate from the malt. The taste is immediately citrus-fruity but then a big kick of hops arrives to add tangy, bitter notes. Dry, lip-smackingly tangy, hop finish. A hop feast.

Ale Mary

ABV 6% **BOTTLE SIZE 500 ml** **SERVE cool**
INGREDIENTS Pale malt/chocolate malt/Progress and Target hops/ginger/cloves/cinnamon/coriander/nutmeg/pimento

Ale Mary is RCH's Firebox (see below), but with spice oils and essences added prior to bottling. It was first 'created' for Christmas 1998 and has remained a festive favourite. CAMRA's *Champion Bottled Beer* in 2001.

TASTING NOTES

Oranges overlaid with exotic, peppery spice dominate the perfumed nose of this strong amber beer. The spices impart an unusual taste, with the bitter citrus qualities of Firebox exaggerated by the coriander in particular, and the other flavourings providing a peppery, gingery warmth. Dry, scented, bitter orange finish with a light ginger burn.

Major stockists Local Tesco and Thresher

Firebox

ABV 6% **BOTTLE SIZE 500 ml** **SERVE cool**
INGREDIENTS Pale malt/chocolate malt/Progress and Target hops

RCH's premium strength cask- and bottle-conditioned beer. Its name reflects the steam-powered nature of the brewery, plus the fascination with the golden age of railways shared by director Paul Davey and brewer Graham Dunbavan.

TASTING NOTES

A flavoursome, red-amber, strong bitter with a fruity, malty nose. The taste is sweet and fruity, backed with hop bitterness and some dark malt. Dry, tangy, bitter fruit finish, with a hint of dark malt.

Major stockists Local Tesco and Thresher

Rebellion

Rebellion Beer Company, Bencombe Farm, Marlow Bottom, Buckinghamshire SL7 3LT. Tel. (01628) 476594 Fax (01628) 476617
E-mail: tim@rebellionbeer.co.uk
Website: www.rebellionbeer.co.uk
Mail order service

Rebellion was the company that brought brewing back to Marlow, following the closure of Wethereds by Whitbread. Opened in 1993, the brewery has since moved locally and expanded, serving a sizeable pub trade. Although the beer featured below is brewed in Marlow, bottling takes place off-site, at Hepworth & Co. in Horsham.

White

● ABV 4.5% ● BOTTLE SIZE 500 ml ● SERVE cold
● INGREDIENTS Pale malt/wheat malt/First Gold and Cascade hops/ coriander/orange peel/lemon peel

This spiced wheat beer was first brewed in 2001 and claimed that year's SIBA (Society of Independent Brewers) *Wheat Beer Challenge* award for Belgian-style wheats, followed up by a category gold medal in the *International Beer Competition* in 2002. In 2003 and 2004, it was voted overall champion in the *Wheat Beer Challenge*. It's not available on draught and, for bottling, the beer is filtered and re-seeded with fresh yeast. The best before date is fixed at 12 months.

TASTING NOTES

Hazy gold with gingery spice in the nose, along with perfumed, bitter orange/lemon and clove. It tastes crisp and bittersweet, with cloves, peppery spice and tart lemon. Dry, scented, bitter citrus and spice finish.

Major stockist Local Waitrose

Red Rose

Red Rose Brewery, Unit 4, Stanley Court, Alan Ramsbottom Way, Great Harwood, Blackburn, Lancashire BB6 7UR.
Tel. (01254) 877373 Fax (01254) 877375
E-mail: beer@redrosebrewery.co.uk
Website: www.redrosebrewery.co.uk

Red Rose was set up by landlord Peter Booth at the Royal Hotel in Great Harwood in 2002 but soon outgrew the premises and moved to a new unit in 2005. In addition to the beers listed below, winter ales may be available in bottle.

Accrington Stanley Ale

● ABV 3.6% ● BOTTLE SIZE 500 ml ● SERVE cool
● INGREDIENTS Maris Otter pale malt/crystal malt/black malt/Target, Challenger, Fuggle and Golding hops

A new beer for summer 2006, to celebrate the return of the local football club to the Football League after more than 40 years.

Bowley Best

● ABV 3.7% ● BOTTLE SIZE 500 ml ● SERVE cool
● INGREDIENTS Maris Otter pale malt/crystal malt/black malt/Target, Challenger, Fuggle and Golding hops

Bowley Hill was the view brewer Peter Booth enjoyed from his bedroom window as a lad, and is also famous for its scout camp.

TASTING NOTES

Tawny-red with a malty aroma. The taste is bitter, with a strong, drying hop presence and soft malt behind. Dry, bitter, hoppy and malty finish.

Quaffing Ale

● ABV 3.8% ● BOTTLE SIZE 500 ml ● SERVE cool
● INGREDIENTS Maris Otter pale malt/crystal malt/black malt/ Challenger and Golding hops

This dark golden ale, like all the other Red Rose beers, is bottled straight from a cask, using a simple, four-head, manual filler.

Treacle Miner's Tipple

● ABV 3.9% ● BOTTLE SIZE 500 ml ● SERVE cool
● INGREDIENTS Maris Otter pale malt/crystal malt/black malt/ Golding and Fuggle hops

This ruby-brown beer celebrates the legend of the so-called treacle mines to be found near the village of Sabden and the Pendle hill area, which also spawned a children's television series.

Felix

● ABV 4.2% ● BOTTLE SIZE 500 ml ● SERVE cool
● INGREDIENTS Maris Otter pale malt/Challenger, Golding and Fuggle hops

A golden ale. Felix is the pub cat at the Royal Hotel. 'He's the real owner,' says Peter. 'He just lets us use it from time to time.'

Old Ben

● ABV 4.3% ● BOTTLE SIZE 500 ml ● SERVE cool

● INGREDIENTS Maris Otter pale malt/Golding hops/coriander

Ben was Peter's dog who passed away a few years ago, aged 16. He features on the label. For a spicy twist, coriander seeds are added late to the copper boil.

TASTING NOTES

A pale golden beer with citrus fruit in the aroma. Grapefruit zest and bitterness leads in the mouth before a dry, very bitter finish.

Lancashire & Yorkshire Aleway

● ABV 4.5% ● BOTTLE SIZE 500 ml ● SERVE cool

● INGREDIENTS Maris Otter pale malt/crystal malt/black malt/Target, Challenger, Fuggle and Golding hops

The Royal Hotel stands close to the site of the old Lancashire & Yorkshire Railway, hence the name of this beer, which is also familiarly known as 'Steaming'.

TASTING NOTES

A red-amber beer with malt and light citrus fruit in the nose. There are more malty, sweet flavours in the taste but also a tart fruitiness and bitter hops. Chocolate and roasted grain appear in the initial maltiness in the finish, with hops taking over for a bitter end.

Care Taker of History

● ABV 6% ● BOTTLE SIZE 500 ml ● SERVE cool

● INGREDIENTS Maris Otter pale malt/crystal malt/black malt/Target, Challenger and Fuggle hops

This strong ale is dedicated to the memory of Jim Ridge, an early CAMRA member who converted Peter from drinking lager to drinking ale. Jim always believed that you'd never made it unless you'd had a beer named after you. He died in 2003.

TASTING NOTES

A ruby ale with a fruity aroma with creamy malt. The lightly warming taste is sweetish and malty but pleasantly balanced by bitterness. Nutty, creamy malt emerges. There are hints of liquorice in the hoppy, bitter, drying aftertaste of roasted grain.

Redburn

Redburn Brewery, Redburn, Hexham, Northumberland, NE47 7EA.
Tel./Fax (01434) 344656
E-mail: redburnbrewery@btinternet.com
Website: www.redburnbrewery.co.uk
Mail order service

Redburn Brewery started production in autumn 2003, and turned to bottling the following year. Many of its beers reflect the proximity of Hadrian's Wall to the brewery, with Latin and Roman connections to the fore. Occasional, one-off bottles complement the regular beers.

Haltwhistle Pride

● **ABV 4.3%** ● **BOTTLE SIZE 500 ml** ● **SERVE cool**
● **INGREDIENTS Maris Otter pale malt/crystal malt/Perle hops**

A celebration best bitter for the town of Haltwhistle, just a few miles from the brewery. Also available in cask form.

TASTING NOTES

A golden beer with orange marmalade and spicy hop in the aroma. Tart fruit and sweet malt feature in the taste. Dry, orange-fruity, bitter finish.

Fortis

● **ABV 4.4%** ● **BOTTLE SIZE 500 ml** ● **SERVE cool**
● **INGREDIENTS Maris Otter pale malt/roasted barley/Perle hops**

Fortis is the Latin for stout! This is also sold as a cask beer.

TASTING NOTES

A deep ruby stout with dark malts in the aroma and bittersweet taste, which also has plain chocolate. Dry, roasted malt, bitter finish.

Solis

● **ABV 4.4%** ● **BOTTLE SIZE 500 ml** ● **SERVE cool**
● **INGREDIENTS Maris Otter pale malt/wheat malt/Perle hops**

Solis, from *solis ortus*, the Latin for sunrise, sums up the sunny complexion of this summer beer. Occasionally sold in cask form.

Bishop Ridley Ale

● **ABV 4.8%** ● **BOTTLE SIZE 500 ml** ● **SERVE cool**
● **INGREDIENTS Maris Otter pale malt/crystal malt/black malt/ Perle hops**

A Scottish heavy-style, red ale, named after Bishop Nicholas Ridley, the 16th-century Protestant reformer, and ultimately martyr, who was born near Haltwhistle. Available in cask in the autumn.

TASTING NOTES

Orange-citrus and dark malt in the aroma. Bitter citrus leads over malt in the mouth. Dry, malty finish with hops and bitterness building.

Twice Brewed IPA

- **ABV 5.3%** • **BOTTLE SIZE 500 ml** • **SERVE cool**
- **INGREDIENTS Maris Otter pale malt/wheat malt/Perle hops**

There are some odd place names in the North-East (Pity Me and No Place, for starters), but Twice Brewed has to be among the strangest, along with neighbouring Once Brewed, of course. Thus the name of this beer has nothing to do with the way it is made. (Redburn also brews a beer called Once Brewed, at 4.7%, for the Once Brewed youth hostel.)

TASTING NOTES

A golden beer with a hoppy nose with some malt sweetness. Tart fruit, hops and malt feature in the taste. Dry, bitter, fruit and malt finish.

Special

- **ABV 6%** • **BOTTLE SIZE 500 ml** • **SERVE cool**
- **INGREDIENTS Maris Otter pale malt/crystal malt/amber malt/black malt/Perle hops**

This dark amber, orange-citrus, strong ale, like the other beers, is bottled directly from a conditioning tank at the brewery, with most of the yeast dropped out but some remaining for the bottle fermentation.

TASTING NOTES

Malt and red berries in the nose. The taste is sweet and malty, with berry-fruit and a little bitterness. Berries and malt in the bitter finish.

Reepham

Reepham Brewery, Unit 1, Collers Way, Reepham, Norfolk NR10 4SW. Tel. (01603) 871091

Reepham is one of the longest established breweries in Norfolk, founded in 1983. Its contribution to the bottle-conditioned beer scene is not entirely conventional, as the beer mentioned is packaged only in 2-litre PET bottles for sale in some local off-licences, with a best before date set at just six weeks after filling.

Rapier Pale Ale

● ABV 4.3% ● BOTTLE SIZE 2 litres ● SERVE cool
● INGREDIENTS Maris Otter pale malt/barley syrup/Fuggle and Bramling Cross hops

Rapier, in its cask form, is a former award-winner at the Norwich Beer Festival and was introduced for that event in 1987. This bottled version is aged in cask for a couple of weeks prior to packaging.

Ridgeway

Ridgeway Brewing, South Stoke,
Oxfordshire RG8 0JW. Tel./Fax (01491) 873474
E-mail: sales@ridgewaybrewery.co.uk

Ridgeway Brewing is run by Peter Scholey, former head brewer at Brakspear, who, in addition to brewing bottle-conditioned beers mentioned elsewhere in this book for other brewers, also brews for his own business, using equipment at Hepworth & Co. in Horsham and other venues. The Ridgeway long-distance footpath passes just a few hundred yards from Peter's front door in South Oxfordshire – hence the brewery name. In addition to the beers featured below, Ridgeway produces six Christmas beers each year for the American market. They vary in strength from 6% to 9% and are occasionally available through independent off-licences in the UK.

Bitter ★

● ABV 4% ● BOTTLE SIZE 500 ml ● SERVE cool
● INGREDIENTS Maris Otter pale malt/Challenger and Boadicea hops

This bitter features the new Boadicea strain of aphid-resistant hops. Like all Peter's bottle-conditioned beers, the beer is sterile filtered before being re-seeded with fresh yeast for bottling. It is also sold in cask.

TASTING NOTES

A golden beer with an aroma of floral hops and a little orange marmalade. The bittersweet taste is also floral and hoppy, with a gentle orange sweetness. Drying, floral, hoppy finish.

ROB (Ridgeway Organic Bitter) ★

● ABV 4.3% ● BOTTLE SIZE 500 ml ● SERVE cold
● INGREDIENTS Vary

Both organic and vegetarian, this new beer also appears in draught form occasionally. The ingredients will vary from year to year, according to the availability of organic materials. However, Peter is confident the flavour will be largely the same. Try it with pizza, pasta or fish, he says.

TASTING NOTES

Juicy oranges and apricots feature in the lightly peppery aroma of this golden ale. The taste is crisp, hoppy and clean, with bitter citrus flavours and always a good malt balance. The bitter, hoppy and drying finish is long and satisfying.

Blue ★

● **ABV 5%** ● **BOTTLE SIZE 500 ml** ● **SERVE cold**

● **INGREDIENTS Maris Otter and Optic pale malt/Challenger, Fuggle and Styrian Golding hops**

A *Tesco Beer Challenge* winner for 2005–6, this new brew has been designed to be drunk cold, not just lightly chilled. Compare it at both temperatures, says Peter, and you'll see what he means. Great with barbecues and spicy foods, he says.

TASTING NOTES

Another golden ale with a clean, grapefruity hop aroma. Grapefruit and orange peel flavours lead in the taste, which is crisp, tangy and clean. Long-lasting, dry, bitter, tangy finish with more grapefruit.

Major stockist Tesco

Ivanhoe

● **ABV 5.2%** ● **BOTTLE SIZE 500 ml** ● **SERVE cold**

● **INGREDIENTS Maris Otter pale malt/chocolate malt/Golding and Admiral hops**

Ivanhoe was first brewed for the Swedish market and then introduced into the UK and USA. The label was designed by a Swedish art student.

TASTING NOTES

A copper-coloured ale with a malty, nutty aroma backed by hoppy fruit. The taste is also malty, nutty and bitter, with light fruit wafting around. The finish is drying and bitter, with roasted, nutty malt.

IPA ★

● **ABV 5.5%** ● **BOTTLE SIZE 500 ml** ● **SERVE cool**

● **INGREDIENTS Maris Otter and Optic pale malt/Challenger, Fuggle, Target and Cascade hops**

The Society of Independent Brewers' (SIBA) *Champion Bottled Beer* for the South-East in 2005–6. This authentic IPA goes really well with curry, according to Peter.

TASTING NOTES

A golden IPA with lots of fresh, sappy hop resins in the aroma, bringing mellow orange and zesty peel notes. Malty sweetness is loaded with tangy, floral hops in the taste, with a tannin-like dryness, too. Yet more hops feature in the bitter, lip-smacking finish.

Ringwood

Ringwood Brewery Ltd., 138 Christchurch Road, Ringwood, Hampshire BH24 3AP. Tel. (01425) 471177 Fax (01425) 480273
E-mail: info@ringwoodbrewery.co.uk
Website: www.ringwoodbrewery.co.uk
Mail order service

Ringwood was set up in 1978 and moved in 1986 to attractive 18th-century buildings, formerly part of the old Tunks brewery. It has since become one of the stalwarts of the UK brewing scene, overtaking in size many established regional brewers. The bottled beers are brewed in the same way as the cask versions, except that a week's cold-conditioning (3°C) is employed to bring down the yeast count prior to bottling (which is carried out under contract at Hop Back Brewery). The beer is then kräusened. Twelve months' shelf life is indicated on the labels. The brewery also ships the beers overseas on request.

Bold Forester

● ABV 4.2% ● BOTTLE SIZE 500 ml ● SERVE cool
● INGREDIENTS Maris Otter pale malt/crystal malt/amber malt/ Challenger and Progress hops

Bold Forester was launched as a cask beer for spring 2003, but was also bottled as a way of commemorating the brewery's 25th birthday. It now continues as an annual spring bottling. The Maris Otter barley included is grown exclusively in Hampshire by farmers directly contracted by the brewery, and then traditionally floor malted. Amber malt helps add dryness to the brew while late and dry hopping (in the conditioning tank) with Challenger hops adds to the spicy fruit character.

TASTING NOTES

Copper, with hops and malt in the nose. Light chocolate, malt, fruit and hops feature in the taste. Dry, bitter finish with lingering chocolate.

Huffkin

● ABV 4.4% ● BOTTLE SIZE 500 ml ● SERVE cool
● INGREDIENTS Maris Otter pale malt/crystal malt/chocolate malt/ Fuggle and Golding hops

Brewed to the same recipe as Ringwood's autumn seasonal beer of the same name that was introduced in 2002. As for Bold Forester, floor-malted Maris Otter barley provides the foundation of this brew. A huffkin is a cake from Kent that includes hops.

TASTING NOTES

A russet ale with light malt and sweet red apples in the aroma. The taste is mix of malt and hops, with a tea-like dryness from the latter, before a bitter, dry, hoppy finish with roasted malt developing.

XXXX Porter

● ABV 4.7% ● BOTTLE SIZE 500 ml ● SERVE cool
● INGREDIENTS Maris Otter pale malt/crystal malt/chocolate malt/ roasted barley extract/Challenger, Progress and Golding hops

Cask XXXX Porter has been a favourite among local drinkers since 1980 but the brewery has only ever brewed it in the winter months. However, following its introduction in bottled form in November 2000, fans can now enjoy this dark brew at any time, as stocks bottled while the cask beer is in production should last through to the next winter run (November to February).

TASTING NOTES

A near-black, dark ruby beer with an aroma of lightly roasted malt. Clean and tasty, it is easy to drink, with hints of orange and pleasantly bitter roasted notes, plus some sweetness throughout. Roasted malt and fruit feature in the dry, bittersweet aftertaste.

Major stockist Local Co-op

Fortyniner ★

● ABV 4.9% ● BOTTLE SIZE 500 ml ● SERVE cool
● INGREDIENTS Maris Otter pale malt/crystal malt/chocolate malt/ Challenger, Progress and Golding hops

Fortyniner first appeared in cask form in 1978, taking its name from its 1049 original gravity. This bottled version only made its debut in 1996 and was increased in strength from 4.8 to 4.9% in 1998.

TASTING NOTES

Orange-gold, with an aroma of oranges and hops. Malt and oranges are

prominent in the mouth, with some sweetness, although bitterness increases as hops kick in. The body is good, but this is an easy drinking and deceptively strong ale. Dry, bitter, hoppy orange peel finish.
Major stockists Tesco, local Co-op and Sainsbury's

St Austell

St Austell Brewery Company Ltd.,
63 Trevarthian Road, St Austell, Cornwall PL25 4BY.
Tel. (01726) 74444 Fax (01726) 68965
E-mail: info@staustellbrewery.co.uk
Website: www.staustellbrewery.co.uk
Mail order service

St Austell joined the band of bottle-conditioned beer brewers in spring 2000, when it won the *Tesco Beer Challenge* with Clouded Yellow. Further bottle-conditioned ales have been added in the last two years. The beers are brewed at St Austell but packaged under contract, by Thwaites in Blackburn, although St Austell has announced plans to install its own bottling line in 2007. The beers are sterile filtered and re-seeded with the original yeast strain prior to bottling. The best before date is set at one year. All are declared acceptable to vegetarians.

Clouded Yellow

● **ABV 4.8%** ● **BOTTLE SIZE 500 ml** ● **SERVE cold**
● **INGREDIENTS Maris Otter pale malt/wheat malt/Willamette hops/ vanilla pods/cloves/coriander/maple syrup**

St Austell stages an annual Celtic Beer Festival, for which it prepared two novel brews in 1999. This beer, known as Hagar the Horrible at the time, was one. Brewer Roger Ryman popped down to his local supermarket to pick up the ingredients to make his vision of a German-style wheat beer become reality. He didn't want foreign yeast strains in his brewhouse, where there might be a chance of St Austell's own prized yeast becoming contaminated, and so set about recreating weissbier flavours artificially, by adding spices to the beer after the boil, as it strained through the hops in the hop back. Vanilla pods, whole cloves and coriander seeds were the key flavourings, as well as maple syrup which was mixed with sugar for priming, and they blended together so well that Roger decided to submit the beer for the *Tesco Beer Challenge*, which it duly won. In 2003, the beer was re-vamped.

The strength was dropped to 4.8% from 5%, the clove content was reduced and a touch more vanilla (four pods per barrel) completed the update, which was packaged in a new, slender green bottle. The name is shared with a rare butterfly, which, just like German wheat beers, is a popular continental visitor to Britain in summer. Drink with lightly spiced foods such as Thai curry, or a dessert like crème brûlée, Roger suggests.

TASTING NOTES

Golden, with rich banana and vanilla in the nose. Crisper and thinner than the earlier version, it still has plenty of banana and vanilla flavour, but noticeably less clove. Dry finish, with light banana and vanilla.

Major stockist Tesco

Smuggler's Ale/Admiral's Ale ★

ABV 5% **BOTTLE SIZE 500 ml** **SERVE cool**

INGREDIENTS Cornish Gold malt/Styrian Golding and Cascade hops

First brewed for the Celtic Beer Festival in 2004, this innovative dark ale was then bottled for the first time at Easter 2005, on both occasions as Admiral's Ale. It is now also sold exclusively in Asda as Smuggler's Ale. The innovation lies in the malt, which has been specially created from Cornish barley for St Austell by Tucker's Maltings in Newton Abbot. The barley is kilned at a high temperature to achieve a dark colour and nutty flavour but with humidity retained so that the sugars in the malt do not crystallize and become useless for brewing. As a result, St Austell doesn't need to include pale malt in the recipe. The same malt is used in St Austell's main cask guest beer, Tribute.

TASTING NOTES

A deep bronze ale with a malty, nutty aroma. The taste nicely balances sweet barley malt with a hop crispness and tropical fruit flavours. Dry, nutty, bitter finish with lingering fruit.

Major stockist Asda

Proper Job

ABV 5.5% **BOTTLE SIZE 500 ml** **SERVE cool**

INGREDIENTS Maris Otter pale malt/Cascade, Chinook and Willamette hops

A new pale, American-influenced IPA, inspired by an exchange visit Roger Ryman undertook with Bridgeport Brewery in Oregon, whose own IPA has won numerous awards. Proper Job was first brewed for the 2005 Celtic Beer Festival and first bottled in 2006.

TASTING NOTES

A golden IPA with fresh citrus notes in the aroma – orange peel, lime and grapefruit. The same full citrus flavours continue in the mouth from the abundant hops, with just a little restraining malt. There's more citrus hop in the long-lasting aftertaste.

Salopian

The Salopian Brewing Company Ltd., The Brewery,
67 Mytton Oak Road, Shrewsbury, Shropshire SY3 8UQ.
Tel. (01743) 248414 Fax (01743) 358866

Salopian began production in 1995. After closing briefly in 1997, it re-opened in new hands, retaining its brewer Martin Barry. Bottle-conditioned beers were introduced in 1996 but the wide range the brewery used to produce has now dwindled to just one, and that is largely for export to the USA. The beer is brewed for Salopian by Peter Scholey, former Brakspear's head brewer, using equipment at Hepworth & Co. in Horsham.

Entire Butt

● **ABV 4.8%** ● **BOTTLE SIZE 500 ml** ● **SERVE cool**
● **INGREDIENTS Maris Otter pale malt/crystal malt/dark crystal malt/amber malt/pale chocolate malt/dark chocolate malt/brown malt/black malt/lager malt/carapils malt/wheat malt/malted oats/roasted barley/torrefied wheat/Fuggle, Styrian Golding and Golding hops**

Count the malts! This mammoth beer is a tribute to a beer style which originated nearly 300 years ago. In the early 1700s, drinkers favoured a blend of three beers – pale ale, brown ale and stock ale – laboriously drawn from three separate casks (or butts). A London brewer, Ralph Harwood, hit upon the idea of combining the three brews in one cask and gave it the name Entire Butt (the brew being entirely in one butt, so to speak). Its popularity with local street porters allegedly saw the new brew re-christened 'porter'.

TASTING NOTES

Dark ruby with a biscuity, grainy, slightly smoky aroma with a little nut and plain chocolate. Smooth malty flavours fill the taste, with bitter chocolate and biscuit, offset by a pleasant, hoppy sharpness. Dry, biscuity, bitter chocolate finish.

Scarecrow

Scarecrow Brewery Ltd., c/o Dairyman's Daughter, Arreton Barn, Newport Road, Arreton, Isle of Wight PO30 3AA.
Tel. (01983) 856161

Scarecrow Brewery is located at Arreton Craft Village, alongside the Dairyman's Daughter Inn, in the middle of the Isle of Wight. The 3.5-barrel brewery can be seen from the adjacent shop, which stocks beers from all the island's breweries, although brewing has been suspended for the time being. The beer below is produced at Ventnor.

Best

● **ABV 4.2%** ● **BOTTLE SIZE 500 ml** ● **SERVE cool**
● **INGREDIENTS Pale malt/crystal malt/wheat malt/Bramling Cross hops**

The brewery that uses the punning slogan 'Outstanding in our field' to advertise its presence. Apparently, this beer 'pulls the birds'.

TASTING NOTES

A golden ale tasting bittersweet, malty and nutty, but with a spritzy hop kick. Dry, roasted nut, bitter finish.

Shakespeare's

Shakespeare's Brewery Ltd., 9 Small Brook Business Centre, Bidford-on-Avon, Warwickshire B50 4JE. Tel. (0845) 838 1564
E-mail: info@shakesbrew.co.uk
Website: www.shakesbrew.co.uk

This small brewery opened in 2005, close to Stratford-upon-Avon, home of the illustrious bard. The beers are all made from organically-grown malt and local hops and the brewery makes a point of its green credentials. Bottle labels declare that electricity used in the process comes from renewable sources and that recycling the bottle will save enough energy to power your TV for an hour and a half!

Noble Fool

● **ABV 3.9%** ● **BOTTLE SIZE 500 ml** ● **SERVE cool**
● **INGREDIENTS Maris Otter pale malt/crystal malt/wheat malt/ rye malt/First Gold hops**

Bottle-conditioned beer was first produced by Shakespeare's in May

2006. All the labels carry a quotation from Shakespeare, in the case of Noble Fool from *As You Like It.*

TASTING NOTES

Dark golden, with malt and grassy hop resins in the aroma. Nutty malt and drying hops feature in the taste, before a bitter, malty, nutty finish.

Taming of the Brew

● **ABV 4.3%** ● **BOTTLE SIZE 500 ml** ● **SERVE cool**

● **INGREDIENTS Maris Otter pale malt/crystal malt/chocolate malt/ wheat malt/rye malt/Challenger and Golding hops**

The Taming of the Shrew, Act II, Scene I, is quoted on the label of this premium ale. As for the other beers, this brew is bottled straight from the fermenting vessel having dropped mostly bright without the use of finings. All the beers are therefore acceptable to vegans. There are no primings, no filtration and no re-seeding with fresh yeast.

TASTING NOTES

Amber, with malt and spicy hop in the nose, then light lemon. The taste is also malty and spicy, but generally bitter. Dry, bitter, hoppy finish.

The Scottish Ale

● **ABV 4.6%** ● **BOTTLE SIZE 500 ml** ● **SERVE cool**

● **INGREDIENTS Maris Otter pale malt/crystal malt/chocolate malt/ wheat malt/Golding and Fuggle hops**

With a quote from *Macbeth*, this 80/- type beer makes allusion to the fact that thespians never mention 'The Scottish Play' by its proper name, for fear of bringing bad luck to the production.

TASTING NOTES

Amber, with an aroma of malt, nuts and plenty of spice, with some juicy fruit. The taste is also malty and spicy, with light, sharp, fruity hops. Dry, malty and hoppy finish.

The Tempest

● **ABV 5.5%** ● **BOTTLE SIZE 500 ml** ● **SERVE cool**

● **INGREDIENTS Maris Otter pale malt/crystal malt/chocolate malt/ wheat malt/rye malt/Challenger hops**

Shakespeare's last fully-completed play is honoured by this robust porter. In addition to selected quotes from individual plays, each bottle label carries the brewery motto: '...for a quart of ale is a dish for a king', a memorable line from *The Winter's Tale.*

TASTING NOTES
A red porter with biscuity dark malts and plain chocolate in the aroma. Bitter dark malts continue on the palate, with hints of liquorice and coffee, plus sweetness for balance. Roasted malt and hops produce a dry, bitter finish.

Shardlow

Shardlow Brewing Co. Ltd., Old Brewery Stables, British Waterways Yard, Cavendish Bridge, Leicestershire DE72 2HL. Tel./Fax (01332) 799188

Shardlow Brewing was set up in 1993 and was taken over by its present ownership in 1996. The beers below are brewed by Shardlow but bottled by Bells Brewery in Ullesthorpe, Leicestershire.

Special Bitter

● **ABV 3.9%** ● **BOTTLE SIZE 500 ml** ● **SERVE cool**
● **INGREDIENTS Maris Otter pale malt/crystal malt/Phoenix and Golding hops**

Formerly Shardlow's Best Bitter, which has been available in bottle since the end of 2003.

Golden Hop

● **ABV 4.1%** ● **BOTTLE SIZE 500 ml** ● **SERVE cool**
● **INGREDIENTS Maris Otter pale malt/Phoenix and Golding hops**

A new golden ale, dry hopped with East Kent Goldings.

Narrowboat

● **ABV 4.5%** ● **BOTTLE SIZE 500 ml** ● **SERVE cool**
● **INGREDIENTS Maris Otter pale malt/crystal malt/Phoenix hops**

A beer recalling Shardlow's history as the one-time busiest inland port in England (on the Trent and Mersey Canal).

Reverend Eaton's

● **ABV 4.5%** ● **BOTTLE SIZE 500 ml** ● **SERVE cool**
● **INGREDIENTS Maris Otter pale malt/Golding and Phoenix hops**

In the early 19th century, the site of the brewery once belonged to the Eaton family, one of whom was also the local vicar. He now gives his name to this dark golden ale.

Five Bells

● ABV 5% ● BOTTLE SIZE 500 ml ● SERVE cool

● INGREDIENTS Maris Otter pale malt/black malt/Phoenix hops

A new strong ale.

Whistlestop

● ABV 5% ● BOTTLE SIZE 500 ml ● SERVE cool

● INGREDIENTS Maris Otter pale malt/Phoenix hops

A pale strong bitter reflecting Shardlow's proximity to the railway city of Derby.

TASTING NOTES

A golden beer with fruit in the nose and taste, back by a soft malty sweetness. Dry, bittersweet, fruity-hop aftertaste.

Shepherd Neame

**Shepherd Neame Ltd., 17 Court Street,
Faversham, Kent ME13 7AX.
Tel. (01795) 532206 Fax (01795) 538907
E-mail: company@shepherd-neame.co.uk
Website: www.shepherd-neame.co.uk**

Kent's largest independent brewer lays claim to being the oldest in the country (established 1698). That year is commemorated now in a return to bottle conditioning at Faversham. In 1993, the brewery was in at the start of the revival of real ale in a bottle, when it launched bottle-conditioned Spitfire (4.5%). Sadly, production problems meant that bottle conditioning was halted a few years later and Spitfire became filtered and pasteurized, as it still is. Now, however, the company has improved its bottling techniques to the point where it is confident enough to supply a bottle-conditioned beer again.

1698 ★

● ABV 6.5% ● BOTTLE SIZE 500 ml ● SERVE cool

● INGREDIENTS Pearl pale malt/crystal malt/Target and Golding hops

1698 was first brewed in 1998, to celebrate Shepherd Neame's 300th birthday. At the time the beer was filtered and pasteurized. This new version, introduced in March 2005, is brewed to the same recipe, except that it is 'thrice hopped'. Target hops go into the copper for bitterness, Goldings are added later for aroma, and yet more Goldings are introduced in the whirlpool, as the beer is being centrifuged to take out unwanted solid matter. The other difference, of course, is in the inclusion of living, fresh bottling yeast, added to the beer after it has been filtered.

TASTING NOTES

A copper-coloured ale with a finely balanced aroma of malt, hops and just a trace of bubblegum. The taste is full and smooth, with rich, sweet malt and a perfumed hoppiness. There are buttery undertones and dried fruit, too. Buttery malt and perfumed hop continue in the drying aftertaste.

Shoes

Shoes Brewery, The Three Horse Shoes Inn, Norton Cannon, Hereford HR4 7BH. Tel./Fax (01544) 318375

Three Horse Shoes landlord Frank Goodwin had been a home brewer long before deciding to brew for his own pub. His bottle-conditioned ales are sold in tiny numbers (no wholesaler calls, please!), with the most famous, Farrier's, smashing its way to the top of the list of the strongest beers featured in this book (even though it's a little weaker now than in the past). All the beers are produced with malt extract, rather than from a full mash. They are bottled in house by Frank with the addition of a little priming sugar.

Norton Ale

● **ABV 3.6%** ● **BOTTLE SIZE 500 ml** ● **SERVE cool**
● **INGREDIENTS Malt extract/Golding hops**

Frank's regular session ale.

Cannon Bitter

● **ABV 4.2%** ● **BOTTLE SIZE 500 ml** ● **SERVE cool**
● **INGREDIENTS Malt extract/Fuggle hops**

The brewery's best bitter.

Peplowe's Tipple

● **ABV 6%** ● **BOTTLE SIZE 500 ml** ● **SERVE cool**
● **INGREDIENTS Malt extract/Golding hops**

A new, powerful ale which Frank readily admits was inspired by the former Gibbs Mew beer, Bishop's Tipple.

Farrier's Beer

● ABV 14% ● BOTTLE SIZE 330 ml ● SERVE at room temperature
● INGREDIENTS Malt extract/Fuggle hops

Beware: this is not a beer for the faint-hearted. Even the brewery's yeast surrenders in the face of so much alcohol, which means Frank needs to finish off the fermentation with a wine yeast. He's now contemplating making a version with green hops.

TASTING NOTES

Amber, with an alcoholic nose. The taste is sweet and fiercely alcoholic, with estery almond notes and a persistent warmth. Warm, sweet, alcoholic finish with a sherry-like dryness.

South Hams

South Hams Brewery Co. Ltd., Stokeley Barton,
Stokenham, Kingsbridge, Devon TQ7 2SE.
Tel. (01548) 581151
E-mail: info@southhamsbrewery.co.uk
Website: www.southhamsbrewery.co.uk

South Hams began life in 1993 as Sutton Brewery, alongside Plymouth's Thistle Park Tavern. In 2004 the brewery moved to Stokenham and the name was changed to South Hams. Two bottle-conditioned beers have been introduced, and a third, Eddystone (4.8%), is planned.

Devon Pride

● ABV 3.8% ● BOTTLE SIZE 500 ml ● SERVE cool
● INGREDIENTS Maris Otter pale malt/crystal malt/chocolate malt/ Bramling Cross and Cascade hops

Formerly known as Plymouth Pride when brewed at Sutton Brewery.

Devon Porter

● ABV 5% ● BOTTLE SIZE 500 ml ● SERVE cool
● INGREDIENTS Maris Otter pale malt/crystal malt/black malt/ Bramling Cross and Styrian Golding hops

A porter that may only be available in winter months. Both beers are brewed at South Hams but bottled by Country Life Brewery.

TASTING NOTES

A ruby porter with biscuity dark malts and sweet liquorice in the peppery nose. Dark malts continue in the taste, with plain chocolate flavours. Mostly bitter and slightly earthy. Roasted notes are obvious in the finish, with more lingering bitter chocolate.

Spinning Dog

Spinning Dog Brewery, 88 St Owen Street, Hereford HR1 2QD.
Tel. (01432) 342125
E-mail: jfkenyon@aol.com
Website: www.spinningdogbrewery.co.uk
Mail order service

Small, family-run brewery established in 2000 and based at Hereford's Victory pub. It was expanded in 2002 to meet demand for its popular beers. The bottled beers are filtered and re-seeded with fresh yeast prior to filling and then matured in the bottle for at least a month before sale. Best before dates are set at 12 months. Both beers are organic and are declared acceptable to vegetarians.

Hereford Organic Bitter

● **ABV 3.7%** ● **BOTTLE SIZE 500 ml** ● **SERVE cool**
● **INGREDIENTS Maris Otter pale malt/Spalt hops**

In its cask version, this beer was the Supreme Champion in the Society of Independent Brewers (SIBA) western region contest for 2005. Note the use of unusual organic German hops.

TASTING NOTES

A golden bitter with a malty, lightly citrus aroma. The taste is clean and well balanced, crisp, bitter and full, with spicy hops to the fore. Dry, hoppy aftertaste.

Organic Oatmeal Stout

● **ABV 4.4%** ● **BOTTLE SIZE 500 ml** ● **SERVE cool**
● **INGREDIENTS Maris Otter pale malt/roasted barley/crushed oats/ Hallertau hops**

An organic variation on the theme of the brewery's draught Muttleys Oatmeal Stout. 'A great accompaniment to strong cheese and game casseroles,' according to the label of this very dark red, near-black beer.

TASTING NOTES

Chocolate and coffee feature in the appealing aroma. Bitter dark malts lead over a gentle malty sweetness in the mouth, with creamy chocolate in support. Bitter dark chocolate takes over in the finish.

Storm

Storm Brewing Co., 2 Waterside, Macclesfield, Cheshire SK11 7HJ.
Tel./Fax (01625) 431234

Storm Brewing was set up in 1998. It supplies around 60 pubs in the Manchester/Cheshire/Peak District area with cask beer and now bottles its beers in house.

Bosley Cloud

● **ABV 4.1%** ● **BOTTLE SIZE 500 ml** ● **SERVE cool**
● **INGREDIENTS Pale malt/lager malt/wheat malt/Cluster and Fuggle hops**

It fits in with Storm's weather theme, but Bosley Cloud is actually named after a rocky outcrop a few miles from the brewery's home in Macclesfield.

TASTING NOTES

A golden ale with a modest malt aroma but plenty of taste. Sweetish orange fruit and a little counter-bitterness from hops ensure a crisp, light drink, with a drying, increasingly bitter and hoppy finish.

Ale Force

● **ABV 4.2%** ● **BOTTLE SIZE 500 ml** ● **SERVE cool**
● **INGREDIENTS Pale malt/crystal malt/chocolate malt/Fuggle hops**

Storm's first ever brew, Ale Force made its debut in cask form in 1998. As for the other Storm entries, bottles are simply filled from the cask, maintaining the same yeast used in primary fermentation, with best before dates set at nine months.

TASTING NOTES

A copper ale with an aroma of malt, oranges and a pinch of chocolate. The taste is full of earthy hops but quite sweet and fruity behind, while the hoppy, drying, bitter finish has hints of dark malt.

Silk of Amnesia

● **ABV 4.7%** ● **BOTTLE SIZE 500 ml** ● **SERVE cool**
● **INGREDIENTS Pale malt/crystal malt/chocolate malt/Cluster and Fuggle hops**

Like Bosley Cloud, this brew features American Cluster hops. Its name, an obvious play on words with a well-known dyspepsia remedy, also reflects Macclesfield's former importance as a major silk industry centre.

TASTING NOTES
A deep amber beer, toffee-flavoured from nose to finish, yet not sweet, with a sharp, balancing bitterness in the taste and a dry, bitter finish.

Strangford Lough

Strangford Lough Brewing Company Ltd., Braidleigh Lodge, 22 Shore Road, Killyleagh, Co. Down BT30 9UE.
Tel. (028 44) 821461 Fax (028 44) 821273
E-mail: office@slbc.ie
Website: www.slbc.ie

An enterprise founded by two management consultants who started to build beer brands in 2004 without running to the cost of setting up a brewery. The beers are contract brewed and are themed around the area of Northern Ireland's Strangford Lough, burial place of Magnus, King of Norway from 1093, one of the area's early invaders.

St Patrick's Best

● **ABV 3.8%** ● **BOTTLE SIZE 500 ml** ● **SERVE cool**
● **INGREDIENTS Pale malt/crystal malt/black malt/Challenger, First Gold and Golding hops**

St Patrick was born the son of a Roman noble, some say in Wales and others in Scotland. However, it is with Ireland that he is closely associated, bringing Christianity to the island and now adopted as its patron saint. He died, and was buried, near Downpatrick in AD 461. This beer was added to the Strangford Lough range in 2004.

TASTING NOTES
A dark golden beer with malt, hops and fruit (tinned peaches) in the aroma. The taste is a malt and hop mix, with a touch of astringency, before a dry, bitter yet still malty aftertaste.

Barelegs Brew

● **ABV 4.5%** ● **BOTTLE SIZE 500 ml** ● **SERVE cool**
● **INGREDIENTS Pale malt/lager malt/caramalt/flaked maize/Northern Brewer, First Gold and Perle hops**

Barelegs was the nickname of Magnus, King of Norway, who was killed in battle near the lough and buried on Downpatrick Marshes in 1103. His Viking ship is seen approaching on the label. Along with Legbiter (below), Barelegs was one of the first two Strangford Lough beers.

TASTING NOTES
A pale golden ale with a big lemon-lime aroma. The crisp, bittersweet taste is lightly warming, a tangy mix of hop fruit and malt. Dry, gently bitter, hoppy aftertaste.

Legbiter

● ABV 4.8% ● BOTTLE SIZE 500 ml ● SERVE cool
● INGREDIENTS Lager malt/caramalt/flaked maize/Northern Brewer, First Gold, Golding and Styrian Golding hops
Legbiter was the name of Magnus's trusty, super-sharp sword, said to have been adorned with ivory and gold-thread.
TASTING NOTES
This pale golden premium ale has spicy hop resins and a little orange in the nose. There's more spicy hop, with malt, in the mouth, rounding off with a dry, bitter, hoppy and tangy, lightly warming finish.

St Patrick's Gold

● ABV 4.8% ● BOTTLE SIZE 500 ml ● SERVE cool
● INGREDIENTS Pale malt/lager malt/wheat malt/Cascade hops/ orange peel/lemon peel
Another beer in honour of the saint, first brewed in 2004. This one is described as a wheat beer, laced with the zest of oranges and lemons, and, according to the label, containing Irish shamrock, too.
TASTING NOTES
Another golden beer, with an aroma of bitter lemons and spices. The refreshing, well-balanced taste is sweet, citrus-fruity and spicy, with lemon and ginger notes. Dry, fruity, lemony and spicy aftertaste.

St Patrick's Ale

● ABV 6% ● BOTTLE SIZE 500 ml ● SERVE cool
● INGREDIENTS Pale malt/crystal malt/black malt/Golding, Progress and Challenger hops
Like all Strangford beers, this is declared as being acceptable to vegans. Further details of Patrick's life are covered on the bottle labels.
TASTING NOTES
Copper-red in colour, this full-flavoured ale has bitter citrus fruit, hop resins and malt on the nose. Powerful liquorice flavours dominate the lightly warming taste, which is also malty and has hints of almond. Dry, malty finish with liquorice and hops.

Suthwyk

Suthwyk Ales, Offwell Farm, Southwick,
Fareham, Hampshire PO17 6DX.
Tel./Fax (023 92) 325252
E-mail: mjbazeley@suthwykales.com
Website: www.suthwykales.com
Mail order service

Suthwyk Ales does not brew itself. It is run by barley farmer Martin Bazeley, who decided to go the whole hog and complete the 'field to table' cycle by commissioning a beer brewed from malt kilned by Warminster Maltings from his own Optic barley. Produced by Hop Back Brewery, Skew Sunshine Ale proved to be a hit and was followed up by a second offering, Bloomfields, and then a third, Liberation. The beers – with best before dates set at 12 months – are now brewed and bottled for Martin by Hepworth & Co. in Horsham (the cask versions are brewed at Oakleaf Brewery in Gosport). Martin is also a partner in Southwick Brewhouse, a bottled beer shop housed in the old Hunt's brewery in Southwick, Hampshire (the brewery is still intact and can be toured).

Bloomfields

● **ABV 3.8%** ● **BOTTLE SIZE 500 ml** ● **SERVE cool**
● **INGREDIENTS Optic pale malt/crystal malt/Challenger, Fuggle and Golding hops**

Sidney Bloomfield was the man who tended Martin's land back in the 1920s, dying at the tender age of 40 in 1926 – a sad consequence perhaps of the fact that the 700 acres in his care were farmed only with horsepower. One field on the estate still bears his name and it is here that the barley turned into crystal malt for this session ale is grown.

TASTING NOTES

Golden, with spicy hop, malt, melon and citrus fruit in the nose. The taste is clean, crisp and spicy, with malt sweetness and a light melon and peach fruitiness. The dry, bitter and fruity finish turns hoppy.

Liberation ★

● **ABV 4.2%** ● **BOTTLE SIZE 500 ml** ● **SERVE cool**
● **INGREDIENTS Optic pale malt/crystal malt/Liberty hops**

Launched to commemorate the 60th anniversary of D-Day, on 6 June 2004. Montgomery and Eisenhower planned Operation Overlord (the D-

Day offensive) in nearby Southwick House and enjoyed refreshments in the local pub after their talks. The label shows the military masterminds examining a bottle of Liberation.

TASTING NOTES

A pale golden beer with a fresh, blackcurrant, hoppy nose, becoming a touch biscuity. The light, bittersweet, slightly perfumed, blackcurrant taste makes it very quaffable. Hoppy, drying finish.

Skew Sunshine Ale

● ABV 4.6% ● BOTTLE SIZE 500 ml ● SERVE cool
● INGREDIENTS Optic pale malt/Challenger hops

The barley for this premium ale is grown in what is known as Skew Field, on Portsdown Hill. The field faces south and catches the sun.

TASTING NOTES

A pale golden ale with a creamy, malty, lightly fruity nose with a hint of sulphur. Light-bodied and fairly spritzy, it tastes citrus-fruity with lightly scented hops crisping up smooth malt. Bitter, fruity, hoppy finish.

Teignworthy

Teignworthy Brewery, The Maltings, Teign Road,
Newton Abbot, Devon TQ12 4AA. Tel./Fax (01626) 332066
Mail order service (via Tucker's Maltings)

Teignworthy Brewery was founded in 1994 by former Oakhill and Ringwood brewer John Lawton, using part of the Victorian malthouse of Edward Tucker & Sons. (Tucker's Maltings is now a fascinating tourist attraction.) The bottled beers are the same as John's cask beers, except that usually they are filtered and re-pitched with new yeast. A 12-month best before date is marked on each bottle. The Willamette hops that used to feature in Reel Ale, Spring Tide and Maltster's Ale have now been replaced by Fuggles. However, the tasting notes below are based on Willamette-hopped samples.

Reel Ale/Edwin Tucker's Devonshire Prize Ale

● ABV 4% ● BOTTLE SIZE 500 ml ● SERVE cool
● INGREDIENTS Maris Otter pale malt/crystal malt/Fuggle, Golding, Bramling Cross and Challenger hops

Reel Ale is Teignworthy's standard cask bitter. When bottle conditioned, it is sold under the same name and also as Edwin Tucker's Devonshire

Prize Ale in the Tucker's Maltings bottled beer shop, largely as an attempt to catch the eye of the holidaymakers the Maltings attracts.

TASTING NOTES

Orange-gold, with fruit, malt and orangey hops in the nose. The taste is dry with more oranges, malt and hops. Dryish, bitter orange finish.

Spring Tide

● ABV 4.3% ● BOTTLE SIZE 500 ml ● SERVE cool

● INGREDIENTS Maris Otter pale malt/crystal malt/Fuggle, Golding, Bramling Cross and Challenger hops

Named after the high tides that wash up the Teign estuary close to the brewery, this best bitter is brewed every four months or so.

TASTING NOTES

A crisp, refreshing and enjoyable, copper beer with a zesty orange nose. Fruit and malt continue into the taste, which has a light, citrus hop balance and grassy, herbal notes. Dry, bitter orange finish.

Old Moggie

● ABV 4.4% ● BOTTLE SIZE 500 ml ● SERVE cool

● INGREDIENTS Maris Otter pale malt/crystal malt/wheat malt/ torrefied wheat/Golding, Bramling Cross and Fuggle hops

Forget brewery cats: this beer, first brewed in January 2000, is named after the Morris Minor motor car owned by former underbrewer Mark Bayley and is a tribute to the heyday of the British motor trade.

TASTING NOTES

An amber ale with a fruity, malty aroma. In the mouth it is toffeeish and malty-sweet with a fruity hop balance. The finish is also sweet and malty, with light hop-fruit.

Beachcomber

● ABV 4.5% ● BOTTLE SIZE 500 ml ● SERVE cool

● INGREDIENTS Maris Otter pale malt/Willamette, Golding, Bramling Cross and Challenger hops

Described as a lager, Beachcomber was devised as a pale beer for barbecues on summer evenings. A bottom-fermenting yeast is used.

TASTING NOTES

A golden beer with a rich, citrus hop nose with sweet malt behind. The full taste combines light malt and excellent hoppiness with hints of blackcurrant. Bittersweet, hoppy, slightly tart finish.

Harvey's Special Brew

● ABV 4.6% ● BOTTLE SIZE 500 ml ● SERVE cool

● INGREDIENTS Pale malt/crystal malt/wheat malt/Golding and Fuggle hops

First brewed to celebrate the birth of John and Rachel Lawton's son, Harvey, on 8 April 2000.

TASTING NOTES

Orange-gold with an aroma of bitter orange peel. The taste is fruity with silky malt and bitter orange peel throughout. Dry, bitter fruit finish.

Amy's Ale

● ABV 4.8% ● BOTTLE SIZE 500 ml ● SERVE cool

● INGREDIENTS Pale malt/crystal malt/wheat malt/Bramling Cross and Golding hops

A beer named after the Lawtons' first child (who drew the label, by the look of it), brewed first in March 1997.

TASTING NOTES

A light amber beer with a floral, honeyed aroma backed with soft malt. The taste is equally flowery, with hints of sweet tropical and citrus fruits. Pleasantly bitter, gently fruity finish.

Maltster's Ale

● ABV 5% ● BOTTLE SIZE 500 ml ● SERVE cool

● INGREDIENTS Maris Otter pale malt/crystal malt/Fuggle, Golding, Bramling Cross and Challenger hops

This was a innovative brew when first prepared in 1996, as it used the new barley strain Regina, but John has now switched to Maris Otter. The beer is sold on draught in winter and is bottled twice a year.

TASTING NOTES

A mellow, bronze beer that lives up to its name with a malty nose that features traces of treacle and citrus. Richly malty in the mouth, it is finely balanced by lemony hops and pear drop flavour. The pleasant aftertaste is gentle, dry and bittersweet.

Martha's Mild

● ABV 5.3% ● BOTTLE SIZE 500 ml ● SERVE cool

● INGREDIENTS Pale malt/crystal malt/amber malt/chocolate malt/wheat malt/Fuggle and Golding hops

Another baby celebration, this time for Martha, born on 27 March 2002.

On the label, John declares that he brewed it as a tonic for Rachel when she was feeding the baby. Now a regular brew for May.

TASTING NOTES

A strong ruby mild with an aroma of coffeeish, biscuity malt. The taste is smooth and quite sweet, with oily roasted malt notes and a hint of hop fruit. Bitterness increases and roasted flavour persists in the finish.

Edwin Tucker's Maris Otter

● ABV 5.5% ● BOTTLE SIZE 500 ml ● SERVE cool
● INGREDIENTS Maris Otter pale malt/crystal malt/wheat malt/ Willamette, Golding, Bramling Cross and Challenger hops

First produced in 1998, as a tribute to the most highly regarded strain of malting barley ('the master brewer's choice around the world').

TASTING NOTES

Dark copper, with bananas and pear drops in the malty nose. The taste is rich and malty, with estery fruit and a hint of lemon. Bitter hops emerge for a pleasant, bittersweet finish with a hint of liquorice.

Edwin Tucker's 175 Ale

● ABV 5.8% ● BOTTLE SIZE 500 ml ● SERVE cool
● INGREDIENTS Westminster pale malt/crystal malt/wheat malt/ Fuggle and Golding hops

A limited edition (only 1,080 bottles) brew to mark the 175th anniversary of the founding of Edwin Tucker & Sons Ltd. in 1831. The beer uses a new spring barley variety called Westminster.

TASTING NOTES

Copper-red, with a lightly vinous aroma of lemon and red berries. The taste is sweet and creamy-malty, with vinous fruit, light hops and a savoury note. Drying, bitter finish, with dark malt and liquorice.

Christmas Cracker

● ABV 6% ● BOTTLE SIZE 500 ml ● SERVE cool
● INGREDIENTS Maris Otter pale malt/crystal malt/Willamette, Golding, Bramling Cross and Challenger hops

This strong seasonal brew is also sold in cask form.

TASTING NOTES

A malty nose, with nuts, chocolate and pear drops, preludes a malty, nutty, chocolaty beer with a firm hop presence and light pear drop notes. Malty, sweetish finish with hop bitterness growing. Red in colour.

Edwin Tucker's Choice Old Walnut Brown Ale

● ABV 6% ● BOTTLE SIZE 500 ml ● SERVE cool

● INGREDIENTS Maris Otter pale malt/brown malt/amber malt/chocolate malt/wheat malt/Fuggle and Golding hops

This dark ale was added to the Tucker's range of historical re-creations in 2004, echoing a style of beer in circulation during the 19th century.

TASTING NOTES

The big malty aroma of this ruby ale has milk chocolate and gentle orange notes. The taste is rich and malty, initially sweet but quickly balanced by a lightly fruity, hoppy bitterness. Milk chocolate creaminess is again evident, along with nut that becomes stronger on the swallow. Roasted malt and tangy, fruity hop feature in the dry, bitter finish.

Edwin Tucker's East India Pale Ale

● ABV 6.5% ● BOTTLE SIZE 500 ml ● SERVE cool

● INGREDIENTS East India malt/wheat malt/Bramling Cross and Golding hops

This well-researched replica of a true India pale ale – bursting with hops and packing the alcoholic punch such beers needed in order to cope with the long sea journey to India – includes malt specially kilned to match the colour of malt used in the Empire days (close to the colour of lager malt).

TASTING NOTES

A copper ale with an orangey aroma and a crisp, zingy, orange-hoppy taste, well balanced with a little sweetness. The same orangey hops add bitterness in the lingering, dry, lip-smacking finish.

Edwin Tucker's Empress Russian Porter

● ABV 10.5% ● BOTTLE SIZE 275 ml ● SERVE cool

● INGREDIENTS Maris Otter pale malt/chocolate malt/oat malt/roasted barley/Willamette, Golding, Bramling Cross and Challenger hops

This re-creation of the Baltic porter style was necessitated in part by the demise of the classic Courage Imperial Russian Stout, once sold in the Tucker's beer shop. It's the sort of strong, warming brew that was shipped to Russia during the 18th and 19th centuries and became known for its medicinal qualities. The beer is not produced every year.

TASTING NOTES

(1998 vintage, tasted after one year) A mellow, very dark brown beer

with caramel and fruit in the nose. Thick, smooth and sweetish on the palate, it has a creamy rum-and-raisin toffee taste with orange-citrus flavours and gentle roasted, bitter notes. Dry, lingering, deep and warming finish, with caramel, toffee and fruit balancing a gentle bitterness.
(2000 vintage, tasted after six months) Near-black, with malt, polished leather and coffee in the nose. The taste is sweetish and deep: strong hops for bitterness, coffee and a little fruit, with persistent malt. Sweetish, roasted, hoppy finish.

Teme Valley

Teme Valley Brewery, The Talbot, Knightwick, Worcestershire WR6 5PH. Tel. (01886) 821235 Fax (01886) 821060
E-mail: info@temevalleybrewery.co.uk
Website: www.temevalleybrewery.co.uk

The Talbot Inn at Knightwick is owned by the Clift family, who farmed hops locally from the 19th century to the year 2000. The hops they cultivated are still used in the pub's brewery, which was set up in 1997. Brewer Chris Gooch produces a range of cask and bottled beers to the same recipes, but beer for bottling is fermented with a dried, bottom-fermenting yeast which remains in the beer when it is bottled, without fining or filtration, by Branded Drinks. There are plans to use the brewery's own yeast in the bottle in the near future, which may produce a 'woollier' sediment. A best before date of 18 months is applied. New 'wood-effect' labels have been introduced to all bottles.

This

● **ABV 3.7%** ● **BOTTLE SIZE 500 ml** ● **SERVE cool**
● **INGREDIENTS Maris Otter pale malt/chocolate malt/wheat malt/ Challenger, Fuggle and Golding hops**

The Talbot Inn's own wine list has included, since spring 2003, a 'Beer and Food' page, suggesting ideal matches for Teme Valley beers. Here, This is recommended as the ideal accompaniment for sandwiches or a ploughman's lunch.

TASTING NOTES

A golden beer with malt and hop-fruit in the nose. The taste balances malt, fruit and crisp, but only moderately bitter, hops before a dry, bitter, hoppy finish with a hint of roast.

The Hop Nouvelle

● **ABV 4.1%** ● **BOTTLE SIZE 500 ml** ● **SERVE cool**
● **INGREDIENTS Maris Otter pale malt/wheat malt/First Gold hops**

Brewed once a year, during the hop harvest, this is an ale equivalent to wine's Beaujolais Nouveau. The hops are plucked from bines less than half a mile from the brewery and, within the hour, without kilning, are cast green into the copper, delivering a sappier, more resin-like flavour to the beer than standard dried hops. Chris also brews five different, single-varietal green-hop beers for the cask each September. They are all showcased at The Talbot's green-hop beer festival in October.

TASTING NOTES

(*2003 version, which also included green Golding hops*) A pale golden beer with a sappy, sweet-lemon aroma. Delicate malt leads in the mouth, overlaid with a sappy, pea-pod hop dominance which has lemon undertones. There's a little burnt flavour in the finish, but bitterness and sappy, green-hop flavours dominate.

That

● **ABV 4.1%** ● **BOTTLE SIZE 500 ml** ● **SERVE cool**
● **INGREDIENTS Maris Otter pale malt/crystal malt/wheat malt/roasted barley/Challenger and Fuggle hops**

A perfect match for stews or game dishes, according to The Talbot's beer menu, the hop bitterness lightening rich sauces and gravies.

TASTING NOTES

Amber, with a big butterscotch, malty, lemony aroma. Gentle hops lie over a clean, nutty, malty, butterscotch base in the taste, with lemon notes emerging. Dry, hoppy, bitter, butterscotch finish with more lemon. Butterscotch notes should disappear with the change of bottling yeast.

Wotever Next?

● **ABV 5%** ● **BOTTLE SIZE 500 ml** ● **SERVE cool**
● **INGREDIENTS Maris Otter pale malt/crystal malt/chocolate malt/wheat malt/Northdown and Fuggle hops**

The complex fruit and roasted malt flavours of Wotever Next? are suggested as ideal partners for a rich chocolate pudding or gateau.

TASTING NOTES

A tawny ale with malt and fruit in the nose (lemon and blackcurrant notes). Hop fruit also dominates the mostly bitter taste and continues into the drying, bitter aftertaste where roasted malt lingers.

Hearth Warmer

● ABV 6% ● BOTTLE SIZE 500 ml ● SERVE cool
● INGREDIENTS Maris Otter pale malt/crystal malt/chocolate malt/ wheat malt/roasted barley/Northdown and Fuggle hops

For Christmas 2002 Teme Valley's Christmas beer, Wass Ale, was made available in bottle, but now this has been renamed Hearth Warmer and is being sold at other times of the year. Sip a glass instead of a port, suggests brewer Chris Gooch.

TASTING NOTES

Red, with dark malts, vinous fruit, almonds and pear drops in the aroma. The taste features liquorice, malt, roasted grain, almonds and light pineapple, while the finish is drier and more bitter than expected as malt sweetness fades and liquorice, hops and roasted grain linger.

Major stockists Local Thresher and Tesco

Thornbridge

Thornbridge Hall Brewery, Thornbridge Hall, Ashford-in-the-Water, Derbyshire DE45 1NZ. Tel. (01629) 641000
E-mail: info@thornbridgebrewery.co.uk
Website: www.thornbridgebrewery.co.uk

Thornbridge opened in October 2004, brewing in the former joiner's and stonemason's workshop in the grounds of Thornbridge Hall, near Bakewell. Filtered beers in bottle are also available.

Jaipur IPA

● ABV 5.9% ● BOTTLE SIZE 500 ml ● SERVE cool
● INGREDIENTS Maris Otter pale malt/Chinook and Cascade hops

A traditional IPA with an American accent, Jaipur was first bottled in December 2005. A multi-award-winner in its cask form.

Saint Petersburg ★

● ABV 7.7% ● BOTTLE SIZE 500 ml ● SERVE cool
● INGREDIENTS Maris Otter pale malt/chocolate malt/roasted barley/Galena and Bramling Cross hops

In 1790, John Morewood bought Thornbridge Hall – which has origins in the 12th century – for the princely sum of £10,000 – money he had made from selling linen to the city of St Petersburg. What better name then to adopt when the brewery created this imperial Russian stout in

September 2005? The beer is matured for 55 days before bottling and primed with a blend of three sugars.

TASTING NOTES

Deep ruby. The aroma is tropical-fruity at first, then light, biscuity coffee and liquorice emerge. The taste is smooth, with more tropical fruits, lots of sweet malt and a notably bitter, roasted grain element as well as a little liquorice. Intense bitter, roasted, hoppy and dry finish.

Three B's

Three B's Brewery, Laneside Works, Stockclough Lane, Feniscowles, Blackburn, Lancashire BB2 5JR.
Tel. (01254) 207686 Fax (01254) 201333

After more than 20 years of making beer, Robert Bell founded Three B's Brewery in 2001 and turns out a range of cask beers, plus the four following bottled brands. The beers – which take their names from aspects of the mill trade that once dominated the brewery's home town of Blackburn – are matured in conditioning tanks then filled directly, keeping the same primary fermentation yeast. A one-year best before date is printed on the bottles.

Tackler's Tipple

● ABV 4.3% ● BOTTLE SIZE 500 ml ● SERVE cool
● INGREDIENTS Maris Otter pale malt/crystal malt/chocolate malt/ torrefied wheat/flaked maize/Progress, Challenger and Golding hops

First brewed in 2004, and also available in cask form. A tackler was the name given to a fitter in a weaving shed.

TASTING NOTES

A red-amber beer with a fruity, floral aroma over malt. The taste is fairly crisp, nicely bitter and fruity, with underlying malt sweetness. Drying, hoppy, bitter finish with malty sweetness dying away.

Major stockists Booths, local Asda

Doff Cocker

● ABV 4.5% ● BOTTLE SIZE 500 ml ● SERVE cool
● INGREDIENTS Maris Otter pale malt/wheat malt/flaked maize/ Hallertau, Challenger and Progress hops

A doff cocker was someone who removed the waste from the shuttle in a weaving machine. Again, this beer is also sold as a cask beer.

TASTING NOTES
Gentle lemon and spice feature in the nose of this golden beer, with soft malt emerging. Blackcurrants and lightly toffeeish malt are evident in the mainly bitter taste. Drying, bitter finish with toffee notes.

Knocker Up

● ABV 4.8% ● BOTTLE SIZE 500 ml ● SERVE cool
● INGREDIENTS Maris Otter pale malt/chocolate malt/black malt/ roasted barley/flaked barley/torrefied wheat/Golding and Progress hops
A dark porter to reflect the dark mornings when the Knocker Up used to rap on doors to arouse folk from their slumbers ready for work.
TASTING NOTES
A ruby porter with creamy, mellow fruit and dark malt in the aroma. The taste is also creamy, with dark malt and barley flavours, plus some pleasant, sweet vinous fruit. Gently bitter, slightly nutty finish.

Shuttle Ale

● ABV 5.2% ● BOTTLE SIZE 500 ml ● SERVE cool
● INGREDIENTS Maris Otter pale malt/crystal malt/flaked maize/ Fuggle hops
Another beer available in draught form that was first bottled in 2005.
TASTING NOTES
An amber ale with a floral, fruity (blackcurrants) aroma, backed by a little toffee. In the mouth, smooth toffee flavours from the malt are offset by the blackcurrant fruitiness of the hops. The finish is fairly thick, malty, bitter and drying.
Major stockists Booths, local Asda

Tindall

Tindall Ales, Toad Lane, Seething, Norfolk NR35 2EQ.
Tel. (01508) 483843
E-mail: greenangela5@aol.com
Tindall Ales is a family-run business founded in 1998 close to historic Tindall Wood (hence its name). In 2002, Tindall moved to new premises in a former stable block, just outside the village of Seething. Bottling began in 1999 and all the beers are kräusened before filling. Best before dates are set at four months later.

Summer Loving

● **ABV 3.6%** ● **BOTTLE SIZE 500 ml** ● **SERVE cool**

● **INGREDIENTS Maris Otter and Fanfare pale malt/Mount Hood hops**

Only brewed June–September, Summer Loving is designed as a refreshing summer beer, and is seasoned with American hops. The brewers suggest it's the sort of beer to drink with Mediterranean food.

TASTING NOTES

A clean and quaffable, golden beer with a fresh, hoppy aroma and plenty of taste for its strength, balancing fruity hop (light bitter orange) and malt sweetness. Gentle, hoppy, dry aftertaste.

Best Bitter

● **ABV 3.7%** ● **BOTTLE SIZE 500 ml** ● **SERVE cool**

● **INGREDIENTS Maris Otter and Halcyon pale malt/Golding hops**

Like the other bottled beers, Best Bitter – Tindall's first ever beer – is also available in cask form.

TASTING NOTES

Copper-coloured, with a hoppy, lightly perfumed nose. Tangy hops and light orange-fruit feature in the taste before a dry, hoppy finish.

Mild

● **ABV 3.7%** ● **BOTTLE SIZE 500 ml** ● **SERVE cool**

● **INGREDIENTS Halcyon and Maris Otter pale malt/crystal malt/ chocolate malt/Golding and Fuggle hops**

The bottled version of a popular cask dark mild.

TASTING NOTES

Attractively ruby, this mild has an aroma of soft, dark malts. The smooth malt and gentle fruit continue in the bittersweet taste, with more fruit arriving on the swallow. Dry, bittersweet finish, with hops emerging.

Liberator

● **ABV 3.8%** ● **BOTTLE SIZE 500 ml** ● **SERVE cool**

● **INGREDIENTS Maris Otter and Pearl pale malt/Cascade hops**

Tindall's new brewery stands opposite Seething USAAF air base, home to the 448th Bombardment (H) Group and their Liberator aircraft from 1943 to 1945 – hence the name of this golden, American-hopped bitter.

TASTING NOTES

Hops and juicy fruit in the nose lead to a crisp, hoppy, tangily fruity, bittersweet taste, with bitterness gradually taking over. Dry, bitter finish.

Resurrection

● ABV 3.8% ● BOTTLE SIZE 500 ml ● SERVE cool
● INGREDIENTS Halcyon pale malt/Cascade hops

A session beer launched at Easter 1999, as implied by its name.

Alltime

● ABV 4% ● BOTTLE SIZE 500 ml ● SERVE cool
● INGREDIENTS Maris Otter and Halcyon pale malt/Golding hops

An unusually-named beer, with a clock-face label. This was a seasonal cask beer brought back permanently because of demand, and hence now available 'alltime'.

TASTING NOTES

A chestnut-coloured beer with a lightly toffeeish, malty aroma. The same malt and toffee feature in the taste, with a gentle fruitiness behind, before a moderate, malty and increasingly hoppy finish.

Christmas Cheers

● ABV 4% ● BOTTLE SIZE 500 ml ● SERVE cool
● INGREDIENTS Maris Otter and Halcyon pale malt/crystal malt/ Golding hops

Available in December, Christmas Cheers is one of the more quaffable festive beers, at a modest 4%.

Ditchingham Dam

● ABV 4.2% ● BOTTLE SIZE 500 ml ● SERVE cool
● INGREDIENTS Maris Otter pale malt/roasted malt/chocolate malt/ Golding and Mount Hood hops/liquorice/ginger

A spiced premium ale, taking its name from an area near the brewery. Ditchingham Dam was a scene of some controversy in 2000 when the local authority proposed to cull the wild chickens that roamed the area, considering them to be a danger to road users. (The chickens had lost their earlier home near Simpson's Maltings when it burned down.) The brewery stepped in and offered to give £5 for every firkin sold of this beer to provide signs to warn motorists of the hazard, and the chickens were saved. Note the picture of a rooster on the label.

TASTING NOTES

A red beer with a fruity, herbal aroma. The taste is fruity, herbal and finely balances bitterness and sweetness, with traces of lemon-ginger throughout. Dry, bitter, herbal finish.

Extra

● **ABV 4.5%** ● **BOTTLE SIZE 500 ml** ● **SERVE cool**
● **INGREDIENTS Maris Otter and Halcyon pale malt/Golding hops**

The brewery's second ever beer, with extra colour, extra flavour and extra strength. It bears much the same label as Best Bitter, featuring a bird on a twig, except the border around the picture is coloured red instead of green.

Norfolk 'n' Good

● **ABV 4.6%** ● **BOTTLE SIZE 500 ml** ● **SERVE cool**
● **INGREDIENTS Halcyon pale malt/Cascade hops**

Be careful how you ask for this stronger version of the 3.8% bitter Resurrection! The cheeky name is derived from a song popular with a local folk band, who have now written a new last verse specifically about the beer.

TASTING NOTES

Dark golden with a floral, peppery hop aroma. Floral hops and soft malt combine in the mouth for a good bittersweet balance. Hops eventually take over and lead in the dry finish.

Norwich Dragon

● **ABV 4.6%** ● **BOTTLE SIZE 500 ml** ● **SERVE cool**
● **INGREDIENTS Halcyon pale malt/Cascade and Golding hops**

A new premium ale named after Norwich's Dragon Hall, a 13th-century merchant's hall that was rediscovered in the 1970s and is said to be the only building of its type still surviving in western Europe.

TASTING NOTES

An easy-drinking, light copper ale with juicy, fruity hops in both the aroma and taste. Hops and bitterness grow in the drying finish.

Honeydo

● **ABV 5%** ● **BOTTLE SIZE 330 ml** ● **SERVE cool**
● **INGREDIENTS Halcyon pale malt/Cascade hops/honey**

A Norwich Beer Festival award-winner, laced with clear honey.

TASTING NOTES

A dark golden beer with floral hops and honey leading over malt in the aroma. The taste is bittersweet, with a honeyed softness, but with hop character to prevent it from cloying. Slightly warming, bittersweet aftertaste with the mellowness of honey.

Tipples

Tipples Brewery, Unit 6, Damgate Lane Industrial Estate, Acle, Norfolk NR13 3DJ. Tel. (01493) 741007
E-mail: brewery@tipplesbrewery.com
Website: www.tipplesbrewery.com

If ever a man was destined to become a brewer, it had to be Jason Tipple. With a name like that, he'd be mad to find another vocation. That said, Jason is relatively new to this game, having previously worked in the financial services and food industries until opening his six-barrel brewery in autumn 2004. His wide range of bottled beers are fined before bottling, with dried yeast added to ensure a secondary fermentation in the bottle.

Longshore

● ABV 3.6% ● BOTTLE SIZE 500 ml ● SERVE cool
● INGREDIENTS Maris Otter pale malt/crystal malt/Bramling Cross, Golding and Cascade hops

Longshore is a pale amber-coloured session bitter.

Ginger

● ABV 3.8% ● BOTTLE SIZE 500 ml ● SERVE cool
● INGREDIENTS Maris Otter pale malt/crystal malt/Bramling Cross and Cascade hops/root ginger

This delicately-hopped ale is enhanced by the addition of fresh root ginger towards the end of the copper boil. It was planned only as a summer refresher, but is now brewed all year-round.

The Hanged Monk

● ABV 3.8% ● BOTTLE SIZE 500 ml ● SERVE cool
● INGREDIENTS Mild ale malt/crystal malt/Bramling Cross, Willamette and Golding hops

The Hanged Monk is the first of three 'ghost beers' Jason has devised (see also Lady Evelyn and Jack's Revenge, overleaf). Each is based on a spooky tale from Norfolk, and this beer relates to St Benet's Abbey, that was built near Ludham in AD 816. The prosperous settlement was envied by William the Conqueror who enlisted the help of an inmate who offered to let the Normans in if they promoted him to abbot in return. His side of the bargain fulfilled, the treacherous monk was pleased to see the Normans being true to their word. But, no sooner had they elevated the monk to abbot status, they promptly elevated him in a different sense, hanging him for being a traitor. It is said that on 25 May each year, his ghost can be seen writhing in agony from a beam above the now-ruined abbey arch.

Lady Evelyn

● ABV 4.1% ● BOTTLE SIZE 500 ml ● SERVE cool
● INGREDIENTS Maris Otter extra pale malt/Bramling Cross, Golding and Cascade hops
The story behind this ale dates back to 1791 when, it is related, Evelyn, Lady Montefiore Carew sold her soul to the Devil in return for the chance to marry Sir Godfrey Haslitt of Bastwick Manor. The Devil stole the bride away in a fiery coach at midnight on the wedding day. The coach crashed and Lady Evelyn perished, her soul surrendered to the Devil. Her cries as the coach smashed into Potter Heigham Bridge over the River Thurne can apparently be heard to this day.

Redhead

● ABV 4.2% ● BOTTLE SIZE 500 ml ● SERVE cool
● INGREDIENTS Maris Otter pale malt/crystal malt/Bramling Cross, Golding and Cascade hops
A best bitter, redder, nuttier and maltier than the other quaffing beers.
TASTING NOTES
An orange-gold beer with bitter oranges in the aroma and bitter grapefruit drying the palate. Hops lead in the dry, lightly nutty finish.

Battle

● ABV 4.3% ● BOTTLE SIZE 500 ml ● SERVE cool
● INGREDIENTS Maris Otter pale malt/crystal malt/Bramling Cross, Golding and Cascade hops
Nelson features on the label of this best bitter, which was first brewed for the 200th anniversary of the Battle of Trafalgar in 2005.

Topper Stout

● ABV 4.5% ● BOTTLE SIZE 500 ml ● SERVE cool
● INGREDIENTS Maris Otter pale malt/crystal malt/chocolate malt/black malt/Bramling Cross, Golding and Cascade hops
A dark stout with the fruity addition of the three hops Jason favours.

Moon Rocket

● **ABV 5%** ● **BOTTLE SIZE 500 ml** ● **SERVE cool**
● **INGREDIENTS Maris Otter pale malt/crystal malt/Bramling Cross, Golding and Cascade hops**

A Jules Verne-style, cartoon space rocket originally featured on the label of this full-flavoured strong pale ale, but the artwork has now changed.

TASTING NOTES

A robust, but well-balanced, orange-gold ale with tart orange peel and sappy hops in the nose. Sappy hop resins fill the mouth with sweet malt in support. The drying finish is bitter and very hoppy.

Jack's Revenge

● **ABV 5.8%** ● **BOTTLE SIZE 500 ml** ● **SERVE cool**
● **INGREDIENTS Maris Otter pale malt/crystal malt/chocolate malt/ Bramling Cross and Willamette hops**

This dark, strong ale recalls the legend of one Jack Ketch, a 17th-century man who was hanged for a murder he didn't commit and who wreaked revenge on the real killer in the afterlife, stabbing him to death on Acle Bridge. Rumour has it that Ketch is still at work because every 7 April fresh blood is discovered on the stonework of the bridge.

Titanic

The Titanic Brewery, Unit 5, Callender Place, Lingard Street, Burslem, Stoke-on-Trent, Staffordshire ST6 1JL. Tel. (01782) 823447 Fax (01782) 812349
E-mail: titanic@titanicbrewery.co.uk
Website: www.titanicbrewery.co.uk

This brewery, named in honour of the *Titanic*'s Captain Smith, who hailed from Stoke, was founded in 1985. A move to larger premises took place in 1992 and new brewing plant was installed in 1995. In 2002, the brewery moved yet again to larger premises next door and in 2005 the 16-barrel brewplant was replaced by new 50-barrel kit.

Stout ★

● **ABV 4.5%** ● **BOTTLE SIZE 500 ml** ● **SERVE cool**
● **INGREDIENTS Pale malt/wheat malt/roasted barley/Fuggle, Northdown and Golding hops**

Titanic Stout (also a cask beer) was the winner of *The Guardian's Best*

Bottle-Conditioned Beer in 1994, and then was voted *CAMRA/The Guardian's Champion Bottled Beer* in 2004 (bronze award also in 2005). The beer is still brewed at Titanic but bottled by Hepworth & Co. in Horsham. There the beer is filtered and re-seeded with fresh yeast (a different strain to that used for primary fermentation). The bottle carries a best before date of 18 months.

TASTING NOTES

Deep ruby with coffee and some liquorice in the biscuity nose. Bitter roasted grain leads in the mouth, but there is a lightly fruity, malty sweetness, too. Smoky coffee, nut and roasted bitterness in the finish.

Major stockist Local Sainsbury's

Christmas Ale

● **ABV 7.2%** ● **BOTTLE SIZE 500 ml** ● **SERVE cool**
● **INGREDIENTS Maris Otter pale malt/crystal malt/wheat malt/ invert sugar/Galena and Golding hops**

Christmas Ale is a bottled version of Titanic's strong ale, Wreckage (7.2%). Only small runs are produced each year, with the bottle size likely to vary. The most recent batch was bottled in house.

TASTING NOTES

Red, with a fruity, alcoholic nose. Slightly tart in the mouth, it is fruity, malty and fairly sweet, with a warming, sweetish, malt and fruit finish.

Tryst

Tryst Brewery, Lorne Road, Larbert, Falkirk FK5 4AT.
Tel. (01324) 554000
E-mail: johnmcgarva@tinyworld.co.uk
Mail order service

Small brewery founded by experienced brewer John McGarva in 2003, in an industrial unit close to the station in the town of Larbert. His bottled beers followed soon after. The bottles are filled in house from prepared casks, the same primary fermentation yeast carrying over to the bottle. Best before dates are set at six–nine months after filling.

Brockville Dark

● **ABV 3.8%** ● **BOTTLE SIZE 500 ml** ● **SERVE cool**
● **INGREDIENTS Optic pale malt/crystal malt/amber malt/chocolate malt/roasted barley/Challenger and Golding hops**

This dark mild was introduced in autumn 2003 and, like the other bottled beers, is also sold in cask-conditioned form.

TASTING NOTES

A garnet beer with dark malts, spice, gentle caramel and plain chocolate in the biscuity aroma. Dark malt flavours continue into the taste, which is fairly thin and mostly bitter, with light citrus/tropical fruit notes. Dry, bitter, chalky finish with roasted malt.

Brockville Pale

● ABV 3.8% ● BOTTLE SIZE 500 ml ● SERVE cool
● INGREDIENTS Optic pale malt/crystal malt/Challenger and Golding hops

Like the Dark, this beer is named after Falkirk's old football stadium.

TASTING NOTES

Citrus and spice (almost gingery) notes feature in the nose of this golden ale. More of the same follows in the mouth, with a peppery warmth and a perfumed note. Dry, bitter, spicy finish.

Festival Red

● ABV 4% ● BOTTLE SIZE 500 ml ● SERVE cool
● INGREDIENTS Optic pale malt/crystal malt/chocolate malt/caramalt/roasted barley/Cascade, Columbus and Golding hops

First brewed in autumn 2004, and bronze medallist in the *Scottish Bottle-Conditioned Beer Championship*, held at Troon Beer Festival in 2005. This is an 80/- style beer with hoppier additions.

TASTING NOTES

Orange-amber, with citrus hops and a little toffee from the malt in the aroma. Sharp hop notes dominate the sweet, buttery malt in the taste, with a little citrus. Darker malt flavours emerge in the dry, bitter finish.

Buckled Wheel

● ABV 4.2% ● BOTTLE SIZE 500 ml ● SERVE cool
● INGREDIENTS Optic pale malt/Fuggle, Golding and Challenger hops

With a name inspired by the Millennium Wheel that connects the Forth and Clyde Canals in Falkirk, this best bitter arrived in autumn 2003.

TASTING NOTES

Pineapple and citrus fruits lead in the aroma of this orange-gold beer. There's a similar fruitiness in the taste, with bitter hops to the fore and continuing into the dry finish, which also has some toasted malt.

Carronade IPA

● **ABV 4.2%** ● **BOTTLE SIZE 500 ml** ● **SERVE cool**
● **INGREDIENTS Optic pale malt/Cascade and Columbus hops**

An IPA named after the famous Carron Ironworks, near Falkirk. Carronade cannon, apparently, was used at the Battle of Trafalgar and is said to have revolutionized portable cannon warfare on ships at the time. This best bitter was winner of the 2005 *Scottish Bottle-Conditioned Beer Championship*.

TASTING NOTES

Golden, with lemon and malt in the nose. The taste is bittersweet with citrus notes. Dry, bitter, hoppy finish with lingering sweetness.

Tunnel

Tunnel Brewery, c/o Lord Nelson Inn, Birmingham Road, Ansley, Nuneaton, Warwickshire CV10 9PQ.
Tel. (024) 7639 4888 Fax (024) 7639 8730
E-mail: info@tunnelbrewery.co.uk
Website: www.tunnelbrewery.co.uk

Brewery set up in 2005 and taking its name from the five-mile railway tunnel that passes beneath the village of Ansley. The pub mentioned in the address is a separate business, but does sell Tunnel's beers. Bottled beers arrived in 2006. Before filling, the beers are generally held in casks for a month and then lightly kräusened with fresh wort. Best before dates are set at six months. All are declared vegan friendly. The back labels of most bottles carry lengthy, light-hearted 'Rumour has it...' stories about the beer's name.

Linda Lear Beer

● **ABV 3.7%** ● **BOTTLE SIZE 500 ml** ● **SERVE cool**
● **INGREDIENTS Maris Otter pale malt/crystal malt/chocolate malt/ black malt/Galena and Bullion hops**

A session beer first brewed in January 2006 to celebrate the 50th birthday of the wife of one of the brewers. Linda, in her formative years, features on the label.

TASTING NOTES

Sharp hops, apples and bitter oranges combine in the nose of this amber-coloured beer, followed by a dry, hoppy and fruity-sharp taste, and then a dry, hoppy, bitter aftertaste.

Ghost

● ABV 4% ● BOTTLE SIZE 500 ml ● SERVE cool

● INGREDIENTS Maris Otter pale malt/lager malt/Pacific Gem, Cluster and Styrian Golding hops

An appropriately pale, golden beer brewed mostly with lager malt.

TASTING NOTES

A big flowery, lemony aroma leads to a dry, bitter, floral-hop taste, then a dry, very bitter and hoppy aftertaste.

Light at the End of the Tunnel/Late OTT

● ABV 4% ● BOTTLE SIZE 500 ml ● SERVE cool

● INGREDIENTS Maris Otter pale malt/crystal malt/Pacific Gem, First Gold and Styrian Golding hops

The brewery's first beer, familiarly known as Late OTT. It took 18 months to progress from initial plans to working brewery, leading the brewers to think they would never see the proverbial illumination.

TASTING NOTES

A dark golden ale with berries and light citrus fruit in the aroma. The taste is bitter, crisp and gently fruity, with a little nut from the malt. Dry, tangy-hop, bitter aftertaste.

Legend

● ABV 4.3% ● BOTTLE SIZE 500 ml ● SERVE cool

● INGREDIENTS Maris Otter pale malt/crystal malt/chocolate malt/wheat malt/Bullion, Golding and Saaz hops

A copper-coloured beer brewed originally in honour of an octogenarian 'legend', Bill Davies, one of the regulars in the Lord Nelson Inn.

TASTING NOTES

The malty, resin-like, lightly citrus aroma preludes a dryish, malty taste with sharp, fruity hops. Dry, bitter finish. Not a sweet beer.

Trade Winds

● ABV 4.6% ● BOTTLE SIZE 500 ml ● SERVE cool

● INGREDIENTS Maris Otter pale malt/wheat malt/Cascade hops

An India pale ale, great for cooking with mussels, say the brewers.

TASTING NOTES

A golden ale with bitter citrus – smoky orange and grapefruit – in the aroma. The taste is hoppy and citrus, backed by sweet malt for a zesty, bittersweet flavour. Bitterness grows in the drying, hoppy finish.

Sweet Parish Ale

● ABV 4.7% ● BOTTLE SIZE 500 ml ● SERVE cool

● INGREDIENTS Maris Otter pale malt/crystal malt/chocolate malt/ Golding and Styrian Golding hops

The brewery's second ever beer, a strong bitter named to poke fun at the local parish council, which lobbied to prevent the brewery opening.

TASTING NOTES

An amber ale with a malty aroma and taste. Bitterness arrives quickly in the mouth thanks to the hops. Dry, bitter and hoppy aftertaste.

Stranger in the Mist

● ABV 5% ● BOTTLE SIZE 500 ml ● SERVE cold

● INGREDIENTS Maris Otter pale malt/wheat malt/torrefied wheat/ Perle and Saaz hops

A cloudy beer, the brewery's take on the German hefeweiss beer style, introduced in June 2006. Wheat malt accounts for 45% of the malt grist.

TASTING NOTES

A hazy yellow beer with a creamy, lightly spicy, toffee nose. The taste is also creamy and toffee-malty, with light spices. Bitter, dry, malty finish.

Nelson's Column

● ABV 5.2% ● BOTTLE SIZE 500 ml ● SERVE cool

● INGREDIENTS Maris Otter pale malt/crystal malt/Cascade and Golding hops

A beer for the 200th anniversary of the Battle of Trafalgar and now a regular brew. Before bottling, it is aged in casks for six months. The cask version was voted *Champion Beer of Warwickshire* by the public in a CAMRA-staged competition which aimed to find the best local beer to complement cheese.

TASTING NOTES

An amber ale with a lightly fruity, hop and malt nose. Bitter oranges lead over malt in the taste. Dry, hoppy, malty finish.

Boston Beer Party

● ABV 5.6% ● BOTTLE SIZE 500 ml ● SERVE cool

● INGREDIENTS Maris Otter pale malt/crystal malt/wheat malt/ Cascade hops

Boston Beer Party, a dark golden, American-inspired pale ale, is matured in casks for two months prior to bottling.

TASTING NOTES
Strong hop resins dominate the aroma, while the taste is citrus-hoppy with decent malt support. Dry, hoppy and bitter aftertaste.

Uncle Stuart's

Uncle Stuart's Brewery, Antoma, Pack Lane, Lingwood, Norwich, Norfolk NR13 4PD. Tel. (01603) 716998
E-mail: stuartsbrewery@aol.com
Mail order service
Stuart Evans has been brewing bottled beers in very small quantities at his home in beautiful rural Norfolk since spring 2002. He has now added cask beer to his selection and has opened The Little Beer Shop in Blofield, selling his own and other bottled beers (see Beer Shops).

Pack Lane

● **ABV 4%** ● **BOTTLE SIZE 500 ml** ● **SERVE cool**
● **INGREDIENTS Pale malt/crystal malt/black malt/chocolate malt/ Golding and Progress hops**
A mild named after the lane that is home to the brewery. Best before dates for this and the other beers are set at one year.
TASTING NOTES
A light-drinking, red-brown ale with a malty, herbal, lightly fruity aroma. The taste and the aftertaste are both sweet and malty.

Excelsior

● **ABV 4.5%** ● **BOTTLE SIZE 500 ml** ● **SERVE cool**
● **INGREDIENTS Pale malt/crystal malt/Golding and Progress hops**
A beer that recalls in its name a fishing smack on which Stuart's grandfather worked and which is still used today by a charity trust.
TASTING NOTES
A dark golden beer with piney hops in the nose and taste, which is light-bodied and has a gentle sweetness. Piney, bittersweet finish.

Buckenham Woods

● **ABV 5.6%** ● **BOTTLE SIZE 500 ml** ● **SERVE cool**
● **INGREDIENTS Pale malt/crystal malt/flaked maize/Golding and Progress hops**
A dark, strong bitter, with a name derived from a local beauty spot.

TASTING NOTES
A deep ruby-coloured beer with a malty, biscuity, herbal aroma. The taste is also malty and herbal, with a touch of coffee, the same flavours carrying through into the bittersweet aftertaste.

Strumpshaw Fen

● **ABV 5.7%** ● **BOTTLE SIZE 500 ml** ● **SERVE cool**
● **INGREDIENTS Pale malt/crystal malt/Progress and Golding hops**
A beer named after a local RSPB nature reserve.
TASTING NOTES
Dark golden, this is another beer with a herbal aroma, mixed with malt and fruit. The sweet, fruity taste is followed by a sweet, malty finish.

Christmas Ale

● **ABV 7%** ● **BOTTLE SIZE 500 ml** ● **SERVE cool**
● **INGREDIENTS Pale malt/crystal malt/black malt/Progress and Golding hops**
A strong old ale, sold only between October and January.

Vale

Vale Brewery Company, Thame Road,
Haddenham, Buckinghamshire HP17 8BY.
Tel. (01844) 290008 Fax (01844) 292505
E-mail: valebrewery@yahoo.co.uk
Website: www.valebrewery.co.uk
Mail order service

Vale Brewery was opened in 1995 by brothers Mark and Phil Stevens. Their brewery is housed in an industrial unit on the fringe of one of the most attractive villages in Buckinghamshire. Bottling began in 1997. All the beers are matured in casks, sterile filtered, primed with sweet wort and re-seeded with fresh yeast. Best before dates are set at nine months. All beers are vegan friendly.

Black Swan Dark Mild

● **ABV 3.3%** ● **BOTTLE SIZE 500 ml** ● **SERVE cool**
● **INGREDIENTS Maris Otter pale malt/crystal malt/roasted barley/ Golding and Fuggle hops**
The name and the label of this mild play on the brewery logo (actually

based on the Buckinghamshire county emblem) of a swan, but making it black to match the beer.

TASTING NOTES

A ruby mild, with a light, chocolaty malt nose and a gentle fruitiness in the taste, balanced by soft, sweetish malt and bitterness from both hops and roasted barley. Dry, bitter aftertaste.

Wychert

● **ABV 3.9%** ● **BOTTLE SIZE 500 ml** ● **SERVE cool**

● **INGREDIENTS Maris Otter pale malt/crystal malt/Fuggle and Challenger hops**

'Wychert', meaning 'white earth', is the substance from which many of the oldest buildings in the lovely village of Haddenham (the brewery's home) were constructed. You see them all around the village green.

TASTING NOTES

An amber ale with orange fruit and a little toasted malt in the aroma. The taste is nutty and lightly fruity, with a good, hoppy, bitter balance. Dry, bitter, hoppy finish.

Black Beauty Porter

● **ABV 4.3%** ● **BOTTLE SIZE 500 ml** ● **SERVE cool**

● **INGREDIENTS Maris Otter pale malt/roasted barley/Fuggle and Golding hops**

A dark horse. Unlike the other beers, there are no Saxon or local connections: the name just describes the beer inside.

TASTING NOTES

Ruby, with subtle dark malt and juicy fruit leading in the nose. The lightish body supports a slightly tropical fruitiness from the hops, roasted barley and gentle bitterness. Dry, bitter, roasted finish.

Edgar's Golden Ale

● **ABV 4.3%** ● **BOTTLE SIZE 500 ml** ● **SERVE cool**

● **INGREDIENTS Maris Otter pale malt/Fuggle and Golding hops**

Edgar is a Stevens family name, passed down to the first son of the first son over the generations. The beer was once sold also as Halcyon Daze.

TASTING NOTES

A clean and tasty, golden beer with a hoppy aroma of 'fruit cocktail'. The same juicy fruit cocktail flavours continue in the mouth, tempered by a crisp, spicy hop bitterness. Fruity, bitter, hoppy finish.

Grumpling Premium

● ABV 4.6% ● BOTTLE SIZE 500 ml ● SERVE cool
● INGREDIENTS Maris Otter pale malt/chocolate malt/roasted barley/ Challenger and Golding hops

Grumpling stones are the large, foundation stones upon which wychert houses are constructed (see Wychert Ale).

TASTING NOTES

A bitter but fruity, amber beer with excellent malty body and a bitter, hoppy finish. The aroma offers both soft, juicy fruit and malt.

Hadda's Head Banger

● ABV 5% ● BOTTLE SIZE 500 ml ● SERVE cool
● INGREDIENTS Maris Otter pale malt/crystal malt/roasted barley/ Challenger and Fuggle hops

Hadda was the Saxon king who settled in (and gave his name to) the village of Haddenham and Hadda's Head Banger is just one of a range of seasonal cask beers Vale produces under his banner. This, however, is the only Hadda in bottle. The label shows a Saxon warrior.

TASTING NOTES

Amber, with malt and fruit in the nose. There's a slightly salty note behind the hops, fruit, malt and lightly roasted bitterness. The same, moreish savoury note lingers with fruit in the dry, bitter finish.

Good King Senseless

● ABV 5.2% ● BOTTLE SIZE 500 ml ● SERVE cool
● INGREDIENTS Maris Otter pale malt/crystal malt/chocolate malt/ Golding and Mount Hood hops

This Christmas warmer is bottled each November.

Ventnor

Ventnor Brewery, 119 High Street, Ventnor, Isle of Wight PO38 1LY.
Tel. (01983) 856161 Fax (01983) 856404
Website: www.ventnorbrewery.co.uk
Mail order service

The former Burts Brewery was put back into production by new ownership in 1996 and now supplies up to 100 pubs on the Isle of Wight with cask beers. However, apart from Old Ruby, the brewery's bottled beers are no longer naturally conditioned. See also Scarecrow.

Old Ruby Bitter

● ABV 4.7% ● BOTTLE SIZE 500 ml ● SERVE cool
● INGREDIENTS Pale malt/crystal malt/wheat malt/Golding and Challenger hops

Old Ruby is bottled for Ventnor by Branded Drinks in Gloucestershire.

TASTING NOTES

Light red/brown, with a malty, fruity aroma (hint of blackcurrant). The palate has lots of clean, nutty malt but is not particularly sweet, and a light fruitiness persists. Toasted malt provides bitterness in the finish.

Warwickshire

Warwickshire Beer Co. Ltd., Queen Street, Cubbington, Leamington Spa, Warwickshire CV32 7NA.
Tel. (01926) 450747
E-mail: sales@warwickshirebeer.co.uk
Mail order service

Warwickshire was set up in 1998 in a former village bakery (an earlier Warwickshire Brewery ran for a couple of years in the mid-1990s producing some beers of the same name). Five bottle-conditioned beers are now available, filled in-house from matured casks primed with sugar. One-year best before dates are set.

Best Bitter

● ABV 3.9% ● BOTTLE SIZE 500 ml ● SERVE cool
● INGREDIENTS Maris Otter pale malt/crystal malt/torrefied wheat/First Gold and Golding hops

One of Warwickshire's first ever beers, depicting the bear and ragged staff emblem of the Earls of Warwick on its label.

TASTING NOTES

An orange-gold beer with earthy malt and hops in the nose. Hops initially shade out malt in the sweetish taste, before a dry, earthy, hoppy, bitter finish, with lingering malt.

Lady Godiva

● ABV 4.2% ● BOTTLE SIZE 500 ml ● SERVE cool
● INGREDIENTS Maris Otter pale malt/amber malt/torrefied wheat/Cascade and Styrian Golding hops

A suitably blonde ale remembering the wife of Leofric, 11th-century

Earl of Mercia, and the stand she made against his high-tax regime, riding naked through the streets of Coventry.

TASTING NOTES

Golden, with a gently malty, hop aroma. Lightly citrus hops lead in the bitter taste, with malty sweetness for balance. Dry, hoppy, bitter finish.

Churchyard Bob

● ABV 4.9% ● BOTTLE SIZE 500 ml ● SERVE cool

● INGREDIENTS Maris Otter pale malt/amber malt/chocolate malt/torrefied wheat/Fuggle hops

Although the label of this porter portrays a rather ghoulish Magwitchian figure, its name actually refers to an old campanology term relating to a ringing call change. The beer was first brewed to commemorate the centenary of the tower and bells at All Saints Church, Leamington Spa.

TASTING NOTES

A red beer with a vinous, malty aroma. The taste is sweetish and malty, with light vinous fruit and soft roasted grain bitterness beneath. Malty, increasingly bitter, slightly liquorice-like finish.

Warwick Market Ale

● ABV 4.9% ● BOTTLE SIZE 500 ml ● SERVE cool

● INGREDIENTS Maris Otter pale malt/crystal malt/torrefied wheat/First Gold and Golding hops

First brewed to commemorate the re-opening of Warwick Market Place in 1999 after major refurbishment. Initially in bottle, the beer was filtered and pasteurized; now it is bottle conditioned.

TASTING NOTES

A dark golden ale with earthy malt in the aroma and taste. Hops provide balance in the mouth, where the spicy bitterness is almost liquorice-like. Dry, bitter finish with lingering malt.

Kingmaker

● ABV 5.5% ● BOTTLE SIZE 500 ml ● SERVE cool

● INGREDIENTS Maris Otter pale malt/crystal malt/torrefied wheat/Challenger and Golding hops

A beer recalling Richard Neville (1428–71), Earl of Warwick, who earned the nickname of Kingmaker because of his influence during the Wars of the Roses (described by Shakespeare in *Henry VI, Part III* as 'Thou setter up and plucker down of Kings', as the purple label explains).

TASTING NOTES

An amber brew with a pronounced malty nose. The taste is full-bodied, malty and gently warming, with fruit and hops for balance, and a trace of liquorice. Hoppy, bitter, drying yet lingeringly malty finish.

Wells & Young's

Wells & Young's Brewing Co. Ltd.,
The Eagle Brewery, Havelock Street, Bedford MK40 4LU.
Tel. (01234) 272766 Fax (01234) 279000
Website: www.youngs.co.uk

This major new name in British brewing came into effect in autumn 2006, with the merger of the brewing interests of Charles Wells and Young's. It followed the closure of Young's Wandsworth brewery which was founded, it is believed, in 1581. Young's two bottle-conditioned beers have survived the move, although the tasting notes and rosette reflect samples brewed in Wandsworth. Charles Wells produces no bottle-conditioned beer, although it provides an excellent take-home alternative in the form of mini-casks of fresh, live Bombardier bitter.

Champion Live Golden Beer ★

● **ABV 5%** ● **BOTTLE SIZE 500 ml** ● **SERVE cool**
● **INGREDIENTS Lager malt/Styrian Golding hops**

Lagered for five weeks at the brewery before being filtered, re-seeded with fresh yeast and kräusened with ale yeast, this beer was the winner of the *Tesco Beer Challenge* in spring 2003 (hence the name).

TASTING NOTES

A pale golden beer with grapefruit, elderflower and lemon in the floral nose. The taste is also floral and fruity-hoppy (more elderflower and lemon), with bitter notes balanced by buttery malt sweetness. Dry, hoppy finish with lingering creamy malt sweetness and lemon.

Major stockists Asda, Tesco

Special London Ale ★

● **ABV 6.4 %** ● **BOTTLE SIZE 500 ml** ● **SERVE cool**
● **INGREDIENTS Maris Otter pale malt/crystal malt/Fuggle and Golding hops**

Special London Ale is the current name for Young's Export, an originally filtered beer once targeted at the Belgian market and, for a while, brewed under licence in Belgium. This bottle-conditioned version arrived in summer 1998. The beer is fermented for seven days and then warm conditioned for up to three weeks over a bed of whole Golding hops. A cold stabilisation period follows before the beer is filtered. The beer is then primed with a hopped wort extract and re-seeded with fresh yeast prior to bottling. A 12-month best before date is marked on the label, with the beer said to be at its prime three–four months after bottling. CAMRA's *Champion Bottle-Conditioned Beer* 1999 and overall champion at the 2002 *International Beer Competition.*

TASTING NOTES

Bronze, with a rich, malty, orangey hop aroma. Smooth, rich and malty on the palate, it has a fine, tangy hop flavour with orange marmalade notes. Dry, long-lasting finish of smoky, orangey Golding hops.

Major stockists Asda, Co-op, Sainsbury's, Tesco, Waitrose

Westerham

Westerham Brewery Co. Ltd., Grange Farm, Pootings Road, Crockham Hill, Edenbridge, Kent TN8 6SA. Tel. (01959) 565837
E-mail: info@westerhambrewery.co.uk
Website: www.westerhambrewery.co.uk

Westerham was set up in 2004 on a National Trust farm close to Sir Winston Churchill's country retreat, Chartwell. Founder Robert Wicks, an ex-City financier, has revived brewing in the area after a gap of nearly 40 years. Yeast strains preserved from Westerham's last operating brewery, Black Eagle, are employed in the new beers.

British Bulldog

● **ABV 4.3%** ● **BOTTLE SIZE 500 ml** ● **SERVE cool**
● **INGREDIENTS Maris Otter pale malt/crystal malt/Northdown and Golding hops**

The Churchill connections show through in the name of Westerham's one bottle-conditioned beer and in the 1940s styling of the label. The beer is brewed at Westerham but bottled elsewhere under contract.

TASTING NOTES

Copper-coloured, with smoky hop and juicy fruit (grapefruit, orange and pear) in the aroma. The taste is hoppy with more juicy citrus fruit and a firm bitterness. Dry, hoppy and bitter finish, with lingering barley notes.

Major stockists Local Tesco and Thresher

White Star

White Star Brewery, 5 Radcliffe Court, 66 Radcliffe Road, Southampton, Hampshire SO14 0PH.
Tel. (023 80) 232480 Fax (023 80) 232580
E-mail: info@whitestarbrewery.com
Website: www.whitestarbrewery.com

Founded by brothers Andy and Chris Ingram in 2003, White Star is Southampton's first commercial brewery for around 50 years. It remembers in its name the famous shipping company that operated out of the port, its most celebrated liner being the ill-fated *Titanic*. All the bottles are hand filled from casks.

UXB

● **ABV 3.8%** ● **BOTTLE SIZE 500 ml** ● **SERVE cool**
● **INGREDIENTS Maris Otter pale malt/hops not declared**

A beer first brewed in autumn 2003 that includes a blend of English, American and New Zealand hops.

TASTING NOTES

A golden ale with oranges in the aroma and bitter orange from the hops in the taste. Dry, bitter, hoppy aftertaste.

Crafty Shag

● **ABV 4.1%** ● **BOTTLE SIZE 500 ml** ● **SERVE cold**
● **INGREDIENTS Malts not declared/Hersbrucker and Saaz hops**

Whatever else you may think, this beer was actually named after a bird watching trip, so Chris declares. It's a pilsener-type brew.

TASTING NOTES

A dark golden beer with a soft malty nose and more soft malt with tangy herbal hops in the mouth. Dry, herbal-hop, bitter finish.

Majestic

● **ABV 4.2%** ● **BOTTLE SIZE 500 ml** ● **SERVE cool**
● **INGREDIENTS Optic pale malt/Northdown hops**

Named after a White Star vessel; the brewery's first ever beer. The cask version was voted best beer at the 2003 Eastleigh Beer Festival.

TASTING NOTES

Light amber, with a malty aroma. The taste is crisp for a malty beer, thanks to a hoppy, bitter edge. Bitter, malty and hoppy finish.

Dark Destroyer

● ABV 4.7% ● BOTTLE SIZE 500 ml ● SERVE cool
● INGREDIENTS Pale malt/roasted malts/hops not declared

Introduced in 2004, Dark Destroyer takes its name from the roasted malts that supply its nutty, dark character. The hops are English, but which ones they are remain a mystery.

TASTING NOTES

A garnet-coloured ale with biscuity malt and coffee in the aroma. There are more dark malt flavours in the taste, with roasted notes on the swallow. Bitter, drying, roasted grain finish.

Starlight

● ABV 5% ● BOTTLE SIZE 500 ml ● SERVE cool
● INGREDIENTS Not declared

Showing Captain Smith of the *Titanic* on its label, Starlight was another of White Star's earliest brews, first arriving in spring 2004.

Capstan Full Strength

● ABV 6% ● BOTTLE SIZE 500 ml ● SERVE cool
● INGREDIENTS Malts not declared/Fuggle hops

Great with sausage and mash, or splashed into a casserole: that's the word from the brewery about the strongest beer in the collection.

TASTING NOTES

A ruby ale with biscuity dark malt and a light herbal note in the aroma. The taste is bittersweet, fruity and gently vinous, with dark malt flavours throughout. There are liquorice notes to the bitterness in the aftertaste, with roasted grain lingering.

Whitstable

Whitstable Brewery, Little Telpits Farm, Woodcock Lane,
Grafty Green, Kent ME17 2AY.
Tel. (01622) 851007 Fax (01622) 859993
E-mail: whitstablebrewer@btconnect.com

Brewery founded in 2003 as part of the Whitstable Oyster company, which also operates a hotel and two restaurants. Bottle-conditioned beer arrived in 2006, filled directly from a conditioning tank after the yeast and fermentability have been adjusted to ensure a good secondary fermentation in the bottle.

East India Pale Ale

● ABV 4.1% ● BOTTLE SIZE 750/500 ml ● SERVE cool
● INGREDIENTS Not declared

A bottled version of a draft India pale ale, noted for its citrus hop zest and fruity flavours, which strongly suggests that the beer is brewed with American hops, although this has not been confirmed. The beer was initially sold in swing-stoppered 750 ml bottles, but 500 ml bottles are now planned.

TASTING NOTES

A golden beer with a strong grapefruit and blackcurrant aroma. Soft malt in the mouth is overlaid with lots of crisp blackcurrant and grapefruit hop notes, before a dry, hoppy aftertaste.

Whittingtons

Whittingtons Brewery, Three Choirs Vineyard, Newent, Gloucestershire GL18 1LS. Tel. (01531) 890555 Fax (01531) 890877
E-mail: info@whittingtonsbrewery.co.uk
Website: www.whittingtonsbrewery.co.uk
Mail order service

Whittingtons Brewery was founded in spring 2003 on the Three Choirs Vineyard. It takes as its theme the character of Dick Whittington, who was born in the area, and his cat: hence the brewery's slogan, 'Purveyors of the purrfect pint'. The beer is still brewed at the vineyard but is now bottled for Whittingtons by Branded Drinks.

Cats Whiskers

● ABV 4.2% ● BOTTLE SIZE 500 ml ● SERVE cool
● INGREDIENTS Maris Otter pale malt/crystal malt/chocolate malt/ sugar/First Gold and Cascade hops

Matured after fermentation, then filtered, primed with sugar and re-seeded with a fresh dose of the brewery's regular yeast, Cats Whiskers carries a nine-month best before date. The cask version was Gloucestershire CAMRA's *Beer of the Year* for 2004.

TASTING NOTES

Amber-coloured, with an aroma of nutty, chocolaty malt until orange-fruity hops take over. Bittersweet and drying in the mouth, with malt, a little lemon, nut and hop; very dry, bitter finish.

Major stockists Local Asda and Thresher

Why Not

The Why Not Brewery, 17 Cavalier Close, Thorpe St Andrew, Norwich, Norfolk NR7 0TE. Tel. (01603) 300786
E-mail: colin@thewhynotbrewery.co.uk
Website: www.thewhynotbrewery.co.uk

This tiny brewery was set up in 2005 by keen brewer Colin Emms, in a purpose-built shed at the rear of his house. He only regularly brewed bottled beers at the outset, but now also supplies cask ale. The bottle labels carry the slogan: 'Fancy a beer? Why not!'.

Wally's Revenge

● ABV 4% ● BOTTLE SIZE 500 ml ● SERVE cool
● INGREDIENTS Maris Otter pale malt/crystal malt/Fuggle and Golding hops

A light ale named in memory of Colin's uncle, an ex-naval officer and keen real ale drinker who died at the time Colin was setting up the brewery. His picture appears on the label.

TASTING NOTES

Amber-orange, with an aroma of malt and hops, plus a light floral note. The taste is a pleasant mix of citrus fruit, hop resins and smooth malt, and there's a firm bitterness to the dry and hoppy aftertaste.

Cavalier Red

● ABV 4.7% ● BOTTLE SIZE 500 ml ● SERVE cool
● INGREDIENTS Maris Otter pale malt/crystal malt/chocolate malt/ Golding and Fuggle hops

A strong bitter with Civil War connections. Like the other three bottled beers, it has been brewed since the start of the brewery's operations.

TASTING NOTES

A moreish red-tawny bitter with creamy malt and light 'fruit cocktail' notes in the nose. Creamy malt also leads in the mouth but with a firm, bitter, hoppy balance, plus a little nut and faint caramel. Nicely bitter and hoppy finish with lingering creaminess.

Chocolate Nutter

● ABV 5.5% ● BOTTLE SIZE 500 ml ● SERVE cool
● INGREDIENTS Maris Otter pale malt/crystal malt/chocolate malt/ Golding and Fuggle hops

This dark ale is, like the other beers, bottled directly from the conditioning tank, with the addition of a little priming sugar. Best before dates for all beers are 12 months.

TASTING NOTES

Garnet in colour, with creamy, chocolaty, nutty malt and a gentle fruitiness in the aroma. The smooth, full flavour is also nutty and malty, with sweet chocolate contrasting with more bitter dark malt and hop notes. Nutty, bitter chocolate and roasted grain linger in the dry aftertaste.

Wicked Hathern

Wicked Hathern Brewery Ltd., 46 Derby Road, Hathern, Loughborough, Leicestershire LE12 5LD.
Tel. (01509) 842585 Fax (01509) 646393
E-mail: beer@hathern.com
Website: www.wicked-hathern.co.uk

It was the Reverend Edward Thomas March Phillips, apparently, who declared that the village of Hathern in Leicestershire was 'Wicked'. The 19th-century cleric despaired at the drunken brawls and the cockfighting that were common place in the village, not least between the gravestones of his churchyard, and after his condemnation of public standards the local nickname of Wicked Hathern stuck. This two-and-a-half-barrel brewery was opened early in 2000.

Doble's Dog

● ABV 3.8% ● BOTTLE SIZE 500 ml ● SERVE cool
● INGREDIENTS Maris Otter pale malt/crystal malt/chocolate malt/wheat malt/Golding and Fuggle hops

An occasional mild, inspired by the unfortunate tale of another of the village's vicars. The Reverend Doble, sadly, died, along with his wife, Violet, attempting to rescue their pet dog in rough seas off Hunstanton. The dog, however, survived. The story is recalled on a plaque in the village church. The late hopping on this beer is with Fuggles, Goldings being used early in the copper.

TASTING NOTES

A ruby beer with a rich, malty aroma. There is light toffee in the sweetish, malty taste, with a touch of burnt grain. Gently bitter, malty finish with a lingering hint of roasted malt.

Hathern Cross

● ABV 4% ● BOTTLE SIZE 500 ml ● SERVE cool
● INGREDIENTS Maris Otter pale malt/amber malt/wheat malt/ Fuggle hops

A light bitter brewed exclusively for the local Hathern Stores and occasionally in draught form for beer festivals. The label depicts Hathern's old market cross.

TASTING NOTES

A golden ale with spicy hops in the aroma. The taste is nicely balanced and bittersweet, with a lemon note from the hops contrasting with malt sweetness. Gently bitter and hoppy aftertaste.

WHB (Wicked Hathern Bitter)

● ABV 4.1% ● BOTTLE SIZE 500 ml ● SERVE cool
● INGREDIENTS Maris Otter pale malt/crystal malt/chocolate malt/ wheat malt/Fuggle and Golding hops

WHB is the brewery's main cask bitter, brewed first in January 2000. Like all the bottled versions, this beer is filled in house, after being conditioned in casks and primed with sugar. Warm conditioning in bottle is then allowed for a week, followed by two further weeks at cellar temperature at the brewery, before the beers go on sale. Twelve months are stated in the best before dates.

TASTING NOTES

Copper in colour, this bitter is robust for its strength. Light malt in the bready, spicy nose; plenty of sharp, hoppy bitterness in the taste, with malt behind. Bitter, tangy-hop, drying aftertaste with roasted malt hints.

Albion Special

● ABV 4.3% ● BOTTLE SIZE 500 ml ● SERVE cool
● INGREDIENTS Maris Otter pale malt/crystal malt/wheat malt/ Fuggle and Golding hops

You can only try cask Albion Special if you visit The Albion Inn at Loughborough, or spot it at a beer festival. However, this bottled version is more widely available.

TASTING NOTES

A copper-coloured bitter with creamy malt in the nose and a bittersweet taste of nutty malt and lightly tart fruit. There's a little smokiness on the swallow before a modest, bittersweet, malty, lightly fruity, drying aftertaste.

Cockfighter

● ABV 4.5% ● BOTTLE SIZE 500 ml ● SERVE cool

● INGREDIENTS Maris Otter pale malt/crystal malt/Golding hops

The 'sport' of cockfighting became extremely popular in this region during the 19th century, and an area on the outskirts of Hathern was the venue for countless challenge contests. These apparently attracted many visitors, including the famous Leicestershire outsize man, Daniel Lambert.

TASTING NOTES

A copper-coloured beer with an aroma of fruit, creamy malt and hop resins. The taste is also malty and creamy, but nicely balanced by lightly fruity hops. The aftertaste is drying and hoppy, with creamy malt lingering.

Hawthorn Gold

● ABV 4.8% ● BOTTLE SIZE 500 ml ● SERVE cool

● INGREDIENTS Maris Otter pale malt/wheat malt/Fuggle and Golding hops

The name Hathern is derived from the Saxon for hawthorn, the bushes that surrounded the village in pre-*Domesday Book* times – hence the title of this golden bitter, which has recently been re-launched at a higher strength (was 3.5%).

TASTING NOTES

A pale golden ale with delicate malt and spicy hop in the aroma. The taste is hoppy and mostly bitter but with good malt support and body. Dry, malt-and-hops aftertaste.

Derby Porter

● ABV 5% ● BOTTLE SIZE 500 ml ● SERVE cool

● INGREDIENTS Maris Otter pale malt/crystal malt/chocolate malt/ wheat malt/Fuggle and Golding hops

First brewed as a special for Derby CAMRA's 25th beer festival in 2002 and known at the time as St Werburgh's Wallop. The Derby Ram features on the label.

TASTING NOTES

A deep ruby porter with a creamy nose of lightly smoky, chocolaty, nutty dark malts. Dark malts dominate the bittersweet, lightly spicy, chocolaty taste but without being too heavy or roasted. Roasted malt increases in the finish, along with bitter chocolate. Drying all the time.

Soar Head

● ABV 5.1% ● BOTTLE SIZE 500 ml ● SERVE cool
● INGREDIENTS Maris Otter pale malt/crystal malt/chocolate malt/ wheat malt/Fuggle and Golding hops
The River Soar flows through Hathern village.
TASTING NOTES
A ruby beer with a fruity, hoppy and malty aroma. The taste is a malty, fruity mix, with a bit of everything from hops to roasted grain. Dry, bitter, roasted malt finish.

Gladstone Tidings

● ABV 5.4% ● BOTTLE SIZE 500 ml ● SERVE cool
● INGREDIENTS Maris Otter pale malt/crystal malt/chocolate malt/ Golding hops
This is Wicked Hathern's Christmas ale, a dark bitter named after the village's Gladstone Street.

Wickwar

The Wickwar Brewing Co., The Old Brewery, Station Road, Wickwar, Wotton-under-Edge, Gloucestershire GL12 8NB.
Tel. (0870) 777 5671 Fax (0870) 777 5672
E-mail: bob@wickwarbrewing.co.uk
Website: www.wickwarbrewing.co.uk
Mail order service
Wickwar was launched in 1990 in the cooperage of the long-gone Arnold, Perrett & Co. Brewery. By 2004, however, the brewery had outgrown these limited premises and moved across the road into the main buildings, expanding capacity at the same time. Regrettably, the bottle-conditioned beer range has been cut back to one, with all other Wickwar bottles now filtered. The beer is brewed at Wickwar and bottled from a conditioning tank by Branded Drinks. Bottles carry a 12-month best before date.

BOB (Brand Oak Bitter)/Dog's Hair

● ABV 4% ● BOTTLE SIZE 500 ml ● SERVE cool
● INGREDIENTS Maris Otter pale malt/crystal malt/black malt/ torrefied wheat/Fuggle and Challenger hops
BOB, one of Wickwar's most popular beers, took its name from Brand

Oak Cottage, where one of the founders was living at the time. This brew – which has also been packaged under the name of Dog's Hair – also exists as a filtered version called BOB Sparkling.

TASTING NOTES

An amber ale with dark berry fruit in the otherwise malty nose. The taste is a berry-fruity mix of malt and hops, rounded off by a dry, moderately bitter, malt and hops finish.

Wolf

The Wolf Brewery Ltd., Rookery Farm, Silver Street, Besthorpe, Attleborough, Norfolk NR17 2LD.
Tel. (01953) 457775 Fax (01953) 457776
E-mail: info@wolfbrewery.com
Website: www.wolfbrewery.com
Mail order service

Brewery founded in 1996 by Wolfe Witham, former owner of Norfolk's Reindeer Brewery, and initially housed in an industrial unit on the site of the former Gaymer's cider orchard. A move to larger, farmland premises took place in 2006. The beers are kräusened prior to bottling and most are now stocked in local Londis stores.

Edith Cavell

● **ABV 3.7%** ● **BOTTLE SIZE 500 ml** ● **SERVE cool**
● **INGREDIENTS Pearl pale malt/crystal malt/wheat malt/Fuggle and Challenger hops**

Brewed primarily for the Norwich lodge of The Buffaloes – the Edith Cavell Lodge – this beer is largely sold at The Beehive, the lodge's meeting place in the city. The label includes a picture of the World War I nursing heroine, who was executed by the Germans.

TASTING NOTES

Amber, with toasted malt and fruity hops in the aroma. The taste is fruity and softly bitter, with malt sweetness. Dry, bitter finish.

Festival Ale

● **ABV 3.7%** ● **BOTTLE SIZE 500 ml** ● **SERVE cool**
● **INGREDIENTS Pearl pale malt/crystal malt/wheat malt/Fuggle and Challenger hops**

Festival Ale is an annual brew for Norwich and Norfolk's Arts Festival, but with the recipe changed from year to year. Flavourings have included lavender honey and blackcurrants.

Norfolk Lavender

● **ABV 3.7%** ● **BOTTLE SIZE 500 ml** ● **SERVE cool**
● **INGREDIENTS Optic pale malt/crystal malt/wheat malt/Golding, Styrian Golding and Cascade hops/lavender honey**

An unusual beer – brewed for Norfolk Lavender Ltd., Heacham – with the scented inclusion of local lavender honey.

TASTING NOTES

Golden, with a perfumed, honeyed aroma. The taste is scented, citrus and bittersweet, with light honey. Perfumed, bitter, hoppy finish.

Wolf in Sheep's Clothing

● **ABV 3.7%** ● **BOTTLE SIZE 500 ml** ● **SERVE cool**
● **INGREDIENTS Pearl pale malt/crystal malt/chocolate malt/wheat malt/Golding and Cascade hops**

From its name, you'd think that this beer had something to hide, but it's essentially just a fruity session ale.

TASTING NOTES

Toffee notes to the malt and a raisin fruitiness feature in the aroma and taste of this ruby ale, which also has a moreishly dry, slight saltiness and finishes with bitter fruit and hops.

Wolf Ale

● **ABV 3.9%** ● **BOTTLE SIZE 500 ml** ● **SERVE cool**
● **INGREDIENTS Pearl pale malt/crystal malt/wheat malt/Golding, Challenger and Styrian Golding hops**

Formerly known simply as Best Bitter in cask and bottle.

Coyote Bitter

● **ABV 4.3%** ● **BOTTLE SIZE 500 ml** ● **SERVE cool**
● **INGREDIENTS Pearl pale malt/crystal malt/wheat malt/Golding, Styrian Golding and Cascade hops**

Cascade hops lend an American accent to this award-winning brew, which explains the presence of the American wild dog in the name. The coyote is featured howling at a desert moon on the colourful label.

TASTING NOTES

Amber with a powerful fruity aroma, laced with hints of pears and juicy oranges. Big, peppery hops, more juicy fruit and a good malt base in the taste; dry, bitter, peppery-hop finish.

Straw Dog

● **ABV 4.5%** ● **BOTTLE SIZE 500 ml** ● **SERVE cool**
● **INGREDIENTS Lager malt/wheat malt/Saaz and Hallertau hops**
Containing 30% wheat, a SIBA *Wheat Beer Challenge* award-winner. Its name comes from its colour and from the fact that it was first brewed in the week that the film *Straw Dogs* was first shown on TV in the UK!

Granny Wouldn't Like It!!!

● **ABV 4.8%** ● **BOTTLE SIZE 500 ml** ● **SERVE cool**
● **INGREDIENTS Pearl pale malt/crystal malt/chocolate malt/wheat malt/Golding and Challenger hops**
This is another acclaimed ale. The label pictures feature Little Red Riding Hood and a menacing, red-eyed wolf.

TASTING NOTES
A red-amber ale with a slightly piney, vinously fruity aroma. The taste is mostly bitter, but with plenty of malt, pepper, roasted malt and a little vinous fruit. Dry, roasted, bitter finish.

Woild Moild

● **ABV 4.8%** ● **BOTTLE SIZE 500 ml** ● **SERVE cool**
● **INGREDIENTS Pearl pale malt/crystal malt/chocolate malt/wheat malt/Fuggle, Golding and Challenger hops**
A strong mild, parti-gyled (brewed as part of the same batch) with Granny Wouldn't Like It!!!

TASTING NOTES
A ruby ale with a fruity, coffeeish nose. Fruit and dark malts feature in the mouth, finishing smoky and bitter, with gentle roasted malt notes.

Timber Wolf

● **ABV 5.8%** ● **BOTTLE SIZE 500 ml** ● **SERVE cool**
● **INGREDIENTS Pearl pale malt/crystal malt/chocolate malt/wheat malt/Golding and Challenger hops**
A warming ale for Christmastime.

TASTING NOTES
Ruby, with a fruity, vinous aroma. Light winey notes continue through this fruity, tangy drink to the finish, with dark malt behind.

Ported Timber Wolf

● ABV 5.8% ● BOTTLE SIZE 500 ml ● SERVE cool
● INGREDIENTS Pearl pale malt/crystal malt/chocolate malt/wheat malt/Golding and Challenger hops/port

Bearing the descriptive sub-title of 'Falling Down Water', this is a doctored version of Timber Wolf, in the style of an Irish stout-and-fortified-wine cocktail (a 'corpse reviver'). A whole bottle of port is added after fermentation to every firkin, and the beer is then left to age for at least nine months before it is bottled (around Christmas).

TASTING NOTES

A ruby beer with an appetising, mellow fruit aroma. The taste is strong and bitter, but the fruitiness of the port shines through amid some roasted malt flavour. Dry, bitter, roasted aftertaste, with hints of winey fruit.

Woodforde's

Woodforde's Norfolk Ales (Woodforde's Ltd.), Broadland Brewery, Woodbastwick, Norwich, Norfolk NR13 6SW.
Tel. (01603) 720353 Fax (01603) 721806
E-mail: info@woodfordes.co.uk
Website: www.woodfordes.co.uk
Mail order service

Woodforde's was founded in 1981 in Drayton, near Norwich, and moved to a converted farm complex in the picturesque Broadland village of Woodbastwick in 1989. It brews a wide range of award-winning beers (including two former CAMRA *Champion Beers of Britain*), many of which are now also bottled. The process has been changed, however, with primary fermentation yeast now allowed to sediment out and the beers re-seeded with fresh yeast. The best before dates are set at nine months (except for Headcracker and Norfolk Nip).

Wherry

● ABV 3.8% ● BOTTLE SIZE 500 ml ● SERVE cool
● INGREDIENTS Maris Otter pale malt/crystal malt/Golding and Styrian Golding hops

This is a bottled version of CAMRA's *Champion Beer of Britain* of 1996, and very well does it reflect the success of its cask-conditioned equivalent, which was also CAMRA's *Champion Bitter* in 2005. A wherry – as depicted on the label – is a type of shallow-draught sailing boat once commonly seen crossing the Norfolk Broads.

TASTING NOTES

A dark golden beer with a lusciously fruity (grapefruit and elderberry), slightly peppery nose. Bitter grapefruit leads the way in the mouth, balanced by malty smoothness, before a dry, bitter citrus finish.

Great Eastern

● ABV 4.3% ● BOTTLE SIZE 500 ml ● SERVE cool

● INGREDIENTS Maris Otter pale malt/lager malt/Progress hops

A golden beer brewed originally to commemorate 150 years of the Great Eastern Railway in Norfolk in 1994.

TASTING NOTES

A light-bodied, pale golden beer with a malty, gently lemony aroma. The taste is smooth, malty and bittersweet, with a pleasant citrus note and peppery hop. Dry, bittersweet, malt and hop finish.

Nelson's Revenge

● ABV 4.5% ● BOTTLE SIZE 500 ml ● SERVE cool

● INGREDIENTS Maris Otter pale malt/crystal malt/Golding and Styrian Golding hops

Nelson's Revenge reflects the famous admiral's associations with Norfolk (the hero of Trafalgar was born in the county, at Burnham Thorpe in 1758). This brew started life as a house beer for the Limes Hotel at Fakenham but was later resurrected for the Norwich Beer Festival and has been kept in production since.

TASTING NOTES

With an appealing, spicy citrus fruit and pears aroma, this copper ale has bags of character right from the first sniff. A fine balance of zesty fruit (orange peel), malt and hop bitterness follows, with a dry, moreish, bittersweet finish.

Norfolk Nog

● ABV 4.6% ● BOTTLE SIZE 500 ml ● SERVE cool

● INGREDIENTS Maris Otter pale malt/crystal malt/chocolate malt/ Golding and Styrian Golding hops

Pre-dating the success of the brewery's Wherry by four years, Norfolk Nog was CAMRA's *Champion Beer of Britain* in 1992. To earn the supreme CAMRA accolade with two different ales is a remarkable achievement, especially for a small brewery. (For the record, only one other brewery, Fuller's, has claimed the top prize with more than one beer.) The only caveat when citing this achievement is that drinkers should be gently reminded that cask beer and bottled beer are not quite the same thing. The level of carbonation can make a difference to the nature of the beer, as can the maturing process in the bottle. A nog is thought to have been an East Anglian type of stock ale, stored for enjoyment many months after brewing.

TASTING NOTES

This is a ruby-coloured, strong mild, with a coffee and chocolate aroma. The taste is rather fruity (light orange) with sweetish dark malts and hints of plain chocolate. The finish is dry and bittersweet, with nut, light chocolate and coffee flavours.

Admiral's Reserve

● ABV 5% ● BOTTLE SIZE 500 ml ● SERVE cool
● INGREDIENTS Maris Otter pale malt/crystal malt/rye crystal malt/ Golding hops

First brewed in April 2002 to commemorate Woodforde's 21st anniversary, Admiral's Reserve is now a permanent member of the bottled range and is also available in cask form.

TASTING NOTES

An amber ale with lightly toffeeish, creamy malt and pears in the nose, before a taste of pears, sweet malt and hop. Bitter, nutty, malty notes hog the dry finish.

Headcracker

● ABV 7% ● BOTTLE SIZE 500 ml ● SERVE at room temperature
● INGREDIENTS Maris Otter pale malt/caramalt/Golding and Styrian Golding hops

Headcracker, as its name suggests, is not a beer to treat lightly but it warrants respect not just because of its strength. It has won CAMRA's *Best Barley Wine* award on no less than three occasions (in cask form). This is one beer to experiment with over a longer period than the prescribed 12 months' shelf life to see how it matures and how the flavours mellow out in the bottle.

TASTING NOTES

This complex barley wine has an orange-gold colour and a fruity (oranges), almost piney, nose. The powerful, fairly sweet taste features oranges with a piney, bitter hop balance. Alcoholic warmth shows through. Dry, tangy, hoppy finish with soft, sweet fruit persisting.

Norfolk Nip

● **ABV 8%** ● **BOTTLE SIZE 330 ml** ● **SERVE at room temperature**
● **INGREDIENTS Maris Otter pale malt/crystal malt/chocolate malt/ roasted barley/Golding hops**

Norfolk Nip closely follows a recipe dating from 1929 for a beer (also called Norfolk Nip) from the much-missed Steward & Patteson brewery in Norwich. The original beer was phased out by Watney's in the early 1960s, but the brew was revived by Woodforde's in March 1992 to commemorate the tenth anniversary of the local CAMRA news journal, *Norfolk Nips*. Brewing now takes place annually on or around St Valentine's Day. The strength and high hop rate should enable this beer to mature long after bottling.

TASTING NOTES

This ruby barley wine has dark malts, treacle, raisin, gentle liquorice, pepper and just a trace of pineapple in its complex aroma. The taste is sweet and malty, with fruity notes throughout (pineapple, orange and raisin) and an underlying roasted barley character. There are tangy hop elements, too, and a dash of liquorice. Malt, roasted grain and tangy hops continue in the dry, warming aftertaste.

Finding a new market for their beers... Forced out of many pubs by major pub chains and the expanding tied estates of regional breweries, many small breweries have taken distribution into their own hands, by bottling their wares. One of the most effective outlets, they have discovered, is the farmers' market. By manning a stall themselves, they cut out the middle man and reach out directly to the public. Some offer free tastings in the knowledge that, once tried, their beers can seldom be resisted. Hundreds of bottles can be sold in one morning.
To find your nearest farmers' market, see www.farmersmarkets.net.

Woodlands

Woodlands Brewing Company,
Units 4, 5 & 6 Creamery Industrial Estate,
Station Road, Wrenbury, Cheshire CW5 8EX.
Tel. (01270) 620101
E-mail: woodlandsbrewery@aol.com
Website: www.woodlandsbrewery.co.uk
Mail order service

Woodlands opened in autumn 2004, using equipment purchased from Khean Brewery. Adding distinctiveness to the beer range is the brewery's water source, a spring that bubbles up through local peat fields. Bottling commenced in January 2006 and the bottles are all filled directly from fermenting vessels, without fining, filtration or priming. They are then allowed four weeks of warm conditioning before leaving the brewery. They are sold at Manchester's farmers' market, among other local outlets. All these beers are also sold in draught form.

Old Willow

● **ABV 4.1%** ● **BOTTLE SIZE 500 ml** ● **SERVE cool**

● **INGREDIENTS Maris Otter and Golden Promise pale malts/pale crystal malt/Cascade, Challenger and Target hops**

The Khean Brewery beers all used to have a cricketing theme and this golden bitter picks up where that brewery left off.

TASTING NOTES

A quaffable golden ale with bitter citrus and floral hops in the nose. The taste is crisp and bittersweet, with hops and citrus fruit coming to the fore. Clean, drying, deeply hoppy aftertaste.

Oak Beauty

● **ABV 4.2%** ● **BOTTLE SIZE 500 ml** ● **SERVE cool**

● **INGREDIENTS Maris Otter and Halcyon pale malts/pale crystal malt/crystal malt/black malt/Northdown, Cascade, Golding and Fuggle hops**

Brewer John Skeaping reckons that this tan-coloured bitter has just a hint of acorn about it.

TASTING NOTES

An amber best bitter with a fresh, lightly fruity mix of malt, hops and a little toffee in the nose. There's more light toffee in the bittersweet taste, well balanced by pleasant citrus fruit from the hops. The finish is drying and malty yet bitter, with a slightly savoury moreishness.

India Pale Ale

● **ABV 4.3%** ● **BOTTLE SIZE 500 ml** ● **SERVE cool**

● **INGREDIENTS Maris Otter pale malts/torrefied wheat/Challenger, Fuggle and Target hops**

'Excellent with curry,' says John about his well-hopped India pale ale.

TASTING NOTES

A golden beer with faint toffee behind the gentle, lemony hops in the aroma. In the mouth it is bitter and hoppy-herbal, with light lemon notes, before a long, dry, hoppy and bitter finish.

Midnight Stout

● **ABV 4.4%** ● **BOTTLE SIZE 500 ml** ● **SERVE cool**

● **INGREDIENTS Maris Otter and Halcyon pale malts/black malt/ roasted barley/Golding and Whitbread Golding Variety hops**

John reckons this easy-drinking stout works well with most meat dishes.

TASTING NOTES

A dark ruby stout with a biscuity, grainy aroma of dark chocolate. The taste is bitter, peat-smoky and grainy, with dark malt flavours. Dry, bitter, slightly chewy finish of bitter chocolate.

Bitter

● **ABV 4.4%** ● **BOTTLE SIZE 500 ml** ● **SERVE cool**

● **INGREDIENTS Maris Otter and Halcyon pale malts/crystal malt/ Challenger and Northdown hops**

John suggests that Woodlands Bitter is rather Bass-like in flavour.

TASTING NOTES

A light amber ale with treacly malt and light, citrus hops in the nose. The taste is malty but not sweet, with gently bitter hops and a light berry fruitiness. Dry, malty, increasingly hoppy finish.

Gold Brew

● **ABV 5%** ● **BOTTLE SIZE 500 ml** ● **SERVE cool**

● **INGREDIENTS Halcyon and Golden Promise pale malts/pale crystal malt/Cascade, Target, Golding and Fuggle hops**

A golden beer to pair up with fish dishes, reckons John, thanks to its crisp, pale character and citrus hop accent.

TASTING NOTES
A dark golden ale with a clean orange aroma. The taste is a bittersweet blast of zesty grapefruit and other citrus fruits, with smooth, malty sweetness beneath. The aftertaste is dry, increasingly bitter and hoppy.

Wychwood

Wychwood Brewery Ltd., Eagle Maltings,
The Crofts, Witney, Oxfordshire OX28 4DP.
Tel. (01993) 890800 Fax (01993) 772553
E-mail: info@refreshuk.com
Website: www.wychwood.co.uk

Wychwood Brewery was founded in 1983 as Glenny Brewery, but changed hands and name in the early 1990s. The brewery is now owned by Refresh UK, a beer marketing company founded by former Bass and Morland sales executive Rupert Thompson. Refresh has also purchased the Brakspear brands, which are now also brewed at Wychwood but have their own, separate fermenting room (see Brakspear).

Duchy Originals Summer Ale

● **ABV 4.7%** ● **BOTTLE SIZE 500 ml** ● **SERVE cool**
● **INGREDIENTS Pale malt/crystal malt/wheat malt/Fuggle, Golding and Target hops**

The Duchy Originals brand was created by HRH The Prince of Wales in 1990, to showcase the quality of organic foods being produced in the UK and to promote the idea of sustainable farming. The duchy in the name refers to the Duchy of Cornwall, an estate held in trust by the Prince under his alternative title of Duke of Cornwall. There are three beers that carry the name, but only the Summer Ale is bottle conditioned (the other two are Duchy Originals Organic Ale and Duchy Originals Winter Ale). Summer Ale was introduced in 2005. It is brewed at Wychwood, bottled at Hepworth & Co. in Horsham and is vegan friendly. Best before dates are set at ten months.

TASTING NOTES
A golden beer with mellow melon, orange and lime in the nose. Earthy, tangy hop takes over in the mouth, supported by the same mellow fruit and a smooth malty base. Dry, hoppy, bitter finish with orange peel.
Major stockist Waitrose

Wye Valley

**Wye Valley Brewery, Stoke Lacy,
Herefordshire HR7 4HG.
Tel. (01885) 490505 Fax (01885) 490595
E-mail: sales@wyevalleybrewery.co.uk
Website: www.wyevalleybrewery.co.uk
Mail order service**

Wye Valley began production in 1985 and, growing substantially, has since moved premises twice, taking up residence in Stoke Lacy in 2002. Wye Valley seasonal cask beers all roll out under the 'Dorothy Goodbody' title. There is not, and never has been, a real Dorothy: she is just a figment of the brewery's fertile imagination, a computer-generated 1950s blonde bombshell dreamt up to market the seasonal range. Three of these seasonal beers are regularly available in bottle-conditioned form, complete with a picture of the seductive Miss Goodbody on the front. The bottles have been stylishly revamped in the past year. Like the other offering, they are now bottled by Daniel Thwaites in Blackburn, having been filtered, re-seeded with fresh bottling yeast and kräusened to ensure good natural carbonation. Occasionally, seasonal and celebration beers may be bottled, too. Best before dates are set at nine months. The US importer is B United.

Dorothy Goodbody's Golden Ale

● **ABV 4.2%** ● **BOTTLE SIZE 500 ml** ● **SERVE cool**
● **INGREDIENTS Maris Otter pale malt/pale crystal malt/wheat malt/ East Kent Golding and Fuggle hops**

Available in cask form March–August. Try it with fish, chicken or pasta.

TASTING NOTES

As its name implies, a dark golden ale with a spicy, pithy, citrus nose, a bittersweet, orange-citrus taste and a soft, malty mouthfeel, plus a dry, fruity, bitter hop finish. Clean and refreshing.

Major stockists Tesco, Thresher, Waitrose, local Sainsbury's

Butty Bach

● **ABV 4.5%** ● **BOTTLE SIZE 500 ml** ● **SERVE cool**
● **INGREDIENTS Maris Otter pale malt/crystal malt/wheat malt/ flaked barley/Golding, Fuggle and Bramling Cross hops**

Mainly aimed at the brewery's Welsh customers, 'Little Friend' has been one of Wye Valley's most successful beers, its cask version voted top beer at the Cardiff Beer Festival three years running.

TASTING NOTES

A dark golden ale with zesty orange peel in the aroma. In the mostly bitter taste there are juicy, orangey hops over a sweet, malty base, and the drying finish is also hop-fruity, with bitterness taking over.

Major stockist Local Sainsbury's

Dorothy Goodbody's Wholesome Stout ★

● **ABV 4.6%** ● **BOTTLE SIZE 500 ml** ● **SERVE cool**

● **INGREDIENTS Maris Otter pale malt/crystal malt/chocolate malt/roasted barley/flaked barley/Northdown hops**

The label claims that Dorothy discovered this recipe in her grandfather's brewing books. The truth is that brewery founder, Peter Amor, once worked for Guinness and was duly inspired to create this award-winning stout. The draught version was CAMRA's *Champion Winter Beer of Britain* in 2002. The best before date for this beer is set at 18 months.

TASTING NOTES

A very dark ruby stout with an aroma of creamy, grainy chocolate. In the mouth it feels rich and nourishing, with an excellent smooth balance of chocolaty malt sweetness and bitter roast flavours. Roasted grain and bitterness dominate the dry finish.

Dorothy Goodbody's Country Ale/ Christmas Ale

● **ABV 6%** ● **BOTTLE SIZE 500 ml** ● **SERVE cool**

● **INGREDIENTS Maris Otter pale malt/crystal malt/amber malt/wheat malt/flaked barley/roasted barley/Bramling Cross and Fuggle hops**

Country Ale is also sold in winter as Christmas Ale and was first bottled for export to the USA under the name of 'Our Glass'. Wye Valley advises you to drink it with cheeses or rich puddings. Eighteen months are declared in the best before date, but the brewers recommend that it enjoy at least six months in the bottle to be at its best.

TASTING NOTES

A red beer with pineapple, gentle pear drops and toffee-malt in the aroma. Bitter, tangy hops lead over sweet, nutty malt and fruit in the mouth, with hints of blackcurrants, orange and lime, and some spicy warmth. Tangy hop resins dominate the dry, bitter fruit finish.

Yates'

Yates' Brewery, Unit 6, Dean Farm, Whitwell Road, Whitwell, Isle of Wight PO38 2AB.
Tel./Fax (01983) 731731
E-mail: info@yates-brewery.fsnet.co.uk
Website: www.yates-brewery.co.uk
Mail order service

Dave Yates used to work for Burts Brewery on the Isle of Wight and also joined the short-lived Island Brewery. Since 2000, he's been brewing on his own, with a five-barrel plant overlooking the sea at The Inn at St Lawrence pub, near Ventnor (the above address is the office and distribution centre). Bottled beers were launched in 2003 and are filled from a cask after being kräusened. Nine-month best before dates are applied.

Undercliff Experience

● **ABV 4.1%** ● **BOTTLE SIZE 500 ml** ● **SERVE cool**
● **INGREDIENTS Optic pale malt/crystal malt/chocolate malt/ torrefied wheat/Golding and Fuggle hops**

The brewery's flagship bitter – taking its name from the area in which the brewery stands – is primarily seasoned with Golding hops, but a charge of Fuggles is added late in the boil. This is contrary to the method of most brewers who use this classic combination: the Goldings are usually added last for aroma.

TASTING NOTES

An amber ale with a bittersweet, malt-and-hop taste and a dry, lemon edge that dominates the bitter finish.

Blonde Ale

● **ABV 4.5%** ● **BOTTLE SIZE 500 ml** ● **SERVE cool**
● **INGREDIENTS Optic pale malt/torrefied wheat/Fuggle and Cascade hops**

'A light ale that won't be eclipsed', declares the label of this new pale brew that Dave suggests will go well with summer barbecues.

TASTING NOTES

A golden beer with a malty aroma, laced with floral, citrus hops. The taste is hoppy and bitter to start, with smooth malt support and light lemon notes. Dry, hoppy aftertaste.

Holy Joe

● ABV 4.9% ● BOTTLE SIZE 500 ml ● SERVE cool
● INGREDIENTS Optic pale malt/crystal malt/torrefied wheat/ Cascade hops/coriander

A glance at the ingredients suggests that this is going to be a citrus beer, with the zesty inclusion of American Cascade hops and powdered coriander added late into the copper. The taste backs this up. The beer is named after a local character from the 1850s who roamed the highways abusing sinners.

TASTING NOTES

Golden, with lots of citrus immediately evident in the aroma, and subtle malt emerging later. Plenty of bitterness features in the mouth along with slightly toasted, sweet malt flavours, pronounced tangy-citrus notes and spicy coriander. Bitter, hoppy, spicy and lightly toasted finish.

Wight Winter

● ABV 5% ● BOTTLE SIZE 500 ml ● SERVE cool
● INGREDIENTS Optic pale malt/chocolate malt/roasted malt/ torrefied wheat/Northdown hops

This is the brewery's seasonal warmer, described by Dave Yates as a stout-like, very dark bitter. Other seasonal beers called A Little Bitter Spring/Summer/Autumn may also be bottled.

TASTING NOTES

A ruby ale with malty milk chocolate at first in the nose, then plenty of orange fruit. It is bitter, malty and roasted to taste, with a perfumed bitter orange note always present. Bitter, roasted, perfumed finish.

YSD (Yates' Special Draught)

● ABV 5.5% ● BOTTLE SIZE 500 ml ● SERVE cool
● INGREDIENTS Optic pale malt/crystal malt/Fuggle and Cascade hops

A strong ale replacing a beer of similar potency called Broadway Blitz in the Yates' range. 'A drink to be respected', declares the label. Bronze medallist in CAMRA's *Champion Bottled Beer* contest in 2004.

TASTING NOTES

Dark golden in colour, with a tart fruit nose, this strong beer has a dry, hoppy, bitter taste that belies its strength to some degree. Fruit notes emerge and linger in the dry, bitter, hoppy aftertaste.

International Selection

WHILE THE NUMBER OF BOTTLE-CONDITIONED BEERS brewed in the UK continues to rise, there is even greater choice for the discerning drinker in the form of more and more bottle-conditioned beers flowing in from overseas. Here is a selection of the best to be found on UK shelves.

The Americas and Australia

Anything goes in America, Canada and even Mexico, as far as brewing is concerned. The craft brewers can turn their hands to beers of all international styles and have even produced outstanding variations of them. It's not all Bud and Miller, by any means. Australian brewers have a poor reputation on the world stage, thanks to the insipid lagers they export or have brewed under licence in other countries, but there are breweries to prove that there is good beer Down Under.

Alaskan Smoked Porter 6.5%, Alaskan
Smoky, bittersweet, roasted porter with just a trace of fruit behind.

Blanche de Chambly 5%, Unibroue
Canadian white beer in the Belgian style, with lemon sharpness and malty-toffee undertones.

Celebration Ale 6.8%, Sierra Nevada
Pungent grapefruit hoppiness dominates this festive offering from northern California.

Coopers Original Pale Ale 4.5%, Coopers
A crisp, lagerish beer with light pear fruit and hops in the taste and an increasingly bitter aftertaste.

Coopers Sparkling Ale 5.8%, Coopers
An Adelaide beer with a sweetish, pear drop flavour, rounded off by a drying, bittersweet finish.

Coopers Stout 6.3%, Coopers
Crisp, clean and lightly bitter stout with roast grain character, although a touch thin for its strength.

Dead Guy Ale 6%, Rogue Ales
Sharp citrus notes feature in this bronze ale that drinks lighter than its strength. None of Rogue's beers are pasteurized and most contain yeast sediment, although they are not officially declared bottle conditioned.
Golden Monkey 9.5%, Victory
A Belgium-influenced, perfumed ale from Pennsylvania, incorporating spices for further mystery.
Goose Island IPA 5.9%, Goose Island
Glorious Chicago-brewed hopfest, filled with juicy fruit.
Honker's Ale 5%, Goose Island
A fresh, full-tasting ale with loads of hop-pocket character.
La Fin du Monde 9%, Unibroue
Canadian 'tripel' blonde, described as the 'beginning of paradise': orange-hoppy and pleasingly acidic.
Little Creatures Pale Ale 5.2%, Little Creatures
Tangy, peppery hops and full citrus fruit feature in this golden ale from Australia. It's been so successful that they're expanding the brewery.
Milennia 8%, Casta
A Trappist-style, spicy, malty ale with a liquorice-like bitterness that proves that not all Mexican beers need a slice of lime for character.
Mocha Porter 5.3%, Rogue Ales
A bittersweet, chocolaty, dark beer with a nutty, coffee finish.
Raftman 5.5%, Unibroue
Whisky malt beer from Quebec, bittersweet, malty and with a lemon-hop overlay. Quite subdued in the smoke department.
Sierra Nevada Pale Ale 5.6%, Sierra Nevada
A crisp, refreshing Californian classic, marrying malt and bitterness with a dry, lime-flavoured hop bite.
Shakespeare Stout 6.3%, Rogue Ales
Despite the strength, not too heavy, with crisp roasted grain flavours.
XS Imperial Stout 11%, Rogue Ales
A stunning recreation of the imperial Russian stout style, full-flavoured and complex, mixing roasted grain and liquorice with sweeter malt.

Belgium

Many of Belgium's most famous beers are bottle conditioned, ranging from potent, nourishing brews supervised by monks in Trappist monasteries, to spicy, fragrant wheat beers (witbiers).

Abbaye des Rocs 9%, Abbaye des Rocs
Not from an abbey, but from a modern brewery set up in the 1980s close to the French border. Rich, fruity and spicy.

Achel Blonde 8%, Achel
The newest of the Trappist breweries, on the Dutch border. The Blonde is peppery, bittersweet and dryish. Look out, too, for the maltier Brune.

Affligem Blonde 6%, Affligem
Soft, sweetish, spicy ale from an abbey-beer producer owned by Heineken. Stronger in its home market (6.8%).

Augustijn Grand Cru 9%, Van Steenberge
A bittersweet, powerful, golden ale with a tropical fruit character.

Barbãr 8%, Lefèbvre
A honey beer that manages to remain bitter rather than sweet, with heavy fruit and malt flavours.

Beersel 7%, Drie Fonteinen
A bittersweet, easy-drinking, citrus blonde containing wheat.

Blanche de Bruxelles 4.5%, Lefèbvre
Lightly toffeeish, spiced, fruity witbier from the makers of Barbãr.

Blanche des Honnelles 6%, Abbaye des Rocs
A strong wheat beer.

Bon Secours Bière Vivante!! Blonde 8%, Caulier
A sweet, warming, slightly earthy, golden beer with a distinct gooseberry flavour.

Bon Secours Bière Vivante!! Brune 8%, Caulier
Spicy, malty and warming, with more than a suggestion of chocolate orange about it.

Brugs Tarwebier 4.8%, Alken-Maes
Quenching, scented, bitter lemon-accented wheat beer, with a dry 'tonic water' finish.

Celis White 5%, Van Steenberge
Pierre Celis, the man behind the early success of Hoegaarden, later created this witbier, now contract brewed: soft, dry, lemony, bittersweet and lightly spicy.

Chimay Rouge/Première 7%, Chimay
Sweetish, malty, spicy beer with a suggestion of cherry, from a Trappist monastery near the French border. Spot its red cap.

Chimay Blanche/Cinq Cents 8%, Chimay
Extremely hoppy, bitter orange- and apricot-accented, zesty stablemate of Rouge, this time with a white cap.

Chimay Bleue/Grand Réserve 9%, Chimay
Blue-capped biggest of the Chimay brothers: full, smooth and malty with fruit notes and a renowned port-like finish.

Corsendonk Agnus 7.5%, Bocq
Commissioned brew for a wholesaler, using a defunct abbey name; classy, refreshing, bittersweet and lemony.

Corsendonk Pater 7.5%, Van Steenberge
A sweet, dark beer with a hint of raisin.

Delirium Tremens 9%, Huyghe
Jokey-named beer served in a stone-effect bottle but far from gimmicky in its mouth-numbing mix of fruit and hop flavours.

Dentergems Witbier 5%, Riva
One of Hoegaarden's competitors and similarly cloudy, but drier.

Duvel 8.5%, Moortgat
'Devil beer', deceptive in its blonde looks. Full zesty bitterness, subtle pear fruit and surprisingly light body for its strength.

Gouden Carolus Classic 8.5%, Het Anker
Mellow, toffeeish beer from 'The Anchor' brewery in Mechelen.

Hoegaarden 4.9%, InBev
Bittersweet, easy-drinking, fruity wheat beer, flavoured with coriander and curaçao. The style's market leader, with a gently peppery, bitter orange and stewed apple character. Now weaker than before.

Hoegaarden Grand Cru 8.5%, InBev
Strong, flowery, spicy, bittersweet strong beer, with hints of mango and orange and a suggestion of whisky. Also reduced in strength.

Kasteelbier Blonde 11%, Van Honsebrouck
A big, alcoholic, almondy beer with a sweetish finish.

Leffe Tripel 8.4%, InBev
Leffe is the market leader in Abbey ales, but only this Tripel, a decent example of the style, is bottle conditioned.

La Chouffe 8%, Achouffe
Coriandered blonde with bitter fruit notes.

McChouffe 8.5%, Achouffe
Ruby-coloured, malty merger of Belgian and Scottish styles.

Orval 6.2%, Orval
World classic ale from a Trappist monastery: bitter, dry and fruitily acidic.

Poperings Hommel Beer 7.5%, Van Eecke
The Belgian hopgardens distilled in one glass. A full-flavoured onslaught of sappy hops well balanced by sweetness, fruit and spice notes.

Reinaert Tripel 9%, Proef
A malty, bittersweet, pleasant tripel with light raisin character.
Reinaert Grand Cru 9.5%, Proef
Dry-finishing, burnished-copper brew, nicely balancing malty sweetness and light fruit, with pear in the aroma.
Rochefort 6 7.5%, Rochefort
Rarely seen away from its Ardennes Trappist homeland, but an amazing malty, spicy confection.
Rochefort 8 9.2%, Rochefort
Light-drinking for its strength, spicy, peppery and fruity.
Rochefort 10 11.3%, Rochefort
Dreamy, peppery and dry, with background fruit.
Silly Saison 5%, Silly
No-joke beer from Silly town, drinking sweet and light despite its deep raisiny, figgy fruit flavours and plenty of malt.
Tripel Karmeliet 8%, Bosteels
Abbey beer from a brewery better known for its 8% beer, Kwak. Sweet malt, strong toffee, hints of lemon, an oaty creaminess and spicy hops.
Val-Dieu Blonde 6%, Val-Dieu
A slightly chewy, lemon-accented, sweetish blonde.
Val-Dieu Brune 8%, Val-Dieu
A perfumed, sweet and malty, red-brown beer.
Val-Dieu Triple 9%, Val-Dieu
Golden, with jammy apricots and oranges in the sweet taste.
Vieille Provision 6.5%, Dupont
Crisp, herbal and gently bitter, with an orange acidity: a leading exponent of the saison style of quenching summer beers.
Westmalle Dubbel 7%, Westmalle
Complex, sweetish brown beer from the largest Trappist brewery. Spice, dark malt, rum and raisin.
Westmalle Tripel 9.5%, Westmalle
A pale, aromatic, classic tripel, with fruit and honey character.
Westvleteren Blonde 5.8%, Westvleteren
Full-flavoured blonde from a Trappist brewery near the Belgian hop fields, close to France.
Westvleteren 8 8%, Westvleteren
A melon-, almond- and liquorice-accented, slightly acidic ruby beer.
Westvleteren 12 10.2%, Westvleteren
A hearty, spicy, sweetish ale with a liquorice-like bitterness.

France

Although the French seem to be ensconced in copy-cat mode, emulating Belgian ales and wheat beers, they do have a classic beer style of their own in the bière de garde. Unfortunately, for purposes of this listing, most such beers – Jenlain, Ch'ti, Trois Monts being the best known – although beautifully matured, are conditioned at the brewery before bottling, rather than in the bottle itself, and are filtered.

Britt Blanche 4.8%, Britt
Spicy, Breton wheat beer, fruity and peppery.

Coreff Ambrée 5%, Deux Rivières
An amber Breton ale with a reasonable hop presence.

Duchesse Anne 6.5%, Lancelot
A strong blonde ale from Brittany.

Gavroche 8.5%, St-Sylvestre
A malty, herbal, fruity brew from close to the Belgian frontier.

L'Atrébate Brune 7%, Bécu
Spicy, malty, brown ale, the most impressive of a small series from the Pas-de-Calais.

La Fraîche de L'Aunelle 5.5%, Duyck
Organic, pale beer from the Nord-Pas-de-Calais brewers of the classic bière de garde, Jenlain.

Lancelot 6%, Lancelot
A Breton brew, featuring biscuity malt and tropical fruit.

Germany and Czech Republic

Germany has a deserved international reputation for quality lager beers, in the hell, export, pils, Dortmunder and other styles, plus fascinating minor styles like Kölsch from Cologne and rauchbier smoked beer from Bamberg. However, when these are bottled they tend to be filtered and usually pasteurized, so it falls to the weissbier, the Bavarian-style wheat beer, to reveal how well Germans can present naturally-conditioned bottled beers. Look out, too, for own-label wheat beers authentically brewed in Germany for some of the British supermarkets. This section also contains one interesting beer from the Czech Republic. Most of the wonderful Czech lagers are filtered and often pasteurized for the bottle, so this beer, from the Bernard brewery in the town of Humpolec, is quite a discovery.

Aventinus 8%, Schneider
Amazingly complex with a full, smooth, fairly sweet and malty taste, well supported by bananas and spice.
Erdinger Weissbier 5.3%, Erdinger
From the world's largest wheat beer brewery, just outside Munich: a mellow, quaffable, mildly clove-spiced, fruity brew.
Erdinger Dunkel 5.6%, Erdinger
A dark wheat beer offering a wonderful, sweet mix of mild clove, soft chocolate and a hint of liquorice.
Franziskaner Hefe-Weissbier 5%, Spaten-Franziskaner
A lightly spicy, fruity wheat beer from Munich.
Franziskaner Dunkel Hefe-Weissbier 5%, Spaten-Franziskaner
An apple-fruity, gently spicy, dark wheat beer.
König Ludwig Weissbier 5.5%, Kaltenberg
Castle-brewed, bittersweet, Bavarian favourite, imported by Thwaites.
Löwen Weiss 5.2%, Löwenbräu
Quaffable, fruit-and-spice-fragranced Munich wheat beer.
Maisel's Weisse 5.7%, Maisel's
Easy-drinking, apple- and orange-fruity weissbier with warming hints of liquorice and clove.
Paulaner Hefe-Weissbier 5.5%, Paulaner
A thinnish weissbier for its strength, from Munich's biggest brewery. Delicate banana, clove and sour notes feature in the taste.
Pikantus 7.3%, Erdinger
Complex, strong wheat beer with sweet, mildly spicy, almond and raisin flavours.
Riegele's Weisse 5%, Riegele
An enjoyably tart and challenging weissbier from a family-owned brewery in Augsburg. Imported by Pilgrim Brewery.
Schneider Weisse 5.4 %, Schneider
Highly-rated Bavarian wheat beer from just north of Munich: spicy, dry and very fruity (banana), with a touch of sourness.
Schöfferhofer 5%, Binding
German national brand weissbier, with a pleasant clove-spice edge.
Svatecni Lezak 5%, Bernard
A bottle-conditioned Czech lager with a full buttery maltiness and tangy, herbal hops for balance. The beer is sold in a tall, swing-stoppered bottle. Bernard's Cerné Pivo, a finely filtered dark lager, is also left unpasteurized.

Weizenland Dunkel **5.1%, Weizenland**
A nutty, spicy dark wheat beer with a mild lemon sourness.
Weizenland Hefetrüb **5.3%, Weizenland**
A fruity, chewy, bittersweet wheat beer.

The Netherlands

The Netherlands shares many of the beery qualities of its near-neighbour Belgium, even if it is best known around the world for its sweetish lager beers.

Hertog Jan Double **7.3%, Hertog Jan**
A Dutch dubbel with tart fruit, dark malts and warming alcohol throughout. Sold in a stone-effect bottle similar to La Trappe's.
Korenwolf **5%, Gulpener**
Named after the Dutch for a hamster (literally 'corn wolf'): a spiced beer in the Hoegaarden mould, brewed with four different cereals. Imported into the UK by Coors.
La Trappe Blonde 6.5%, **Schaapskooi**
A fruity blonde from a brewery now back officially in the Trappist fold (the monks sold the brewery to Dutch giant Bavaria but have won the right to be declared Trappist again).
La Trappe Dubbel **6.5%, Schaapskooi**
A sweet, malty, spicy and nourishing dubbel.
La Trappe Tripel **8%, Schaapskooi**
A well-regarded, bittersweet, fruity tripel.
La Trappe Quadrupel **10%, Schaapskooi**
Sweetish, spicy, malty and warming, with marzipan undertones.
La Trappe Witte **5.5%, Schaapskooi**
Witbier with a tart apple and lemon, spicy taste. Not too sweet.
Robertus **6%, Christoffel**
Unusual dark lager in the Munich style with roasted malt flavours.
Wieckse Witte **5%, Ridder**
Refreshing, lightly lemony, slightly toffeeish, spicy wheat beer, Heineken's bid to steal away Hoegaarden drinkers.
Zatte Tripel **8%, IJ**
A tasty, fruity (bitter orange) tripel with a gently bitter aftertaste.

Dictionary

A reference guide to the technical terms used in this book and on bottled beer labels.

ABV: Alcohol by Volume – the percentage of alcohol in a beer.

Abbey beer: a beer brewed in the style of monastic beers by commercial companies. Only authentic Trappist monasteries have the right to call their beers 'Trappist'; others producing beers in similar style under licence from a clerical order have adopted the term 'Abbey'.

adjuncts: materials like cereals and sugars which are added to malted barley, often to create a cheaper brew but sometimes for special flavours or effects.

aftertaste/afterpalate: see finish.

ale: a top-fermenting beer (the yeast mostly sits on top during fermentation).

alpha acid: the bittering component of a hop; the higher the alpha acid content, the fewer hops are needed for bitterness.

aroma: the perfumes given off by a beer.

barley: the cereal from which malt is made, occasionally used in its unmalted form in brewing, primarily to add colour.

barley wine: a very strong, sweetish ale.

bitter: a well-hopped ale.

body: the fullness of the beer, generally indicative of the malt content.

bottle-conditioned: beer which undergoes a secondary fermentation in the bottle ('real ale in a bottle').

brewery-conditioned: beer with a fermentation completed at the brewery and usually pasteurized.

bright: filtered (often pasteurized) beer.

burtonize: to adjust the salts in brewing water to emulate the natural, hard waters of Burton upon Trent.

carbon dioxide: a gas created by yeast during fermentation and vital to the drinkability of a beer; see also condition.

cask: container for unpasteurized beer.

cask-conditioned: beer given a secondary fermentation in a cask ('real ale').

condition: the amount of dissolved carbon dioxide in a beer. Too much and the beer is gassy; too little and it is flat.

decoction: a continental mashing system in which parts of the extract are moved into a second vessel and subjected to a higher temperature, before being returned to the original vessel. The aim is better starch conversion into sugar.

dry hopping: the process of adding hops to a beer after it has been brewed, usually in the cask or in a conditioning tank prior to bottling, in order to enhance the hop character and aroma.

dubbel: a Trappist or Abbey 'double' ale of about 7% ABV, generally dark brown and malty, with low hop character. Tripel ('triple') beers are stronger (around 8–9%), fruity and often pale in colour.

80/-: see shilling system.

esters: organic compounds comprised of an alcohol and an acid, produced during fermentation. These have unusual – often fruity – aromas and flavours.

filtered: a beer with its yeast and other sediment extracted; sterile-filtered beer has passed through a very fine filter.

finings: a glutinous liquid that attracts yeast particles and draws them to the bottom of a cask (or a conditioning tank in the case of many bottled beers), leaving the beer clear. Finings are usually made from the swim-bladder of a tropical fish. Also known as isinglass.

finish: the lingering taste in the mouth after swallowing beer.

framboise/frambozen: see kriek.

green beer: beer not fully matured.

green hops: hops picked fresh from the bine and used without undergoing the traditional drying process that allows them to be stored for months. Green hops provide a pungent, sappy character.

grist: crushed malt ready for mashing. The term also refers to a mix of cereals, or hops, used in the brew.

gueuze: see lambic.

hop: fast-growing plant, a relative of the nettle and cannabis. Its flowers are used to provide bitterness and other flavours in beer. Hops also help preserve beer.

isinglass: see finings.

keg: a pressurized container for storing usually pasteurized beer. Brewery-conditioned beers, or 'keg' beers, need gas pressure to give them artificial fizz.

kräusen: to add a small quantity of partially fermented wort to a beer in order to provide fresh sugars for the yeast to continue fermentation. It helps generate extra condition.

kriek: a Belgian lambic beer undergoing a secondary fermentation with the addition of cherries or cherry juice. Similar beers incorporate raspberries ('framboise'/'frambozen') and other fruits. See also lambic.

lager: a bottom-fermented beer (the yeast sinks to the bottom of the wort during fermentation) that is matured for several weeks (months in the best instances) at low temperatures.

lambic: a Belgian wheat beer fermented by wild yeasts and aged in casks. Blended lambic is known as gueuze. See also kriek.

late hopping: the process of adding hops late to the copper boil, to compensate for any aroma that may have been lost from hops used earlier in the boil.

malt: barley which has been partially germinated to release vital sugars for brewing, then kilned to arrest germination and provide various flavours.

malt extract: commercially-produced concentrated wort, used by some brewers to save mashing, or to supplement their own wort.

mash: the infusion of malt and water in the mash tun which extracts fermentable materials from the grain.

mild: a lightly-hopped, usually lowish-strength ale, often dark in colour.

mouthfeel: the texture and body.

nose: see aroma.

OG: Original Gravity – a reading taken before fermentation to gauge the amount of fermentable material in a beer. The higher the OG, the more fermentables and the greater the likely strength of the finished brew.

old ale: a strong, dark beer; traditionally, a beer set aside to mature.

original gravity: see OG.

oxidation: the deterioration in beer caused by oxygen, usually manifested in a wet paper or cardboard taste.

palate: the sense of taste.

parti-gyle: method of brewing more than one beer at the same time, using one standard brew that is then adapted – often by adding water to change the strength, or by using the first runnings from the mash tun to make a heavy beer and later runnings for a lighter beer.

pasteurized: beer which has been heat treated to kill off remaining yeast cells and prevent further fermentation.

porter: a lighter-bodied predecessor of stout, usually dry, with some sweetness.

rack: to run beer from a tank or a cask.

real ale: an unpasteurized, unfiltered beer which continues to ferment in the vessel from which it is dispensed ('cask-conditioned' or 'bottle-conditioned').

sediment: solids in beer, primarily yeast but also possibly some proteins.

shilling system: a Scottish system of branding beers according to style and strength, derived from Victorian times when the number of shillings stated referred to the gross price payable by the publican on each barrel. 60/-, or light, is the Scottish equivalent of a mild; 70/-, or heavy, is a Scottish bitter; and 80/-, or export, is a stronger beer again.

SIBA: The Society of Independent Brewers, a trade body representing the interests of the small brewing sector.

single-varietal: a beer using just one strain of hops or one type of malt.

sterile-filtered: see filtered.

stock ale: a very strong beer intended to be kept and matured for several months.

stout: traditionally, a strongish beer, usually dark in colour and tasting dry and bitter, often with roasted barley flavour.

sunstruck: beer which has been over-exposed to bright light. This can cause a chemical reaction, leading to unsavoury aromas and flavours.

Trappist ale: see Abbey beer.

tripel: see dubbel.

weissbier: a Bavarian style of wheat beer, known for its fruit-and-spices character. Hefeweissbiers are naturally cloudy; kristalweissbiers are filtered to be clear. Also called weizenbiers.

wheat beer: a style of beer originating in Germany and Belgium, brewed with a high percentage of wheat and often served cloudy with yeast in suspension.

witbier: a Belgian-style, spiced wheat beer; also known as bière blanche.

wort: the unfermented sweet liquid produced by mashing malt and water.

yeast: a single-celled micro-organism that turns sugar in wort into alcohol and carbon dioxide.

Beer shops

CAMRA is delighted to welcome Sainsbury's as sponsor of the *Good Bottled Beer Guide*, a move that happily reflects just how far British supermarkets have come in terms of the bottled beers they offer. Naturally, we think Sainsbury's has one of the best selections at the moment, including some excellent foreign beers, but other major chains are worth checking out, too. Booths in the North-West has an exceptional range, and Asda and Waitrose are also improving their choice. Tesco, Morrisons, the Co-op and Somerfield, as well as Thresher in the multiple off-licence sector, all carry some beers of note. For an even wider selection, it may pay to seek out a specialist independent off-licence. The following shops all stock bottle-conditioned beers and should prove a useful starting point. Some of these also offer mail order services, as indicated by the abbreviation (MO) after the address. Additionally, there are a number of internet companies that offer mail order beer sales. Some of these are listed at the end.

Bedfordshire

Parkland Wines
142 High Street, Cranfield.

Berkshire

Palmer Wines
61 Wokingham Road, Reading.
Tel: (0118) 935 3555

Wickcroft Farm Shop
Pangbourne Road, Theale.
Tel. (118) 930 5159
www.wickcroftfarmshop.co.uk

Bristol

The Bristol Wine Company
Transom House, Victoria Street, Bristol. (MO)
Tel. (0117) 373 0288
www.thebristolwinecompany.co.uk

Corks of Cotham
54 Cotham Hill, Cotham.
Tel. (0117) 973 1620
www.corksof.com

Humpers Off-Licence
26 Soundwell Road, Staple Hill.
Tel. (0117) 956 5525

Buckinghamshire

The Grape & Grain
84 Broad Street, Chesham.
Tel. (01494) 791319

Cambridgeshire

Bacchanalia
79 Victoria Road, Cambridge. (MO)
Tel. (01223) 576292

Bacchanalia
90 Mill Road, Cambridge. (MO)
Tel. (01223) 315034

Wadsworth's
34 The Broadway, St Ives.
Tel. (01480) 463522

Cheshire

deFINE Food & Wine
Chester Road, Sandiway, Northwich. (MO)
Tel. (01606) 882101
www.definefoodandwine.com

Cumbria

Open All Hours
5 St Johns Street, Keswick. (MO)
Tel. (0176 87) 75414
www.personalbeer.co.uk

Derbyshire

Chatsworth Farm Shop
Pilsley, Bakewell. (MO)
Tel. (01246) 583392
www.chatsworth.org

Goyt Wines
1A Canal Street, Whaley Bridge.
Tel. (01663) 734214
www.goytwines.co.uk

La Cave Robert
34 Market Hall, Derby.
Tel. (01332) 242403

The Original Farmer's Market Shop
3 Market Street, Bakewell.
Tel. (01629) 815814

Devon

Green Valley Cyder at Darts Farm
Topsham, Exeter.
Tel. (01392) 876658

Tucker's Maltings
Teign Road, Newton Abbot. (MO)
Tel. (01626) 334734
www.tuckersmaltings.com

Dorset

Turbary Wines
5 Turbary Road, Ferndown.
Tel. (01202) 861514

Durham

Binns Department Store
1–7 High Row, Darlington.
Tel. (08701) 607237

Essex

Beers Unlimited
500 London Road, Westcliff-on-Sea. (MO)
Tel. (01702) 345474
www.beersunlimited.co.uk

Bottles
37 Broomfield Road, Chelmsford. (MO)
Tel. (01245) 255579
www.onlyfinebeer.co.uk

The Turnpike Off Licence
1206 London Road, Leigh-on-Sea
Tel. (01702) 476028

Hampshire

Bitter Virtue
70 Cambridge Road, Portswood,
Southampton. (MO)
Tel. (023 80) 554881
www.bittervirtue.co uk

Hops & Grapes
220 Shirley Road, Southampton.
Tel. (023 80) 333951

Southwick Brewhouse
Southwick.
Tel. (023 92) 201133
www.southwickbrewhouse.co.uk

Herefordshire

Gwatkin Cider
Moorhampton Park Farm, Abbey Dore.
Tel. (01981) 550258

Hertfordshire

Boxmoor Vintners
25–27 St John's Road, Boxmoor.
Tel. (01442) 252171

Isle of Wight

Scarecrow Brewery and Beer Emporium
Arreton Craft Village, Arreton.
Tel. (01983) 856161 (Ventnor Brewery)

Kent

The Bitter End
107 Camden Road, Tunbridge Wells. (MO)
Tel. (01892) 522918
www.thebitterend.biz

The Cask & Glass
64 Priory Street, Tonbridge.
Tel. (01732) 359784

Lancashire

Hop & Vine Experience
2 Queen Victoria Road, Burnley.
Tel. (01282) 454970

Rainhall Drinks
18–22 Rainhall Road, Barnoldswick.
Tel. (01282) 813374

Real Ale Shop
47 Lovat Road, Preston.
Tel. (01772) 201591

Leicestershire

Bells Brewery & Merchants
The Workshop, Lutterworth Road, Ullesthorpe. (MO)
Tel. (01455) 209940
www.bellsbrewery.co.uk

Melton Wines
Unit 5, Bell Centre, Nottingham Street, Melton Mowbray.
Tel. (01664) 410114

The Offie
142 Clarendon Park Road, Leicester. (MO)
Tel. (0116) 270 1553
www.the-offie.co.uk

Lincolnshire

The Beer Cellar
2 Gordon Road, Bailgate, Lincoln. (MO)
Tel. (01522) 524948
www.beercellarlincoln.co.uk

Poachers Off-Licence
457 High Street, Lincoln.
Tel. (01522) 510237

Greater London

The Bitter End
139 Masons Hill, Bromley. (MO)
Tel. (020) 8466 6083
www.thebitterend.biz

Ex-Cellar
775 Fulham Road, SW10. (MO)
Tel. (020) 7736 2038

Kris Wines
394 York Way, N7.
Tel. (020) 7607 4871

Nelson Wines
168 Merton High Street, Merton, SW19.
Tel. (020) 8542 1558

Real Ale
371 Richmond Road, Twickenham. (MO)
Tel. (020) 8892 3710
www.realale.com

Utobeer: The Drinks Cage
Unit 24, Borough Market, London Bridge, SE1. (Fri pm and Sat only) (MO)
Tel. (020) 7394 8601
www.utobeer.co.uk

Greater Manchester

The Bottle Stop
136 Acre Lane, Bramhall, Stockport.
Tel. (0161) 439 4904

Carringtons
322 Barlow Moor Road, Chorlton. (MO)
Tel. (0161) 881 0099

Carringtons
688 Wilmslow Road, Didsbury. (MO)
Tel. (0161) 446 2546

Unicorn Grocery
89 Albany Road, Chorlton-cum-Hardy. (organic beers) Tel. (0161) 861 0010
www.unicorn-grocery.co.uk

Norfolk

Beers of Europe
Garage Lane, Setchey, King's Lynn. (MO)
Tel. (01553) 812000
www.beersofeurope.co.uk

Breckland Wines
80 High Street, Watton.
Tel. (01953) 881592

Castles
2 Mere Street, Diss.
Tel. (01379) 641863

Elveden Ales
Elveden Estate, Thetford.

Iceni Brewery
3 Foulden Road, Ickburgh.
Tel. (01842) 878922

The Little Beer Shop
Blofield Leisure Village,
58 Yarmouth Road, Blofield.
Tel. (01603) 717197

The Real Ale Shop
Branthill Farm,
Wells-next-the-Sea.
Tel. (01328) 710810
www.therealaleshop.co.uk

Oxfordshire

Classic Wines and Beers
254 Cowley Road, Oxford. (MO)
Tel. (01865) 792157

SH Jones & Co. Ltd.
27 High Street, Banbury. (MO)
Tel. (01295) 251179
www.shjones.com

SH Jones & Co. Ltd.
9 Market Square, Bicester. (MO)
Tel. (01869) 322448
www.shjones.com

The Grog Shop
13 Kingston Road, Oxford.
Tel. (01865) 557088

Shropshire

The Marches Little Beer Shoppe
2 Old Street, Ludlow.
Tel. (01584) 878999

Somerset

Dunster Village Shop and Deli
11 High Street, Dunster.
Tel. (01643) 822078

Open Bottles
131 Taunton Road, Bridgwater.
Tel. (01278) 459666

Suffolk

Barwell Foods
39 Abbeygate Street, Bury St Edmunds.
Tel. (01284) 754084
www.barwellfoods.com

Memorable Cheeses
1 The Walk, Ipswich.
Tel. (01473) 257315

Surrey

Arthur Rackham Emporia
216 London Road, Burpham, Guildford.
Tel. (0870) 870 1110
www.ar-emporia.com

Hogs Back Brewery Shop
Manor Farm, The Street,
Tongham. (MO)
Tel. (01252) 783000
www.hogsback.co.uk

Osney Lodge Farm
Byers Lane, South Godstone
Tel: (01342) 892216
www.osneylodgefarm.co.uk

Sussex (East and West)

The Beer Essentials
30A East Street, Horsham.
Tel. (01403) 218890

Southover Wines
80–81 Southover Street, Brighton.
Tel. (01273) 600402

Trafalgar Wines
23 Trafalgar Street, Brighton.
Tel. (01273) 683325

The Wine Store Ltd
50A America Lane, Haywards Heath
Tel. (01444) 456600

York House Wines
8 Richardson Road, Hove.
Tel. (01273) 735891

Warwickshire

SH Jones & Co. Ltd.
121 Regent Street,
Leamington Spa. (MO)
Tel (01926) 315609
www.shjones.com

West Midlands

Alexander Wines
112 Berkeley Road South, Earlsdon,
Coventry. (MO)
Tel. (024 76) 673474
www.alexanderwines.co.uk

Bernie's Real Ale Off-Licence
266 Cranmore Boulevard, Shirley.
Tel. (0121) 744 2827

Da'Costa Wines and Beers
84–86 Edgewood Road, Rednal,
Birmingham.
Tel. (0121) 453 9564

Global Wines
2 Abbey Road, Smethwick,
Birmingham.
Tel. (0121) 420 3694

Laurel Wines
63 Westwood Road, Sutton Coldfield.
Tel. (0121) 353 0399

Rai Wine Shop
337 Harborne Lane, Harborne,
Birmingham. (MO)
Tel. (0121) 472 7235

Stirchley Wines and Spirits
1535–37 Pershore Road, Stirchley,
Birmingham.
Tel. (0121) 459 9936
www.stirchleywines.co.uk

Wiltshire

Magnum Wines
22 Wood Street, Old Town, Swindon.
Tel. (01793) 642569
www.magnumwineshop.co.uk

Worcestershire

Hop Pocket Wine Company
The Hop Pocket Craft Centre,
New House, Bishops Frome.
Tel. (01531) 640592
www.hoppocketwine.co.uk

Tipplers
70 Load Street, Bewdley.
Tel. (01299) 402254

Weatheroak Ales
25 Withybed Lane, Alvechurch.
Tel. (0121) 445 4411
www.weatheroakales.co.uk

Yorkshire

Ale Shop
79 Raglan Road, Leeds.
Tel. (0113) 242 7177

Archer Road Beer Stop
57 Archer Road, Sheffield.
Tel. (0114) 255 1356

Beer-Ritz
17 Market Place, Knaresborough. (MO)
Tel. (01423) 862850
www.beerritz.co.uk

Beer-Ritz
Victoria Buildings, Weetwood Lane,
Far Headingley, Leeds. (MO)
Tel. (0113) 275 3464
www.beerritz.co.uk

Dukes of Ingleton
Albion House, 6 High Street, Ingleton. (MO)
Tel. (0152 42) 41738

Fabeers
31 Goodramgate, York. (MO)
Tel. (01904) 628344
www.fabeers.com

Fabeers
39 High Street, Wetherby. (MO)
Tel. (01937) 588800
www.fabeers.com

Jug and Bottle
Main Street, Bubwith.
Tel. (01757) 289707
www.jugandbottle.co.uk

Mitchells Wine Merchants
354 Meadowhead, Sheffield. (MO)
Tel. (0114) 274 0311

Wells Wine Cellar
94–100 St Thomas Street, Scarborough.
Tel. (01723) 362220

York Beer and Wine Shop
28 Sandringham Street, York.
Tel. (01904) 647136
www.yorkbeerandwineshop.co.uk

Scotland

Cornelius
18–20 Easter Road, Edinburgh.
Tel. (0131) 652 2405

JA Mackay Ltd.
4 Traill Street, Thurso, Highland. (MO)
Tel. (01847) 892811
www.getwhisky.com

Peckham's
(licensed delicatessen with several branches in Glasgow, Edinburgh and Stirling: MO)
Tel. (0141) 445 4555
www.peckhams.co.uk

Peter Green and Co.
37A/B Warrender Park Road, Edinburgh.
Tel. (0131) 229 5925

Wales

Conwy Fine Wines
19 High Street, Conwy.
Tel. (01492) 573050

The Jolly Brewer
Stall 21, Butcher's Market, Henblas Street, Wrexham.
Tel. (01978) 263338

Thirst for Beer
Unit 2, Y Maes, Pwllheli, Gwynedd.
Tel. (01758) 701004

The Treehouse
14 Baker Street, Aberystwyth.
Tel. (01970) 615791
www.treehousewales.co.uk

Northern Ireland

The Vineyard
375–377 Ormeau Road, Belfast.
Tel. (028) 9064 5774
www.vineyardbelfast.co.uk

The Vintage
33 Church Street, Antrim.
Tel. (028) 9446 2526

Isle of Man

The Vineyard
Prospect Terrace, Douglas.
Tel. (01624) 663911
www.thevineyard.co.im

Internet Sites

The following internet companies sell beer via the web, but check also the websites of the shops listed above for more mail order options.

www.beer4home.co.uk
www.livingbeer.com
www.orchard-hive-and-vine.co.uk
www.pitfieldbeershop.co.uk
www.realbottledale.co.uk

Real Ale in a Bottle Index

S

T

Breweries Index

Join CAMRA

Do you feel passionately about your pint? Then why not join CAMRA. Just fill in the application form (or a photocopy of it) and the Direct Debit form on the next page to receive three months' membership FREE. If you wish to join but do not want to pay by Direct Debit, fill in the application form below and send a cheque, payable to CAMRA to: CAMRA, 230 Hatfield Road, St Albans, Hertfordshire, AL1 4LW.

Please note that prices will change from January 1st 2007. See www.camra.org.uk for new prices.

- Single Membership (UK & EU) £18
- Concessionary Membership £10 (under 26 or 60 and over)
- Joint membership £21
- Concessionary Joint membership £13
- Life membership information is available on request.

Title______ Surname______________________________

Forename(s)______________________________

Address ______________________________

____

____

Postcode__________ Date of Birth______________________

Email address______________________________

Signature______________________________

Partner's details if required

Title______ Surname______________________________

Forename(s)______________________________

Postcode__________ Date of Birth______________________

Email address______________________________

Please tick here ☐ if you would like to receive occasional emails from CAMRA (at no point will your details be released to a third party).
Find out more about CAMRA at **www.camra.org.uk**

Instruction to your Bank or Building Society to pay by Direct Debit

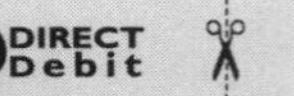

Please fill in the form and send to: Campaign for Real Ale Ltd. 230 Hatfield Road, St. Albans, Herts. AL1 4LW

Name and full postal address of your Bank or Building Society

To The Manager — Bank or Building Society

Address

Postcode

Name (s) of Account Holder (s)

Bank or Building Society account number

Branch Sort Code

Reference Number

Originator's Identification Number

9	2	6	1	2	9

FOR CAMRA OFFICIAL USE ONLY
This is not part of the instruction to your Bank or Building Society

Membership Number

Name

Postcode

Instruction to your Bank or Building Society
Please pay CAMRA Direct Debits from the account detailed on this Instruction subject to the safeguards assured by the Direct Debit Guarantee. I understand that this instruction may remain with CAMRA and, if so, will be passed electronically to my Bank/Building Society

Signature(s)

Date

Banks and Building Societies may not accept Direct Debit Instructions for some types of account

detached and retained this section

DIRECT Debit

This Guarantee should be detached and retained by the payer.

The Direct Debit Guarantee

- This Guarantee is offered by all Banks and Building Societies that take part in the Direct Debit Scheme. The efficiency and security of the Scheme is monitored and protected by your own Bank or Building Society.
- If the amounts to be paid or the payment dates change CAMRA will notify you 7 working days in advance of your account being debited or as otherwise agreed.
- If an error is made by CAMRA or your Bank or Building Society, you are guaranteed a full and immediate refund from your branch of the amount paid.
- You can cancel a Direct Debit at any time by writing to your Bank or Building Society. Please also send a copy of your letter to us.

ATLANTIC BREWERY
Blue
Organic Dark Ale
BREWED IN CORNWALL
Chocolate NUTTER
Brewed using Chocolate Malt
The WHY NOT BREWERY
Alc 5.5% vol
NORWICH
POUR CAREFULLY TO ENSURE A CLEAR GLASS OF BEER
BREWSTER'S BREWING Co
WICKED WOMEN
JEZEBEL
1 PT 9 FL OZ ALE
BOTTLE CONDITIONED ALE FROM THE VALE OF BELVOIR
GOOD KING
www.valebrewery.co.uk
SENSELESS
...LAST PASSED OUT, ON A PINT OF STEVENS
500 ml ℮
Alc. 5.2% Vol.
This traditionally brewed Christmas Ale blends Pale, Crystal and Chocolate Malts with Choicest English Hops producing a classic Winter Warmer.
Bottle Conditioned for Flavour
DOROTHY GOODBODY'S
NELSON'S REVENGE
NELSON'S REVENGE
WOODFORDE'S NORFOLK ALES
Alc. 4.5% Vol.
COTLEIGH BREWERY
BUZZARD
DARK ALE
FINEST SOMERSET BEERS
THE GRAINSTORE BREWERY
TEN FIFTY
DAVIS'ES BREWING Co Ltd
BLACK ISLE
ORGANIC